In Praise of the Common

In Praise of the Common

A Conversation on Philosophy and Politics

Cesare Casarino and Antonio Negri

University of Minnesota Press
Minneapolis
London

Portions of "Vicissitudes of Constituent Thought" were originally published in Cesare Casarino and Antonio Negri, "It's a Powerful Life: A Conversation on Contemporary Philosophy," *Cultural Critique* 57 (Spring 2004): 151–83; reprinted with permission from the University of Minnesota Press. "The Political Monster: Power and Naked Life" first appeared as "Il mostro politico: Nuda vita e potenza," in *Desiderio del mostro: Dal circo al laboratorio alla politica*, ed. Ubaldo Fadini, Antonio Negri, and Charles T. Wolfe (Rome: Manifestolibri, 2001), 179–210. "Time Matters: Marx, Negri, Agamben, and the Corporeal" is a slightly revised version of Cesare Casarino, "Time Matters: Marx, Negri, Agamben, and the Corporeal," *Strategies* 16, no. 2 (Fall 2003): 185–206.

Published by the University of Minnesota Press
111 Third Avenue South, Suite 290
Minneapolis, MN 55401-2520
http://www.upress.umn.edu

Library of Congress Cataloging-in-Publication Data

Casarino, Cesare.
   In praise of the common : a conversation on philosophy and politics / Cesare Casarino and Antonio Negri.
      p. cm.
   Includes bibliographical references (p.   ) and index.
   ISBN 978-0-8166-4742-2 (hc : alk. paper) — ISBN 978-0-8166-4743-9 (pb : alk. paper)
   1. Political science—Philosophy. I. Negri, Antonio, 1933– II. Title.
   JA71.C3288 2008
   320.01—dc22

                                             2008024171

Printed in the United States of America on acid-free paper

The University of Minnesota is an equal-opportunity educator and employer.

15 14 13 12 11 10 09 08   10 9 8 7 6 5 4 3 2 1

Contents

Surplus Common

A Preface

Cesare Casarino

Conversation as Language of the Common

The common speaks: a conversation unfolds . . . Unlike Folly—the garrulous, auto-encomiastic, first-person narrator of Desiderius Erasmus's *In Praise of Folly*—the common abhors monologues. Arguably, the exuberant, joyful *Stimmung* and the dramatic, polyphonic structure of Erasmus's monologue could be understood as belonging to the dialogic in their own right. A conversation, however, is no more a dialogue than it is a monologue. Neither monologic nor dialogic, the common converses. For the common is that which is always at stake in any conversation: there where a conversation takes place, there the common expresses itself; there where we are in common, there and only there is a conversation possible. Conversation is the language of the common.

Thus far, I have used the term "dialogic" in the Platonic rather than in the Bakhtinian sense. Mikhail Bakhtin writes: "Dialogic relations are . . . much broader than dialogic speech in the narrow sense of the word. And dialogic relations are always present, even among profoundly monologic speech works."[1] For Bakhtin, the dialogic relation constitutes the matrix of the entire dialogue–monologue binary opposition: such a relation inheres in both dialogues and monologues alike—with the difference, presumably, that the former materialize it by acknowledging and affirming it, whereas the latter materialize it by foreclosing it. Importantly, in the same essay Bakhtin defines the dialogic relation in terms of response:

> For the word (and, consequently for a human being) there is
> nothing more terrible than a *lack of response* . . . Being heard as
> such is already a dialogic relation. The word wants to be heard,
> understood, responded to, and again to respond to the response, and
> so forth *ad infinitum*.[2]

1

If the dialogic relation is understood in this way, then a conversation is indeed dialogic, for it involves *response* to and from—rather than *sublation* of—the other. Once sublated, the word and the body who speaks it are not heard, not understood, not corresponded. Sublation is the attempt to interiorize and to assimilate that which is different, which is why it can never constitute a real response. It is in this sense that conversation is the language of the common: it is that form of language that brings us together as different from rather than identical to one another.

I continue to prefer the term "conversation" rather than the term "dialogue," even in the Bakhtinian sense, for two reasons. I find "dialogue" to be irrecuperable not only because of its Platonic determinations but also because of the more pernicious subsequent philosophical and political history of such determinations. This history has culminated in the now hegemonic liberal-democratic discourse of identity and in its suffocating invocations of "dialogue" as a means of negotiating and reconciling differences among various and sundry identities (as if there was actually any real difference rather than sheer equivalence among identities, even despite the incommensurable inequities that they always index and that they are meant to redress in the realm of representation alone, and as if, hence, anything like a real dialogic relation—that is, anything like dialogue at the level of the real—could even begin to take place among them). I find also that "conversation" takes us directly to the problematic of the common (the Latin noun *conversatio*, after all, derives from the medial verb *conversari:* to keep company with, to live together), and hence points to a set of concepts as well as to a history altogether different from dialogue's Platonic and post-Platonic ones. To converse is to be in common, to produce the common.

This book wishes to be a conversation precisely in this sense. Despite the fact that at times—while working together on this book—Negri would refer teasingly to me as Socrates and to himself as the Sophist, there is nothing Platonic about our conversation. In his *Architecture as Metaphor: Language, Number, Money,* Kojin Karatani has argued that Platonic dialogues ought to be understood as monologues. While discussing Ludwig Wittgenstein, Karatani comments thus on Plato's *Meno:*

> A dialogue carried on within a common set of rules cannot be
> identified as a dialogue with the "other." Such a dialogue, or internal
> dialectic, can be converted into or considered a monologue . . .
> In the work of both Aristotle and Hegel, dialectics became a

monologue. And though Plato's dialogues were written in the form of conversations, finally they must be considered monologues. Western philosophy thus began as an introspective—that is, monologic—dialogue . . . Wittgenstein . . . questioned the Platonic dialogue because it is *not* inclusive of the other, and often becomes a monologue. In order to interiorize the other, that other must share a set of common rules. But doesn't the other by definition designate only those who do not share a set of rules? Is not the dialogue only with such an other? Wittgenstein attempted in his *Philosophical Investigations* to introduce this other that could no longer be interiorized, that is, the otherness of the other.[3]

The Bakhtinian echo here is unmistakable. On the relation between dialogue and dialectics, Bakhtin writes:

Take a dialogue and remove the voices (the partitioning of voices), remove the intonations (emotional and individualizing ones), carve out abstract concepts and judgments from living words and responses, cram everything into one abstract consciousness—and that's how you get dialectics.[4]

Our conversation is an attempt to think otherwise. Wary and weary of the introspective and dialectical dialogues with which the history of Western philosophy is replete, we tried to think together by making up rules as we went along rather than by appealing to a supposedly shared set of rules posited a priori, as well as by letting asymmetries and differences of all sorts come to light and be visible rather than by reconciling them, resolving them, and then shoving them under the carpet of sublation.

This conversation was born as an interview. The original idea was to reconstruct Negri's early intellectual and political formation—from the end of World War II to 1968—so as to give a sense to the Anglophone reader of the milieu from which his philosophical project emerged. It became clear soon, however, that neither of us would be satisfied with the limiting parameters of the interview as a genre, that neither of us would feel at home in the roles of interviewer and interviewee. On the one hand, Negri was more eager to think in the present and for the future rather than about the past. On the other hand, I was more eager to question his current projects, so as, possibly, to push them further. And both of us were eager to have exchanges on a conceptual rather than solely biographical level. Before we even knew it, we were stepping beyond the confines of the interview, we were thinking together, we were having fun. The different parts of this book correspond to various shifts in our language game.

"A Class Struggle Propaedeutics, 1950s–1970s" remains faithful to the original idea: it consists of an interview focused on the three decades that were most crucial in defining Negri's intellectual and political trajectories. What concerned me most here in my role of interviewer was to inquire into the complex relay of interactions among his early experiences as a student, as a teacher, as a thinker, as a writer, and as a political militant. It is here that Negri relates the beginnings of his philosophical research (ranging from Georg Lukács to Karl Marx, from G. W. F. Hegel to René Descartes, from Kantian philosophy of right to German historicism as articulated in Heinrich von Treitschke, Friedrich Meinecke, Wilhelm Dilthey, and Max Weber) as well as of his political commitments (ranging from brief involvements with militant Catholicism and with socialist political organizations to his visits to the Soviet bloc and his work in the petrochemical factories of the Italian Northeast). What transpires from this inquiry is that for Negri the realms of philosophy and of politics have been inseparable and mutually determining all along.

"Sounding the Present" marks a shift to some of Negri's most recent writings, and primarily to his collaborative works with Michael Hardt, *Empire* and *Multitude: War and Democracy in the Age of Empire* (as well as, to a lesser extent, *Labor of Dionysus: A Critique of the State-Form*). Here too, however, the original intention was modified in the process of conversing. We had meant to focus our attention on these works, and soon we realized that in order to attend to their complexities we had to expand the scope of the discussion by questioning those concepts that constitute their shared episte-mological and ontological framework (such as the concepts of "the com-mon," "the singular," "empire," "multitude," "democracy," "communism," "subjectivity," "sovereignty," "constitution," "freedom," "poverty," "war," and "void"). In questioning the conceptual framework of these works, it became necessary also to engage selectively with the past and present histories of these concepts (including their contemporary reformulations in thinkers ranging from Maurice Blanchot to Jacques Derrida, from Jean-Luc Nancy to Giorgio Agamben, from Paolo Virno to, above all, Gilles Deleuze and Félix Guattari). In short, this part of the book attempts at once to explicate and to excavate the philosophical foundations of Negri's understanding of our contemporary historical and political conjuncture.

"Vicissitudes of Constituent Thought" denotes another shift. As we engaged with the philosophical and political histories of the aforementioned concepts, it became clear that a more sustained engagement with the history of Western philosophy, and, in particular, with Negri's past and present interlocutors, was needed. In short, here the primary question became first of all to situate Negri vis-à-vis the contemporary thinkers with whom he has most affinities as well as crucial disagreements (namely, Deleuze, Guattari, Agamben, and Michel Foucault), and second to ask Negri to engage—however briefly—with a variety of past and present thinkers with whom one might not usually associate his thought and about whom he has commented seldom, if ever, in writing (from Giordano Bruno to Pier Paolo Pasolini, from Giovanni Gentile to Antonio Gramsci, from Ernesto Laclau to Chantal Mouffe, from Walter Benjamin to Theodor Adorno, from Franz Rosenzweig to Jacques Lacan, from Bruno Latour to Paul Virilio, etc.). Ultimately, this series of exchanges culminates in a critique of philosophy—from antiquity to the present—as instrument of sovereign Power.

"Notes on a Politics of the Future Anterior" marks yet another shift, after which we continue our conversation by different means. It had become apparent that the rules of our game were such that, on the one hand, we would let asymmetries and differences emerge and stand unresolved, and, on the other hand, we would be unable at times to articulate them fully and adequately. (In particular, Negri noted that at times I was being too polite or inhibited in my disagreements, and that I ought to try to express them more explicitly and effectively.) This is why we decided to conclude the book with two essays—one by Negri and one by myself—that engage in more detail with some of the questions and thinkers we had been discussing. Negri's essay—"The Political Monster: Power and Naked Life"—constitutes an attempt to produce a communist teratology. Starting with a critical genealogy of the philosophical discourses of eugenics from antiquity to modernity as well as from modernity to postmodernity, he traces the emergence and development of the necessary complement and inescapable nightmare of such discourses, namely, the figure of "the monster." This—Negri argues—has always been a political figure, whose myriad metamorphoses have haunted sovereign Power by confronting it from within as an intractable and indomitable force of resistance. While following the monster in its various transformations and confrontations, Negri articulates the most sustained critique he has undertaken thus far of Agamben's concept of "naked life"—which he denounces as a mystifying ideological apparatus that supports rather than refutes the eugenic imperatives of sovereign Power and that, in the end, constitutes the very opposite of the concept of potentiality, that is, of the potential to be and to act. Ultimately, Negri understands the contemporary—now fully biopolitical—monster as the power of the multitude, as the production and constitution of the common. My essay—"Time Matters: Marx, Negri, Agamben, and the Corporeal"—constitutes an attempt to think a communist temporality, namely, a way to understand and to practice time as existing nowhere outside of, and as fully incorporated in, our singular and common body, a way to live time as incorporation of the common. To this purpose, I stage a confrontation between Agamben's and Negri's very different articulations of a theory of revolutionary time—the former in his essay "Time and History: Critique of the Instant and the Continuum," and the latter in his *The Constitution of Time*—both of which I find at once very productive and yet inadequate. First of all, I argue that what is different in their theories of temporality is more usefully understood as complementary. Second, I argue that—differences notwithstanding—they both, on the one hand, sense the fundamental importance of the question of corporeality for any theorization of revolutionary time, and, on the other hand, are impeded by their own theorizations of time when it comes to attending to this crucial question in a convincing manner. This is why in the end I turn to Marx—and, in particular, to his discussions of the money form and of the temporality of capitalist circulation in the *Grundrisse*—in order to show that he had already not only encountered but also pointed in the direction of a possible solution to the problem into which both Agamben and Negri run. In short, this part of the book gives both of us the chance to offer the reader further clarifications and elaborations of our—at times convergent, at times divergent—positions.

Because the diachronic demands its share, it would be remiss of me not to spend a few words on the circumstances of our conversation. Our exchanges took place in Negri's apartment in Rome, were recorded on tape, and subsequently were transcribed, edited, and translated from Italian into English. "A Class-Struggle Propaedeutics, 1950s–1970s," "Sounding the Present," and "Vicissitudes of Constituent Thought" were recorded in July 2001—during the days of the infamous G8 summit in Genoa—with the exception of the second section of "Sounding the Present" ("On *Multitude*"), which was recorded in July 2004. The first section of "Vicissitudes of Constituent Thought" appeared in 2004 under a different title in the journal *Cultural Critique*.[5] Negri's essay "The Political Monster" was originally published in

Italian in 2001 and appears here in English for the first time, in a translation by Maurizia Boscagli.[6] My essay "Time Matters" is a slightly revised version of an essay by the same title that was published in 2003 in a special issue on Negri of the journal *Strategies*.[7]

As the title of this book indicates, the concept of the common constitutes the concatenation of all its sections: it is engaged explicitly in the sections of "Sounding the Present"—yet our conversation hovers like a swarm of thoughts around this concept throughout. In *What Is Philosophy?*, Deleuze and Guattari write that all "concepts are connected to problems without which they would have no meaning and which can themselves only be isolated or understood as their solution emerges."[8] The problem that is found here to constitute the condition of possibility as well as the raison d'être of the concept of the common can be formulated as a question: how can we be in common, how can we live together, today? I will let the reader decide what kind of solution—if any—emerges from our book. Deleuze and Guattari point out also that concepts are never given a priori, are not ready-made and ready-for-use; rather, they need to be produced anew each and every time.[9] This is why I have felt it necessary to offer here further elaborations of the concept of the common. (In many respects, they complement my essay "Time Matters.") These elaborations, on the one hand, owe an immense debt to Negri's entire philosophical and political trajectory (including our conversing together), and, on the other hand, are ultimately my own and hence do not reflect necessarily Negri's own thoughts on the common (which may well differ significantly from what I write here). In the following section of this preface, I engage selectively with some of the thinkers I have found to be most productive when thinking about the common—primarily, Dante Alighieri, Marx, Aristotle, Spinoza, as well as Hardt and Negri—so as, in the end, to try to sketch the contour of a concept of *surplus common*. In the final section of this preface, I reflect very briefly on the relation among friendship, thought, and the common by expressing my gratitude to the friends who produced thought in me while I was writing these pages.

On Surplus Common

The common is legion. Many are its manifestations and definitions. This is not the place to retrace the multifarious genealogies of the concept of the common, whose origins hark back at least to the dawn of the early-modern era. It might constitute an instructive exercise nonetheless to foreshorten the distance separating us from that dawn, and to juxtapose one of the earliest and one of the latest attempts to produce such a concept, namely, on the one hand, Dante's writings on politics and on language, and, on the other hand, Hardt and Negri's *Multitude*.[10]

According to Agamben's compelling claim, modern political thought begins with Averroist philosophy—and, in particular, with Dante's 1313 treatise *De monarchia* (On world government). Agamben's claim is based on this philosophy's attempt to define the intellect as a potentiality for thought common to all human beings, as well as to define thought not at all as the solitary activity of separate individuals, or even as the activity of particular communities in isolation from one another, but as the collective, incessant, and incremental practice of a common humanity, that is, of humankind posited in its totality.[11] To Agamben's claim I will add that prior to elaborating explicitly such an argument with respect to thought, Dante had made implicitly a similar argument with respect to language approximately a decade earlier in his treatise *De vulgari eloquentia* (On the Eloquence of the Vernacular). On the first page of this treatise—when positing the superiority of *locutio prima* (namely, vernacular language as we all learn it first by hearing and imitating adults) over *locutio secundaria* (namely, grammar, or, scholarly language, as the few learn it later through formal instruction)—Dante writes:

> Of these two types of language, the more noble is the vernacular:
> because it was the first to be used habitually by humankind
> [*humano generi*]; because the whole world employs it, even though
> it is divided into different pronunciations and into different words;
> and because it is natural to us, while the other appears artificial
> instead.[12]

The three reasons adduced here for the superiority of the vernacular have the combined effect of revealing what Dante is after—or has stumbled upon—in grappling with the question of the vernacular in the first place. First of all, the second reason given here crucially modifies the first: the vernacular, in other words, was the first language "to be used habitually by humankind" not in the sense that it constituted a common or universal language (i.e., in the beginning, everybody spoke the same language) but in the sense that it constituted a common linguistic *habitus* (i.e., in the beginning everybody learned and used language in the same manner). Second, to assert, on the one hand, that "the whole world employs it," and, on the other hand, that it does not exist as such outside its myriad different forms and manifestations, is tantamount to saying that this "it" refers to the very fact that there is language rather than to a specific kind of language or even to language in and of itself intended as structure or system. Moreover, to insist that "it is natural to us, while the other appears artificial"—after having explained in the immediately preceding paragraph that *both* are learned—suggests that the predicates "natural" and "artificial" do not refer to two different types of language but to two different ways of learning, using, and conceptualizing language. In short, Dante's protestations to the contrary notwithstanding, the vernacular is not a type of language at all and is not even language per se. The vernacular, rather, is at once a linguistic potential (that is, the capacity to learn language) and a linguistic practice (that is, the process by which such a capacity comes to its fruition through acquisition and usage) common to all human beings. Even though later in the treatise Dante will deploy the term and concept of vernacular in a different way—as he proceeds to produce a taxonomy of the fourteen different types of vernacular spoken across the Italian peninsula—in these opening pages the vernacular constitutes a common potential for language as well as a common practice of language.

When speculating on the emergence of the vernacular thus conceived, however, Dante specifies further what exactly the object of investigation is in this treatise:

> Since, therefore, human beings are moved not by their natural instinct but by reason, and since that reason takes different forms in single individuals, according to their discrimination, judgment, or choice—to the point where it appears that almost everyone enjoys the existence of a unique species—I hold that we can never understand the actions or passions of others by reference to our own, as the baser animal can. Nor is it given to us to enter into each other's minds by means of spiritual contemplation, as the angels do, because the human spirit is concealed by the opacity and weighed down by the heaviness of the mortal body. So it was necessary that humankind, in order for its members to communicate their conceptions among themselves, should have some rational and sensory [*sensuale*] sign. Since this sign was needed to take from reason as well as to give back to reason, it had to be rational; but since nothing can be conveyed from a reasoning mind to another

except by sensory means, it had to be also sensory. For, if it was purely rational, it could not transmit or travel [*pertransire*]; if purely sensory, it could neither take from nor deliver back to reason. This sign, then, is the noble subject that I am going to discuss; for it is sensory inasmuch as it is a sound; and it is also rational inasmuch as it is taken to signify, by common agreement.[13]

Much ought to be said about this remarkable proto-Saussurean investigation into the nature of the linguistic sign. For the moment, I would like simply to point out that the sign is posited here as a translating—and, indeed, transvaluating—apparatus. First of all, this passage reveals that the vernacular and the sign are, for all intents and purposes, equivalent to one another. It is the case not only that both are identified explicitly as the "subject" of this treatise (the latter in this passage and the former as early as in the title). It is the case also that the way in which the sign is articulated here constitutes in effect a way of considering *locutio prima* in itself rather than in relation to *locutio secundaria*. (Importantly, both the vernacular and the sign are qualified by the same adjective: the former at this point in the treatise has been referred to as "the more noble type of language" twice already, while the latter is referred to in the passage quoted above as "the noble subject" of the treatise.) Second, the power of the sign is such that it is able to translate and to transcend even those individual differences that are so radical that they turn each and every human being into a veritable species unto itself. Third, the sign is described here as taking and giving (i.e., as medium of exchange), as transporting and traveling back and forth (i.e., as medium of circulation). Fourth, and most important perhaps, the sign is at once sensory and rational, and hence is delicately poised between body and spirit—belonging fully to both as their interface and mediator, and yet already representing *in potentia* some sort of semiautonomous entity unto itself. I am suggesting, in other words, that for Dante the linguistic sign functions already like the modern sign of value par excellence, namely, *money*.

In this respect, Dante seems to anticipate a host of structural homologies between language and capital at least by five centuries (if one understands Marx's work to constitute implicitly one of the earliest such homologies).[14] Let me emphasize, however, that Dante's articulation of the sign is at once (largely) precapitalist and (marginally yet crucially) protocapitalist. On the one hand, the sign in this passage is characterized as medium of exchange and circulation, and, as Marx explains in detail in the *Grundrisse,* as long as money is no more than medium of exchange and circulation—which is to say, as long as money has not yet become the independent and general form of wealth—we are still fully within precapitalist modes of production.[15] On the other hand, there is one specific characteristic of the sign here that already hints at this future development in the money form: the sign fluctuates in a zone of indistinction between body and spirit. In order to clarify this last point, I will quote from Kiarina Kordela's succinct and powerful thesis regarding the advent of secular capitalist modernity:

> Albeit in different ways, antiquity and all the subsequent presecular eras of Hellenistic and medieval theocracy were organized around one and the same persistent opposition: *matter* versus *spirit*. The secular era of capitalist modernity, by contrast, constitutes itself around a radically new opposition: *matter* versus *value*. The displacement of spirit by the secular function of value entails an unforeseen expansion of the realm of *representation*, insofar as value is an immaterial, abstract symbol that is determined through its differential relation to all other homogeneous symbols. While spirit could manifest itself only in the Word, value has two manifestations: a *semantic* one, as the word or the signifier representing the concept that refers to a thing; and an *economic* one, as the equivalent exchange-value representing the relevant value of a thing (commodity). The advent of secular capitalism amounts to the transformation of the economy into a representational system.[16]

Dante's sign is pivotal in at least two respects: it lives and mediates not only in between matter and spirit but also in between the two eras marked by the matter–spirit theocratic opposition and the matter–value secular opposition, respectively. In Dante's sign we can already catch a glimpse of a possible third term that might undo the binary opposition of matter and spirit from the inside by making its living contradiction manifest and—ultimately—untenable, unlivable. In the context of this paradigm, matter and spirit by definition do not share anything in common and do not communicate, and yet the sign partakes of both and enables their exchanges, that is, the circulation of meaning or differential semantic value. Incidentally, it bears witness to the difficulties posed by this contradiction that Dante, when running into the problem of having to explain how Adam learned language in the first place, corners himself into asserting, on the one hand, that language was given to Adam by God, and, on the other hand, that the divine Word has nothing at all to do with anything that "we would call language."[17] In short, Dante's sign constitutes one of the earliest harbingers and proto-typical manifestations of that secular, capitalist, abstract, differential, and self-referential symbol of value that will eventually displace spirit altogether and usher forth a dispiriting modernity that is still very much with us.[18]

Let us return now to Dante's intuitions regarding the vernacular as constituting a common potential for language as well as a common practice of language. We can already begin to draw three related and provisional conclusions from these early moments in the conceptualization of the common. First of all, *the common is defined according to two fundamental Aristotelian categories, namely, potentiality and actuality.* Steeped as it is from its very beginning in Averroist philosophy—whose powerful investments in reelaborating the Aristotelian problematic are well known and well documented—the common comprises two related elements or aspects: at once potential and actual, the common lives of a double life. It is crucial to stress, in other words, that for Dante that which brings human beings in common is at once a shared potentiality for thought and for language *as well as* the collective process of actualization of such a potentiality in the first place: the common precedes us as much as we precede it, it produces us as much as we produce it—at one and the same time. Second—because of its intimate relations to thought, to language, and to their modalities of transmission and circulation—*the common is defined in terms of communication rather than in terms of community.* Indeed, to the extent to which communication—in both its semantic and nonsemantic forms—is understood as a collective and cooperative process of actualization of common intellectual and linguistic potentials that entails necessarily the mobilization of humankind in its totality, to that extent it is also identified as that process that undermines the very condition of possibility for the emergence both of separate, discrete, unitary individualities, and of separate, particular, homogeneous communities.[19] (It is worth noting that for Dante the first instances of linguistic communication are nonsemantic rather than semantic, performative rather than constative: according to his myth of linguistic origins, Adam's first utterance was "God!"—intended specifically as "a cry of joy"—while the first utterance of each and every human being after the Fall is "woe!"—a cry of suffering and pain. This means that for Dante the expression of affect—including that which seems most solitary, personal, and intimate—not only is collective, impersonal, and extimate, but also needs to be understood as part and parcel of communication and of the common.)[20] In short, the common (understood at once as the cause and as the effect of intellectual, linguistic, and affective communication) and community (understood as *Gemeinschaft*) are not only mutually exclusive with but also profoundly inimical to each other. Third, such a conceptualization of the common emerges from and is symptomatic of a certain type of heretical, protosecular, rationalist, medieval—Christian as well as Islamic—universalism. For better and for worse, *the common is defined from its very inception as a universalist concept.*[21]

It is hardly a coincidence that one of the latest and most comprehensive attempts to produce a concept of the common—namely, Hardt and Negri's *Multitude*—bears a striking family resemblance to Dante's initial intuitions; for in philosophy, much as in friendship, one is given the chance to create one's own "family" according to the principle of elective affinities. Such affinities may be elected in a variety of ways. I have been always unsure about Walter Benjamin's assertion that "[t]here is a secret agreement between past generations and the present one," that "[o]ur coming was expected on earth," and that "[l]ike every generation that preceded us, we have been endowed with a *weak* Messianic power, a power to which the past has a claim."[22] I am not sure that the past and its generations were waiting for our arrival, but I am sure that some of us still wait for *theirs*. I am sure that some of us wait and work for our own past to happen in the form of the future anterior. Some of us search for, stake a claim on, and elect as our own past that bygone moment when what we desire now was first anticipated and deferred, when what we now want as our future might have taken place but never did.

Elective, however, does not mean arbitrary. The historical condition of possibility for identifying nowadays in whatever way with certain thinkers of the late-medieval and early-modern eras consists of a specific, momentous event. What those thinkers had begun to sense as the driving force and operative principle of the common, namely, a common intellectual, linguistic, and affective capacity along with its appertaining forms of realization, circulation, and communication—or, in short, thought, language, and affect, in both their potential and actual aspects—has become the prime motor of the capitalist mode of production in its current, fully global, and tendentially universal phase. If those past eras and their heretics are at all intelligible as well as urgently relevant for us today, that is so because that which they had envisaged as the condition of possibility for a common humanity has become the increasingly dominant and determining form of labor in the era of the real subsumption of all forms of life and of *bios* itself under capital, also known as postmodernity. What had been identified long ago as our best (and possibly our only) chance for being in common has been turned into communicative labor and has been put to work for postmodern capitalism instead: it is not only harnessed, expropriated, and exploited for the extraction of surplus value; it is also posited as the paradigmatic feature of a mode of production that brings us together precisely to the extent to which it tears us apart.[23]

It is such an indentured and postmodern avatar of the common that concerns Hardt and Negri in *Multitude*. In this work, they attempt to rethink the common in the wake of the event of our time—namely, the capture of the common by capital.[24] What matters most is not merely that the three fundamental features of the common in its earliest definitions—namely, its exhibiting potential and actual aspects simultaneously, its being rooted in intellectual, linguistic, and affective communication rather than in homogeneous communities, as well as its being posited hence as a universalist concept—are to be found almost unaltered in *Multitude*.[25] Precisely because such echoes resound so clearly across the diachronic abysses separating our postmodern present from that protomodern past, it is necessary, rather, to tune in on the less audible refractions, on the more muted distortions. What matters most, in other words, is to identify the difference in Hardt and Negri's repetition of the common. In one of the most valuable sections of *Multitude*, "Method: In Marx's Footsteps," Hardt and Negri at once recapitulate and reformulate an argument they had made already in *Empire*, namely, that the capitalist mode of production in its current phase—driven as it is by intellectual, linguistic, and affective communication—is to be understood as having its proper "foundation in the common":[26]

> A theory of the relation between labor and value today must be based on the common. The common appears at both ends of immaterial production, as presupposition and as result . . . The common, in fact, appears not only at the beginning and end of production but also in the middle, since the production processes themselves are common, collaborative, and communicative. Labor and value have become biopolitical in the sense that living and producing tend to be indistinguishable. Insofar as life tends to be completely invested by acts of production and reproduction, social life itself becomes a productive machine.[27]

We begin to see here already a subtle modification of the early conceptualization of the common as articulated by Dante. (Arguably, such a modification amounts to a full explication of an insight regarding the thought—language—affect assemblage as common praxis that was already implicit in Dante's formulations.) No longer only potential (i.e., "presupposition") and actual (i.e., "result"), the common here is identified as the process by which the former is turned actively and continuously into the latter. Situated as it is "not only at the beginning and end of production but also in the middle," *the common is now (its own self-producing, self-positing, and self-referential) production.* This reformulation of the common has two crucial consequences.

First of all, to reconceptualize the common also as production in its entirety is tantamount to saying that nowadays the common no longer has any outside. This is another way of saying that nowadays the common is virtually indistinguishable from that which continually captures it, namely, capital understood as a fully—that is, intensively and extensively—global network of social relations. In short, the common has no outside and is virtually indistinguishable from capital to the extent to which "living and producing tend to be indistinguishable." Hardt and Negri proceed to argue that to reformulate the relation between labor and value in such a manner means also to conceive of "exploitation as *the expropriation of the common.*" "The common," they write, "has become the locus of surplus value," and hence exploitation is to be understood as the privatization "of the value that has been produced as common."[28] If, therefore, a necessary component of any anticapitalist political project today is the reappropriation of the common—whose precondition consists in resisting capital's current and rampant privatization of the common in all of its forms—I would argue that such a precondition itself rests on another more fundamental precondition. The condition of possibility for any such resistance and reappropriation consists in being willing and able paradoxically to distinguish capital from its own "foundation in the common" *precisely because it is capital rather than the common that posits and needs to posit itself and the common as indistinguishable from one another.* On the one hand, this would be a purely analytic distinction—given that there is no longer any outside, either to the common or to capital. On the other hand, such a distinction would be no less significant and effective for being analytic or even merely heuristic. For example, at the very least such a distinction might have important performative functions: the very fact of being willing and able to posit it might very well transfigure the way in which I look at and live in the world—which is no small matter, if it is the case that today "life tends to be completely invested by acts of production and reproduction," and "social life itself" is "a productive machine." Put differently, the act of positing such a distinction might constitute at once the cause and the effect of a radical transformation in the form of subjectivity I inhabit such that I would *want* to reappropriate the common in the first place: this desire, after all, cannot be taken for granted as being there a priori. In short, I am arguing that any project of reappropriation of the common from capital needs to begin from an attempt to distinguish—that is, to articulate the difference—between the two.

Second, the emergence of this "middle" term in the passage just quoted— namely, the common as production—raises a host of other questions. Is this "middle" the common-in-itself as opposed both to the common-for-itself (the common as "presupposition") and to the common-for-others (the common as "result")? Is the common as production the condition of possibility of both the common as "presupposition" and the common as "result"? Is this middle term in effect the matrix of both potentiality and actuality? My provisional answer to these questions is yes. I am suggesting that Hardt and Negri articulate the common here as a triadic structure (and, as we shall see, this structure is to be understood more precisely as tetradic rather than triadic). Within such a structure, the term of production—precisely to the extent to which it is now fully self-producing, self-positing, self-referential, and hence without any outside—constitutes the only truly potential term that, on the one hand, is immanent in all forms of actualization, and, on the other hand, is never actualized in and of itself. Contrary to what I stated at first, the common as "presupposition" is not to be understood as a potential term; or, more precisely, it is to be understood as a potential term *only relatively,* that is, only as relative to its successive "result." Put differently, both "presupposition" and "result" constitute different types of actualization because they function within strictly relative and diachronic parameters: far from constituting potentiality as such, the former is a *past* actualization of the common, while the latter is a *present* actualization that is based on the former and that will provide in turn the basis for a number of possible *future* actualizations. Potentiality, however, functions according to strictly absolute rather than relative, synchronic rather than diachronic parameters. In short, the common in its tetradic reformulation consists of (a) an element of potentiality—that is, production—that constitutes the condition of possibility of (b) past, (c) present, and (d) future actualizations, all of which partake of and determine (a) potentiality. The latter (actualizations) provide one another with elements of relative potential within a diachronic succession, thereby constituting building blocks in the edifice of the history of the common. The former (potentiality) is that absolute, synchronic, transhistorical, ontological structure of the common-in-itself which functions as absent cause immanent in its own effects.[29]

And, one might ask, so what? Why does any of this matter? The point is that any project of reappropriation of the common is bound to fail if it is directed solely to its past, present, or future actualizations. We may well be successful in resisting the privatization of this or that specific element of the common, and even in claiming back for the common one or more of its elements that already had been expropriated and privatized successfully by capital. There is nothing in such a success, however, that in principle will impede capital from proceeding to expropriate some other element— or even those very same elements—of the common once again. Any project of reappropriation of the common, in other words, needs always to address itself also to the common understood as indiscernible yet distinct from its myriad actualizations. To reappropriate the common means to claim back and seize not only its products but also its means of production, that is, the common as (its own self-producing, self-positing, and self-referential) production.

And yet, one might insist, doesn't this entail, in effect, seizing potentiality qua potentiality, that is, potentiality in its absolute, synchronic, transhistorical, nonrepresentable, nonactualizable state? Isn't such a seizure by definition not only impossible but also nonsensical? When recast in terms of potentiality, however, the seizure of the means of production is no Leninist project. To claim back and seize the common as production entails a drastic reorientation of subjectivity such that one might begin to distinguish between, on the one hand, the common as its own foundation, and, on the other hand, the common as the foundation of its own negation in capital. It entails the production of a form of subjectivity constitutionally unable any longer to be interpellated by and to identify with the capitalist desire to posit itself as indistinguishable from the common. It entails the production of a form of subjectivity constituted by a counterdesire. Such a counterdesire is *the desire to be in common*—as opposed to the desire to be for the common-as-captured-by-capital, the desire to be for the common-as-negated-by-capital, the desire to be captive of one's own negation—in short, as opposed to *the desire not to be*. (Incidentally, the desire not to be is not to be confused with the desire to die. On the contrary, the desire not to be is the desire to foreclose and transcend death altogether: it is the desire to live forever as always already dead. This is the desire to live as pure dead labor in perennial exchange, as pure commodity in perpetual circulation: under capital, *the desire not to be is the desire to be money.*)

Arguably, the form of subjectivity I am envisioning here exists already in many of us (albeit in various degrees of intensity and in various modalities of expression, according to radically different geopolitical and socioeconomic determinations). It is the case, for example, that the vast global network of so-called antiglobalization movements—which have emerged during the last two decades, and which are well documented and discussed in *Multitude*—bear witness to a form of subjectivity constituted precisely by the desire to be in common.[30] I am in full agreement with Hardt and Negri when they assert—in light of such political movements—that "a common political project is *possible*," that "it is important to remember that another world, a better, more democratic world, is possible," that it is important "to foster our desire for such a world" (even though "democratic" is not the term I would use to describe a better world).[31] Leaving aside the question of how exactly such a desire is to be fostered, what is to be done when the desire to be in common is not there, when what is there instead is what I have been calling the desire not to be? Isn't it also the case that vast portions of the world's population are driven by the desire not to be, and that they constitute the actual limit and concrete walls up against which any desire to be in common repeatedly shatters? What is to be done about the fact that many are those who not only are enslaved but also actually desire their own enslavement—thereby, willy-nilly, supporting the imposition of a global system of enslavement on all those who do not desire their own enslavement in the least? (The fact that these two different types of desire and their corresponding forms of subjectivity often coexist in the same body does not simplify matters.) Obviously, if everybody everywhere were driven already, however minimally, by the desire at once to disidentify with the capitalist imperative to posit itself as indistinguishable from the common and to identify instead with the common as qualitatively different from capital, then we would already be in a different world—a world beyond the desire not to be and beyond capital altogether.

If the desire not to be is to change in any way, it needs first to be taken seriously and confronted as an actual, real, true desire in its own right: it needs to be understood as actually existing, as really produced, as truly desired just like any other desire—including the desire to be in common. Put differently, just like any other desire, the desire to be in common has no ontological primacy: it does not correspond to an ontological dynamic intrinsic to the common as production; it is not inscribed a priori in the order of being; it is not the logic of potentiality as such. If that were to be the case, the reappropriation of the common in all of its aspects would be not only a foregone conclusion in terms of historical development but also an ontological necessity *tout court*—and, on the contrary, it is neither. The reason why other worlds (including better and worse ones) are possible— which is also to say the reason why none of them is inevitable—is that potentiality is nothing necessarily: namely, it is necessarily nothing outside its actualizations or effects. Being is being-together only to the extent to which we (as desiring effects) strive to make it so. The reappropriation of the common—including the seizure of the common-in-itself, of the common as production, of potentiality—entails not only fostering our desire to be in common whenever and wherever it is already there in whatever degree and in whatever form. It entails also producing such a desire there where it is not, namely, transforming its own negation, transfiguring the desire not to be. And because the desire not to be feeds on the capitalist fantasy of identity with the common, the transfiguration—at once metamorphosis and radicalization—of such a desire demands that that fantasy be neutralized, deactivated, and substituted by the qualitative difference between capital and the common instead. Undoubtedly, such a qualitative difference is a fantasy too, but at least it is not a murderous one. There is something to be said for a fantasy that does not support and materialize the necessary double gesture of capital: at once to exploit and to foreclose the common as production, thereby not only separating potentiality from its effects but also commanding us to live as if potentiality were sheer nothing rather than nothing outside its effects. There is something to be said for a fantasy that, on the contrary, embodies a life-affirming gesture—a fantasy congruent with a body willing and able to affirm and to incorporate the common as production in all of its gestures, thereby rejecting any separation whatsoever. This is all to say that the seizure of the common as production entails nothing less than a revolution in desire and subjectivity—which is to say, an ideological revolution.[32] In short, my point is that it is first of all by taking the risk of acknowledging, knowing, affirming, engaging, and, indeed, living potentiality as absent cause immanent in its effects and as nothing outside its effects that such a qualitative difference and its attendant and constitutive desire may be produced in the first place.

We might begin to articulate the qualitative difference between capital and its own "foundation in the common" by pointing to a fissure in Hardt and Negri's formulations—a fissure that may prove to be productive for further elaborations of the concept of the common. On the one hand, they argue that capital and the common have become virtually indistinguishable from each other to the extent to which nowadays "living and producing tend to be indistinguishable." On the other hand, they also argue that there is a remainder, a gap, between the two. When characterizing the common as "the locus of surplus value" and hence "exploitation as *the expropriation of the common*," in fact, they add that production and its products "are by their very nature common, and yet capital manages to appropriate privately *some* of their wealth."[33] This last sentence introduces an important qualification: namely, *there is a common wealth that is not appropriated by capital*. It turns out that capital and the common are not identical, and hence that they might be distinguishable after all. This qualification begs several crucial questions. What exactly is the nature of this common wealth that is not appropriated by capital? Is it something that capital has not been able to appropriate yet, or is it something that capital cannot appropriate by structural necessity and by definition? In short, are we faced here by a difference of degree or by a difference of nature, by a quantitative and relative difference or by a qualitative and absolute difference?

In order to try to answer these questions, let us turn to another section of *Multitude*—titled "Mobilization of the Common"—in which Hardt and Negri discuss the relations among exploitation, antagonism, revolt, and struggle:

> We have already noted how antagonism results from every relationship of exploitation, every hierarchical division of the global system, and every effort to control and command the common. We have also focused on the fact that the production of the common always involves a surplus that cannot be expropriated by capital or captured in the regimentation of the global political body. This surplus, at the most abstract philosophical level, is the basis on which antagonism is transformed into revolt. Deprivation, in other words, may breed anger, indignation, and antagonism, but revolt arises only on the basis of wealth, that is, a surplus of intelligence, experience, knowledges, and desire. When we propose the poor as the paradigmatic subjective figure of labor today, it is not because

the poor are empty and excluded from wealth but because they are included in the circuits of production and full of potential, which always exceeds what capital and the global political body can expropriate and control. This common surplus is the first pillar on which are built struggles against the global political body and for the multitude.[34]

The common had been identified earlier as "the locus of surplus value" and hence of exploitation. Here, however, Hardt and Negri explain that the common is also the locus of a different kind of surplus altogether. But what exactly is the difference? If surplus value is the specific difference of capitalism as a mode of production, this other surplus may well hold the key to the specific difference of the common as other than capital—and hence it is crucial to explain Hardt and Negri's explanation in turn.[35]

Aside from the first sentence, the other five following sentences in the paragraph just quoted function like so many tesserae in a possible and as yet incomplete mosaic of another surplus, like so many complementary parts toward a general architectonics of its specific difference. About such a surplus, we read sequentially: (1) it is that which in "the production of the common always" is unexploitable; (2) it is the condition of possibility for the transformation of "antagonism" into "revolt"; (3) it is a common "wealth" of "intelligence, experience, knowledges, and desire"; (4) it is that "potential, which always exceeds what capital" can exploit; (5) it is that "common surplus" which serves as the foundation of "struggles . . . for the multitude" and hence for the reappropriation of the common.[36] I will rearrange the pieces of this philosophical-political jigsaw puzzle by drawing attention to the fact that this other surplus is posited here as the cause of (what Deleuze and Guattari would call) a revolutionary becoming: it may lead us from exploitation to struggle, from expropriation to reappropriation, by effecting a shift from a form of subjectivity capable only of "anger, indignation, and antagonism" to a form of subjectivity in "revolt." How does this surplus effect such a subtle yet vertiginous, momentous shift? Whence does it derive such a transfiguring power? The power of this surplus lies in the fact that, as we have seen, it can *never* be exploited by capital, that is, it cannot be exploited by structural necessity and by definition: it is precisely because this surplus is other than capital, thus, that it may enable revolutionary forms of subjectivity. But how does this surplus escape the increasingly ubiquitous, penetrating reach of capital? In what sense does it exceed capital's indefatigable capacity to extract surplus value, to exploit, to expropriate, to capture? I believe the passage just quoted answers this question in the following way: the surplus of the common can never be exploited by capital in the sense that it is "potential."[37] I believe also that this answer is accurate and yet incomplete: the surplus of the common exceeds capital not only insofar as it is potential but also insofar as it is an absolute rather than a relative potential. (This means that such a surplus can be defined as common "wealth" of "intelligence, experience, knowledges," "desire," and much else besides, only if the term "wealth" is disengaged completely from its capitalist determination. This common wealth is not relative wealth that is measurable or even comprehensible in terms of value; it is, rather, absolute wealth, or, as Marx would put it, labor power as "*not-value*," that is, at once as "absolute poverty" and as "the *general possibility* of wealth.")[38] In short, if "the production of the common always involves a surplus that cannot be expropriated by capital," that is so because this surplus is the common-in-itself, the common as (its own self-producing, self-positing, self-referential) production, the common as potentiality as such. This surplus not only is not measurable or quantifiable but also is not a thing or collection of things at all. The qualitative difference between the common and capital understood as the regime of surplus value consists of this other surplus, which, for lack of a better term, I would like to call *surplus common*. Revolutionary becoming is living the common as surplus.

Surplus is potentiality qua potentiality.[39] Thus far, I have characterized surplus value and surplus common as two different surpluses altogether, which are irreducible to one another. Such a characterization needs to be qualified. The point is that *there is only one surplus,* which may effect and be effected in different ways. On the one hand, surplus is that which capital strives to subsume absolutely under surplus value and yet manages to do so only relatively because it is structurally unable to subsume without at the same time negating and foreclosing that which it subsumes—thereby enabling the emergence of surplus common. On the other hand, surplus is also that which envelops and subsists in the common as surplus common, that is, as the common's distinct yet indiscernible element of potentiality, and hence also as the condition of possibility of all the common's fully exploitable and subsumable actual elements—thereby enabling the emergence of surplus value. This may sound like a suffocating, unbreakable, vicious circle—but it is not necessarily one at all. Being is not a serpent swallowing its own tail. The solution to this apparent stalemate is not to shy away from actualizations altogether: it lies, rather, in actualizing without foreclosing that which enables us to actualize in the first place. This is tantamount to saying that surplus value and surplus common name two radically different ways of materializing the one and only surplus. *The qualitative difference between capital and the common consists in positing surplus in different ways, in engaging surplus to different ends. Surplus value is living surplus as separation (in the form of value par excellence, namely, money). Surplus common is living surplus as incorporation (in the forms of the common, including and especially our bodies).* Wasn't this already one of Marx's most revolutionary intuitions? It may be instructive here to turn to (arguably) the most important thinker of surplus, namely, Marx. If indeed the *differentia specifica* of capitalism as a mode of production is the extraction of surplus value, that is, the self-contradictory process of subsuming surplus under value, let us inquire into the ontological status of "value" and "surplus value" in Marx.

In the *Grundrisse*, Marx asks: "In and for itself, is value as such the general form, in opposition to use value and exchange value as *particular* forms of it?"—and, as he proceeds to show, this is, in effect, a rhetorical question.[40] There is no such a thing as value, which nonetheless inheres in its particular manifestations. But what exactly is the mode of existence of that which inheres in its manifestations? What is the materiality "of value . . . as general form"? When analyzing the double life of the commodity in *Capital*, Marx qualifies such a materiality in no unclear terms:

> Not an atom of matter enters into the objectivity of commodities as values; in this it is the direct opposite of the coarsely sensuous objectivity of commodities as physical objects. We may twist and turn a single commodity as we wish; it remains impossible to grasp it as a thing possessing value.[41]

Value does not have "an atom of matter" in the specific sense that it constitutes "the direct opposite" of matter. In this stunning turn of phrase, Marx identifies the difference between precapitalist antiquity and capitalist modernity. The invocation of the "atom" in this context could hardly be more laden with significance for someone who had written his doctoral dissertation on ancient Greek atomism.[42] Unlike the ancient conception of matter as composed of atoms, modern matter is not only made of atoms but also haunted by something other than atoms, by something other than itself, by its uncanny mirror image, by its photographic negative, by its inverse, by antimatter, namely, value. To the extent to which it is commodified, matter has its doppelgänger in value.

This crucial insight—namely, that value constitutes the difference between ancient and modern materiality—is made explicit shortly thereafter, in those luminous pages in which Marx discusses Aristotle's pathbreaking yet incomplete analysis of the form of value in the *Nicomachean Ethics*. Marx argues that "Aristotle . . . himself tells us what prevented" him from proceeding "any further" in his analysis: namely, "the lack of a concept of value" understood as the equalizing representation of that "common substance" which is "human labour."[43] Marx argues in effect that Aristotle discovers "value" by not discovering it. I will return to this epistemological paradox. It is essential first to relate Marx's explanation of Aristotle's impasse: "Aristotle . . . was unable" to discern in "the form of value" the fact that in commodities "all labour is expressed as equal human labour and therefore as labour of equal equality . . . because Greek society was founded on the labour of slaves, hence had as its natural basis the inequality of men and of their labour-powers."[44] Marx reaches the conclusion, therefore, that only under capital—that is, "in a society" in which "the commodity-form is the universal form of the product of labour" and hence in which "the dominant social relation" is the exchange relation—it becomes possible to decipher exactly what value represents: "namely the equality and equivalence of all kinds of labour."[45] In short, value is the representation of a social relation of exchange that presupposes the commensurability of all things on the basis of that which is equal in them and which produces them. The emergence of value as representation enables a posteriori the visibility of its inverse, that is, of labor as common substance, of production as substance of the common.

What concerns me here, however, is also what Marx does not say rather than only what he does say. On the one hand, Marx identifies accurately the—at once historical and structural—reasons why Aristotle lacks "a concept of value." On the other hand, Marx does not tell us what the condition of possibility, as well as the significance, might be of the fact that "Aristotle . . . himself tells us" that he lacks "a concept of value." Marx explains why Aristotle did not and could not discover value, without, however, explaining why Aristotle paradoxically did discover it nonetheless by not discovering it.[46] Let us look at the text more closely. Marx comments thus on the fact that for Aristotle the equation "5 beds = 1 house . . . is indistinguishable from" the equation "5 beds = a certain amount of money":

[Aristotle] sees that the value-relation which provides the framework for this expression of value itself requires that the house should be qualitatively equated with the bed, and that these things, being distinct to the senses, could not be compared with each other as commensurable magnitudes if they lacked this essential identity. "There can be no exchange," he says, "without equality, and no equality without commensurability" . . . Here, however, he falters, and abandons the further analysis of the form of value. "It is, however, in reality, impossible [*adynaton*] . . . that such unlike things can be commensurable," i.e. qualitatively equal . . . Aristotle's genius is displayed precisely by his discovery of a relation of equality in the value-expression of commodities. Only the historical limitations inherent in the society in which he lived prevented him from finding out what "in reality" this relation of equality consisted of.[47]

On the threshold of that which is equal in the bed and in the house and which is represented by money, Aristotle "falters." But one does not stumble without stumbling upon *something*: Aristotle here stumbles upon something that he declares to be "impossible." Put differently, Aristotle would not have faltered had he not sensed something rather than nothing at all, however impossible that something might have seemed to him. As described by Marx, the trajectory of Aristotle's thought is one of advance toward, arrest in the face of, and then retreat from *not nothing, but something whose mode of existence is the direct opposite of the possible, of the potential*. Matters become more complicated, in fact, when we note that the adjective used by Aristotle to describe this something that exists in the modality of the "impossible" is *adynaton*, namely, without *dynamis*, without potentiality: in the passage quoted by Marx, Aristotle has encountered something that is *adynaton*, something that has no potential. My point here is not that Marx mistranslates the adjective in question: although literally *adynaton* means "without potential," it could be used to mean either "impossible" or "weak," "impotent," "impotential"—much as *dynaton* could be used to mean either "possible" or "mighty," "potent," "potential." My point is (a) that what Aristotle declares to be "impossible" happens to be—from a conceptual standpoint—precisely something that has no potential, and hence (b) that *adynaton* here is at once more appropriate and more significant of an adjective than it may seem at first.

This crucial adjective, in fact, takes us directly to the heart of the matter of Book Theta of the *Metaphysics,* in which Aristotle elaborates the relation between potentiality and actuality. In Part I of Book Theta, Aristotle defines potentiality (*dynamis*) as an "originative source" of change, as a transformative principle, that inheres in matter.[48] Moreover, he differentiates between two types of potentiality, namely, the potentiality to act, to change—which he defines as primary—and the potentiality to be acted on, to be changed.[49] It is in reference to potentiality thus defined that Aristotle raises the possibility of the impossible, namely, impotentiality (*adynamia*): "Impotentiality [*adynamia*] is a privation contrary to potentiality. Thus all potentiality is impotentiality of the same and with respect to the same."[50] Because, for Aristotle, potentiality can be only potentially, the statement "all potentiality is impotentiality" cannot but imply that all potentiality is impotentiality *potentially*. This is tantamount to saying that all potentiality involves the possibility of its own privation, that all potentiality has the potential to be deprived of itself. Neither actuality nor potentiality, *adynamia* adheres nonetheless to both and hence constitutes a third term in the shadow of the relation between the two.[51] Neither actuality nor potentiality, *adynamia* designates the subtraction from (both potential and actual) matter of its double property of acting or changing and being acted on or being changed: it subtracts from matter its power to transform, its power to produce. Neither actuality nor potentiality, *adynamia* does not have one atom of matter and indeed constitutes the very undoing of matter: *adynamia* is privation or nonbeing par excellence.

For Aristotle, thus, *adynamia* is, strictly speaking, nonexistent, impossible. Or is it? Such impossibility, somehow, is important enough for Aristotle to define it as well as to devote to it the entire conclusion of Part 1 of Book Theta. In that conclusion, in fact, he proceeds to define the various meanings of the term "privation"—and he defines it strictly in terms of the absence of a quality: that is, privation "means (1) that which has not a certain quality and (2) that which might naturally have it but has not it," etc.[52] After having completed this definition, however, Aristotle adds one last sentence—almost as an afterthought, almost as if he feels that there is something amiss or lacking in his definition after all, almost as if there continues to persist something in privation that does not cease to trouble him: "And in certain cases if things which naturally have a quality lose it by violence, we say they have suffered privation."[53] This sentence constitutes an implicit commentary on the preceding definition: for Aristotle it is not sufficient to define privation as the absence of a quality without also inquiring into the condition of possibility or the coming into being of such an absence in the first place. Moreover, the sudden appearance of "violence" in this sentence recasts the definition of privation also in terms of relations of Power, thereby adding to the definition proper a crucial corollary: privation designates not only the absence of a quality but also the violent process by which that absence may be actively produced, by which a quality may come to not be. In short, privation names also the subtraction of a quality by force. And such is the case also for that privation par excellence which is *adynamia:* it is not only always a real possibility but also "in certain cases" a real actuality. The possibility of the impossible is identified here in no unclear terms: it is potentially and actually possible to be deprived of the capacity for production, to be deprived of labor power.

Marx's definition of labor power, after all, is strictly Aristotelian: labor power "is the aggregate of those mental and physical capabilities existing in the physical form, the living personality, of a human being, capabilities that he sets in motion whenever he produces a use-value of any kind."[54] Labor power is precisely what Aristotle would define as primary and rational potentiality: the potentiality of human beings to act on and change something other than themselves. "Aristotle's genius" lies not only—as Marx puts it—in "his discovery of a relation of equality in the value-expression of commodities" but also in his discovery of the fact that labor power always involves the potential to be subtracted from itself, that labor power always may be wrested away by force. If Aristotle did discover value by not discovering it in the *Nicomachean Ethics,* that is precisely because that which he declares to be impossible in that work is posited as a concrete possibility in the *Metaphysics.* In the *Nicomachean Ethics,* he states, on the one hand, that commensurability does exist in the realm of exchange, and, on the other hand, that it is "impossible [*adynaton*] . . . that such unlike things can be commensurable"—namely, as Marx puts it, "qualitatively equal"—because to be commensurable would mean for these things to suffer the privation of those qualities that make them unlike one another, and indeed unlike any other. In the *Metaphysics,* however, *adynamia* names precisely such a privation, which is posited implicitly as the third term inherent to potentiality and actuality designating the privation of all their qualities, including and especially the power to produce: *adynamia* names already the potential for a general equalizer, the possibility of a universal nullifier. In short, in the *Nicomachean Ethics* Aristotle discovers *the concept* (in the exchange relation) without being willing and able to name it, whereas in the *Metaphysics* he discovers *the name* without being willing and able to conceptualize it (in terms of exchange). These two moments in Aristotle's thought are at once separated and related by *adynamia* as an unthinkable aporia: they constitute the open circuit that Marx closes and completes by positing the equalizing and expropriating relation between labor power and value, between potentiality and impotentiality. What remains truly unthinkable in Aristotle—namely, what he did not discover at all—is that the realm of the metaphysical and the realm of the economic could be related in any way, that the exchange relation could involve privation as violent expropriation, that *adynamia* could force its way into the realm of exchange in and as the general form of value.[55]

After this Aristotelian excursus, the materiality of value as such can be defined in a more precise manner. In Marx, value has the materiality of an absent cause immanent in its potential and actual effects, that is, in all particular use values and exchange values. For Marx, however, the concept of value does not suffice to understand the exchange relation under capital: a complementary concept of surplus value, of course, is also needed. In the *Grundrisse,* he writes:

> Surplus value in general is value in excess of the equivalent. The
> equivalent, by definition, is only the identity of value with itself.
> Hence surplus value can never sprout out of the equivalent.[56]

Obviously, as Marx points out immediately after these sentences, both value and surplus value "arise from the production process of capital itself."[57] This, however, does not explain the nature of the relation between the two. In other words, what does it mean to say that excess is not born out of that which it exceeds? In what sense, then, is surplus value "in excess" with respect to value? (And in this problem too the Aristotelian echo is unmistakable, as the question of excess plays a crucial role in Aristotle's theorization of the realm of the economic in the *Politics.*)[58]

In order to answer the question of the relation between value and surplus value, it is important to note first of all that for Marx the relation between surplus value as such and its particular forms is the same type of relation that binds value as such to its particular forms. In the *Grundrisse,* for example, he writes:

> *The surplus value which capital has at the end of the production*
> *process* [is] a surplus value which, as a higher price of the product, is

realized only in circulation, but, like all prices, is realized in it by already being *presupposed* to it, determined before they enter into it.[59]

Surplus value is found here to constitute at once the presupposition and the result of one of its particular forms, namely, profit. And again:

> If capital increases from 100 to 1,000, then 1,000 is now the point of departure, from which the increase has to begin; the tenfold multiplication, by 1,000%, counts for nothing; profit and interest themselves become capital in turn. *What appeared as surplus value now appears as simple presupposition etc.,* as included in *its simple composition.*[60]

In short, the quantifiable result (i.e., a specific surplus value) "counts for nothing" and yet reappears as presupposition (i.e., surplus value as such), that is, *it reappears as that nothing which counts as presupposition, it reappears as determinate absence.* Indeed, Marx felt that the distinction between surplus value in general and its quantifiable modes of realization constituted one of his most important discoveries. Commenting on the first volume of *Capital* in an 1867 letter to Engels, Marx writes that one of the "best points" of that work is "the treatment of surplus value independently of its particular forms as profit, interest, ground rent, etc."[61] If one compares this statement to the aforementioned rhetorical question that Marx asks in the *Grundrisse*—namely, "is value as such the general form, in opposition to use value and exchange value as *particular* forms of it?"—one sees clearly that for Marx value and surplus value function in exactly the same way. Or—to rephrase Althusser in *Reading Capital*—for Marx, neither value nor surplus value is "a measurable reality" as such because neither of them is "a thing, but the concept of a relationship . . . visible and measurable *only in its 'effects,'*" in which it is "present" "as a structure, in its *determinate* absence."[62] In Marx, both value and surplus value have the same structure and function according to immanent causality. Thus, the relation between the two— in which one is "in excess" of the other—can be described in the following manner: surplus value as such is the absent cause immanent in the general effect (value) that is itself absent cause immanent in its potential and actual effects (use value and exchange value), which, in turn, make it possible to turn value and surplus value into measurable, quantifiable, exchangeable, visible, and tangible magnitudes of violent expropriation of labor power in the form of money. In short—just as Aristotle had foreseen already, not without a shudder of horror—excess or surplus governs the entire machinic assemblage of capital from start to finish, in the first place and in the last instance. This is why Marx can write in the *Grundrisse* that "the creation of surplus value is the presupposition of capital" itself.[63] This is also how Negri—when reading the *Grundrisse* in *Marx beyond Marx*—can reach the conclusion that the "theory of value . . . can exist only as a partial and abstract subordinate of the theory of surplus value."[64]

I have undertaken this brief passage through Marx not to demonstrate that his "immense theoretical revolution" was to produce the concept of capital in terms of immanent causality: such a demonstration, after all, was articulated already, elegantly and incontrovertibly, by Althusser in *Reading Capital*.[65] My point has been more specifically to show that capital consists of a tetradic structure, whose four elements—namely, surplus value, value, use value, and exchange value—indeed relate to one another according to the logic of immanent causality. My point has been to show, in other words, that *both* capital and the common are tetradic structures governed by the logic of immanent causality, that they *both* determine a posteriori and are determined a priori by the one and only surplus, and that they constitute nonetheless two radically different modalities of surplus (neither despite nor because of the fact that they share in the same structure and in the same logic, for all other possible modalities of surplus likewise would share in such structure and logic). The singular difference that makes all the difference on this plane of immanence is the impossible nexus between its two sides, namely, the nonrelation between surplus value as locus of exploitation of the common and surplus common as unexploitable surplus, the nonrelation between impotentiality as violent separation of labor power from all its products—including "the physical form" and "living personality" of human beings—and potentiality qua potentiality as lived and incorporated in our bodies.

Arguably, it is such a difference, such a nonrelation, that drives Marx's philosophical and political project, and that he strives to identify and to articulate throughout his works. I will invoke here only one such articulation (and I will return to Marx's engagement with this difference at the end of this book).[66] In the *Grundrisse*, he writes:

Capital as such creates a specific surplus value because it cannot create an infinite one all at once; but it is the constant movement to create more of the same. The quantitative boundary of the surplus value appears to it as a mere natural barrier, as a necessity which it constantly tries to violate and beyond which it constantly seeks to go.[67]

When Marx writes in *Capital* that the movement of capital is limitless and infinite, he means this in the specific sense that capital is the constant movement to create more of the same.[68] Marx's point here is that the "quantitative boundary"—far from being "a mere natural barrier," or, as he calls it in a footnote to this passage, "an accident"—constitutes rather the insurmountable structural limit of capital. In capital, Marx discovers repetition without difference: capital is infinite repetition of the same whose structural limit is precisely qualitative difference. Capital "creates a specific surplus value because it cannot create an infinite one all at once." What would such "an infinite" surplus value be? And what would it mean to "create" it "all at once"? Such "an infinite" surplus value would not be surplus value in any sense whatsoever: being infinite, it would be immeasurable; being immeasurable, it would be unaccountable in terms of value—in short, *it would be surplus without value.* Moreover, to "create" it "all at once" would mean to produce it synchronically, to produce it in no time and without time, *to produce it without having to pay for necessary labor time.* This is to say that the production of such surplus would no longer belong to the capitalist mode of production. Capital strives for surplus—namely, for the infinite, for the synchronic—yet can construe it only in finite, diachronic, quantifiable terms. Capital attempts to posit itself as the plane of immanence yet cannot do so because absolute immanence is synchronic and infinite movement beyond any separation, division, or measure.[69] Capital reaches for that which is beyond measure yet can grasp it only in terms of measure, of equivalence, of value.[70] In this passage, Marx is envisaging a way to think surplus outside the form of value and within relations of synchronicity, a way to live surplus beyond capital altogether.

This intuition of a surplus beyond value constitutes one of the most important, and as yet not adequately explored, links between Marx and the thinker of immanence and of the common par excellence, namely, Spinoza.[71] To "create" infinite surplus "all at once" would be an act of love, in the sense that Spinoza gives to this term in Part V of the *Ethics.* I am suggesting, in other words, that Marx's formulation describes accurately the operation of Spinoza's third kind of knowledge, from which "there necessarily arises the intellectual love of God"—a love *sub quadam aeternitatis specie,* a love that "is eternal."[72] To substantiate this claim fully would take me well beyond the scope of this preface. Let me nonetheless point in the direction I would take were I to proceed further on this path. Before doing so, however, it may be useful to summarize Spinoza's theory of knowledge. In brief, Spinoza conceives of three different kinds of knowledge (which ought to be understood not only epistemologically but also ontologically, in the sense that each of them instantiates different modes of subjectivity).[73] The first— which Spinoza calls "imagination"—includes all forms of sensory and representational knowledge (i.e., knowledge based on corporeal perceptions, on images, on signs). The second—which he calls "reason"—is knowledge of the common: it proceeds from "common notions," namely, from the ideas of that which is common in two or more modes, including those "ideas . . . which are common to all human beings." The third—which he calls "intuitive knowledge"—I will discuss shortly.[74] Genevieve Lloyd has encapsulated succinctly the differences among these kinds of knowledge:

> The first way of knowing is focused on singular things, but is inherently inadequate. The second is inherently adequate, but unable to grasp the essences of singular things. The third and highest kind of knowledge is inherently adequate and able to understand singular things.[75]

It is important to note that Spinoza's concept of "essence" is a strictly nonessentialist and immanentist one, insofar as essences are not in common by definition: a singular essence appertains to each mode as well as to substance, whose essence is existence itself.[76] (This has important implications for the concept of the common.)[77] Even though essences cannot be shared, they can be known. They cannot be known adequately either through the first kind of knowledge (which conceives of them in an incomplete or distorted manner) or through the second kind of knowledge (because this kind of knowledge is not concerned with essences but with that which is common to all modes). Essences can be known adequately only through the third kind of knowledge.[78] Indeed, it is because both the first and the second kinds of knowledge fail to grasp the essence of things that the third kind—which builds nonetheless on the previous two—is needed. In short, even though there is a clear hierarchy among these different kinds of knowledge, all three are necessary and strictly complementary.[79]

SURPLUS COMMON · **33**

Let us return now to the third kind of knowledge and to the love it produces. Spinoza writes:

> Although this love of God does not have a beginning . . . yet it has all the perfections of love, just as if it had come into being . . . Nor is there any difference here, except that the mind will have had eternally these same perfections that we have just supposed to be added to it, with the accompaniment of the idea of God as an eternal cause. So if happiness consists in a transition to a greater perfection, beatitude must assuredly consist in the fact that the mind is endowed with perfection itself.[80]

This love comes into being in the same way in which Marx conceives of the production of infinite surplus, namely, "all at once." Or—which is to say the same thing—we experience this love "as if it had come into being" in such a way, because, strictly speaking, it has neither beginning nor end, given that it belongs to the realm of the eternal. In short, to achieve this love is to produce an experience of synchronicity from within and through the diachronic. Furthermore, this love involves surplus at least in two ways. First of all, it involves all the "perfections" appertaining to love, in the sense that, as soon as we achieve it, not only do we experience such perfections as an addition to our mode of being but also we experience them retroactively as having been there always already in us. In other words, to be in love here means to determine a posteriori and to be determined a priori by "the perfections of love" as forms of surplus.[81] Second, such an experience of love is accompanied by "the idea of God as an eternal cause"—namely, by the idea of substance as immanent cause of itself as well as of modes. But, as I have been implying all along, surplus is itself immanent cause, or, more precisely, immanence as such. I will return to this matter. For the moment, I wish to point out that as soon as Spinoza reconceptualizes substance as absent cause immanent in its effects, the world (i.e., substance and modes) is no longer *either* the theocratic world whose transitive cause used to lie outside of this world and used to mediate all relations among modes from afar *or* the world as sheer mass of unrelated modes without any cause, rhyme, or reason whatsoever. Spinoza's world, rather, is the self-positing and self-producing plane of immanence consisting of modes *and* their cause (which they determine and through which they relate). In Spinoza, the world includes and determines its own cause as surplus. *It is in this sense that the third kind of knowledge produces surplus as love, that the intellectual love of God is love of surplus.*

And yet—one might object—doesn't one often experience love precisely as excess? Isn't love always a modality of being in excess of one's own otherwise identical, equivalent self? Isn't love always that difference which breaks with and goes beyond all identity and all equivalence? In short, isn't love always an experience of surplus? What exactly differentiates the intellectual love of God from all other experiences of love? Spinoza explains this difference thus:

> Then it is to be noted that the sicknesses and misfortunes of the
> mind derive their origin chiefly from an excessive love for a thing
> that is subject to many changes, and which we can never possess
> [e.g., a thing such as money, as Marx might say!]. For no one is
> concerned or anxious about any thing except one that he loves, nor
> do injuries, suspicions, enmities, etc. arise except from love for
> things which no one can truly possess.[82]

This is love based solely on the first kind of knowledge, on the imagination—which Spinoza also calls "knowledge from inconstant experience."[83] This is love subjected to the tyranny of contingency, limited by the anxiety of loss. Indeed, for Spinoza what we experience as love is most often an experience of love as possession, which is haunted by the (past, present, or future) loss of that which we love. This is love as an experience of privation, as an experience of lack. This is love minus X (where X is the cause of love). By contrast, when we experience love without the concomitant loss of that which causes it, we experience love plus X, that is, we experience love and its own surplus. In short, *love of surplus occurs when the subject no longer suffers privation of potentiality, no longer experiences lack in being.* This is why Spinoza calls this love "perfection itself."[84] It goes without saying that this is no longer love as possession (of that which we love as other than oneself) because its cause is now immanent.[85] Indeed, this is also love beyond exchange and beyond measure altogether. Or, as Theodor Adorno and Max Horkheimer put it: "In the world of commercial exchange, he who gives over the measure is in the wrong; whereas the lover is always he who loves beyond measure."[86]

Nowhere does Spinoza imply that we cannot go from love as the experience of lack to love as the experience of surplus—hence his reference to "transition to a greater perfection."[87] Neither does he imply that the path from the former to the latter is a necessary, inevitable one: this path does not constitute a teleological trajectory.[88] The point, in any case, is that these two types of love are related, in the sense that it is possible to build on one in order to achieve the other, to turn one into the other: were this not to be the case, the love of surplus would be sheer mystical epiphany. The third kind of knowledge and the love that arises from it do not involve a flight into transcendence because one cannot achieve them directly and immediately, because they build on the previous two kinds of knowledge without ever leaving them behind. Spinoza, after all, insists that both body and mind are involved equally in the third kind of knowledge and in its love (which is why, despite Spinoza's own characterization of the intellectual love of God precisely as intellectual, Althusser argues that this "is in no way an 'intellectual' love").[89] Moreover, as Deleuze as shown, the second type of knowledge—the knowledge of the common—on the one hand, involves the first, and, on the other hand, constitutes the immanent cause of the third.[90] The knowledge of the common thus perfects the imperfections of the first kind of knowledge by finding its fullest realization in the third kind of knowledge and in the experience of love that arises from it. This is what I have been arguing all along: the common finds its highest degree of perfection—namely, its own determination beyond capital—in surplus common, that is, in producing its own surplus beyond value, in living its own surplus as love, in the love of surplus. It is from such a singular and common experience of love that any reconceptualization of love as a political concept within and against capital ought to start.[91]

It is in this common intuition of another way of living surplus that Spinoza and Marx are at their most revolutionary. The condition of possibility of such an intuition lies in an understanding of surplus as immanence itself. If both capital and the common share in a tetradic structure governed by immanent causality, that is because immanence itself consists of a tetradic structure that may be determined in different ways. Such is the structure of immanence in Spinoza, who was the first to think it in and for philosophy. In *What Is Philosophy?*, Deleuze and Guattari define philosophy as the practice of "forming, inventing, fabricating concepts"—in short, as the production of concepts.[92] In this context, they write:

> [Spinoza] fulfilled philosophy because he satisfied its prephilosophical presupposition. Immanence does not refer back to the Spinozist

substance and modes but, on the contrary, the Spinozist concepts of substance and modes refer back to the plane of immanence as their presupposition. This plane presents two sides to us, extension and thought, or rather its two powers, power of being [or power of acting] and power of thinking [or power of knowing].[93]

Plane of immanence, substance, modes of extension, modes of thought: such are the four components of immanence, where the plane of immanence is posited as the presupposition of the entire structure, as its surplus. Not only is surplus not a thing; it is, philosophically speaking, not even a concept, because it is prephilosophical. Deleuze and Guattari write:

Prephilosophical does not mean something preexistent but rather something *that does not exist outside philosophy*, although philosophy presupposes it . . . Precisely because the plane of immanence is prephilosophical and does not immediately take effect with concepts, it implies a sort of groping experimentation and its layout resorts to measures that are not very respectable, rational, or reasonable. These measures belong to the order of dreams, of pathological processes, esoteric experiences, drunkenness, and excess. We head for the horizon, on the plane of immanence, and we return with bloodshot eyes, yet they are the eyes of the mind . . . THE plane of immanence is, at the same time, that which must be thought and that which cannot be thought. It is the nonthought within thought . . . Perhaps this is the supreme act of philosophy: not so much to think THE plane of immanence as to show that it is there, unthought in every plane, and to think it in this way as the outside and inside of thought, as the not-external outside and the not-internal inside—that which cannot be thought and yet must be thought.[94]

What Deleuze and Guattari argue for philosophy is true of any practice and above all, perhaps, of the practice of politics, namely, of the practice of the desire to be in common: "not so much to think" surplus "as to show that it is there" as the extimate unthought in each and every one of our singular, common gestures. Elsewhere, Deleuze credits Spinoza with the "discovery of the unconscious, of an *unconscious of thought* just as profound as *the unknown of the body*."[95] Crucially, he adds: "The entire *Ethics* is a voyage in immanence; but immanence is the unconscious itself, and the conquest of the unconscious."[96] Immanence is the unconscious *and* its own conquest just as immanence is substance *and* modes. Far from being a Cartesian "conquest"—namely, a transcendent triumph of the mind and of its reason over the body and its nonreason—such a conquest names the act by which we incorporate our immanent cause in a supreme gesture of self-determination; such a conquest names love of surplus. Surplus, potentiality, production, unconscious, plane of immanence: these are all names for immanence degree zero; these are all names for what Negri in the pages of this book refers to as "the void," as "the nonontological absolute."[97] It is up to us to decide what to build on this void. It is up to us to turn this zero into a minus or a plus.

Acknowledging the Friend

> La pensée de l'amitié: je crois qu'on sait quand l'amitié prend fin (même si elle dure encore), par un désaccord qu'un phénoménologue nommerait existentiel, un drame, un acte malheureux. Mais sait-on quand elle commence? Il n'y a pas de coup de foudre de l'amitié, plutôt un peu à peu, un lent travail du temps. On était amis et on ne le savait pas.
>
> —Maurice Blanchot, *Pour l'amitié*

> The thought of friendship: I believe that one knows when friendship comes to an end (even if it still continues). One knows as much because of a disagreement that a phenomenologist might call existential, because of a tragic event, because of an unfortunate act. But does one know when friendship begins? There is no thunderbolt of friendship; there is, rather, a little by little, a slow labor of time. We are friends—and we did not even know it. (My translation)

Erasmus opens *In Praise of Folly* with a letter of dedication to his dear friend Sir Thomas More:

> Coming out of Italy a while ago, on my way to England, I did not want to waste in idle talk and popular stories all the hours I had to sit on horseback, but chose at times to think over some topics of the studies we share in common, or to enjoy my memories of friends—and I had left some here in England who were wholly learned and wholly gracious. Among them you, More, came first to mind.[98]

The friend comes first. Indeed, the friend precedes the dedication itself, given that the Latin title of this work, *Moriae Encomium,* means also "In Praise of More." More important, the friend precedes and enables thought itself: "the studies" Erasmus and More "share in common" are the source of thought. That one never thinks alone, that one always thinks in common, is an ancient truth of thought—as Agamben has shown elegantly.[99] And the friend is the other with whom one is in common when thinking. Or (as Deleuze and Guattari put it in *What Is Philosophy?*) the friend is "a presence that is intrinsic to thought, a condition of possibility of thought itself."[100] The friend precedes and enables thought much as the plane of immanence is the prephilosophical condition of possibility of philosophy itself: "Prephilosophical does not mean something preexistent but rather something *that does not exist outside philosophy,* although philosophy presupposes it."[101] The friend comes first in the sense that it is a synchronic rather than diachronic, intrinsic rather than extrinsic, immanent rather than transcendent presence of thought. My friend is my surplus thought: it is with my friend that I may come to think anew and differently, it is in my friend that I may become different from what I thought I was in the first place. Indeed, it is in friendship that this I ceases to be an I and turns into one who is many. Deleuze and Guattari begin *A Thousand Plateaus* by writing: "The two of us wrote *Anti-Oedipus* together. Since each of us was several, there was already quite a crowd."[102] One can think only as many, one can think only among friends, one can think only in the common.

The friends who made me think while writing on the common are—much like the common itself—legion. Among them, there are friends who not only made me think anew and differently but also were subjected to my often feverish, inchoate words, either in writing or in speech or in both, while I was working on this preface: Murat Aydemir, Kristin Brown, Richard Dienst, Bishnupriya Ghosh, Vinay Gidwani, Ron Greene, Michael Hardt, Qadri Ismail, Eleanor Kaufman, Saree Makdisi, Tim Malkovich, John Mowitt, Bhaskar Sarkar, Hans Skott-Myhre, Nick Thoburn, Kathi Weeks. And then there are two friends whose presence is so immanent here as to have become undetectable to me: it is not a hyperbole to say that I have experienced writing this preface as a common project involving, in different ways, Kiarina Kordela and Brynnar Swenson—with the crucial proviso that the limits of this project are only my own. Each in their various ways, all these friends helped me give these pages and the thoughts they try to express whatever substance or value they may have. Each in their various ways, all these friends are part and parcel of an infinite conversation of which this book is only one effect, only one form. To this common legion of friends—named and unnamed—I offer my gratitude.

My thanks also go to Jon Hoofwijk, who not only came up with the title for this book but also helped me write this preface in ways that he will never know; to Richard Morrison, my editor at the University of Minnesota Press, whose patience and tact in dealing with the countless hiccups and delays of this project were always impeccable and always enabling; to the two anonymous readers whose comments and suggestions were invaluable; and to an institution, namely, the College of Liberal Arts of the University of Minnesota, which provided time—which is money—by granting me a research leave in the fall of 2006, during which most of this book was completed.

There is always the friend who comes first and last: it is with everlasting, immeasurable gratitude that I dedicate this preface to Toni, who has shown me his life in the common and who has taught me how to learn from it.

Amsterdam—Venice—Minneapolis 2007

A Class-Struggle Propaedeutics, 1950s–1970s

CESARE CASARINO: I would like to begin by asking you to reflect on the most significant moments and events of your political and philosophical formation from the 1950s onward.

ANTONIO NEGRI: Besides the indelible marks left by the war when I was a child, my first moment of politicization as an adult took place during my brief involvement with Azione Cattolica [Catholic Action] in the early 1950s.[1] At the time, I was already studying philosophy at the University of Padua. But while the department of philosophy there was dominated by fairly conventional interpretations of Thomistic doctrine, with the leftist priests of Azione Cattolica we discussed theology by immediately relating it to political issues: we brought the question of class struggle to bear on theology in ways that already anticipated 1960s liberation theology. We were a motley and enthusiastic group; as I recall, Umberto Eco was part of it, among others. Of course, some bishop eventually took notice of what was going on, disbanded our discussion group, purged the relevant priests, and so on.

CC: Besides these theological readings, what were you reading back in those days? What readings proved to be particularly important for you?

AN: It was in those years that I began to receive a good training in philosophy. I began to read right away primary sources—and this is something for which I have to thank my philosophy teachers at the time. I remember that I read the Greeks very well during that period—especially Plato, and less so Aristotle.

CC: Were you reading these thinkers already in high school?

AN: Yes, I am talking about high school right now. It was also at that time that I read Saint Augustine as well as the classics of the Italian Renaissance, including Marsilio Ficino as well as more recondite figures such as Leonardo Bruni.[2]

CC: What about Giordano Bruno?

AN: As far as Giordano Bruno is concerned, every day I couldn't wait for school to be over so that I could rush back home in the evening and read his books there!

CC: And Spinoza?

AN: This is also the time when I began studying Spinoza. After that, I dealt with Kant and Hegel. I did all this while I was still in high school, and I must say that we studied all these thinkers really well there. After that, I continued with more advanced studies at the university level—and even though I was in a clerical department, they did make us read primary sources. There was, for example, an excellent professor who defined himself as a Christian existentialist—his name was Stefanini—and who introduced me to Martin Heidegger already in the 1950s: this was quite a strange thing to do in Italy at the time—and not only in Italy! He gave us to read *Sein und Zeit* [Being and Time] as well as several essays as if it was the most normal thing in the world to do—and even though he criticized these texts ferociously, he did give us the chance to read them. Likewise, several people there were already stirred and roused by Ludwig Wittgenstein. This is all to say that there was great disorder in my education: my studies were scattered and chaotic. This was due to several factors. First of all, the tragedy of the war as well as several deaths in the family were terribly important for me at the time, and they had the effect of sparking in me a great craving for life, a ferocious desire to get to know the world: this was the time, hence, when I traveled all over the world in search of experiences of all sorts. Furthermore, I had the good luck of winning a scholarship for the Scuola Normale di Pisa[3] at the end of high school, but at the time my mother was very ill and I was the only one who could be in the house with her, and hence I couldn't go. However, they immediately offered me instead a scholarship for an exchange program with the École Normale in Paris for a later date. So, in 1954 I went to Paris for a whole year, where I studied with Jean Hyppolite and I began my thesis on the young Hegel.

CC: But what about your studies in Padua? Did you interrupt your studies there in order to go to Paris?

AN: Yes, I did. Then I returned to Padua and I graduated from there in 1956—earlier than I was supposed to. I went through my studies very fast. I have always had the good luck of being an excellent student: this is one of those very strange things in my life that I have never been able to understand! I really was such a nerd [*secchione*]! And I used this quality of mine so as to save time, since in those days the idea of saving time and of growing up quickly was extremely important. At any rate, Paris constituted a parenthesis in my studies, which accelerated and anticipated many of my future developments. Once I was back in Padua I decided not to graduate with the thesis on Hegel that I had written in Paris, and instead I wrote yet another thesis, which dealt with German historicism, that is, with Dilthey, Treitschke, Weber, and Meinecke. At first I published only the parts dealing with Dilthey and Meinecke in 1959, and I rewrote and published the parts dealing with Weber only much later, in 1967.[4] In the meanwhile, my thesis on Hegel had been turned into a book and published in 1958. And between 1958 and 1959 I translated Hegel's 1802 texts into Italian, which were published in 1962. So, in this period I devoured massive quantities of philosophical knowledge: I followed what was fundamentally a dialectical-humanist trajectory. If I look back on this trajectory from the standpoint of the results it yielded—which perhaps is not the correct way of going about it—I think that what I was looking for in that period was an escape from an epoch that at the time I was absolutely convinced constituted its values as so many entelechies, as so many forms of shutdown. I was looking for a way out of the modern. This is why I was so annoyed then by those attempts to come up with a *philosophia universalis,* which I experienced in all those Thomistic philosophers, Christian philosophers, or natural law philosophers who surrounded me and who were hegemonic in the philosophy department at Padua. And this is also why I began to forge strong ties with the French and German philosophers whom I had gotten to know while traveling and who helped me to develop in a direction that could be characterized as some sort of existentialist—or, perhaps, phenomenological—humanism.

cc: You say that in this period you devoured massive quantities of philosophical knowledge. But what stood out? What was most formative for you at the time?

an: Clearly, there was Hegel—whom, I must say, I studied really well. He was the pivot, the great passage—and I would have to reckon with him and struggle against him in later years. At the same time, there was Sartre. In this sense, I don't think my *Bildung* was very original. Anybody who had an alert, lively mind at the time basically had this same formation. And after that I read Freud, even though I must add that psychoanalysis has remained always foreign to me—and I don't know whether this is a limit or an advantage. In the meanwhile, throughout this period I was strangely also involved in the analysis of language. This is the time when neo-empiricist currents of thought are being introduced in Italy: they were fundamentally linked to pragmatism, which I continue to be quite fond of in some ways, having read in those days much John Dewey, William James, and Charles Peirce. And then the English arrived. In particular, many of my friends went to Oxford—and I was there too for a brief period—and we started reading Wittgenstein together, which for us was pretty much like reading James Joyce: we would gather around these texts without being able to understand anything! So, we began by evaluating his poetics, his rhythms. But then there was that madman of Enzo Paci—an existentialist at first and subsequently a phenomenologist—who came down to Padua and energized us greatly. His circle—which eventually founded the journal *Aut Aut*—became very important for me, especially because I made many friends there whom I reencountered later in the context of political militancy. While in Padua, Paci undertook a very strange philosophical project: he attempted to put together phenomenology, Husserlianism, and Wittgesteinianism. Of course, it didn't work—but it did nonetheless enable us to study Wittgenstein in depth for the first time. At any rate, the point is that—even though all these readings were extremely important for me, and I was terribly passionate about them, and I built my whole life, friendships, and even loves around them—I was nonetheless looking for something else, for something practical. I felt the tremendous need to turn all these studies into something practical. In particular, my brief passage through Catholicism had showed me that it was possible to link thought and action.

cc: You are referring to your time in the Azione Cattolica, right?

an: Yes. What interested me most at the time was to try and think forms of community that would enable us to go beyond the crisis of values that I had experienced first as a child during the war and then as an adult in the misery of the world around me after the war. This was the first time, in other words, that the problematization of the common came into being and became a question for me. What is a community? What is to be together? What is to express ourselves together? What is to give a hand? What is charity? What is the love of others? What is to act according to all these questions?

cc: It seems to me that what's at stake in what you are saying is a conception of how to live thought. Can you say more about this need you felt to bring your theoretical investigations to bear on all other aspects of lived experience?

AN: I think we all seek a practical outcome for our studies—otherwise we would feel unfulfilled. In my case, I had no choice: I was forced to seek practical outcomes by the enormous confusion of the times, which was not only theoretical but also human. During the Cold War, in Italy, we did not get any sense of what life in common might be, of what political life might be. Something that was very important for me—and that in a sense constituted a decisive moment in my theoretical life—was the fact that I became communist before becoming Marxist. I gradually became communist without knowing what Marxism was. Or, rather, I knew Marxism in the form in which I had learned it in school: there they had taught it to me as dialectical materialism pure and simple, as a dogma that did not interest me in any way whatsoever.

CC: You say that you became a communist before becoming a Marxist. Is this assessment entirely retroactive? In other words, did you at the time think of yourself as a communist without being a Marxist? Did you call yourself communist as opposed to Marxist?

AN: No, I thought of myself as a communist thinking that I was also a Marxist. In any case, I certainly did not call myself communist; rather, I felt I was becoming communist. Immediately after the expulsion from Azione Cattolica, in fact, I joined the PSI [Italian Socialist Party]—without, however, participating in any of its political activities. It was only around 1958 that I began to get involved in politics. That was also the year in which I passed the exam that enabled me to begin teaching at the university level [*esame di abilitazione alla libera docenza*], and I passed it by presenting my book on the young Hegel. This was a book that built on Lukács and, in particular, on his major book on the young Hegel. But it's not as if I plagiarized Lukács: my research had started with Hyppolite and with the French analysis of Hegel. To get a sense of how really taken with Hegelianism I was, just imagine that the book that became fundamental for me around that time was Lukács's *History and Class Consciousness*. You see, after Grigory Zinoviev condemned it at the 1923 Communist International, this work was thrown out of circulation; nonetheless, I found a copy of it in the Munich library, I spent much time studying it, and I decided to translate it into Italian. In the end, however, it was Giovanni Piana, a friend of mine, who translated it shortly thereafter.

cc: You are characterizing this period of your life as a Hegelian phase, during which Lukács in particular was crucial for you. But were you already
critical of Hegelianism and of the dialectic then? Or was it only later, in
the 1960s, that you began your critique of dialectical thought?

an: That critique took place later. My theoretical situation in the 1950s was
such that those were the only instruments at my disposal: you continue
to use them, and yet you are profoundly dissatisfied with them. So,
here was this thing called the dialectic: sometimes it worked; and yet
some other times it seemed to be a false key, a false solution. It opened
any door—and only a false key opens all the possible doors. It lacked a
conception of singularity. It had a very unclear relation to the question
of nature. It lacked radical antagonism. In short, Hegelianism was reactionary. But it was so precisely because it was reactive with respect to real
and important matters—which is why I have always believed that it is
only from reactionaries that one learns what is most fundamental. Even
though it annoyed me, I continued to use Hegelianism because it was
a philosophy of modernity. What made me suspicious of Hegelianism
eventually was the fact that it lacked any internal obstacles; rather, there
were only limits that could always be overcome. It was extremely difficult
to bring practical materiality back into these philosophical schemata.
Keep in mind also that at the time the hegemonic current of thought in
Italy was still Gentilian.[5] This powerful cultural substratum was everywhere: it lived on in theoretical philosophy, in historicism, as well as in
the cynicism of the PCI [Italian Communist Party]. Incidentally, this was
also the case with Gramscism: what we were being offered was precisely
a Gentilian Gramscism. In any case, I think that in the end it is historically accurate to say that Antonio Gramsci fed himself much more on
Gentile than on Benedetto Croce. Even though, of course, Gramsci was
trying desperately to use these schemata within a communist practice—
because this is precisely the practice that forces one to confront such a
materiality. In the end, communist practice was quite different from this
thing that enabled you to sublate, to overcome, to tumble upside down,
to do somersaults in the air and come back down always perfectly on
your feet.

cc: Are you saying, in other words, that you began to be dissatisfied with the
dialectic because it made everything too easy?

an: Yes, precisely, everything was too easy. And, in fact, I wrote way too
quickly then!

cc: When did you first read Gramsci?

an: I always already read Gramsci! And always badly! There was no way to get rid of him. There wasn't a film you could watch without having already been told by the critics: "This is a classic example of the hegemonic usage of such and such a concept!" There wasn't a play you could go to without having been given twenty pages of Gramsci to read in advance! It was all really suffocating and terribly dogmatic. But what was most absurd was the fact that somehow Gramsci had inevitably foreseen and approved of each and every political move of the communist party![6]

cc: I find it interesting that while outlining your *Bildung* you have not yet mentioned Marx even once. Am I to surmise, then, that you read Marx only much later?

an: I began to read Marx in 1962. Around 1959—after the book on Hegel and after the Hegel translations—I had embarked on two other projects: I started working with the journal *Quaderni Rossi* [Red notebooks] and at the same time I started writing a major study on the formalism of Kantian jurists. Incidentally, it is also at this time that I began to get significantly involved with the Socialist Party in Padua. My research on Kantian jurisprudence took me for long periods of time to Germany, where I needed to consult archives. But at the same time this project took me repeatedly to Turin and to the Martinetti library: Piero Martinetti was a Kantian professor at the University of Turin who had collected an enormous amount of texts by late-eighteenth-century Kantian philosophers of right. And it is while I was in Turin for my research that I met Raniero Panzieri and Renato Solmi for the first time. The point I am trying to make is that my intellectual barycenter had suddenly shifted: whereas up until this time it had been located between Padua and Milan, and had been marked by phenomenology as well as by this strange Lukacsian Hegelianism, now it moved toward Turin and toward Panzieri—and it was Panzieri who insisted that I read Marx.

cc: So, after this Lukacsian-Hegelian phase, you became interested in Kantian jurisprudence. Why? What was so compelling about the philosophy of right for you at that moment? In other words, was there something in Kantianism that perhaps helped you move away from the dialectic?

an: First of all, I began my academic career teaching philosophy of right, and, of course, I had studied some jurisprudence—especially Roman law and constitutional law. What interested me was the formation, the coming-into-being, of the dialectic. The main thesis of my book on the young Hegel was that political thought had been central and fundamental in Hegel's formation: the critical question was to understand how Hegel had confronted the various forms and modes of Kantian formalism. In Kant, the law is defined as a form that organizes certain social relations. In Hegel, this form becomes a transformation: at the same time that it organizes these various elements, it transforms them and raises them to a higher level of social constitution and of spiritual constitution. What interested me was to ascertain what kinds of alternatives had emerged within Kantianism, understood as that absolutely central site in which all the political-philosophical—and hence also juridical—currents of the time had converged. What I started excavating within Kantianism, therefore, were the various ways in which the philosophers of law—and especially the practical jurists who directed and shaped the massive codifications that were taking place at the time—interpreted the Kantian form, that is, the juridical qualification of social facts.

CC: In a sense, this is what you were saying earlier when you spoke about your need to find practical outcomes for your theoretical investigations. In this case too, what seems to have interested you most in the Kantian problematic was precisely the way in which the philosophy of right was immediately translated into juridical practice through a process of codification.

AN: A theoretical problem acquires any sense only when you move into the real. In this specific case, the theoretical problem was inextricable from the French Revolution. The subtitle of my study on Kantian jurisprudence was "A Study of the Genesis of the Concept of Form in Kantian Jurists from 1789 to 1802"—and 1802 here was taken as the moment at which the constitution of Hegel's dialectic reached its full maturity. So, this is what I found: there were those who apprehended the Kantian form as a transcendental belonging to natural law, that is, as a transcendental that repeats itself eternally—much as Leo Strauss would maintain later in our times; then there were those who intended it in neo-Kantian terms, that is, in terms of community (à la Charles Taylor) as well as in terms of contract (à la John Rawls); then there were those who historicized it in hermeneutical terms, such as, for example, Friedrich von Savigny. And then there was Hegel. And Hegel cleared them all off the stage by saying: "No, my dear gentlemen, what we have here is the different levels of the historical constitution of the social, which change time after time and provide us each time with new paradigms for the interpretation of social complexity." This study, in other words, was extremely relevant to our contemporary situation: in fact, it had an enormous success and it brought me tenure immediately in 1963 at the age of thirty. This is when I stopped being a member of the faculty of law and I moved to the Department of Political Science, where I became professor of Doctrine of the State, which was the name under which philosophy of right was taught within the Department of Political Science.

CC: I do want to return to Marx and Marxism, however.

AN: My need for Marxism stemmed from a desire to understand the real. I chose to espouse Lukacsian Hegelianism probably because I believed that it would have given me the chance to confront the real. Such a choice, in other words, was motivated by a belief that philosophy and politics ought to go together, that community-affirming values are the telos of the dialectical process, that the dialectic, after all, does enable one to analyze things, that is, to interpret things as social relations. In short, leftist Hegelianism constituted my first introduction to Marxism. But the most important introduction to Marxism that I had was through my relationship with Panzieri. And around him there were other figures who also became important for me: Solmi—who at the time was translating Benjamin as well as the *Grundrisse;* Giovanni Pirelli—an extraordinary man who belonged to the Pirelli family, who basically financed all of us, who had a fantastic knowledge of the Third World and in particular of Africa, and from whom I learned much about anticolonial struggles; and, of course, Franco Fortini. Through Panzieri, I also got to know Vittorio Foa—the principal union organizer in Turin, who introduced me to the world of FIAT—as well as Mario Tronti, Alberto Asor Rosa, Romano Alquati, all of whom became extremely important for me. I must confess that even though I was really fascinated by all these figures and by what they had to say, I was very cautious and prudent when I first came into contact with this world. But this was also due to the fact that at the time I had to deal with a whole series of urgent practical matters, such as the beginning of my university career, the decision to get married (which I did in 1961), etc. In the meanwhile, I was elected to the lists of the Social-ist Party to the Padua city council in 1960—without campaigning, and, in fact, without doing much of anything, really. The socialists in Padua were leftists within the Socialist Party: they had struck an alliance with the Communist Party at the local level and eventually they would become part of the PSIUP [Italian Socialist Party of Proletarian Unity].[7] This means that when the 1960 revolts took place, I found myself there in the front lines doing political work of all sorts. And, as a prize, I was sent to the USSR. I was there also with Armando Cossutta, Abdon Alinovi, and Pio La Torre.[8] In any case, this was truly an upsetting trip.

cc: In what ways was it so? Could you be more specific?

an: I was completely disturbed by the contacts I had with the Communist Party there. You see, during the 1950s I had been to Yugoslavia many times: in 1956, I had attended an important conference on self-management in Belgrade; later, I attended a long seminar on management methods in the socialist economies in Dubrovnik. This is to say that I had had some exposure to the political environments and discourses of the socialist countries. But my impact with the USSR was nonetheless traumatic: I was fundamentally a communist, and there I found myself in front of a world of bureaucrats. We were welcomed first by Mikhail Suslov—who was in effect the manager of Soviet ideology—and then by various other party officers who dealt with the West. Later, we were taken to some sort of sanatorium on the Black Sea, which was full of Communist bureaucrats who did nothing else but pig out. At any rate, eventually I had a ferocious psychosomatic reaction to this environment: I came down with a terrible case of asthma and I almost died. Once I got better, I went to Leningrad and then I returned to Italy—cured of any sympathy for the outcomes of the Soviet project.

cc: And once you were back in Italy?

an: The most important event of this period for me was my involvement with *Quaderni Rossi,* which was in the process of doing research on the working class. The first thing that I learned in this context was precisely how to conduct a workers' inquiry [*inchiesta operaia*].[9] I began to use my privileged position as secretary of the Socialist Party in Padua so as to meet and work with the union organizers, to make as many contacts as possible with the workers, as well as to introduce my friends to this world. I was driven by curiosity: I wanted to understand exactly what work was, what its forms of organization were, what the working class was, what exploitation was, what the wage was, etc. And it was at this point that I began to read Marx. I studied systematically all his works over the course of two years—and I still have and use the notes I took then. And reading Marx coincided with the end of my Hegelianism. Then I embarked on different research projects, even though I did not publish anything between 1962 and 1969.

cc: Why is it that reading Marx marked a break with Hegel?

AN: Because I began to see Marxism not at all as the end of history but rather as an alternative to modernity. Marx was not perfecting modernity. He did not present us with an ideal that would exalt the not-state as opposed to the state, that would advance communism as an organic force as opposed to the realm of the communalized individual. No, Marx was nothing of the sort: he was already something other than that. What Marx was about was the fact that struggles—or, rather, activities—are what produce and make the world. Everything else for me—and Hegelianism above all and first of all—started to look like the conclusive element and indeed the end of philosophy, started to look like a mystifying schema, like a screen. I started to exit this Hegelian world, to go down below, and to move into the real. My great Cartesian doubt, my great Husserlian caesura consisted precisely in going in front of the factory doors to verify what really was going on there. But what I realized there was also the fact that Marx's *Capital* probably needed to be rewritten, and that such a rewriting needed to start from the discovery of subjectivity, from an investigation of such a subjectivity. The factory was an extraordinary adventure for me. Interestingly, this was also the time when I basically stopped traveling: all my discoveries and explorations were focused on the factories of Porto Marghera.[10] This was my favorite place back then: Porto Marghera had been built at the end of World War I, but it was in the late 1950s and early 1960s that the great chemical plants and oil refineries were built there. I was introduced to this world by friends of mine who were socialist union organizers and who were a marginalized minority there: that area, in fact, was a Christian Democratic stronghold, and to find a job in those factories was regarded as an immense privilege. I am sure you are familiar with these classic situations from your native Sicily. At any rate, there were no union organizations in the area; or, rather, union organizations did exist but were mostly external to the factory—and when they were internal they were very corrupt, that is, they had been put together by the boss so as to fulfill the need of pretending that there was some form of dialogue and mediation. As I became more familiar with this environment, I started inviting my friends from Turin (Panzieri, Foa, etc.) as well as the comrades who were working with me at the University of Padua (Massimo Cacciari, Luciano Ferrari Bravo, and, much later, Lauso Zagato) to come down to our factory meetings. In the meanwhile, I founded a newspaper by the name of *Progresso Veneto* [Veneto's progress] and I invited many of these young factory workers to describe and indeed advance their struggles there. And, as I was saying earlier, these are the years—from 1962 to 1969—when I stopped writing.

CC: Deleuze writes somewhere that he was always fascinated by the gaps in the lives of thinkers, by the long periods of silence during which they did not write or publish. And surely he must have had Foucault in mind, among others; he must have been referring to those long eight years after the publication of the first volume of *The History of Sexuality*, during which Foucault interrupted his planned project and reoriented his whole research. At any rate, Deleuze claims that it is precisely in such gaps that what's most important happens. Do you think that this was also the case with you?

AN: Perhaps so. The factory was my archive—and it was an exceptional one at that. My research consisted of arriving in front of the factory door at 5:00 a.m. and staying there till 8:00 a.m. handing out leaflets, talking, and getting drunk on grappa with the workers, while surrounded by thick winter fog and unbearable oil stench. Then I would go and teach at the university in Padua. And then I would return to Porto Marghera at 5:00 p.m. to meet again with the workers so as to write the leaflets we would be handing out the next day. There were around sixty thousand factory workers in that area at the time.

CC: While you were involved in this kind of political activism, what were you teaching at the university?

AN: I think I was teaching courses on the theory of state planning. Basically, my research has always developed in the following way: I teach first what I write about later; but once I have written a book, I neither teach it nor read it again! In any case, back then I was trying to construct a theoretical model so as to analyze and understand those amazing twenty years of economic development and of political struggles in Europe: the 1950s and the 1960s. I was very much in contact at the time with the scholars of the Regulation School in Paris (such as Michel Aglietta, Benjamin Coriat, etc.), and I found many parallels between their project and my own—even though they were fundamentally economists, while I was working on the morphology of sociojuridical and sociopolitical systems. At the same time, I was beginning a critique of the tradition of the philosophy of public law: namely, the major texts of German constitutionalism—from Carl Gerber up to Carl Schmitt; the thinkers of juridical formalism—such as Hans Kelsen; as well as the great American constitutionalists and philosophers of public law—Oliver Holmes, Benjamin Cardozo, etc. This is basically what I was teaching at the time. In those years, I did no philosophy up until 1968, when I started writing my book on René Descartes—*Political Descartes: Reason, Ideology, and the Bourgeois Project*—which was published in 1970.[11]

cc: But how exactly did you get to Descartes from these investigations into the juridical constitution of the state-form?

an: In between those investigations and the study on Descartes, I wrote an essay on the genesis of the modern state as a way of preparing myself for the latter—an essay that was also the result of my engagement with the Annales school, which I was reading at the time. These too were all elements, however, that I was putting together so as to be able to distance myself from them. In other words, I wouldn't want the story I am relating to become teleological. I wouldn't want to give the impression that all my research at the time was somehow awaiting the arrival of 1968. And yet, it is true that there was some sort of destinality in what I was doing! It's a bit creepy, really. All I did from 1958 to 1968 truly was a great propaedeutics to class struggle.

cc: In other words, you reached 1968 with all the appropriate instruments to make sense of the state-form and of its repressive apparatus.

an: Yes, of course! But, you see, the state-form *is* class struggle.

cc: What do you mean exactly? Throughout its history, Marxism has mostly focused on the analysis of class struggle, while it has often neglected the analysis of the state. And even when the question of the state has undergone analytic scrutiny, such an analysis has usually been kept separate from the question of class struggle. But for you the state-form and class struggle somehow are one and the same? When and how did you reach this conclusion?

an: At the time, I was following two different paths at once. On the one hand, I persevered with the analysis of class struggle. Much of this analysis was conducted by investigating the world of the factory workers at Porto Marghera, as I was explaining earlier. Alongside this investigation, however, I studied much relevant sociology. When, for example, I noticed in 1962 an enormous wave of wildcat strikes at the FIAT factories in Turin, I started looking through the sociological literature and I discovered that already a few years earlier a book detailing this kind of phenomenon had been published in England. This discovery encouraged me to find out whether similar phenomena had ever been analyzed in the USA. And, in fact, it was then that I learned about Facing Reality—a group of U.S.

Trotskyists who at the end of the 1930s had broken with Trotsky and had decided to spend all time and effort on the factories. They were all rank and file,[12] and they wrote a series of splendid analyses of the class movements within the factories. What especially interested me was the fact that they were dealing with Fordist factories and, in particular, with oil and chemical plants. I learned about them in *Socialisme ou barbarie*—the journal that Cornelius Castoriadis and Claude Lefort published in Paris, which became my daily bread in that period. Such research developed further when we—that is, Ferrari Bravo, Alquati, and I—started studying the self-destruction, or, rather, the self-critique of American functionalism and the passage to conflict analysis. All these different cultural elements were investigated and ultimately directed toward our primary goal, that is, they were all brought together so as to understand what exactly took place in the factory. On the other hand, we were also studying the classics of the theory of the state—even though I started to get interested in Soviet juridical theory quite late: I read Evgeny Pashukanis, for example, in the 1970s. In any case, the point is that my research method has always consisted in starting first of all from a phenomenon that you want to explain: for example, you see that suddenly the state intervenes on a determinate set of social relations, or, perhaps, that capital exerts pressure on the state so as to make sure that such an intervention happens; but then you also note that things don't really go in the way in which either the state or capital had planned; rather, what takes place actually mediates between class struggle and whatever it was that state and capital were looking for in the first place; and then you see that these mechanisms gradually spread throughout the articulations of state administrative action; and hence you watch the law transform itself under your very eyes into conflict procedure, that is, into codified conflict management. So, on the one hand, we advanced our investigation of the factory, and, on the other hand, we studied the forms—juridical and otherwise—through which the state manages conflict. In other words, we were studying class struggle from two opposite points of view at once.

cc: And this explains the need for delving into several different disciplinary domains simultaneously.

AN: Yes, I have always worked in a completely interdisciplinary context. For example, I don't think I have ever studied a juridical text without keeping historiographical and sociological texts nearby.

CC: Undoubtedly, this must have also been Marx's method. It seems that in order to take class struggle seriously one must conduct interdisciplinary research, that class struggle breeds interdisciplinarity!

AN: Yes, and that is one of the reasons why Marx became so important for me. In those years, we really felt we were discovering a new Marx—and that certainly wasn't the Marx of the first book of *Capital,* volume 1. I always find Marx very annoying when he spins all these tales about the commodity form. Of course, they are all true tales! But in order to understand them, one needs to get to them only later, that is, after the analysis of class struggle! Otherwise, all we are left with is Derrida's version of the commodity! In any case, our study of Marx was immediately related to the analysis of class struggle and was made answerable directly to the realities of struggle. We always proceeded on two fronts simultaneously: political work in the factory and theoretical work on the factory—and we insisted maniacally on linking the two. There was no meeting that did not begin with an analysis of what was taking place in the factory at that particular moment; or, as we used to say then: "Whoever does not conduct investigations in the factory has no right to speak." This is how a whole new generation of intellectuals was born who had no longer anything to do with the Communist Party. Except for that brief "vacation" in the USSR, I have never had anything to do with the Communist Party. I don't think of myself as particularly libertarian! I am not even minimally an anarchist! I am very fond of discipline and of groups that organize so as to come to a common understanding. I adore the fact that there exist organizations that put order in all aspects of reality! What I absolutely detest is that all of this might be done in a stupid manner! Having said that, my assessment of the USSR is not entirely negative. While I was watching yesterday that bunch of buffoons who rule our world at the G8 in Genoa, I couldn't help but think: "I wish the USSR was still around!" I know it's cruel and absurd to say such a thing, and yet . . .

CC: Let's go on to the 1970s.

AN: You think I am done with the 1960s? It was such a rich period! You have no idea what it meant, for example, to travel from Porto Marghera to all the other major oil and chemical plants in Italy—from Gela in Sicily to Porto Torres in Sardinia, from Milan to Taranto, etc.—and to put together groups of comrades in all of these places. Undoubtedly, 1962 constituted the pivotal moment and the point of no return for many of us. This is when the wildcat broke loose: the workers left the FIAT factory in Turin and took the streets—and then we had three or four days of fierce clashes with the police all over the city, and especially at Piazza Statuto. The point is that this strike was fundamentally a revolt against the unions: it was conducted against FIAT, but its main target in effect was the unions, which were widely perceived as having swindled the workers. And this is when they started accusing us very harshly of all sorts of things: this is the first time they called us fascists . . .

cc: Where did such accusations come from?

an: They came from the Communist Party, from the CGIL [Italian General Confederation of Labor], and from *L'unità*.[13] They were so kind to us! In any case, this is also when the shit hit the fan at *Quaderni Rossi*: this is when Panzieri got scared, as he understood suddenly that the political path we were following in the journal would have taken us completely outside of the traditional workers' movements. You see, he was ten or fifteen years older than I and he had lived in those movements: he had been the head of the Socialist Party in Sicily, he had worked in the unions, etc. And hence he got scared. Among other things, he was also one of the editors at the Einaudi publishing house; during that period, he published many great politically radical works, but he started getting enormous pressures from the press to stop doing so. Basically, most people who looked at us from the outside saw a bunch of savages! I have never really been able to understand how I got tenure; I mean, they knew perfectly well who I was and what I was up to. In any case, they made me pay for it eventually. They made me pay for it all at once later. I suppose they gave me tenure in the attempt to co-opt me. I am sure you know how these mechanisms of co-optation work: they ask you to be faithful to the corporation, or else . . .

cc: All the more so nowadays, when the university is being restructured according to corporate models—especially, but not exclusively, in the USA. In other words, I suspect that the type of co-optation you experienced then was quite different from the current corporate type, which is perhaps more subtle, as well as more effective in the end.

an: In any case, after this first break with Panzieri, our group—that is, mainly Tronti, Asor Rosa, Cacciari, Ferrari Bravo, and I—founded the journal *Classe Operaia* [Working class], which was active from 1963 to 1966 and which marked the foundation, or, rather, the consolidation, of Italian workerism. Then there was another break when Tronti and some others decided to join once again the Communist Party—which they had left when they were very young. At this point, in 1967, we made one last attempt and we founded yet another journal, namely, *Contropiano* [Counterplan]—which lasted only one year, because 1968 marked the end of the propaedeutics to the working class and, in fact, marked the end of all propaedeutics. So, this is how we got to 1968. But I must also point out that we all reached 1968 differently. Take, for example, Ferrari Bravo. He was a bit younger than I—as he was born in 1940, while I was born in 1933—and was still a student when I met him. What really struck me about him was the fact that he was already a different life-form, that he already belonged to a different epoch from mine: he hadn't experienced the war. And the war in northern Italy had been particularly intense and complex: besides having been a war against the fascists, the partisan war in the north had been also very much a class war. In any case, Luciano had not lived through it. He was—as he used to say—a communist *naturaliter*. He had no need to delve into himself, to detach himself from the past. This was also the case with Cacciari, who was younger than Ferrari Bravo: I met him when he was seventeen, and, in fact, I can say I basically raised him! It was a strange revelation to encounter such extraordinary people: in the early 1960s, I got to know a whole young generation that had reached already that level of political and theoretical development which I had had to struggle so much to reach. They had arrived there almost naturally and without any effort: they just were there—and they were ready for the great adventure of 1968. It is precisely when one looks back at that generation that one best realizes the folly of the political repression that swept Italy in the 1970s: an extraordinary generation of intellectuals—which was also the first postwar generation—was swept away, destroyed.

cc: This is perhaps a good moment to turn to the 1970s. How did you experience this decade? How was it different for you from the two preceding decades we have been discussing?

an: First of all, I started writing again—and I did so for reasons having to do fundamentally with my involvement in political movements. With the study on Descartes, I had begun to introduce certain historiographical criteria in my research: for example, it was in that work that I elaborated for the first time a concept that has become increasingly important for me, namely, the concept of the two modernities.[14] I saw Descartes's project—his "reasonable ideology"—precisely as an attempt to mediate between these two modernities. I must say, however, that my arguments in that work were still quite confused, much as my first attempt at a critique of Hegel in the early 1960s had not been very well defined and articulated. All these concepts were not yet precise: they began to appear in the study on Descartes thanks to my engagement with a certain kind of historiography, but they were still somewhat uncertain. In any case, the point is that, after dealing with Descartes, I started writing—and continued to do so for a long period of time—strictly on the basis of the movement's needs: in a sense, these were writings made to order. This was the case with my writings on the New Deal, as well as with all those pamphlets that are now collected in *Books for Burning* and that in the end constituted the main reason why they sent me to jail.[15] During this period, I also put together a volume of essays under the title *La forma stato: Per la critica dell'economia politica della Costituzione* [The state-form: For a critique of the political economy of the Constitution].[16] Among these essays, one in particular was extremely important for me, namely, "Il lavoro nella Costituzione" [Labor in the Constitution], which has been collected also in *Labor of Dionysus: A Critique of the State-Form.*[17] I cannot overemphasize how crucial and fundamental this essay was in my political development. I actually wrote it in 1962–63, but I kept it in the drawer till 1977, when I finally published it by inserting it in *La forma stato.*

cc: Why did you wait so long before publishing it? Why did you feel the need to wait?

an: I was really scared—that's why! This essay was so important for me because in it I had been able for the first time to take the critique of labor all the way to the Constitution, to unhinge the constitutional apparatus using the critique of labor as a lever, to critique the role played by the bourgeois concept of labor in the juridical formation of the state.

cc: What exactly scared you about all this?

an: I was afraid that my arguments did not hold up; I was afraid that I had not been able to make them theoretically coherent. Keep in mind that when you come up with a good idea, you need to be careful about letting it out.

cc: In other words, you finally published the essay only when historical developments themselves had confirmed and supported its arguments. Is this a fair assessment of what you are detailing here?

an: Yes, it is. Today, however, I would probably not be as prudent as I was then—and not because I have become particularly imprudent but because now I would be better able to recognize that something so new for me would index a passage, would signal the anticipation of a new period. That early essay was precisely the first piece of writing anticipating and already belonging to a distinct period in my research that actually began only fifteen years later and that was characterized by an attempt to push the critique of labor to its most extreme and most logical conclusions. That is why that essay was so fundamental for me: in it, by critiquing the Italian Constitution and by unveiling the paradox of a republic founded on labor,[18] I had attacked the very roots of the New Deal state-form, which is the republic founded on the relation between big business and big labor.[19]

CC: Such a critique of labor had already emerged in the early 1960s but had to wait till the mid-1970s to be fully articulated.

AN: Yes—although this critique was already under way in my essay on John Maynard Keynes and the New Deal. And I will always associate this essay with a funny story, a peculiar event. In 1968, I, along with the other editors of *Contropiano,* organized a small symposium on Keynes at the University of Padua, and we invited various groups of comrades to participate. We had scheduled several papers: in particular, Ferrari Bravo delivered a very important paper on the juridical-administrative forms of the New Deal, whose main theses at once enabled and were later reconfirmed and supported by my "Keynes and the Capitalist Theory of the State," which is now a chapter in *Labor of Dionysus.*[20] At any rate, the point is that, as the symposium was taking place, the first student occupation of the university took place: the students burst into the classroom in which we were meeting and kicked us out! At the time, I thought it was a beautiful coincidence! As I recall, it was Alisa Del Re—later to become my teaching assistant—who burst into the classroom and interrupted our meeting, shouting: "Out! Out! All of you! Out!" We all left very amused and went to continue our discussion somewhere else. So, 1968 coincided with the first conclusion of a research that had silently developed for ten years. And then the 1970s came, which preeminently were years of political struggle.

CC: What I find interesting is that the theses you first put forth in the early 1960s and later took up again in the mid-1970s came into being as the direct result of your continued involvement with the workers' movement at Porto Marghera, and that it is only later that your study of Marx and of the *Grundrisse* confirmed such theses.

AN: Yes, that's right.

CC: In other words, it was the political movements that took you to Marx rather than the other way around. This fact alone, of course, does not explain the nature of your arguments regarding the *Grundrisse* in *Marx beyond Marx*—which you published in 1979; however, it seems to me that it is nonetheless an important fact to take into consideration when studying and evaluating this work. What do you think about this? Could you talk about the genesis of *Marx beyond Marx*?

AN: I had been arguing for someone to translate the *Grundrisse* into Italian already in the mid-1960s. Then, one of our comrades—Enzo Grillo— took this task upon himself and the translation was finally published in 1976. Those pages of the *Grundrisse* dealing with the question of machines, however, had already been translated by Solmi, and we had published them in the second issue of *Quaderni Rossi*. So, even though I had already studied and worked on the *Grundrisse* in the 1960s, it was finally only in 1977 and 1978 that I started writing on this text—and the circumstances that led me to write on it are significant in their own right. I had to run away from Italy to Paris because of a first arrest warrant relating to the Bologna events of March 1977.[21] Once there, I found a job immediately at the University of Paris VII, where I continued my work with the Regulation School: we conducted research around the questions of imperialism and unequal exchange, and while I dealt with the juridi- cal aspects of the research, they dealt with the economic aspects. (Inci- dentally, these were the same topics that Ferrari Bravo was working on back at the University of Padua at the time.) It was precisely while I was working on these matters that Althusser invited me to give a series of lectures on the *Grundrisse:* he knew that we had been working on this text at the University of Padua; he felt strongly that the way in which this text had been read in Paris up until that moment was simply awful; and hence he insisted that we reintroduce it and discuss it anew there. I accepted, and those were the lectures that constituted the bulk of *Marx beyond Marx.* The moral of the story is that whenever they force me to abandon political practice, I have nothing else left to do but to start writing once again! I have told the judges many times already: "Why do you want to force me to write? Don't put me in jail and leave me alone, so that I don't have to write!"

CC: Leaving these important circumstances aside for the moment, could you be more specific regarding the political and conceptual genesis of *Marx beyond Marx*? How did you conceive of this work? What exactly were the relations between your political experiences and the arguments of this work?

AN: In *Marx beyond Marx*, I summarized from a theoretical standpoint all that I had done in the 1970s, without the militant rhetoric. This work—which was conceived fundamentally as a commentary on the *Grundrisse*—allowed me for the first time to create links across a whole series of different elements of analysis: analysis of methodology, analysis of struggles, analysis of cycles, analysis of classes, analysis of the state.

CC: But how did the *Grundrisse* enable you to put all these things together? Why was it this text in particular rather than others that allowed you to accomplish this?

AN: If the *Grundrisse* constituted such a condition of possibility for me, that was due perhaps to the very nature of the text: the *Grundrisse* in effect was a formidable probe, an extraordinary sounding line that Marx had plunged into the real phenomena of his time.

CC: Are you referring specifically to the 1857 financial crisis, which was unfolding while Marx was writing the *Grundrisse*?

AN: Yes, of course, it's in the midst of all that that the Marxian theory of revolution is born. In fact, to fully appreciate the importance of the *Grundrisse* for me, you have to keep in mind that the 1970s not only saw the political advancement and intensification of our struggles but also marked the moment when we discovered that capitalistic structures had undergone profound transformations. From the early 1970s onward, capitalistic initiative started up once again and was forced to make great leaps forward. Several factors contributed to this: first of all, 1968; second, the U.S. defeat in Vietnam; third, the great development of workers' struggles; fourth, the oil crisis—understood as the first expression of the victory of anticolonial movements and as a formidable demand that global revenues be redirected toward the South; fifth, the brilliant American maneuver by which the dollar was detached from gold—a maneuver that paved the way for unbridled deregulation and that in effect decreed that money has value solely insofar as it is exchanged, or, put differently, solely insofar as it is overdetermined by Power.[22] This complex configuration of events had the result, on the one hand, of unhinging the power of the working class, and, on the other hand, of forcing capital to shift and to move outside of its traditional territory. What exacerbated this situation from a working-class standpoint was the fact that the unions simply refused to see that anything had changed, and completely denied the existence of these new phenomena and realities—even as the workers, and especially the new generations of workers, were living them. In particular, factory workers started witnessing at once the exponential computerization of the labor process as well as capital's increasing reliance on social circuits of production. In other words, as the factory began to undergo profound restructurations, the whole of society began to be turned into a factory: capital saturated the social through and through. It was during this period that I put forth for the first time my theses regarding the emergence of what I called the socialized worker [*operaio sociale*].[23] And that was the second time in my life that they called me a fascist! They accused me of being against the unions because I was affirming that a new type of labor force was emerging. The unionist political line at best amounted to an attempt to bring all these people, all these new forms of subjectivity back into the fold of the factory. But the unions simply did not have the strength to do that. Our political line was quite different: we felt that it was much better to try and run ahead of these new processes within capitalism; we felt that it was much better to try and anticipate these developments so as to be able to organize this new type of external labor force—external, that is, to the factory. In any case, I have discussed such developments in detail elsewhere.[24] Let's return now to the *Grundrisse*. In the context of the historical and political conjuncture I have just outlined, our reading of the *Grundrisse* constituted also an attempt to recuperate and reelaborate *Capital*'s volume on circulation, in which Marx had begun to understand and foresee such a socialization of production. Whereas the first volume of *Capital* had been fundamental in the 1960s, it was the *Grundrisse* and the second volume of *Capital* that became fundamental in the 1970s. In a sense, the research we were conducting in the 1970s meant to redress some crucial gaps in *Capital*, namely, the missing chapters on the wage and on the state. It was only later—in the age of empire—that the third volume of *Capital* became newly relevant.

Sounding the Present

On *Empire*

CESARE CASARINO: In many respects, *Empire* stands out as an anomaly among your works. Many of your other books are works of textual analysis, that is, works that produce concepts and put forth arguments on the basis of detailed analyses either of a specific text (such as your books on Marx's *Grundrisse,* on the biblical book of Job) or of a specific constellation of texts (such as your books on Spinoza, on Descartes, on Lenin, on Giacomo Leopardi). These are all works that—among other things—attempt a radical reevaluation of a thinker by undertaking intensive and extensive close readings of his textual production. *Empire,* on the other hand, is a work of synthesis, that is, a work that interrelates and brings together numerous different texts, thinkers, historical formations, and disciplinary discourses, so as to produce a specific philosophical concept— the concept of empire—and, in this sense, this book also constitutes something like a summa of your previous work and, indeed, of your life experience. Moreover, something similar could be said also about *Empire*'s place in Hardt's research. Likewise, in fact, his first book is very different from *Empire,* given that it consists of an original assessment of Deleuze's thought that is centered on and based on a careful analysis of three specific, crucial, early texts by this philosopher.[1] Given that before *Empire* both of you wrote for the most part books that relied significantly on detailed analyses of highly circumscribed textual domains, what compelled you to write a work of synthesis such as *Empire,* whose scope is as vast as it is diverse? What convinced you of the urgency and necessity of this type of book?

ANTONIO NEGRI: Before trying to analyze the fundamental motives that compelled us to write *Empire,* I would like to mention the specific occasion that lies at the origin of this work: namely, I was asked to write a textbook on modern political thought by the French publishing house Seuil. I accepted the invitation, and I drafted a detailed outline for a work on the concept of modern sovereignty. Suddenly, however, the series in which the textbook was supposed to appear was canceled and the whole project fell through. In a sense, *Empire* began with the outline for this textbook.

CC: This certainly explains why *Empire* often reads like a pedagogical overview, or, in any case, like a text that is driven by pedagogical imperatives.

AN: This is the case only for the first two parts of *Empire,* namely, the historical parts: these are the sections of the book, in fact, that derived essentially from the outline I had drafted for Seuil. But there was also another occasion—an occasion of a different type—that motivated us to write *Empire* and that inspired especially the third and fourth parts of the book: it consisted of the series of debates that took place on the pages of the French journal *Futur Antérieur* regarding the question of globalization in the aftermath of the fall of the Berlin Wall and of the first Iraq war.[2] It was while participating in these debates that Michael and I first began formulating what later became the central hypothesis of *Empire,* and that we finally came to the conclusion that we needed to elaborate and refine this hypothesis in writing. More than formulating a hypothesis, at first we were simply asking ourselves a question: what is the character of the emergent global unification that corresponds to and is sponsored by American unilaterality? It was, thus, essential for us to understand the role that other capitalistic forces—such as Europe or Japan—were playing in such a process of unification. In particular, one of the issues that was most discussed in *Futur Antérieur* was the protracted and ferocious trade war between the United States and Japan that took place on and off throughout the 1980s and 1990s, largely due to different levels of development in the electronic industries of these two countries. There were definitively moments when everything seemed to indicate that Japan was on the verge of winning this war. And yet, even at such moments, we never ceased to argue that the United States would have won this war in the end because the level of social development of the technologies in question was infinitely more advanced in the United States—and we were right.

CC: You are implying that it is the level of *social* development—as opposed to the more specifically technical or scientific development—of a given technology or industry that produces value. Put differently, that which produces value in the end is always social relations—that is, modes of social organization and cooperation—rather than technology per se; if anything, technology is secondary to and expressive of certain social relations. In short, the social always comes first—which is, of course, what Marx was saying all along.

AN: Yes, I agree. The reason why at times it seemed as if Japan would win this fight was that Japanese companies focused all their efforts on the technological means of production—which often are highly visible and tangible, and which, hence, draw much attention in the media and elsewhere.

CC: While the social determination of technology and, more generally, the social means of production are more difficult to detect, describe, and analyze.

AN: And it was precisely on the basis of the social means of production that we were convinced that the United States would eventually come out victorious: nowhere more than in the United States, in fact, were the figure of the socialized worker and the role of immaterial labor more developed and productive at that point.[3] It was this crucial insight that constituted the point of departure of our arguments in *Empire*.

CC: There is a fundamental continuity, thus, between the arguments you and Michael develop in *Empire* and the hypotheses regarding the moment of real subsumption of society by capital—hypotheses that you and others had been elaborating and refining at least from the late 1960s onward. In effect, the insight that constituted the kernel of *Empire*'s arguments— namely, that the United States would eventually win in the struggle against Japan—was the final confirmation of those earlier hypotheses.

AN: Yes, but if there was continuity between *Empire* and the hypotheses on real subsumption, and if the insight regarding the relations between Japan and the United States was able to provide us with the starting point of our arguments in *Empire*, that was also thanks to a crucial intervention made by Michael: I am referring to his beautiful review of Giovanni Arrighi's *The Long Twentieth Century*, in which he used those hypotheses in order to argue against Arrighi's cyclical understanding of the development of capital as well as against his conviction that the United States eventually would have to abdicate economic supremacy to Japan.[4] In any case, the point is that in the early 1990s Michael and I were in fundamental agreement on two crucial theses, which constituted the basis of our collaboration: we were convinced, first of all, that immaterial labor had reached the point of hegemonic primacy and, second, that we were witnessing the emergence of a supranational form of governance—that is, a structure of order and command—corresponding to and supportive of the processes of globalization.

CC: The problem with Arrighi's account is that it does not sufficiently take into consideration the development of social forces; reading his book, one is left with the impression that capitalism is some kind of *perpetuum mobile* that moves, functions, and develops all by itself, rather than being pushed, driven, and determined by class struggle and by social antagonisms of all sorts.

AN: This is also, by the way, the conception of capitalism that one finds in the Frankfurt School; in fact, this is the classical conception of capitalism one finds in all purely objectivistic interpretations of Marxism. Such an interpretation—which by now has been fully absorbed, incorporated, and deployed also by Wall Street—amounts to an understanding of Marxism as a set of formidable instruments for the analysis of social relations: this is, however, a purely objective analysis, according to which the emergence of any kind of transformative force is enabled exclusively by capitalist crisis; put differently, this type of analysis is founded on the premise that only a crisis in capital can produce the possibility of radical change. According to my reading of Marx, on the other hand, there are always two opposing forces—capital and labor—that can never reach a synthesis; at most, they can temporarily reach more or less stable equilibriums.

CC: According to you, in other words, capitalist crisis is induced by labor in the first place, and hence it is actually labor—that is, the pressure that labor exerts on capital—that enables any possibility for change.

AN: Yes. This is—if you will—a Machiavellian reading of Marx. Put differently, the dualism constituted by these two forces is not at all a metaphysical dualism; it is, rather, an empirical as well as materialist dualism, which cannot be sublated in any way. Moreover, this is a dualism that is redetermined over and over again—and each and every time it is redetermined by exploitation. And exploitation is always a machine for the production of subjectivity, is always a process of subject formation.

CC: And hence class struggle is the process par excellence through which subjectivity is produced. In any case, the point is that your analysis of capitalism gives priority to the question of subjectivity, and that you always analyze capitalism from the standpoint of the production of subjectivity. A subjectivist analysis of capitalism?

AN: I am not sure whether the term "subjectivist" adequately describes the way in which I analyze capitalism, but, clearly, the question of subjectivity does play a crucial role in my conception of capitalism. One of the things that I did to earn a living in Paris was from time to time to write sociological reports for government ministries as well as for private companies. Once I cowrote with two other comrades—Maurizio Lazzarato and Beppe Cocco—a detailed and purely technical report on the political consequences of the information highways in Europe. While working on this report, I had a series of exchanges with both American and European computer scientists, and, in particular, I had many conversations with a Silicon Valley computer scientist who used to visit the Soviet Union regularly during the mid-1980s. I remember that he always came back with very ambivalent reports on the state of Soviet computer science: on the one hand, he was extremely impressed with how advanced computer science was there, especially when it came to hardware and infrastructure; on the other hand, he was puzzled by how perfectly useless all of this scientific and technological advancement was. Exception made for intercontinental ballistic missiles and other computerized weapon systems, they had not been able to find any other use for their computers.

CC: In short, there was astounding scientific and technological potential, but the social conditions of possibility for the actualization of such a potential were simply not there.

AN: More specifically, it was the subjective condition of possibility that was lacking: the subjects who corresponded to this new technology—that is, who could and would help concretize as well as expand its possibilities—simply did not yet exist in Soviet society at the time.

CC: You are saying, in other words, that the actualization of any type of potential—scientific, technological, and otherwise—always depends on appropriate and enabling forms of subjectivity. Undoubtedly, this is the reason why you privilege the question of subjectivity in your work.

AN: And, in particular, this is the reason why Michael and I pay so much attention to the question of subjectivity in *Empire*. If *Empire* is a work of synthesis, as you suggested earlier, it is so only in the following sense: it interrelates, on the one hand, a series of critiques of modern sovereignty, and, on the other hand, a series of investigations into the production of subjectivity that attempt to trace the anthropological mutations of modernity, which, as we know, are always determined by struggle. *Empire* is not a synthesis in the sense that it brings all the different aspects of our past research together, thereby finally completing them, realizing them, and transforming them by subsuming them into an organic whole;

it is a synthesis in the sense that it juxtaposes all these different elements in such a way that they resonate with one another—and by resonating they produce a surplus [*eccedenza*]. If we say something new in *Empire*—and I think we do—that new element consists of a surplus that comes into being through a process of mutual resonance. And it is on the basis of such a surplus that I defend this book as a creative synthesis, as a transdisciplinary and transmaterial synthesis.

CC: Would you say, then, that *Empire* constitutes what for lack of a better term I would call a nondialectical synthesis? Your defense of this book—as well as of the method that you and Michael adopted in it—seems to indicate something of the sort.

AN: I would simply say that in *Empire* we created the monster, not unlike the one I write about in "The Political Monster."[5] *Empire* is a product of hybridization and metamorphosis: we hybridized all the different parts of our past research and life experience, and such hybridization produced a metamorphosis, a monster.

CC: I would like to return to the question of method in *Empire* and, in particular, to the way in which this book is written and organized. Earlier I pointed out that *Empire* is quite different from your previous works in terms of its scope as well as of its style, and you replied that much of the book was based on an outline for what you had conceived originally as a textbook. This explains its expository tone, its pedagogical style—doesn't it?

AN: No, I don't think so. The tone and style to which you refer are actually Michael's doing. He is very good at organizing topics in a coherent manner and at explaining difficult concepts in clear and simple terms.

CC: Very well. You should perhaps tell me, then, who is responsible for what in *Empire*. Exactly how did the two of you write this book together?

AN: First of all, we discussed the overall structure of the entire book at length—including the chapter subdivision—and we came up with a table of contents. After that, each one of us picked an item from the table of contents—sometimes a whole chapter, sometimes a section or even just a paragraph in a chapter—and proceeded to write an outline of that item. We then exchanged, criticized, and very often completed each other's outlines, till when all the writing was basically done. At that point, we spent much time moving some of these materials around: for example, we would move a section of a chapter to another chapter, and so on. We realized then that there were several sections or paragraphs that did not quite belong anywhere or did not fit very well in the logical flow of the discussion; this is when we came up with the idea of inserting separate sections at the end of some chapters—sections which at first we used to call scholia. When finally we were able to find the right place for each of these sections and to pull everything together, we rewrote and edited the whole thing a couple of times.

cc: There are parts of this book, though, that seem as if they had been written much earlier, as well as for different purposes and contexts.

an: Oh, yes. There are even whole articles that were lifted in their entirety from earlier works and inserted in *Empire*. For example, most of those historical parts dealing with the development of imperialism derive from documents that had been published already in *Macchina Tempo* [Time machine];[6] all the stuff about capitalist cycles had been written by Michael earlier and was thrown in almost without any changes; and so on and so forth.

cc: In this respect, *Empire* is similar to your previous collaboration with Michael—*Labor of Dionysus*—with the difference that there you acknowledge explicitly the presence of older materials. Does this mean, by the way, that the writing of *Empire* did not take as long as one might imagine given the length and scope of the book?

an: The bulk of the work was all done in one year, and then we kept on revising and editing for two more years. So, yes, the new parts did not take too long to be elaborated and written down.

cc: All in all, what do these new parts add to the older materials that you integrated from elsewhere? What would you say are the entirely new insights and elements in *Empire* that had not been articulated yet in your previous works?

an: Among the new elements, two or three stand out as being fundamental, in my opinion. The first is the critique of the type of universalism that finds its political expression par excellence in the United Nations, and the second is the analysis of the crisis, obsolescence, and disintegration of international law. Moreover, while the analysis of the American constitution was present already in *Insurgencies*,[7] all the materials dealing with the USSR in *Empire* are completely new.

cc: But you and Michael had already written at length about the USSR in *Labor of Dionysus*.

an: Yes, true. The way we frame and discuss the question of the USSR in *Empire*, nonetheless, is quite different.

cc: I agree with you on what is new here with respect to your previous work—especially when it comes to the first two points you just made. What I find also to constitute a significantly new element in *Empire*, however, is the way in which the relation between capitalism and sovereign Power is conceptualized in it. When you compare modern sovereignty with the new and emergent form of sovereignty that you call empire, you describe the latter as a reelaboration of the expansive and expansionist constitutional project of the USA, as the immanent constitution of an open space, and as a movement that goes beyond all barriers and limits, only to find or to produce new ones farther along the way. I suppose it is not a coincidence that such a description of this new form of sovereignty—which, in a sense, due to its immanent character, is no longer a form of sovereignty strictly speaking—is remarkably similar to Marx's description of the development of modern capitalism in the *Grundrisse:* there, in fact, he writes of capitalism as producing a tendentially global and open space from the very start, and, above all, as a movement that overcomes its own limits by pushing them always farther along.[8] And, importantly, these are the arguments and passages from the *Grundrisse* that Deleuze and Guattari invoke when elaborating their concept of "apparatus of capture" in *A Thousand Plateaus*[9]—a concept that you elaborate further in *Empire*. The point, in any case, is that, on the one hand, you and Marx are dealing with two quite different objects—that is, sovereignty and capitalism, respectively—and, on the other hand, the structure being described in both cases is virtually identical. I wonder, then, whether it would be feasible to say that capitalism and that form of sovereignty which is empire have a certain type of movement in common, that they develop and move across time and space in similar or even homologous ways, that they share in the same spatiotemporal categories, or—in short—that they conceptualize, structure, and measure time and space in the same ways. Aren't we dealing here with what Foucault would have called a diagram, that is, with an abstract mechanism and matrix that does not originate either in capitalism or in empire but that both nonetheless have in common? If the answer to this question is affirmative, then it would follow that, even though empire arguably has emerged later than even late capitalism, the latter never constituted a model for the former in any direct way; the blueprint for empire, rather, would consist of an abstract principle whose myriad manifestations would include also the various and sundry apparatuses of real subsumption.

AN: Yes, but how does such an abstract principle emerge? Understandably, you are trying to avoid getting caught in the proverbial chicken-and-egg impasse. Your solution, however, does not account for—indeed, does not tell us anything about—the emergence of that principle you invoke. The point is that the diagrammatic figure is the product of struggle. The diagram is born out of struggles as well as out of the capitalist acknowledgment of the impossibility to control such struggles according to previous parameters, to contain them within older dimensions. Try to look at these dynamics no longer from a perspective of development, that is, from within a movement of development; try, rather, to conceive of them like someone who sits on the margins of such a development or event and looks at what is taking place. Think of a Dutchman standing on a beach, staring at the sea, with the intent of building a dike. What is he doing? How does he proceed? First, he gauges [*misura*] the strength of the waves that rush at him; then he builds a system of dikes in a certain place; then he builds another one ten kilometers behind the first one; and so on. And he does all this fully knowing that the sea will rush at him with increasing strength and will bring all dikes down eventually, and that he or others will have to start all over again and build another network of dikes at some point.

CC: I am not sure I am in full agreement with this parable, which—if I understand it correctly—suggests that the diagram is something like a strategy of containment of struggle. It is certainly that . . . but is it only that? Is the sole function of the diagram to contain? It seems to me that this is a purely negative, limiting function. I think that in Foucault the diagram fulfills also a positive, productive function.

AN: Whether its function ends up being negative, positive, or both, the fundamental point for me remains that the diagram emerges always in relation—and as a response—to struggle (and it goes without saying that at times this is a double response, in the sense that it constitutes a reaction to past struggles as well as a preventative, preemptive measure against future ones). In any case, empire and capitalism do have a diagram in common. This is a diagram that fundamentally concerns the spaces and times of domination as well as the forms of control: in this respect, it constitutes indeed a negative response, a blockage. And this diagram emerged because the previous one was no longer tenable: wage demands—which is to say, life needs [*i bisogni di vita*], or, more precisely, those desires that would anticipate and constitute needs, and hence that would determine the quantities of the wage—could no longer be satisfied on the basis of the previous diagram's internal monetary norms. Under such pressures, the prices of commodities increased to the point that they were no longer competitive, and hence the alternatives became either to quit production altogether or to go back to what had been fascism's solution to this problem, namely, autarky—a solution that had failed in the end. To put it differently: the diagram's first and foremost problem was that the nation space [*lo spazio nazione*] no longer held, no longer functioned. The second problem was that internal contradictions as well as wealth had been moved to the colonial territories. But the same mess happened in this case too! In other words, it's not as if wealth could be recouped in the colonial territories and then transferred to the national proletariat—thereby producing some sort of fraternal bond with the latter, thereby reducing internal contradictions, thereby enabling internal reformism. None of this was possible because the national proletariat too continuously raised the bar, demanded more. The nation-state and colonialism collapsed together simultaneously.

cc: But in what sense did they collapse? The nation-state, for example, may well be subordinate to the emergent imperial networks and global institutions nowadays; it is, nonetheless, still present, necessary, and functioning in various—old as well as new—capacities. If to collapse in this case does not mean to disappear, what does it mean exactly?

an: What I mean is that the nation-state and colonialism failed as economic possibilities, and that, hence, they failed also as possibilities for exercising sovereignty over limited spaces. Capital cannot live in limited spaces for too long, and hence eventually it has to look for different types of sovereignty as well as for different norms that would enable its massive quantities of accumulated labor to move around the world. This is precisely what happened at the beginning of the 1970s, when the dollar cut loose from the gold standard. In this sense, Richard Nixon and Henry Kissinger—who masterminded this extraordinary political-economic maneuver—were truly two geniuses: they constituted the Lycurgus of capital, that is, they laid the political foundations of postmodern capitalism.

cc: The dollar's break with the gold standard, in other words, enabled the crystallization of that new diagram which capitalism and sovereignty now have in common. And this explains why it is practically impossible nowadays—if it was ever possible, that is—to produce a critique of sovereignty without producing also a critique of capitalism and vice versa.

AN: More precisely, the critique of political economy nowadays can continue to fulfill the functions it had in Marx's time only if it constitutes at one and the same time also a critique of the social in all of its aspects, that is, a critique of contemporary forms of life.

CC: Let me pursue a little further this matter of the new diagram, and, in particular, of the crucial role the USA played in its emergence and formation. It seems to me that the USA occupies an ambiguous position in empire as well as in *Empire*. On the one hand, in *Empire* you insist on the fact that empire is not American and that the USA does not constitute the center of empire precisely because the latter is a form of sovereignty that has no center by definition. On the other hand, in the same book you also insist on the centrality of the USA for empire, especially as a constitutional model (and I don't mean this only in terms of the juridical constitution but also in terms of the social one, that is, in terms of the material fabric of social relations). In principle, there is no contradiction here; this is not to say, however, that there are no tensions at all between these two positions. There could be no empire without the USA, and yet empire is not American: how do we make sense of this paradox?

AN: Well, there could be no empire without a unified Germany either. Nonetheless, yes, of course, the USA does play a primary role in the emergence and ongoing development of empire. That aside, however, you are quite right to point out that there is something problematic about the way in which we deal with the USA in our book; in fact, there are several unresolved problems there when it comes to this matter. First of all, to the extent to which the American constitution turns into the imperial constitution—and I am using "constitution" here in the formal, juridical sense of the term—it affirms and indeed reinforces its own fundamentally aristocratic character. This is a point that does not come across very clearly in our book.

CC: Could we say perhaps that the moment when the American Constitution becomes the imperial one is also the moment when it becomes clearer than ever that the American Constitution had been an aristocratic rather than a democratic one all along?

AN: Yes, I suppose so. The American Constitution is an aristocratic constitution in the sense that it asserts in an extremely precise and uncompromising manner that Power belongs to the virtuous, that Power accrues to virtue, and that virtue is by definition the virtue of those who hold capital. Under this respect, therefore, the American Constitution immediately posits itself as a set of norms that is wide open to global deployment: being virtuous, after all, cannot provide the basis for national character; being virtuous, rather, constitutes a Classical, Hellenic, Enlightenment character.

cc: Could we return to the paradox I mentioned earlier?

an: Undoubtedly, it is difficult to imagine a transformation of the present world order that would not entail a capsizing of the American order. In other words, it is probably the case that the empire is nowhere and everywhere; it is also true, however, that it is impossible nowadays to imagine any type of truly radical event—positive, negative, or both—that would not take place on the highest point of capitalist development. The Seattle movement, for example, would never have started had it not started precisely in Seattle, that is, in one of the world capitals of information technology and communication industry. No anticolonial movement will ever turn into a worldwide anti-imperial movement without producing first a Malcolm X who would bring such a struggle deep inside American society. Etc.

cc: It strikes me somehow that the political elites that rule the USA at present do not share your understanding of empire. Don't you think that at least some among them will attempt to turn the empire into a strictly national matter, that is, will attempt to rule over the empire in a colonial as well as imperialist manner rather than in an imperial one? Looking back on the early 1990s, it seems to me that the "New World Order" was the term that the first Bush administration used precisely in order to identify the emergent reality you later called empire as well as to stake out a claim on such a reality in the name of the USA understood as an imperialist nation-state.

an: There is no doubt that right now the American ruling classes are tempted very much to transform the empire into an entity over which the USA could rule no longer as a republic but specifically as a nation. Such a split between republic and nation, of course, is nothing new in the history of the USA: it has always been there—from its foundation to the present day. I am convinced that at present Bush the son represents the nation while a large portion of the American people still represents the republic. I am convinced also that all the current political developments will turn the USA into what, in a recent article for *Libération*, I referred to facetiously as Byzantium: this—mind you—would not constitute merely the triumph of the American nation against the American republic; it would also decree the end of the American constitutional aristocracy and the beginning of a monarchy that would rule in the name of the globalized interest of large capital.

cc: So, you are saying that Bush the son is a nationalist monarch who exercises global sovereignty in the name of multinational corporations! Quite a hybrid creature! I must confess that this sounds a bit too paradoxical somehow.

an: Yes, I am saying something like that, and, unlike you, I see no paradox in any of it. In any case, the point is that empire is a tendency, and, much like all tendencies, it can be guided in a variety of ways. At present, we are witnessing the struggle for the ways in which empire will be headed in the future. What Michael and I did in our book was to record one of these ways—namely, globalization—which, as far as I am concerned, is irreversible. However, precisely to the extent to which globalization is determined by struggles, and precisely to the extent to which struggles continue to take place within globalization, empire could be configured in a different way. As Tacitus shows us, after all, there is an enormous difference between the Roman Empire in its earliest phase—which, in some ways, was a democratic phase—and the Roman Empire under Tiberius.

cc: What are you referring to exactly when you invoke these struggles that live within, feed on, as well as determine globalization?

an: When I speak of struggles, I am not really referring to people going to demonstrations, and the like. I am referring, rather, to wage levels, to cost of living—in short, to the distribution of wealth.

cc: You are referring to quotidian antagonism, to the world of needs and of their expression.

an: Yes, precisely. Macpherson once wrote a splendid book on English postrevolutionary political thought in which he refers to the period after the English Revolution as the appropriative age.[10] Well, I believe that the modern begins precisely with the appropriative age of the bourgeoisie and extends up until and including the age of distribution, or, rather, the multiappropriative age. The Keynesian equilibrium, after all, was a multiappropriative equilibrium. Today, all of this is over, finished, and done with. Today, there is no longer any measure, and hence there is no longer any reasonable appropriation either. Today, we are outside measure—and that is so because we are in a state of productive surplus. We could easily satisfy all the needs of all the populations in the world: this is not a potentiality; this is a calculable, economic possibility. Once upon a time, we used to say: "Let's try the impossible." Today, all we need to do is to try the possible!

CC: What used to constitute both a political and an economic problem is now exclusively or primarily a political problem. In theory—and in theory only—such a development ought to make it easier to solve the problem. In practice, however, the problem is at least just as difficult to solve as it ever was: what has changed is that the difficulties we are facing now are of a different type—but they are no less difficult for being different.

AN: Today, we are dealing with a completely different problem: it is a problem that concerns specifically political formulas. We need to create political formulas that would be able to have a powerful impact on both capital and empire, on both economic production and political representation, at once. As far as I am concerned, the Luxemburgian version of the councils, of the sovietist formula, still constitutes one of the lesser evils, one of the most decent solutions.

CC: I would like to focus for a moment on the historical scope of *Empire*. In particular, I am struck by the way in which the present and the past are interwoven and related to each other in this work. On the one hand, this is very much a book about the contemporary historical conjuncture: its main purpose consists of naming a new form of sovereignty that has broken with all previous incorporations of sovereign Power—including the nation, the people, the proletariat, etc.—as well as of identifying the multifarious manifestations of this new form in the present. On the other hand, in this book you also feel the need to trace the earliest origins, ancestries, and antecedents of this contemporary form of sovereignty: the archaeology of empire takes you as far back into the past as the Middle Ages and the world of classical antiquity. In short, in your account of empire there is a tension between, on the one hand, radical breaks and ruptures, and, on the other hand, continuities that span vast periods of time. This is, of course, a fairly common tension in works that wish to understand how we came to be so as to become different from what we are, in works that think historically and ontologically at one and the same time. Obviously, this is not a tension that should be resolved necessarily—but this does not mean that it should not be questioned at all. For example, I think that, since some of empire's elements and characteristics seem to be quite ancient according to your account, it is legitimate to wonder whether you are suggesting that empire has always existed in some form or other—that is, as a latency—and that it

crystallized and became fully actual only once certain conditions materialized in our present (and these are conditions that you analyze in detail).
In any case, this is just one example of the type of questions that are produced by this tension in your work.

AN: No, I don't agree. Michael and I never suggest that empire has always
existed—as latency, as potential, or as whatever else. That which has
always existed is the thought as well as the practice of resistance (and I
believe that the practice has occurred more often than the thought). That
which constitutes continuities across all sorts of breaks and ruptures in
history is resistance understood as creative element, as unceasing ability
to build the coming peoples [*popoli a venire*]. There is this beautiful passage somewhere in Deleuze in which he explains that he doesn't care at
all about demography, populations, peoples, etc., and that all he wants,
rather, is to build a people, to pursue a coming people. The subject—that
is, the form of subjectivity—which Michael and I are after in our book is
precisely such a coming people.

CC: It seems to me that what you are calling here a coming people has been
always already coming as well as always already there—which is why you
and Michael chase after it not only in the present and the future but also
in the past. It seems to me, in other words, that this coming people is the
same as the people of resistance: isn't the coming people the subject of
that thought and practice of resistance which you claim constitutes the
only possible basis upon which one can speak of historical continuity in
the first place?

AN: You may well be right.

CC: And isn't this subject of resistance also that which constitutes continuities in your own work, that is, across all the—otherwise quite different—
research projects you have undertaken during more than half a century?

AN: Yes, I suppose so. In this sense, much of my earlier work constitutes the
referent and condition of possibility for the type of arguments Michael
and I pursue in *Empire* regarding what you call the subject of resistance.
Starting from my work on Descartes up until and including my work
on Spinoza, all I did in effect was to build the thesis of the two modernities. What does this thesis assert? At the end of the humanist revolution
of the Renaissance—which constituted the first modernity proper—the
Counter-Reformation blocked the development of thought as well as the
structure of property at one and the same time (and, under this respect,
the Counter-Reformation thereafter influenced and even included also

much of the Protestant Reformation). Between the sixteenth and the seventeenth centuries, in other words, we witness a general refeudalization of society in all of its main aspects—and, importantly, such a refeudalization expelled revolutionaries of all sorts to the East as well as, above all, beyond the Atlantic. This is to say that the reactive blockage of the Counter-Reformation, on the one hand, posited itself as a second and rightful modernity, and, on the other hand, was never able to erase that other, prior, and alternative modernity completely. The revolutionary energies of that first modernity lived on and found their theoretical expression in the Spinoza–Marx line of thought.

CC: There and only there did that first modernity find its expression?

AN: No, no, that's not what I mean at all. It found many other expressions. The very idea of this other modernity, after all, came to me as I was working my way through Delio Cantimori's beautiful studies on Socinianism and on the religious heresies that swarmed throughout Europe before and after the Reformation.[11] Here you have truly a formidable phenomenon: a bunch of Tuscan artisans suddenly assert that the Trinity does not exist because it is not possible to turn the idea of God into a logical schema, and that, rather, the only thing that really exists and counts is charity. These are the Socinians: the most technologically advanced bronze artisans of their time, who take off from Tuscany and go to Prague, from Prague they go to Poland, from Poland they go to Holland, from Holland they go to England, and from England they go to America—thereby living through all the phases of the struggle against the Counter-Reformation and against the restoration of the status quo.

CC: Yes, this was undoubtedly a formidable phenomenon—and yet, as you know, it was not an isolated one. Socinianism was not the only extraordinary, radical heresy of its time. Why exactly are you so taken with the Socinians in particular? What is it about them that leads you to include them among the revolutionary expressions of that other modernity?

AN: The reason why I like them so much is that they were artisans! You know how much I care about the question of artisanship, about the question of the tool, and, moreover, about the question of science understood as one great, enormous, complex artisanship. If I put my own affinities and proclivities for artisans aside for a moment, however, there is no doubt that Socinianism was not alone in expressing radical needs and revolutionary exigencies of all sorts at the time. In fact, there are many stories of struggle and revolt in this era—all of which end with defeat. They are very beautiful, Nietzschean stories—in the most positive sense of the term, that is, in the sense that there is no rancor or resentment in them. These heretics wandered around Europe like so many Zarathustras: they did not have, however, the Romantic, orientalizing traits of that Nietzschean character; they had, rather, that stunning clarity which is to be found in Tuscan painting. They constituted so many flashes of lightning, so many illuminations.

CC: Illumination from below?

AN: Yes, absolutely! And such earthly illuminations, of course, were not born out of nothingness: they emerged, rather, out of a rich, radical culture of revolt, which had been already Girolamo Savonarola's culture, Saint Francis's culture, Dante's culture. Dante was certainly one of the founders of modernity: one witnesses in him a profound ambivalence, as he was pulled in opposite directions by those emerging forces which later will give rise to and crystallize into the two modernities; he was torn between, on the one hand, the productive construction of modernity, the poetry of matter, and, on the other hand, the sovereign construction of modernity, the retranscendentalization of labor. And as far as Saint Francis is concerned, I have always believed that his influence on later movements of resistance has been underestimated. Lately, a dear old friend—Giorgio Passerone, who has written on Dante, among other topics—has reconfirmed my long-standing hunch on this matter, and, in fact, we have been having repeated exchanges and discussions on the question of political Franciscanism, which is his main field of research at present. I must confess that these are just the kinds of things I would like to write about right now—but I am too old for such a project at this point. If I were younger I would write a history of the other European civilization. And it is precisely this other civilization—with all its stories, characters, needs, and exigencies—which was reborn with extraordinary power in Spinoza, which found its most eminent interpreter in Spinoza. A moment ago we were saying that the historical factor on the basis of which we are able at all to conceive of continuities across even the most radical discontinuities is nothing other than the subject of resistance. I think that now I might be in a position to put all of the above more precisely: the only real continuity to be found throughout this myriad of highly discontinuous and heterogeneous struggles is the constitution of the common.

cc: I don't think it is a coincidence that the passage from the subject of re-sistance to the constitution of the common in this conversation has taken place via Spinoza. In his work, in fact, the two are intimately related to one another.

an: The idea that the common is more important than the individual spans the whole history of modernity from its very beginning to its very end—and undoubtedly Spinoza marked a pivotal moment in the development of this idea. As Deleuze explained a thousand times, the problem with the individual is not at all that it is a singularity; the problem is, rather, that it is *not* a singularity!

cc: This is another way of saying that the common includes and is consti-tuted by singularities, while the individual contains only the same and more of the same, that is, that which is self-identical.

an: Precisely. The individual is repetition, while singularity in the common is difference.

cc: And that is why any type of community founded on identity in the end always goes hand in hand with individualisms of all sorts—all protesta-tions to the contrary from all concerned parties notwithstanding.

an: Yes, that's obvious. The common is the exact opposite of *Gemeinschaft:* the latter is the organic community—a Romantic and completely reac-tionary concept that constituted and continues to constitute the basis for any concept of the nation.

cc: And it constituted the basis also for the concept of people.

an: No, not really. The concept of people is rather French, while the con-cept of *Gemeinschaft* is completely German. And—let me emphasize this once again—*Gemeinschaft* is an absolutely reactionary and unredeem-able concept. Think, for example, of all those people nowadays who are antiglobalization in a truly coherent manner: whether they like it or not, what they do in effect is to invoke the original *Gemeinschaft*—which is why, as far as I am concerned, they are a bunch of fascists.

cc: Let us return to the common. If I understand you correctly, the concept of the common much precedes the concept of *Gemeinschaft* (and I am referring specifically to the concepts rather than to the terms here).

an: Yes. What I am saying is that the common—understood as that which contains singularities rather than individuals, difference rather than rep-etition—can be found already in revolutionary Franciscanism, in the Anti-Trinitarian heresy, in most peasant sects during the Thirty Years War, in Dutch Anabaptist and communitarian circles, among Comenius's disciples, and often even in the English Revolution. By contrast, the idea of a community sharing in and founded on identity is a relatively recent one.

cc: The constitution of the common too—much like the formation of identitarian types of community—presupposes a sharing as its logical condition of possibility. If it is not identity or essence, what do singularities share so as to constitute the common? What brings us together in the common [*cosa ci accomuna nel comune*]? Or—to put it differently—what exactly is common in the common?

an: Common is that which enriches the productivity of singularities [*dei singoli*]! Common is the fact that a lot of ideas come to me when you and I talk about something! Common is the fact that if I love you, we invent things together!

cc: The fact that as singularities we are essentially different—from one another as well as from ourselves—is that which may bring us together in the common (and this same fact, I suppose, has the potential also to keep us away or to tear us apart from one another). The common in question here, in other words, is difference.

an: Yes, but I would put it differently. That which brings us together and constitutes the common is not difference per se; it is, rather, activity, that is, the activity that builds this thing, that thing, any thing. In short, it is *alma venus*.[12] In a sense, this is the crucial difference between me and Deleuze. The questions I have been raising here—namely, the questions of the common, of its constitution, of its activities and practices—were certainly present in Deleuze. He never felt, however, that they were fundamental questions (except when he dealt with a specific political issue once in a while). Deleuze's as well as Félix's need to destroy the repressive machine of structural thought—within which they rightly included also orthodox Marxism—was extremely intense, and hence it distracted them from those other questions. Their fundamental aim was to break the dike and to let the flood come through—so to speak.

cc: And difference was the explosive they used to bring it all down. In short, you are suggesting that—given the specific enemy they were facing and the specific weapons they had at their disposal in that historical conjuncture—they had to put much more emphasis on the question of difference, on the explosion of difference, on its destructive force, rather than on its constructive potential.

an: Yes—but I am suggesting also that our struggle is different from their struggle. Today, we need to pay attention above all to the intentional, powerful constitutivity of contemporary subjectivities. Today, we have no other choice but to bring into play, as well as to gamble on, this desire for constitution.

cc: It is especially in the final sections of *Empire* that you take this gamble: I am referring in particular to the political proposals that you put forth in the last chapter and that you present as the concrete expressions of such a desire for constitution.[13] Perhaps it is not a coincidence that—as far as I am concerned—these are also the most problematic sections of the whole work.

AN: Undoubtedly, the end is the most confused and open-ended part of the book.

cc: Nonetheless, there is also much in it that is compelling. For example, I was struck by the notion of a nonteleological telos, which you only begin to elaborate there, and which I find potentially very productive. I would like to pause for a moment on this paradox of a telos without teleology: isn't this simply what we used to call a project, a political project—in the best possible sense of the term?

AN: Yes, but the problem is that the idea of project—as well as the idea of planning [*progettualità*]—has been used almost exclusively in a teleological sense, in politics and elsewhere. A telos is not teleological to the extent to which it is able to modify itself, to change. Above all, such a telos does not have any necessity. As you know, teleology is defined by the complex of Aristotelian causation: the world must develop according to the mechanism of the four causes—the most fundamental of which is the teleological one. Such a cause functions in the following manner: each and every nature or being has a prescribed end that it must pursue. All of Western thought is dominated by this idea of a necessary end or goal. A nonteleological telos, on the other hand, is not necessary in the same sense: if we conceive of the world from the standpoint of such a telos, there is nothing for us to pursue in it aside from freedom.

cc: Including the freedom not to pursue anything at all, I imagine! And yet, how is freedom here not a necessary telos? First of all, by appealing to an intrinsic striving for freedom, aren't you reintroducing a teleological structure of sorts once again, aren't you taking it away with one hand and putting it back with the other? Furthermore, isn't freedom the name or figure of the teleological telos par excellence, that is, that necessary telos which Hegel attributes to Spirit?

AN: But Hegel's is a completely different type of freedom!

cc: What do *you* mean by freedom, then?

an: Believe it or not, I have never asked myself this question. The problem is that whenever people have asked me this question, they have asked it in strictly liberal or liberalist terms: in short, I refuse the very terms in which the question is posed, because I believe that there has always been another idea of freedom—prior to and incompatible with the bourgeois idealist conception of freedom.

cc: All the more reason to ask this question now in a different way, then.

an: Let's give it a try. First of all, freedom is not chaos, is not chaotic choice. Each one of us chooses certain things and determines specific finalities within the scope of given possibilities or parameters.

cc: Yes, I understand. And yet I feel, somehow, that if it makes any sense to speak of freedom at all, it makes sense only to speak of that freedom which can be found in the struggle to turn something contingent into something necessary, something relative into something absolute.

an: But isn't that what I am saying too? The type of necessity you invoke here, after all, is precisely not posited as such a priori: it is not ready-made; rather, it has to be produced actively out of a set of conditions that cannot be experienced at first but as arbitrary and contingent. The point is that the struggle to posit the contingent as necessary is a common one, is a struggle in common. And the common too is not given a priori: rather, it is constituted by subjectivities. Any eventual, possible, variable, aleatory telos comes only afterwards, is given only later: namely, it is determined and redetermined over and over again in the quotidian activity of verifying our productive abilities, of putting such abilities to the test.

cc: This means that exercising our ability to produce the new is tantamount to reformulating our common projects—thereby diverting them in a different direction, if needed. Moreover, if I understand you correctly, such moments of determination or redetermination are the moments when this nonteleological common telos, on the one hand, is posited as necessary, and, on the other hand, is kept open to the possibility of being put into question, to the possibility of change—which is why you call it aleatory, which is why it continues to remain variable even after having been turned into a necessity. In other words, something that has been actively turned into and produced as necessity is liable forever after to change once again—that is, to be redetermined anew as necessary each and every time—while something that is given as necessary a priori cannot change ever again by definition.

AN: Yes, but let there be no misunderstanding about production here. To produce the new or whatever else may well be the most common way to put our telos to the test—that is, to redetermine it—but certainly it is not the only way. To produce the new is a choice too: it is something that is not given a priori; it is something that, if and when we want it, we need to make our own.

CC: And this means that we can also not want it. Productivity or creativity is not destiny.

AN: Nowhere in human nature is it written, after all, that we must produce more and more, better and better. Only one thing is truly in our nature: being common. And this means above all that our language wants, strives to be as rich as possible.

CC: I would like to bring you back to the matter of freedom: you still haven't really answered my question.

AN: When I say freedom, I mean common freedom. I don't need to tell you what I think about the bourgeois definition of freedom—that is, merely formal freedom—because it is precisely what Marx thought about it already a long time ago. This is why in my entire life I have never inflicted philippics in defense of civil rights on anybody—not on my readers, my students, my comrades, or even my judges. During my numerous trials, I never asked the judges that they let me free. I simply discussed with them, rather, whether or not it was advisable to use liberticidal laws against me as well as against the political movement in which I operated. I always tried to make them understand simply that what they were doing was not useful for anybody concerned. I never claimed to be entitled to freedom in absolute terms or argued in the name of freedom from the standpoint of natural law. You ask me what freedom is? Freedom is power. Freedom is power in the Spinozist, Nietzschean, Deleuzean sense of the term. But—and this is crucial—it is power that organizes itself in the common. It is power that constitutes itself at the highest level of equality and in the fullness of solidarity, that is, of fraternity, that is, of love.

CC: *Liberté, égalité, fraternité*? I don't think you mean it in this way, and yet this is all beginning to sound like an Enlightenment slogan.

AN: Yes, of course, there is an Enlightenment echo in what I am saying: the terminology is similar but I use it quite differently, which is why I qualified it further by specifying that solidarity and fraternity need to be understood as love. Solidarity, otherwise, is a rather disgusting term— a Christian rather than an Enlightenment term, by the way. Fraternity is indeed an Enlightenment term and at least is already more expressive than solidarity: it harks back to medieval fraternities, to corporative fraternities, to artisan associations; it expresses an organic link, namely, the blood bond to the brother; etc. This also means, of course, that whenever one speaks of fraternity one is always a little bit of a mafioso. Love— on the other hand—is another thing altogether: it is a free virtue; or, better yet, it is a naive virtue; or, better yet, it is a virtue of receptivity, of availability. It is making oneself truly available. It is openness to an extreme degree.

cc: It strikes me that you are not alone here. During the last two decades or so—and especially after 1989—several thinkers whose common source of inspiration and crucial reference point often is Heidegger have insisted on continuing to use Enlightenment terms and concepts so as to interpret them in ways quite different from their original ones, that is, have been trying at once to critique and to redeploy the intellectual legacy of the Enlightenment so as to work toward a refoundation of all the most important modern political categories. I am thinking here of works such as Derrida's *Politics of Friendship*, Jean-Luc Nancy's *The Inoperative Community*, Maurice Blanchot's *The Unavowable Community*, Agamben's *The Coming Community*, and so on. In particular—much like *Empire* as well as *Labor of Dionysus*—these works engage with concepts such as the common, community, communism, even love, in an attempt to imagine new forms of being-in-common that would differ radically from *Gemeinschaft*. In short, these thinkers share with you much common ground, or, at the very least, many common concerns: how would you characterize the relation between their attempts to rethink the common in our present historical conjuncture and your own attempts to do so?

an: There is at least one fundamental difference between my work and the work of the thinkers you mention here. In none of them subjectivity— and especially militant subjectivity—is central. This is the case even for Nancy, who is the most *gauchiste* among them. This is also the case for a thinker like Roberto Esposito, whose book on community owes much to Nancy and constitutes something like a synthesis of all these Heideggerian reflections on community.[14] Among such attempts to reconceptualize community, as a matter of fact, Esposito's book stands out as a truly pernicious work, due to its absolutely total refusal of subjectivation.

cc: Is such a refusal really any more total in Esposito than in these other thinkers? It seems to me, actually, that the rejection of any hypothesis of subjectivation or moment of constitution is most uncompromising in Blanchot—and I would not call his work pernicious because of that.

AN: Blanchot is certainly the most uncompromising among these thinkers in more ways than one. In fact, Blanchot constitutes an exceptional, unique case—and this is due in no small measure to his astonishing foresight, namely, to the fact that he was the first to anticipate the direction and to trace the main contours of this discourse on community and of much else besides. After 1968—which was the period of his great conversion— we used to read Blanchot as an intensification of contemporary conducts and behaviors, as an exacerbation of historically manifest forms of subjectivity. What differentiates Blanchot radically from all these other thinkers is his singular sense of corporeality, that is, his propensity and ability always to posit forms of being above all as corporeal. In Blanchot, all essences refer back to corporeal presences—and this is not at all the case in any of these other thinkers. In them, language becomes abstract, whereas in Blanchot one witnesses a concrete and poetic language— which is why, in spite of everything, I still find him to be a very compelling thinker. I would want to make also a further differentiation between, on the one hand, Nancy and Agamben, and, on the other hand, Derrida. The latter has worn himself out in the attempt to articulate an intellectual project that has never been able to exit the stage of literature, to move beyond the literary domain (and under this respect too Blanchot, who never moves beyond the *poetic* rather than the *literary* domain, is much preferable). Moreover, one finds in Derrida also another, and extremely dangerous, intellectual component, namely, Emmanuel Levinas— who is lethal for any type of thought that would be truly open. In Levinas, one faces a theological blockage, a mysticism that closes thought down rather than opening it up. Nancy and Agamben are very different from all this: they struggle on an altogether different front, and hence it is still important to engage with them—Agamben's limitations notwithstanding.

CC: I am pleased to see that you share my admiration for Blanchot as well as my sense that he is fundamentally a poet.

AN: Yes, each and every one of Blanchot's texts is a poetic text. He has a poet's rather than a mystic's concreteness: the mystic creates the void, whereas the poet fills it. I love Blanchot enormously, even though probably I don't agree with him on anything. But one doesn't need to agree with, say, Arthur Rimbaud in order to live the passions he expresses along with him!

CC: In a sense, this—namely, the fact that we don't need to agree on anything in order to be able to live the same passions, possibly even with the same intensity—is a perfect definition of the common.

AN: Yes, there is no doubt about that.

CC: The common that is brought about by poetry is a nonhomogenizing common, or—to reformulate a famous sentence by Georges Bataille— the common of those who have nothing in common. And this is why I continue to believe that, if there is hope, it lies in poetry—intended in the widest possible sense, which for me includes literature.

AN: I just finished rereading *Moby-Dick,* by the way. Just as I remembered, it is an absolutely extraordinary work.

CC: And it is also one of the best works I know about the common![15] Before we get too sidetracked by our favorite novels, though, let us return to *Empire.* There is yet another concept that I find striking in this work: you only begin to elaborate it in *Empire* and you define it more precisely in *Kairòs, Alma Venus, Multitudo*—namely, the concept of poverty.[16] If I invoke it at this point, that is because I feel it is intimately related to your understanding of the common. All your pagan leanings notwithstanding,[17] this concept of poverty is also a decidedly Christian concept; in fact, it is a foundational Christian concept, given its importance in the canonical Gospels. I want to discuss the role of a certain—terminological as well as conceptual—religiosity in your thought at a different time. For the moment, however, let me simply point out that if yours is a religiosity of labor as the producing product—or, as you put it elsewhere, a religiosity of making [*del fare*]—it is not immediately evident how the concept of poverty fits into such a religiosity.[18] For example, what is the ontological relation between poverty and that incarnated force which is labor? If such a religiosity implies a conception of the subject as producing subject, what type of subjectivity is constituted in and as the poor? Etc. But let me begin to try and answer some of these questions myself. When I first encountered the concept of poverty in *Empire,* I was rather perplexed. On the one hand, you and Michael are perfectly aware of the fact that poverty is shit, that the poor of the planet increasingly live in hunger, suffering, and destitution, etc. On the other hand, you immediately posit such destitution as strength and possibility: you write of the poor as power, as the immanent divine, as God on earth. In principle, I would have found this almost Nietzschean reversal of value (i.e., it is the poor who are truly rich, it is the powerless who are truly powerful, etc.)

to be very compelling. The way in which such a reversal was executed, however, I found to be problematic. First of all, I felt that this reversal was executed a bit too easily and quickly, in the sense that it was being presented almost as an article of faith without enough substantiation or elaboration—thereby sounding a little pat. Second, I also felt that other categories—such as, for example, the exploited—would have been more suitable for the type of argument you were articulating there: I did not understand, in other words, what exactly there was to be gained, conceptually or otherwise, from referring to the exploited as the poor. When I read *Kairòs, Alma Venus, Multitudo*, however, many of my initial perplexities were dispelled: in this text, poverty finally becomes what it wasn't yet in *Empire*—namely, a full-bodied, effective, and rigorous ontological concept. I would go so far as to say, in fact, that the later conceptual elaborations found in *Kairòs, Alma Venus, Multitudo* are logically prior to what we read in *Empire*, and that, in any case, it was only retroactively—that is, from the standpoint of the later text—that the invocation of the poor in *Empire* became for the first time fully intelligible as well as convincing for me. And yet, a nagging question still remains—and perhaps this is more of a terminological rather than a conceptual question. Why choose poverty as the common name of the multitude? Why call such richness of life and such fullness of being with the name of poverty, when this name is so burdened with privative connotations, with connotations of lack?

AN: If it is the case that the working class as such—that is, as it was first defined in the nineteenth century—has disintegrated and is now extinct, it is also the case that what is still very much with us nowadays is, on the one hand, the fact of exploitation, and, on the other hand, an enormous mass of poor people. This is a completely materialist and economic definition of poverty, which does not posit any value in poverty at all. But there is another definition of poverty, which is implied and called for by a positive concept of power: according to this definition, the poor are understood also as partaking of such a positive power to the extent to which they participate in social production and reproduction. Often, the poor engage actively in the mechanisms of production (and they still remain poor). At times, however, even when they are excluded from such mechanisms, they still participate in them in other ways, and not only as a mere reserve army of potential workers.

cc: The poor, in other words, are always included in the process of production, at the very least as the leftover, the refuse, the excess of such a process—an excess that is always potentially threatening and explosive.

an: Yes, sure. But the poor are part and parcel of this process not only in the sense that they constitute its excess. First of all, the poor reproduce themselves: they produce children, that is, they produce people who can be put on the market. Moreover, they produce languages, ways of being, forms of life!

cc: Indeed, the poor are in some ways at the cutting edge of linguistic production nowadays—and this is particularly crucial, given the increasingly important roles that language and communication play in the global economy today.

an: The poor produce so much that is absolutely vital to the contemporary process of production that even their exclusion from this process constitutes, paradoxically, an inclusion. It is in this sense that the poor are always included in the global and imperial productive process. So, on the one hand, there is this enormous mass of poor people, who exist and are dispersed within the multitude, even though they do not constitute multitude and are not subjectivity; on the other hand, there is a systematic and relentless attempt to exclude, segregate, and ghettoize poverty *tout court*, or, at the very least, to absorb, organize, and corporatize certain strata of this mass of poor people, and then to throw the rest away—and this is the case at the national level as well as at the global level. The point is that poverty is essential for the reproduction of the economic system: the singularity of the poor consists of the fact that they are pure labor power [*forza lavoro*] at the disposal of the capitalist machine of production and reproduction. Poverty is naked power [*nuda potenza*].[19]

cc: You are implying that this naked power is not to be confused with Agamben's naked life, right?

an: Precisely. And nowadays this naked power is always plugged in and essential to the economic process in some way or other. In this sense, poverty is the ubiquitous backdrop of globalization.

cc: I see now my mistake: earlier, I was suggesting that poverty needs to be understood as residual waste; you are saying, however, that poverty is not only the residual waste but also the condition of possibility of the contemporary process of production. One of the problems with understanding poverty only as sheer refuse and waste is that poverty then can be mistaken more easily as a phenomenon that, while being linked to the contemporary process of production in the sense that it constitutes one of its inevitable outcomes and by-products, nonetheless exists outside such a process for all intents and purposes. Your point, however, is that poverty nowadays is never outside production.

AN: Yes—and here lies the difference between my position and a Marxist conception of poverty. For a Marxist, the poor are outside the economic system as soon as they can no longer be hired, that is, as soon as they can no longer be formalized in the process of production. As far as I am concerned, however, such an understanding of the question of poverty is completely wrong. It is not true that the poor are excluded from production once they can no longer be turned into wage laborers. I believe, on the contrary, that they too are plugged into the circuitries of the global economy, regardless of whether or not they can still function profitably as workers.

CC: What you say about poverty makes much sense to me. What I still find unclear, however, is the following: given all that you say about poverty, what exactly is the relation between poverty and multitude? Earlier, you spoke of the poor, on the one hand, as being dispersed within the multitude, and, on the other hand, as not constituting multitude—thereby implying, obviously, that there is a specific difference between the two. And yet, when you speak of poverty as constituting naked power and of the poor as never being excluded from production by definition, it is then difficult for me to understand what difference—if any—there might be between poverty and multitude. Could we say that they are distinct yet indiscernible from one another? Could we say, in other words, that they name two different attributes of the same entity?

AN: The problem here is that the concept of multitude is terribly unclear . . .

CC: While the concept of poverty is for you a clearer and more precise concept at this point?

AN: Yes. First of all, it is important to note that when Michael and I introduced the concept of multitude in *Empire*, we were not producing it from scratch; we were at once reporting and reelaborating a series of exchanges and discussions that we had been having with numerous other comrades over a long period of time. In these discussions, the multitude was being identified as the dissolution of the concept of people: while we understood the latter to be essentially a modern and Hobbesian concept, we increasingly posited the multitude as a postmodern form, and, in particular, as a postmodern form of movements of population. In this sense, the multitude came to be conceived of as a set—an almost infinite set—of singularities. So, how does the concept of poverty adhere to the concept of multitude? On the one hand, poverty adheres to the multitude only in part; on the other hand, however, poverty integrates the multitude as tendency. In any case, the concept of multitude is not yet very clear to me, and hence I use it—as well as advise others to use it—with much caution. This is why the current simplifications of this concept make me shiver! I am referring, for example, to the way in which the phrase "the multitude against empire" has been rapidly appropriated and deployed as a slogan by some antiglobalization movements, as we have seen in the past few days on leaflets and banners at the demonstrations against the G8 in Genoa.

CC: Simplifications aside, let's keep the focus on the relation between multitude and poverty. The more I listen to what you are saying, in fact, the more I become convinced that the key to the multitude lies in poverty, and that one cannot hope to clarify fully the concept of multitude without first examining the relation between these two concepts. It is not sufficient, perhaps, to try and define the multitude only by contrast and in opposition to the people: one should also define it in terms of its overlaps with and divergences from the poor. Put differently, if one defines the multitude exclusively in terms of its relation to the people—namely, in terms of a concept that historically has constituted its ontological and political rival—then one ends up determining the multitude entirely by negation, thereby running the risk of neglecting to identify and to foreground its positive characteristics; given that poverty and multitude are not opposed but symbiotic or perhaps complementary concepts, however, a careful investigation of the complex play and interaction between the two might offer valuable insights into the positive and affirmative attributes of the multitude. In short, if the people determine what the multitude is not, I wonder whether poverty might help us determine what the multitude is, what its singularity consists of.

AN: One of the reasons why it is difficult to define the relation between multitude and poverty is that the former is still a concept *in fieri*, whereas the latter is a concept *in actu*. This difficulty notwithstanding, I think that the relation between these two concepts can be defined adequately in the following manner: poverty is the radical of the multitude—in the sense that poverty constitutes at once that which holds revolutionary political potential in the multitude as well as the root and source of the multitude. As far as the concept of people is concerned here, matters are more complicated than you have just presented them. You need to remember, after all, that the concept of people and the concept of poverty are related to each other too—and that this relation has a long history. If it is the case, in fact, that the concept of people was produced by Hobbes as ordered and hierarchized multitude—that is, as that political form which would result from restructuring the multitude according to transcendent parameters—it is also the case that later the concept of people was reinterpreted by Voltaire as the overcoming of poverty, namely, as the biopolitical guarantee of survival, reproduction, and historical continuity. The point, however, is that as soon as the concept of poverty is related to the concept of multitude, it turns into something quite different from the poverty Voltaire hoped would be overcome by producing the people.

cc: In other words, the people's poverty is not the multitude's poverty.

an: Precisely. Whereas when poverty is related to the people it is posited as lack and privation, when it is related to the multitude it turns into the fundamental element of resistance and rebellion—and this is why poverty is so terribly important. Poverty is the point that you cannot grant: it is that with respect to which you cannot not rebel, that with respect to which you must rebel! I think it is possible today to return to the concept of poverty and to endow it with materialist characteristics, such as resistance. It is possible to do so because the type of poverty we are witnessing nowadays is a phenomenon that has already absorbed and incorporated its own integration in the totality of the system: it is being continuously reproduced as integral and integrated to the system.

cc: You are saying that today the poor are not only not outside the system but also not even at its margins or in its periphery. In short, poverty is central: it lies at the heart of the world of globalization.

an: Today, there is nothing marginal about poverty—which is why the harder they try to ghettoize it, the more impossible they find it to do so. This is poverty in exodus: this is a poverty, for example, that escaped from the Third World and entered the First World, but was then reimpoverished and once again "third-worldized" in the First World, etc. The point is that as the poor go through this series of movements, passages, and transformations, they always carry along with them—in their minds and bodies—not only the tools that will enable them to work wherever they go but also the capacity to resist.

CC: People, multitude, poverty . . . Judging from the way in which you juggle, interrelate, and reconfigure all these concepts, it seems to me that what we are dealing with here is also an unspoken engagement with the concept of class. I think that one of the main reasons why you find it necessary to give new life to concepts like multitude and poverty, after all, is that the traditional concept of class is no longer adequate for understanding and defining the current realities of globalization, such as the movements of population you just mentioned. To say that class as a concept is not equal to the task of dealing with the realities facing us today, however, is not to say that we no longer need to think about class, or, more precisely, that we no longer need to think about those structural inequalities and antagonisms which the concept of class was meant to describe in the first place and did describe more or less adequately for quite a while: those inequalities and antagonisms, after all, are still very much with us. I am wondering, in other words, how this concept—as well as its analytic function and usefulness—might need to be rethought in light of what we have been saying about multitude and poverty. If— as you stated earlier—contemporary poverty has emerged from the disintegration of the modern working class, isn't it then the case that your concept of poverty is necessitated and determined also by the obsolescence and unserviceableness of the traditional concept of class? And doesn't your understanding of the relation between poverty and multitude too constitute an attempt to remedy some of the shortcomings of class as a concept?

AN: Undoubtedly, the traditional concept of class is no longer very useful. This concept was based on the centralization of the site of production and on the homogenization of the forms of reproduction, that is, on the homogenization of the styles of life. Such an understanding of class is what you find in Émile Zola or in certain Russian novels, where we are told precisely what the proletariat is—down to the last detail. Nowadays, however, we are faced with the full dissolution of this concept's unity and coherence: social hierarchies are no longer determined and ordered strictly according to differences in production and reproduction; rather, they crisscross and permeate the social through and through.

CC: But that is so because production permeates the social through and through in the first place. What has made the concept of class obsolescent, in other words, is the fact that production has spread throughout the fabric of the social.

AN: True. The point is, in any case, that all this in the end constitutes a great victory of the working class, which wanted to erase itself as such. In the postwar period—and especially from the 1960s onward—the refusal to work truly constituted a destructive machine: it had severe effects on the capitalistic systems of organization of the labor force. And this was the case both in so-called developed countries—where the working class in effect brought a default action on the very possibility of continuing to be organized according to such systems—and in colonial countries, where a complete break with the classical colonial disciplinary system took place.

CC: What you have just said could well serve as a preliminary or partial definition of the multitude. Whatever else it is, in fact, what you have been calling the multitude seems to be also the self-erasure of the working class. Isn't the multitude precisely what emerges when the working class abolishes itself as such? The multitude as the abolition of the proletariat rather than as the dictatorship of the proletariat?

AN: Yes, sure—but there is much more to the multitude than such a definition. In order to solve the problems and ambiguities of the concept of multitude, we need a new Paris commune—much as Saint Paul used to say of ancient Greek philosophers that they needed a Christ in order to invent the concept of redemption.

CC: In other words, you are saying that only political practice truly creates and produces.

AN: Yes. And right now all of my work is focused on the problem of what form of political practice—which is to say, what form of subjectivity—produces the multitude. In some way or other, all I think, say, write, or do is an attempt to understand what decides of a production of subjectivity that is adequate to the multitude, namely, what are the mechanisms of decision that can posit the multitude as subjectivity. Such a subjectivity—that is, that subjectivity which is adequate to the multitude—can never constitute the one and only subjectivity; it is, rather, a forming form in which all other multiplicities and articulations play as such and yet are able to govern themselves. The main problem is to try and figure out both the dynamics and the statics of these multitudes—that is, the internal mechanisms that stabilize and conform behaviors or, instead, potentiate, transfer, and metamorphose them—as well as what passions and virtues one needs to have within such processes. But the fundamental question, perhaps, is this: How does the multitude behave in case of war? What does the multitude become in the face of all-out antagonism? At this point, war defines the relation between multitude and empire.

CC: It makes sense that you would want to deal with the question of war now. In a sense, this development was already announced and anticipated in the preface to *Empire,* in which you and Michael draw attention to the fact that that book was written between two imperial wars. When you speak of war now, however, do you mean to refer to imperial wars, that is, to that war which is waged *against* the multitude?

AN: I am referring both to the war that is waged against the multitude *and* to the war that the multitude wages against empire. It's not a coincidence that both the theme of war and the theme of poverty are becoming essential in our sequel to *Empire,* which will deal primarily with the production of subjectivity. In this second volume, the first task will be to demolish entirely the theoretical models of war and of strategy that were elaborated from Carl von Clausewitz onward, so as then to be able to engage with what we could call—using a Machiavellian expression— the new arts of war, namely, the novel forms and practices of war that are emerging on this edge of history which is our present. The most important reason why I am so concerned with the question of war right now is that I am absolutely convinced that the multitude will not be able to unfold without having won a war, that the exercise of constituent power will not become hegemonic unless such a moment of decision takes place. *Mala tempora currunt!* [We live in dire times!]

CC: *Mala tempora currunt!* Coming from you, such pessimism is surprising, uncharacteristic.

AN: I am not feeling very optimistic right now. I feel as if we are rapidly heading toward some sort of definitive showdown.[20] And I am scared about the possibility that the politics of somebody like Bush—or the politics of American conservatism in general—might accelerate this process tremendously.

CC: On the one hand, the possibility of such acceleration and of such a showdown scares you. On the other hand, you also feel that the multitude will not be able to constitute and assert itself as a coherent subjectivity without having waged and won a war. I assume that your ambivalence— if it is indeed ambivalence—is due to apprehension regarding just how high the losses will be in this war or showdown no matter who comes out victorious, if terms such as victorious are even applicable here.

AN: My apprehension is about the type of showdown that might take place due to the enormous historical accelerations that we are witnessing right now. The point is that the showdown resulting from such accelerations might end up being not only a terribly bloody but also a completely fake showdown, namely, a foregone conclusion meant precisely to preempt the coming-into-being of the multitude.

CC: Are you saying that only empire can benefit from such accelerations?

AN: I am saying actually that the war that might result from these current accelerations will have absolutely no winners—and that this is yet one more reason why it is so urgent to rethink the concept, theory, and practice of war. This is another way of saying that that war which the multitude will wage and win will have little in common—if anything at all—with what has been understood, waged, and experienced as war in modernity. The multitude needs to reinvent war—and in doing so, it will also constitute itself.

On *Multitude*

CESARE CASARINO: I would like to begin our discussion of *Multitude* by addressing the relation between democracy and communism in this work. In many respects, the question of democracy—of what it can still mean nowadays, of how to achieve it, etc.—is posited explicitly as the central question of this work. When it comes to the question of communism, however, matters become more complicated. On the one hand, from a lexical point of view communism is marginal at best: the term "communism," in fact, appears only twice in the whole work.

ANTONIO NEGRI: Only twice?

CC: Yes, I think so—and I was just as surprised to realize this as you are now. On the other hand, from a conceptual point of view communism is everywhere in this work. Given that your understanding and definition of democracy are based on the constitution of the common, it seems fair to say that such a democracy would be at the very least intimately related to communism, and hence that whenever you discuss democracy in this work you bring communism into play implicitly as well. When it comes to communism, in other words, the gap between the lexical level and the conceptual level is a veritable abyss: communism is virtually omnipresent as a concept and almost completely absent as a term. I find this gap perplexing, problematic. I suppose one could argue that in the end concepts are more important—that is, effective—than terms as such, and even that concepts at times are all the more effective the more implicit they remain. This is all true, of course. And yet what I still find problematic is the fact that in *Multitude* the term "communism" for all intents and purposes has been substituted by the term "democracy." Why was such a substitution necessary?

AN: First of all, I must confess that I am very surprised: I thought somehow that the term "communism" was much more present in *Multitude* than what you are telling me. The fact that this term appears only twice in the whole book is indeed an important fact: it constitutes a *lapsus* in reverse, that is, a *lapsus* of absence. As far as I am concerned, in other words, this was not—either on my part or on Michael's—a willed or planned omission. It is possible, nonetheless, that there might have been moments in the text when we consciously decided not to use the term "communism" so as to avoid misunderstandings, that is, so as to make sure that the reader would not mistake our usage of this term for the way in which it has been used by socialism in its various manifestations. The issue, in other words, is to dissociate the term "communism" from the ways it has been used, which have constituted misappropriations for the most part.

CC: There are two important matters here that need to be clarified further. First of all, what you call a *lapsus* of absence still remains to be explained: to be able to name it is certainly an important and necessary step, and yet simply to be able to do so does not necessarily tell us much yet about its causes. A generous interpretation of such a *lapsus* might be simply that both you and Michael have absorbed the term "communism" in the very fabric of your thought to such an extent that you no longer feel the need to use it; or, put differently, you took so much for granted that your definition of democracy in this work is tantamount to communism that it didn't even occur to you to mention this term. I imagine, though, that there could be other interpretations. Second, as far as those moments of conscious omission are concerned, I find your explanation to be some-what unconvincing: if it is the case that one might want to avoid using the term "communism" because of the particularly pernicious ways in which it has been used in the past, it is also the case that one could say and do the same with respect to the term "democracy." As far as I am concerned, in fact, the past and present political history of the term "democracy" has been often at the very least as baneful as, say, the tendentious and oppor-tunistic socialist misappropriations of communism—starting from the Athenian version of democracy, which excluded women and slaves, and ending with the various and sundry contemporary forms of Western parliamentary democracy, which by now exclude just about everybody from the political process, in the sense that they no longer represent any-thing or anybody at all, if they ever did at some point. Not to speak, of course, of recent slogans and shibboleths such as "exporting democracy to the Middle East"—which at least have the unintended merit of reveal-ing that "democracy" nowadays is conceived of as just another form of commodity regulated by the laws of capitalist exchange, and hence as indissoluble from the current and ongoing processes of globalization.

AN: Yes, of course, this is all true. There is, nonetheless, at least one important reason why the question of democracy still needs to be addressed, and why democracy both as a concept and as a term all in all can still be used in significant, powerful, positive ways. This reason consists of the alternative history and definition of the term "democracy." Allow me for a moment to reiterate the obvious and to make recourse to what I feel by now constitutes a commonplace: the term "democracy" has a double history. On the one hand, there is democracy defined as form of government, that is, as the government of the many. But what exactly do the many govern according to this definition of democracy? They govern the One. Such a democracy, in other words, has always constituted the government of the One by the many—exactly in the way in which monarchy is the government of the One by the one, aristocracy or oligarchy is the government of the One by the few, etc. On the other hand, there is another side to such a definition of democracy, which indexes a radical break or rupture in the history of the concept of democracy. This other side that indexes and indeed constitutes a rupture is absolute democracy—as opposed to constitutional democracy or to those definitions of democracy that are philologically related to the government of the One by the many in its various forms. Absolute democracy is our definition of democracy in *Multitude*. Keep in mind, after all, that the word *democracy* literally means "government of the people"—and you know very well how ferociously Michael and I critique the concept of the people. At the very heart of that definition of democracy which Western political tradition has handed down to us, in other words, there lies a profound mystification: *demos* is posited in it, in fact, as the basis of political legitimation—that is, as the foundation of Power—whereas in actuality *demos* is the product of sovereignty and hence of the disciplinary harnessing of Power.

CC: Democracy, in other words, is the term that sovereign Power has used in order to hide that the concept of people is actually its own invention, as well as to perpetuate the myth that it is the people who produce, support, and legitimate the sovereign—regardless of whether the latter is a monarch, an elected representative of the people, or a dictatorship of the proletariat.

AN: Yes, precisely.

cc: All the more reason not to use this term, then!

an: I don't agree. I think it is possible to reconquer and to reverse the concept of democracy by reconfiguring it in a different—and perhaps more naive—manner: to do so means to conceive of democracy as the expression of the multitude. It is essential to take care, however, that such a constituent expression of democracy not be posited without forms. To say that democracy is the government of the multitude, in other words, is not enough. On the one hand, democracy is not the government of the One by the many: this is merely the form through which the many are attempting to express the One, namely, the mediation, articulation, and alienation of the many in the One. On the other hand, democracy intended as a proliferating, multiple, and absolute form of the multitude—absolute in the sense that it does not have any outside—cannot be an anarchical form. This is why the common—or, if you like, communism—is terribly important for us: democracy intended as the expression of the multitude is nothing other than the expression of the common.

cc: It is the common, in other words, that guarantees that democracy as the expression of the multitude would not disperse itself in sheer anarchy.

an: It is the common as ontological substratum that constitutes such a guarantee. Let me put it more bluntly: Michael and I argue that no form of government whatsoever could possibly exist without a commune of citizens, that is, without a strong institutional capacity to organize relations among citizens. The analogy with language is absolutely crucial here, in the sense that social relations are analogous to linguistic relations. What is a linguistic relation? It is the common acceptance of a set of signs that enable the elaboration of the social. If one pays close attention to this matter, one will see that the set of signs, or, if you like, the set of customary habits and behaviors, that constitutes the social adds up to something like 90 percent or 95 percent of the reality of being-in-the-world, of inhabiting the world—in short, of life. Communism and democracy are intimately related—and even linked—to one another on the basis of the realization that such an ontological precondition or substratum is immensely powerful. All traditional forms of government are perfectly aware of the existence of such a substratum; they consider it, however, as something extraneous to government dynamics, that is, they relativize it.

cc: While in your definition of democracy such a substratum is posited as absolute.

AN: More precisely, democracy means to reconstruct and reassemble that substratum that preexists government. In this sense, democracy is not even a form of government: it is simply the form of being-together. To believe in this definition of democracy, in other words, means to believe that the old adage *homo homini lupus* [man is a wolf to man] is completely false.

CC: It strikes me that the structure of your argument regarding democracy is exactly the same as the structure of your thesis of the two modernities.[1] In both cases, you assert that there is a double history, as opposed to what we have always been told, namely, that there is only one and uniform history. The latter (that is, modernity as we know it, democracy as we know it, in short, the official story) is nothing more than the transcendentalizing reaction to the other—logically, if not temporally—prior history (that is, modernity as the discovery of immanence, as the affirmation of the productivity of being; democracy as absolute democracy, as the ontological substratum of any form of government, as form of being-together). In short, in both cases you excavate a latent, alternative, and repressed history at the very heart of the dominant and official one. In this respect, *Multitude* translates and articulates your thesis of the two modernities into the specific language and problematic of democracy. Put differently, in *Multitude* you reiterate in different words what you have been saying already for quite a while.

AN: Yes, sure. And just as there are two different genealogies of thought when it comes to the articulation of modernity, there are also two distinct genealogical lines when it comes to democracy: on the one hand, what you might call the Hobbes-Rousseau-Hegel line, and, on the other hand, the Machiavelli-Spinoza-Marx line—in which one could also include Nietzsche perhaps. The point is that the latter series of thinkers developed the concept of democracy not at all as a specific form of government among others but as the form of living together that constitutes the condition of possibility of governing *tout court.* And since 1968, it is precisely *this* concept of democracy that has been increasingly affirming itself as the only possible, viable, true meaning of democracy. Nowadays more than ever, on the one hand, hardly anybody anywhere believes any longer in the virtues and possibilities of representative democracy, and, on the other hand, whenever people [*la gente*] speak positively and hopefully of democracy it is this *other* democracy that they have in mind.

cc: The crisis of the traditional concept of democracy, in other words, is specifically a crisis of political representation: if hardly anybody believes in democracy any longer, that is so in the sense that hardly anybody feels represented by and in it. In short, you are saying that it is the concept of political representation that people [*la gente*] no longer take seriously rather than the concept of democracy per se: while the latter can still be recuperated because it has also another and alternative history, the former is simply unredeemable.

an: That is exactly what I am saying. What has become perfectly clear to all concerned is that the traditional—which is to say modern—social and political institutions of representation are profoundly corrupt, and, indeed, that political representation itself by now is ethically bankrupt. Nobody even tries to make a secret out of any of this any longer: all over the planet, people [*la gente*] realize and remember this very well.

cc: Though, of course, this generalized—and, indeed, common—realization of the total bankruptcy of political representation can be expressed in all sorts of different ways. This widespread feeling of mistrust with respect to the social and political institutions of modernity, this increasing lack of credibility—and hence crisis of legitimacy—of such institutions, in other words, can and does take all of us in very different directions.

an: Yes, but in whatever different directions such a realization may take us, what nonetheless does remain extremely valuable for any possible constitution of the common is the fact that whenever and wherever people [*la gente*] remember all this, they unveil. *This* is the true meaning of unveiling: unlike what Heidegger tells us, unveiling has little to do with Being as an ontological entity; unveiling, rather, is related to praxis—in the sense that only collective praxis unveils as well as that the only thing collective praxis can unveil is itself. Unveiling is never unveiling of Being; it is, rather, always unveiling of collective praxis, of the common nature of social life, of a teleology internal to social existence. Unveiling in and of itself, however, is only half the story: as soon as such an unveiling is about to take place, the fundamental question becomes to find the specific, adequate, historical form through which it should determine itself.

cc: The implication here is that unveiling in and of itself does not constitute the primary goal of collective praxis, does not constitute a telos unto itself. Unveiling is simply a by-product of collective praxis: it is what happens when we do things together. Whenever we pursue common projects, we also unveil.

AN: Yes. One of the most beautiful things that happened while Michael and I were writing *Multitude* was that we quickly realized that the real challenge was not to unveil or to reveal the multitude; the point, rather, was to do it, to make it, to produce it. As we wrote, the increasingly recurrent refrain for us became to make the multitude [*fare la moltitudine*]. Since you are so fond of counting words, perhaps you can go through the whole book and tell me how many times the phrase "to make the multitude" occurs! Lexical and philological analysis aside, I believe that making the multitude—as opposed to revealing it or to explaining it—constitutes the central theme of this work.

CC: I would like to return to the question of communism, since I still find its role in *Multitude* to be unclear. Earlier, you suggested that communism and democracy are indissolubly bound to each other by a realization or recognition that the common understood as ontological substratum is powerful, and that perhaps all power inheres to and emerges from the common. One could say, then, that the term "democracy" in *Multitude* functions in effect as some sort of Trojan horse containing the concept of communism. The question for me remains, however, why is the term "communism" for all intents and purposes absent in this book? As I admitted earlier, it is probably true that concepts matter more than terms in the end. It is also the case, however, that terms have their own importance too: every term has a history, and that history too is a history of class struggle; a term, in other words, is the object and the product of struggles. In short, I find it very important to continue to insist on the term "communism" and to continue to use it, even if just heuristically, so that it—as well as the struggles that produced it—not be forgotten. Obviously, such an insistence on my part does not indicate nostalgia for any of those regimes that used to call themselves communist or allegiance to any of the few remaining regimes that continue to identify themselves as such. As you know, I belong to a generation that came to political consciousness in the 1970s, a generation for which the Soviet Union and even Maoist China never constituted any model or any hope whatsoever. As a matter of fact, I was never even a member of or voted for the Communist Party in Italy, since the latter too represented for me a betrayal of anything I could associate with communism—albeit a betrayal quite different from, say, the Soviet one. Having said all this, nonetheless, often I have found it and I continue to find it important to call myself communist. Before the disintegration of the Soviet Union, I was hesitant at times to use the term "communism" lest I be misunderstood as sympathizing in any way with the Soviet project. After that project collapsed under its own dead weight, however, I felt the need to use this term with renewed urgency because—among other reasons—that collapse could have the potential finally to disengage communism both as a term and as a concept from its stifling Soviet connotations and misappropriations. In short, I felt with much relief that the disintegration of the Soviet Union afforded us a unique chance to reclaim and rethink communism much more freely—and I would be the first one to admit that there was much naïveté in all this. After all that has occurred during the last decade, however, I still feel this way—and I think that it is possibly more important than ever to continue to use the term "communism" at the very least as a heuristic device for indicating past, present, and perhaps even future forms of being-in-common, for characterizing any struggle for the reappropriation of the common from its current and rampant privatization. And let me add that much of what I am saying about communism here I learned from you anyway! I still remember, for instance, the thrill of reading a book like *Communists Like Us* in 1990.[2] Is the term "communism" still important for you? Or does *Multitude* perhaps signal a shift—in the sense that the term "democracy" has now become more urgent or useful for you in this particular historical conjuncture?

AN: I do think it is extremely important to use the term "communism." And it is just as important to assess how the two distinct genealogies of thought in question here—namely, the thought of radical democracy and the thought of communism—might meet, complement, and even reinforce each other.

CC: I assume you are implying that *Multitude* constitutes an attempt at such an assessment. But why exactly is it so important to enable the intersection or confluence of these two distinct political and philosophical genealogies? I suppose one could argue that we cannot afford not to use all the weapons at our disposal—if the legacy of radical democracy turns out to constitute a weapon at all, that is.

AN: I believe that the problem of the relation between democracy and communism ought to be posed within the larger context of a new communist patristics. Patristic philosophy, as you know, constituted an attempt on a large scale at reassembling and reformulating a specific set of religious forms—all of which shared in two foundational elements, the acceptance of Christianity and the liberation of slaves (that is, the affirmation of the freedom and the equality of all subjects before God). The brilliance of patristics consisted in reassembling these religious forms in a way such that they could be approached from very different routes, could be reached from very different points of departure. In this way, for example, even a school of thought as internal and essential to the very structure of Latin thought as the most advanced forms of Stoicism could be encompassed within and blended into the main currents of Christian theology. I believe that nowadays—after a heroic and defeated first phase in the assertion of communism—we find ourselves in a phase of vast ecumenical reconstruction of the foundations of communism. This is a phase in which what is being recovered and reelaborated is not merely the revolutionary element of communism—namely, all that links communism immediately to struggle, to specific antagonisms, etc.—but also an enormous cultural context that includes extremely diverse elements, from the genealogies of radical liberalism to the oppositional reappropriations of certain Asian religions such as Buddhism. In short, we are living through a constructive phase in which a set of formalized desires is being reassembled on a global scale—and it is this set or assemblage that I call new communist patristics. From the standpoint of such an assemblage, terms such as "democracy" and "communism" are absolutely interchangeable. Even though, as I said earlier, I do find it important to continue to use the term "communism," I have no nostalgia for the sectarianism that characterized the first phase of the history of communism—a phase in which communist militants often would waste precious time and effort fighting and even killing each other over the true meaning of the term "communism." I find that nowadays such sectarianism is obsolete. This doesn't mean, of course, that from now on people won't kill each other over the meaning of words, of systems of thought, etc.; it simply means that right now the fundamental tendency is one of recomposition. And the crucial point for me is that such a recomposition is possible precisely because nowadays the concept of democracy increasingly is no longer a concept of management of the One by the many but a concept of management of the All by everybody.

cc: Yes, I see your point. It strikes me, though, that such a patristics may run the risk of constituting only a new school of thought rather than constituting also a new political movement. In any case, let me probe this question of the interchangeability of democracy and communism a little further, since this is a point that I believe could lead easily to dangerous misunderstandings.

AN: Let me address immediately one such possible misunderstanding: democracy and communism are interchangeable only to the extent to which they are revolutionary, that is, only to the extent to which they have posited a radical break with any concept of government of the One. As long as democracy and communism are conceived of as two specific forms of government of the One, not only are they not interchangeable but also they are not revolutionary at all.

CC: Yes, I agree, but let me pose this question in a different way. As I was reading *Multitude,* I did feel that in this work democracy and communism—the relative scarcity of one of these terms with respect to the other notwithstanding—increasingly refer to the same phenomenon or event, that is, the constitution of singularities in the common. At times, I also felt, however, that these two different concepts or names refer to this same event in different ways—and that this difference may be a temporal one. Could one say perhaps that in *Multitude* democracy refers to the constitution and reappropriation of the common from the standpoint of diachrony (and hence from the standpoint of history), whereas communism expresses this same event *sub specie aeternitatis,* that is, from the standpoint of synchronicity (and hence from an ontological standpoint)? Could one say that democracy at its best is one of the specific historical manifestations or forms of that transhistorical desire for the constitution of the common that goes by the name of communism? Are there specific types of temporality that subtend or are intrinsic to democracy and communism?

AN: I am not sure that I would pose the problem in the way that you do, that I would ask these types of questions in the first place. The point for me is that the concept itself of temporality is in crisis nowadays—which is why I don't think I can answer these questions as long as they are formulated in this way. Moreover, I find your characterization of the specific temporalities appertaining to democracy and to communism to be problematic to the extent to which it can be misunderstood easily along the following lines: on your reading, democracy begins to sound like some kind of reformist temporality, while communism begins to sound like some sort of utopian temporality. The problem is that it is precisely this type of distinction that can no longer be made: nowadays, each and every reform is radically transformative because we live on an ontological terrain, because our lives are pitched immediately on an ontological level; and for this same reason each and every utopia stands behind rather than ahead of us, is posited not at all as something to come, and constitutes, rather, the actual psychological content of our quotidian experience.

CC: I am not sure I understand fully what you are saying here.

AN: All I am saying is that we live in a world without mediations. Reforms and utopias—as well as their appertaining temporalities—used to be structures of mediation. Under a fully realized regime of biopolitical production, any reform can be radically transformative because it no longer constitutes mediation, or, put differently, any reform stands to change immediately the ontological substratum of our lives if it stands to change anything at all.

CC: This means, if I understand you correctly, that during the modern era reforms always changed something—although that something never could be what you call the ontological substratum and hence reforms never could be revolutionary—while nowadays reforms at one and the same time have the potential to change everything as well as the potential to change nothing at all. Lest your assessment of our present historical conjuncture not be misunderstood as implying that reforms nowadays are always already necessarily revolutionary, in other words, I would make sure to put as much emphasis on both sides of the coin: it is precisely to the extent to which reforms stand to change nothing at all that that they stand to change everything, and vice versa—and it's difficult to know in advance what the outcome of a specific reform will be. In any case, this is the only way I can make sense of your position.

AN: Yes, this is what I am saying—more or less. I am beginning to suspect, however, that you don't really agree with my way of posing these questions: judging from what I have heard from you here, I think you find my arguments largely unconvincing. Did you like *Multitude*? What did you think of the book?

CC: I liked the first section on war very much. I also liked the second section—especially the excursus on Marx—even though I thought that there was not much in this section that could not be found already in *Empire* and elsewhere. And, yes, as you can tell from all that I have been saying and asking so far, I did not find the third and last section on democracy to be compelling.

AN: I must confess that I have similar misgivings: whereas I can see the point of the first and—to a lesser extent—of the second sections, I am not really sure what it is that we achieved in the third section of the book.

CC: I should qualify my cursory assessment, however, with two further points. First of all, possibly what I find most valuable in *Multitude* from a conceptual standpoint—that is, in terms of its conceptual elaborations and achievements—is the way in which you and Michael critique several foundational dialectical binaries of bourgeois idealism, such as, among others, the binary oppositions of Identity and Difference, of the Particular and the Universal, of the Public and the Private. Obviously, the critique of such binaries—no matter how thorough and radical—is nothing new in and of itself: many are the thinkers who have undertaken it before you at least since Marx and especially during the second half of the twentieth century. It is, however, the *particular* way in which you undertake this critique that I find very valuable. In fact, you don't really spend much time critiquing these binaries at all—probably because you are well aware of the fact that such a critique has been done before in various effective ways. What you do, rather, is to substitute all these dialectical binary oppositions with one complementary dyad—namely, the dyad of singularity and commonality, of the singular and the common—and this substitution as well as these two concepts I do find quite compelling and powerful. Arguably, Deleuze had laid the foundation already for much of what you say about singularity here and elsewhere. The complementary relation between the singular and the common, however, is articulated far more clearly and productively in your thought, and, in fact, is uniquely yours. In Deleuze, after all, we hear much more about the singular than about the common—or, put differently, we hear often about the singular without hearing about the common, we are faced with a conceptualization of the singular in isolation from the common—while in *Multitude* these two concepts are always indissoluble from each other. But I would like to return to the dyad of the singular and the common—to its merits as well as to its shortcomings—later in more detail. My second point is that possibly what I find most disappointing about *Multitude* is the way it's written—that is, its language, its style.

AN: What exactly about the style bothers you?

CC: Well . . . this is not easy to explain, to pinpoint. As a shortcut, let me make recourse to the conceptual categories of form and content—which, admittedly, in the end are not terribly useful or adequate, and, in fact, I regularly discourage my own students from using them as anything other than mere heuristic devices for jump-starting textual analysis, as anything more than the starting point rather than the end point of an investigation. (On these categories too, Deleuze—in the wake of Louis Hjelmslev—has important lessons to impart.) And let me add that what I am about to say is a commentary on both *Multitude* and *Empire,* since these two works are quite similar when it comes to those very general aspects that concern me here. From the standpoint of content, I have two main points to make about these works. On the one hand, I believe that when it comes to providing an adequate, accurate, detailed analysis of our contemporary historical conjuncture as well as of how we got to it— that is, when it comes to understanding our present and our past—these two works are second to none: I have not encountered more incisive and powerful analyses anywhere so far. On the other hand, when it comes to the political conclusions you draw from such an analysis—that is, when it comes to articulating proposals and demands, to outlining projects and projections in the present as well as in the future, as you do, for example, in the final sections of both these works—I feel much more ambivalent, as I have made clear several times already. From the standpoint of form—including linguistic expression, writing style, etc.—I have one general remark to make about both works: often, they are not a pleasure to read—and I find this to be the case less for *Empire* than for *Multitude,* by the way. Unlike all your previous books, as well as unlike Michael's book on Deleuze, I find them boring to read at times. And I must confess that I find it embarrassing to put the matter in these terms, because, after all, I don't see why anybody should care about what bores me and what doesn't.

AN: Aren't you just saying that you feel—rightly or wrongly—that these books were not written for you? And why should they have been, anyway? Let's be very clear about this: *Multitude* was meant to be a book that could be sold on the supermarket shelves! This, at least, was our original idea and goal. I am not sure, though, whether we were successful in the end—for better or for worse!

CC: Thankfully, you weren't successful! In any case, I don't think that all I am trying to say here is merely that these books were not meant for me— although, to be sure, that's part of it. And I don't think either that what I am saying can be put to rest entirely by invoking the proverbial maxim "de gustibus et de coloribus non disputandum est" [about tastes and about colors, one cannot argue]. I see myself as part of an intellectual tradition for which form is historical and ideological—namely, that it has its own implicit content regardless of whatever other explicit content it is supposed to articulate in representation; this is also a tradition for which, hence, matters of taste may well be indisputable and yet are hardly unquestionable or insignificant in terms of their political conditions of possibility as well as of their political effectivity.

AN: Yes, fine, but what is your point here?

CC: Your choice of expository style in both these works indicates that you meant to write not only or not exactly pedagogical texts but also works of popularization [*divulgazione*]—in short, not only books for beginning students of, say, political philosophy or critical legal theory but also for a much wider educated public. Your invocation of the supermarket shelves reconfirms all this. I find this type of project to be a defensible, commendable, necessary, and urgent political project—even though it has never been my project, largely due to the fact that I have neither the proclivity nor the talent for it when it comes to my writing (while I hope I have both when it comes to teaching in the classroom or elsewhere!). I don't have any problems with the project per se, in other words—on the contrary. And I also grant that, if you speak five languages and I speak only one among those five, when you want to tell me something, you have no choice: you must speak my language. This does not mean, however, that you must speak my language *in the same way* in which I do—especially if you believe that my language is crippled by clichés, that is, if you believe that my language has been colonized through and through by the commodity form and by its mortifying repetition of the same. In other words, you cannot, on the one hand, argue that under our fully realized regime of biopolitical production even the most constitutive core of the common—that is, language in all of its forms—is being taken away from us, expropriated, exploited, and reified, and, on the other hand, argue all this precisely through such a reified language without attempting to transform it and reelaborate it—in short, without attempting to produce something new out of all the clichés that surround us and saturate our sensorium. Undoubtedly, I am exaggerating in order to make my point as clear as possible: I don't think that *Empire* and *Multitude* ever make recourse to linguistic clichés, for instance. But my point is that to be a writer—which is what you, Michael, and I also are—means to have a craft as well as to have ethical responsibilities toward that craft:

paramount among such responsibilities is to be able and willing to produce the new out of reified language, that is, to enable our language to
become different from what it is. Incidentally, I believe this is one of the
main lessons to be learned from Deleuze when he writes about the culture of the cliché in *Cinema 2*.[3] Under this respect, your other books are
very different from *Empire* and *Multitude*. Take, for instance, books such
as *Marx beyond Marx*—which to this day I consider in many ways to
be your best book as well as the book that has influenced me most—or
Kairòs, Alma Venus, Multitudo: these are books that experiment with
writing. It's not just that they are difficult books: there are plenty of difficult and uninteresting books out there! The point is that in these other
books you take risks with writing, you treat writing as an experiment,
you are very inventive and creative—and you are so precisely where you
show, for example, just how inventive and creative Marx was both stylistically and conceptually in the *Grundrisse*.

AN: You raise very important issues here—even though I do think you are
exaggerating in your characterization of the writing style we adopted
in *Empire* and *Multitude*. Moreover, I am not sure whether it is entirely
accurate to understand the genre, so to speak, of these two books in the
way that you do, namely, as works of popularization [*divulgazione*]—
even though I have nothing against this type of works in principle. Obviously, we were trying to reach a wide audience with them, but not all
books that are trying to achieve that are to be considered automatically
works of popularization [*divulgazione*] because of it. It seems to me that
your main point here is that something important is lost or sacrificed
when trying to reach a wide audience in writing. I don't think this is
necessarily the case. And even if it were the case, this fact would raise
many other questions. First of all, it is not self-evident or immediately
clear what this certain something that gets lost is exactly. Theoretical
nuance? Conceptual precision? Philosophical purity? Political effectivity?
All of the above? Something else altogether? I am not sure—and there
is nothing in what you said that provides an answer to this question.
Second, this could be said of any form or style of writing: something important is always lost in the sense that no type of writing can achieve
everything or reach everybody. I am sure that something of the sort could
be said precisely of a book like *Marx beyond Marx*, for instance—a book
that, after all, was conceived as a series of lectures to be delivered in a very
specific setting and for a very specific audience, namely, academic ones.

Having said all that, however, let me add that, of course, I agree with you on a crucial point, namely, on the fact that the question of style is a very important historical, political, and ideological question.

CC: Could one say, perhaps, that what I am pointing to here has to do with our specific historical conjuncture, in the sense that there are certain compromises one needs to make nowadays if one wants to reach a wide audience? A work as beautifully, inventively, powerfully, and uncompromisingly written as *The Communist Manifesto,* after all, did reach a very wide audience in its own time—and I wonder whether anybody at all could achieve such a feat nowadays.

AN: I am not sure. In any case, I don't think that we made any damaging or significant compromises in *Empire* and *Multitude* in order to reach a wider audience. *Empire,* for example, did reach a very wide audience— a fact that to this day greatly surprises as well as amuses me—but the reasons for its success, as far as I am concerned, are not attributable to compromises or the like. I do agree with you that this work does not say much that either Michael or I had not said before already, and even that this work in a sense does not say much that is new to anybody at all—and I don't find this to be a problem. In fact, this is possibly the main reason for its success: *Empire* reached the audiences it did because it was able to seize upon, to express, as well as to interrelate a whole series of needs, desires, and aspirations that nowadays are very common and very widespread among the multitudes of the planet. This is what it means truly to sound the present.

CC: Yes, I agree that both *Empire* and *Multitude* constitute such soundings. But let me push this matter further by way of a comparison. In *Empire,* you and Michael explicitly point to *A Thousand Plateaus* as one of your main sources of inspiration—both methodologically and conceptually. Now that you have written *Multitude,* however, it strikes me that a different parallel could be made, namely, between, on the one hand, *Empire* and *Anti-Oedipus,* and, on the other hand, *Multitude* and *A Thousand Plateaus.* Much as *Anti-Oedipus* constitutes in many ways the *pars destruens* while *A Thousand Plateaus* constitutes the *pars construens* of Deleuze and Guattari's project, *Empire* in many ways presents itself as a work of critique while *Multitude* posits itself explicitly as a moment of construction and constitution. Earlier, you corroborated at least the latter part of this comparison when you emphasized that the main problem you were facing in writing *Multitude* was precisely to make the multitude rather than revealing or analyzing it. I believe, however, that this comparison holds much more conceptually rather than methodologically—and not at all stylistically. What I mean is that these four works are in some ways very similar when it comes to the concepts they elaborate and deploy, as well as similar perhaps when it comes to the methods of investigation they employ, and not comparable at all when it comes to the ways in which they are written—which is why I brought this comparison up in the first place. For example, while Deleuze and Guattari felt the need to change radically their style of writing—as well as their method of inquiry, to some extent—in the passage from the *pars destruens* to the *pars construens* of their project, under this regard there is instead a fundamental continuity between *Empire* and *Multitude*. In short, the passage from *Anti-Oedipus* to *A Thousand Plateaus* constituted, among other things, a metamorphosis of style, an exponential leap in linguistic experimentation—and, for better or for worse, this cannot be said about the passage from *Empire* to *Multitude*. It is possible, however, that I am pushing this parallel too far.

AN: Your parallel leaves me somewhat perplexed. I experienced the relation between *Anti-Oedipus* and *A Thousand Plateaus* as a passage very different from the one that brought Michael and me from *Empire* to *Multitude*. Much like you, I too think of *Anti-Oedipus* as a true *pars destruens*—in the specific sense that it destroyed structuralism. *Empire*, however, is not at all a *pars destruens*, and, if it can be compared to any of these works at all, it is rather comparable to *A Thousand Plateaus*. In some ways, actually, it is *Multitude* that could be said to be similar to *Anti-Oedipus*—although, in a fundamental sense, Michael and I have yet to write our *Anti-Oedipus*. *Anti-Oedipus*, after all, was an attempt to recover the deepest or highest level of ontological causality, namely, an attempt to reintroduce desire within postmodern philosophy, to rediscover desire as foundation of the postmodern, so as to counter that last great Marxist heresy which was structuralism. If I characterize structuralism in this way that is because it constituted the last in a long series of efforts to articulate the relation between base and superstructure against and yet from within purely dialectical parameters. I believe this is what the most important figures within structuralism—namely, Claude Lévi-Strauss and Jacques Lacan—were after: an articulation of consciousness and matter, of consciousness and life, that would be at one and the same time within and against the dialectic. *Anti-Oedipus*'s answer to the structuralist articulation can be summarized in the following way: there is no longer any dialectic; there is only a production of consciousness that cannot be dialectically prefigured—as it is, for example, within Freud's schemata—and that, rather, can only be free, open, that is, uncompromisingly non-teleological. *A Thousand Plateaus*, then, constitutes a further development of this argument in the sense that while *Anti-Oedipus* brought the redis-covery of this productive force to bear on the question of conscious-ness—thereby marking a radical break with structuralism—*A Thousand Plateaus* brought it to bear on the whole of history and of life, that is, on the common. The relation between *Empire* and *Multitude*, on the other hand, is different from all that I have just described—and that is so above all because there is much more continuity between our two books than there is between Deleuze and Guattari's books. Unlike *Anti-Oedipus*, *Empire* is an incomplete project: it continuously drops hints about the multitude without ever saying anything about it.

cc: In a sense, *Empire* looks at and describes our present from the stand-point of the multitude without saying so explicitly and hence without forcing itself to clarify and to develop such a standpoint fully. In some respects, hence, *Multitude* actually precedes *Empire*: even though *Multi-tude* was written later, much of what you actualize in that text was a latency that not only was already present in *Empire* but also constituted the condition of possibility for your thinking and writing *Empire* in the first place. It is not a coincidence, then, that in *Multitude* you engage with the relation between *Forschung* and *Darstellung*: by doing so, in fact, you also thematize and address implicitly the inverse temporal relation between *Multitude* and *Empire*.[4] Much the way Marx says in the *Grun-drisse* that the anatomy of the human is the key to the anatomy of the ape, we could say perhaps that the anatomy of the multitude is the key to the anatomy of empire.[5]

an: Yes, I completely agree. And I would add that, to the extent to which *Multitude* completes a project that had begun already in *Empire*, the relation between these two works is one of complementarity—which I don't believe can be said about the relation between *Anti-Oedipus* and *A Thousand Plateaus*.

cc: Since you have invoked the concept of complementarity to describe the relation between *Empire* and *Multitude*, this might be as good a moment as any to return to the complementary dyad of the singular and the com-mon. As I said earlier, I find these two concepts not only to be extremely valuable but also to constitute a significant step forward with respect to Deleuze's theorizations of singularity, which often neglect its indispensable link to the common. I find the way in which you make recourse to complementarity, however, to be perplexing. While I would agree with you that the relation between *Empire* and *Multitude* could be argued to be one of complementarity, I am not sure I understand what it means to say that the relation between the singular and the common is a complementary one. I associate the concept of complementarity—perhaps wrongly—with dialectical relations. Or, at the very least, a complementary dyad for me always points to a concept of lack, in the sense that X constitutes the necessary complement of Y to the extent to which Y lacks something necessary, something that makes it radically incomplete—and vice versa. However, if singularity as a concept makes any sense at all, in your work as well as in Deleuze's work, it makes sense only as a concept referring to something that lacks nothing whatsoever and that is absolutely perfect (and I use the term "perfect" here in the Spinozian sense).[6] Moreover, if this is the case for the concept of singularity, I would argue that it is all the more the case for the concept of the common.

AN: There are several points to be made here. First of all, I would caution against stressing the continuity between, on the one hand, Deleuze's concept of singularity, and, on the other hand, the dyad of the singular and the common—even though in both cases we are dealing with attempts to displace the binary opposition of identity and difference. More precisely, one has to be very careful in specifying exactly what type of continuity there is in general between their thought and mine. You know very well how intimate and intense the bond that links me to Félix and to Gilles is—a bond that is personal as much as it is historical. The sources of their thought, however, are radically different from the sources both of my thought and of Michael's thought, since for the two of us Marxist philosophy was fundamental from very early on. Undoubtedly, Deleuze and Guattari articulated their thought within a Marxist domain, deployed their concepts in the context of a Marxist problematic—and yet such a domain and such a problematic were neither primary in nor internal to their intellectual formation. The sources of their thought were never Marxist: they were, rather, Henri Bergson, Freud, etc. I—and, to a lesser extent, Michael—on the other hand, started from Marx. It is essential to stress that the relation between, on the one hand, Deleuze and Guattari, and, on the other hand, myself was never one of filiation: it was, rather,

an encounter—an encounter pure and simple. If one mistakes this relation for filiation, one will never be able to understand, for example,
the extent to which Deleuze, Guattari, and I often use the same terms
in extremely different ways. In short, what binds us all to one another is
the continuity of an encounter rather than the continuity of a filiation.
Frankly, I cannot think of a type of relation that is worse than filiation.
The family must be destroyed!

CC: I am in complete agreement with you, and I hope I did not give you
the impression that I was implying otherwise. The only reason why I
am insisting so much on comparing your collaborative works to Deleuze
and Guattari's collaborative works is that in the preface to *Empire*
you and Michael state explicitly that Marx's *Grundrisse* as well as Deleuze
and Guattari's *A Thousand Plateaus* are your primary methodological
models.[7]

AN: Obviously, I am not trying to claim authenticity, originality, or any such
bullshit. I am trying to say simply that this is how things went: it was
an encounter. There is no doubt that Deleuze is my most privileged
interlocutor among all contemporary thinkers. There is no doubt that
Deleuze and Guattari constituted a crucial moment in my theoretical
elaborations: they became my *passe-partout* of postmodernity. Likewise,
their discovery of the philosophical as well as political articulations of
real subsumption constituted a pivotal moment in their project. The intellectual traditions from which we emerged, however, were profoundly
different from each other—and this fact determined the divergences as
well as the convergences of our respective projects to a significant extent.

CC: Shall we return to the conceptual dyad of the singular and the common?

AN: Yes. My second point is that the common constitutes indeed the crucial
element differentiating my theorization of singularity from Deleuze and
Guattari's theorization—which is what I believe you were suggesting
earlier. It is not only the case that in Deleuze and Guattari the concept of
the common is present far less than the concept of the singular. It is also
the case that whenever the common is present in them it constitutes a
dialectical element. I have the distinct impression, in other words, that
the overcoming of the dialectic in Deleuze and Guattari is certainly radical and complete, but that it is an overcoming that leads them to a purely
horizontal conception of the relations among singularities. Deleuze and
Guattari's overcoming of the dialectic leads them to dismiss or ignore
synthesis as a problem altogether, that is, leads them to deny the fact that

synthesis is a problem to be contended with regardless of one's position with respect to the dialectic. The solution they find to this nonproblem of synthesis—which is to say, the solution they find in order not to deal with the question of synthesis in any way whatsoever—is in effect to hypothesize a continuous displacement of the levels of knowledge [*conoscenza*] as well as of the levels of action [*agire*]. As far as I am concerned, this is at best a nonsolution to a very real problem—a nonsolution that, nonetheless, did serve them well for a while. By the time they write *What Is Philosophy?*, however, this solution becomes very problematic, that is, it is revealed fully as a nonsolution, as a conceptual device that simply doesn't work. In that book, in fact, they struggle continuously to avoid producing precisely that which brought them to write that book in the first place—namely, a concept of synthesis. In *What Is Philosophy?*, they were looking for a synthesis, and they were not able to find it because by then they had made it impossible for themselves to conceive of any synthesis whatsoever.

cc: One could argue that their theorization of the brain at the end of *What Is Philosophy?* is tantamount to an attempt to produce a concept of synthesis, since the brain is that producing product of the intersection of the three fundamental instances of the intellect, namely, philosophy, art, and science.

an: Yes, I suppose so. And yet, it is such an inadequate attempt. Their concept of the brain yearns and yet fails to be a concept of the producing product of the common. The problem is that the very idea of the production of the common is nowhere to be found in Deleuze and Guattari.

cc: It seems to me that you are implying several important things at once here. First of all, you are saying that Deleuze and Guattari avoid the question of synthesis because this question has been conceptualized always in dialectical terms and, indeed, has represented the very hallmark of the dialectic as a discourse and as a problematic. Their engagement—or lack thereof—with the question of synthesis, in other words, amounts to throwing the baby away with the bathwater. Moreover, you are saying that just because the concept of synthesis has been so essential and definitional for the dialectic, it does not follow that one can do away with this concept and that one cannot reconceptualize it differently; on the contrary, the concept of synthesis is indispensable for any thought of the political, and it ought to be disengaged from the dialectic as well as reconceptualized in a nondialectical manner. Lastly, you are implying that this is precisely what you have been trying to do for a while, namely, to produce a nondialectical concept of synthesis, and that such a concept in your work consists of the production of the common—which is why the common in the end is that which differentiates most your thought from Deleuze and Guattari's thought.

AN: Yes. And I am saying also that all of this—including the nonengagement or inadequate engagement with the question of synthesis, with the production of the common, etc.—becomes most apparent in *What Is Philosophy?* I never thought this was one of their best works; on the contrary, I thought of it as a bit of a botch, as somewhat of a messy compromise or retraction. Originally, they had conceived of it as a work on the philosophy of nature, but I don't think they were able to pull it off. Undoubtedly, there are very valuable things in it: extremely beautiful pages on aesthetics, ferocious critiques of the postmodern, and so on. When it comes to what they present possibly as the most important question of the work—that is, the question of the concept, of its consistency, of its emergence, etc.—though, they have nothing useful to say. But I want to return to the complementary dyad of the singular and the common, since I have not addressed yet your most crucial objection, namely, the purportedly dialectical nature of the concept of complementarity. So, my third point is simply the following: contrary to what you assert, a relation of complementarity is not a dialectical relation. A complementary relation does not go through negation; rather, it goes through the void. There is only one thing that faces and confronts the *kairòs*, and that is the void. And it is on the void that the *kairòs* builds that which brings together, that which is in common.[8]

CC: The complementary relation, in other words, is the one and only relation that brings together in producing something that is shared in common: if you and I are complementary, that means that we are bound to each other by the activity of producing something in common as well as by that something, namely, by the product of that activity. It might be more accurate, then, to resort to complementarity in order to describe the relations among all the singularities that constitute the common rather than in order to characterize the relations between the singular and the common itself—but perhaps I am being a bit too nitpicking. What is crucial, in any case, is that for you this type of relation can be built only on the void.

AN: Yes. And this is another way of saying that a relation of complementarity marks a transformation rather than a dialectical synthesis, that each and every process of conceptual production is a metamorphosis rather than an *Aufhebung.*

CC: All that you are saying makes sense, however, only to the extent to which what you are calling the void is something other than a limit.

AN: The void and the limit are completely different concepts.

CC: I understand what a limit is. But what is the void exactly?

AN: The void is that thing which we don't know, which is over there, which is beyond reach.

CC: Yes, but can the void be said to exist? How can the void be?

AN: Of course the void exists! The void is in each and every instant. Each and every moment of our lives, we risk: that is the void. The void is the risk we run each and every step we take.

CC: Actually, I mean something else. Does the void have any ontological consistency? Can one speak of it as an ontological entity?

AN: No. One can speak of it, rather, as the nonontological absolute. Right now, for example, you and I are speaking on the void, that is, in the self-unfolding or self-exposure of the void [*nell'esporsi del vuoto*]. Each and every word we speak is thrown there—in the void—so as to reinvent itself. And in ethical terms, not to risk the void is the very definition of evil.

CC: Yes, I agree. And I would add that your definition of the void as the nonontological absolute is not a negative one, is not determined by negation: on your reading, in fact, the void reveals itself to be there only to the extent to which we throw something in it, the void makes itself felt—that is, becomes perceivable, palpable—only to the extent to which we affirm, build, produce something.

AN: Moreover, if one acts at the level of immanence, duration—that is, the duration of existence—has any meaning and makes any sense only to the extent to which one risks it as void. Any of our experiences verifies and attests to our exposure to the void, to chance, to a truly regal contingency. And that's what materialism is! If materialism were not this absoluteness of our precarious condition, this absoluteness of a coming or future condition founded on doing, making, producing—materialism would simply not exist. Each one of us builds on the void: any form or presence is a bridge that we cast over the void.

CC: I must confess that your concept of the void as the nonontological absolute in some ways is beginning to sound analogous to Lacan's concept of the Real—not necessarily in the sense that they are two names for the same concept, but more in the sense that they fulfill similar functions and occupy similar positions in your different philosophical systems and intellectual projects.

AN: Well, I don't see the analogy between these two concepts at all.

CC: Fine. Let me invoke, then, another—perhaps more pertinent and certainly related—analogy. Toward the end of his life, Althusser had begun to articulate a theory of what he called "aleatory materialism"—in which concepts such as void, contingency, and risk play central roles.[9] It seems to me that much of what you have been saying here with respect to materialism bears a striking resemblance to Althusser's late formulations.

AN: Yes, I see the similarity, even though I must say that those formulations are very confused and inconclusive. I am afraid that toward the end of his life Althusser was no longer very lucid or coherent.

CC: All these analogies and similarities aside, what I find very interesting about your current insistence on the importance of a concept such as the void is that it comes in the wake of decades during which you spent considerable time and effort on the affirmation of the fullness of being.

AN: But there is no contradiction at all between, on the one hand, the void as indispensable element in the production of being, and, on the other hand, the richness and fullness of this process of production.

CC: I agree. I am not implying that there is any contradiction here. I am remarking, rather, on the sequence of events, that is, on the fact that you have felt the need to elaborate a concept of void only quite recently.

AN: Don't we all need to do one thing at a time? Who knows what things are coming next, what things still need to be done, how many or how few other things one will never get to do! This is why fullness is eternity. Eternity is chance: it is made up of things that can never be unmade once they have been made. Whatever bullshit we come up with endures and shall never be unmade, because we have built it on this enormous void that faces us, on this enormous task that life confronts us with in each and every instant. That's why the dialectic is shit! It always tries to recombine and reconcile everything, to bring everything together, to make everything fit together, to force everything to make sense—so as to please everybody, to make everybody happy, and to pacify us all! Perhaps even more than Hegel, the master of this dialectical charade was your Sicilian compatriot, Gentile—a great philosopher, a true genius, compared to whom Croce was a rather dull academician. Gentile tries it all: he scrambles Spirit, nation, praxis, transcendence, immanence, and even the common all together—even though the common in his thought is no more than spiritual essence.

cc: Since we have returned once again to the common, I would like to try and investigate this concept further in a different way—that is, no longer from the standpoint of its relation to the singular but from the standpoint of its relation to the multitude itself. And I would like to approach this matter by way of yet another comparison, namely, by way of comparing your concept of multitude and Deleuze and Guattari's concept of multiplicity in *A Thousand Plateaus* and elsewhere. In some ways, these two concepts are very similar, even though, of course, they have very different genealogies: multitude's genealogy is primarily political and ontological (Machiavelli, Spinoza, Marx, etc.), while multiplicity's genealogy is primarily mathematical (Georg Riemann, Benoit Mandelbrot, Bergson, etc.).[10] Genealogies aside, however, I think that there are other important differences. When attempting to elaborate multitude as a class concept, for example, you and Michael write: "A multitude is an irreducible multiplicity; the singular social differences that constitute the multitude must always be expressed and can never be flattened into sameness, unity, identity, or indifference. The multitude, however, is not merely a fragmented and dispersed multiplicity."[11]

an: If you are implying that in this passage—and possibly elsewhere in *Multitude*—in effect we are dissociating ourselves from a dispersive concept of multiplicity that we attribute to Deleuze and Guattari, I believe you are correct. This is just another way of expressing some of those fundamental differences between our positions and Deleuze and Guattari's positions—especially with respect to the common—which we discussed earlier.

cc: Yes. There might be, however, yet another fundamental difference between your multitude and Deleuze and Guattari's multiplicity. In *Multitude*, you and Michael repeat several times that the multitude is not divided or divisible according to differences of nature—and I take this to mean also that the multitude is divided and divisible only according to differences of degree. Let me give you two examples. In the first, you write: "[T]he concept of multitude is meant to repropose Marx's political project of class struggle. The multitude from this perspective is based not so much on the current empirical existence of the class but rather on its condition of possibility . . . Such a political project must clearly be grounded in an empirical analysis that demonstrates the common conditions of those who can become the multitude. Common conditions, of course, does not mean sameness or unity but it does require that no differences of nature or kind divide the multitude."[12] In the second, you add: "In order to verify this concept of multitude and its political project we will have to establish that indeed the differences of kind that used to divide labor no longer apply, in other words, that the conditions exist for the various types of labor to communicate, collaborate, and become common."[13] It strikes me that exactly the opposite is the case for Deleuze and Guattari's multiplicity! Whereas differences of nature are foreign to your multitude, their multiplicity undergoes a radical metamorphosis each and every time it is divided, that is, it changes in nature as soon as any type of division takes place in it. For Deleuze and Guattari, in fact, whereas a magnitude is an entity that can always be divided in extensive, quantifiable, and commensurable parts, a multiplicity can only be divided in intensive, nonquantifiable, and incommensurable parts; in short, magnitude allows only for differences of degree, while multiplicity allows only for differences of nature. My point is the following: if your multitude is to make any sense, it ought to be a multiplicity; you define it, however, in terms of magnitude.

AN: These are extremely important issues. I suspect that in the end, however, the multitude has little or nothing to do with either magnitude or multiplicity. I am not yet sure, in any case, that your point is completely clear to me, and hence I need you to explain it more in detail before saying anything further. In particular, you have not specified yet what exactly any of this has to do with the question of the common—which was your initial claim, I believe.

CC: First of all, it seems to me that to the extent to which the multitude is the becoming-common of singularities, it must involve difference of nature. Singularity, after all, indexes absolute and primary difference as opposed to relative and secondary difference—and I understand difference of nature precisely to be absolute and difference of degree merely to be relative. It seems to me, in other words, that only difference of nature might constitute an adequate guarantee against commensurability, equivalence, and exchange—which is what I imagine the multitude and its constitutive singularities do not index. Second, I think that—contrary to what you state in the last passage I quoted—not only is it possible for entities that are different in nature to be in common and to communicate but also it is only among such entities that being-in-common and communication are at all possible. Spinoza is very clear about this matter: the fact that modal essences can never be shared, can never be in common, and hence constitute singularities, does not mean at all that modes cannot exist in common or cannot communicate; modes do communicate adequately, for example, through the common notions, even though their essences are absolutely different from one another. Furthermore, not even the essence of substance is shared with modal essences, and yet substance and modes do exist in common and do communicate, thanks to, for example, the third type of knowledge.[14] Spinoza aside, what I am trying to say is that you cannot assert, on the one hand, that the singular and the common are complementary to one another, and, on the other hand, that entities that are different in nature or essence—namely, singularities— cannot "communicate, collaborate, and become common," or, in short, cannot constitute the common.

AN: Your objections are certainly very subtle, complex, pertinent—as well as very useful for clarifying and refining further the concept of multitude. I believe, though, that several of these objections are already addressed— albeit indirectly, perhaps—in *Multitude* and elsewhere.

CC: Certainly. As a matter of fact, when you discuss the concept of multitude with Anne Dufourmentelle in *Negri on Negri*, you define this concept in ways that are more congruent with Deleuze and Guattari's concept of multiplicity and hence that would make it much more difficult to raise the type of objections I have raised here.[15]

AN: Let me try, nonetheless, to address your concerns here. I must begin by saying that I find it difficult to accept the terminology you employ, which derives more from the poststructuralist Deleuze than from the Deleuze of *A Thousand Plateaus*. As you point out, the genesis of Deleuze's concept of multiplicity is a mathematical one. Such a genesis, in other words, is inextricable from a level or type of analysis that is so formal as to impose a dimension on the concept of multiplicity that is itself purely formal too. Our concept of multitude, on the other hand, is born of the analysis of the singularization of labor. While the references to Machiavelli and Spinoza are undoubtedly important, our concept of multitude starts specifically from the analysis of the contemporary passage and transformation from Fordist labor to post-Fordist labor, from mass labor (in which labor is ordered and defined according to Taylorist principles so as to meet the requirements of industrial mass production) to what lately I like to call "swarm labor" (in which labor increasingly comes to be identified in and as social activity *tout court*). Michael and I, in other words, start our investigation from within material rather than formal determinations: we are not dealing with the dissolution of a set or of another type of logically conceived and abstractly defined unit; we are dealing, rather, with the dissolution of a mass, of a concretely defined mass, and, in particular, we are concerned with the expressive or materially constituent element of this mass, namely, with its organizational and productive apparatus [*dispositivo*]. There is a huge difference between, on the one hand, considering an infinitely subdivisible set that is reassembled each and every time a division occurs over and over again, and, on the other hand, considering an infinitely subdivisible mass that produces and that is bound up with the emergence of infinite singularities, each of which is itself productive. I am grateful to you for your objection, since it is able—starting from a philological standpoint—to seize upon the essential element that separates me from Deleuze and Guattari. Moreover, I must add that you have seized upon an aspect of Deleuze and Guattari's thought that I have found always to be quite annoying: even at those times when our projects were closer to each other than ever, I could not stand the fact that Deleuze and Guattari would forget punctually and systematically that there are certain material phenomena such as exploitation or class struggle that cannot be formalized in any way. My understanding of the constitution of singularities is Aristotelian rather than Platonic, materialist rather than mathematical. In spite of everything, there are nonetheless several mathematical as well as Platonic-Bergsonian residual elements that continue to be operative within Deleuze's conception of singularity, which, on the one hand, is decidedly formalist, and, on the other hand, does strive to become increasingly concrete and historically determined. I believe we need to discard such residual elements so as to be able to foreground that constitutive, dynamic, formative apparatus [*dispositivo*] which is essential in the constitution of singularity. Each singularity expresses—and such expression cannot be captured by any formalism whatsoever. It is not a coincidence that Michael and I continuously refer to language rather than to mathematics: language has an expressive—that is, innovative—nature; linguistic circulation is not a circulation of formal elements but a circulation among expressive elements that say, speak, tell. The foundational component of the concept of multitude is not simply a formal concept of set that breaks up into singularities or reassembles into unity; it is, rather, a concept of singularities that continuously reassemble and reconfigure themselves into a language. The common, thus, is not presupposed a priori as identity, as compacting element, or even as that site in which singular modalities reassemble into a being. The common, rather, is that which takes place when singular modalities reassemble into a specifically discursive and proliferating being. Your objection or question, then, could be rephrased in the following terms: Does the common function as the foundation or background of this discursive proliferation? Does the common have ontological consistency? Is the common determined ontologically in any way? The answer is unequivocal: No. Michael and I are saying that all we have is a continuous construction, a continuous process of dissolution and recomposition, and that in order to give a figure to such a process—which is to say, in order to understand how this process works—we need to posit an analogy between the constitutive behavior of the multitude and language understood as the expressive social activity par excellence. As a way of clarifying our position further, let me contrast it with Paolo Virno's recent work, since he too understands the common in relation to language. Virno, in effect, ends up at once dehistoricizing and naturalizing the process I have just described: he undermines the nonteleological historicity of the self-determination of singularities by asserting that the constitutive relations—including linguistic relations—that produce as well as bind these singularities together can be defined only in terms of faculty.[16] To recapitulate: I have identified here three distinct propositions. The first is Deleuze's proposition, according to which the relation between multiplicity and totality simply dissolves into a myriad of singularly differentiated positions or entities. Ours is the second proposition, according to which all these differentiated positions—namely, this multiplicity—reassemble constitutively through language and through social activity in general. The third is Virno's proposition, according to which such a linguistic and social recomposition can take place exclusively on the basis of preexistent natural faculties, which follow specific laws. As far as I am concerned, the third proposition represents a step backwards with respect to the first. Virno's argumentations index a slippage toward Chomskyan positions, that is, toward that formal or structural naturalism that Deleuze had refuted and defeated already a long time ago; moreover, we must keep in mind that every time one naturalizes processes such as the ones we have been discussing, one sooner or later ends up falling back into identity discourse.

cc: There is much to say here. First of all, I am not sure I agree fully with your characterization of Virno's position. On the one hand, I do agree that in Virno the constitution of the common takes place on the basis of faculty—even natural faculty. On the other hand, I think that the type of faculty he invokes cannot be construed as preexistent; in fact, in Virno this faculty cannot be said even to exist at all; on the contrary, this faculty is, strictly speaking, nonexistent, to the extent to which he defines it as pure potentiality immanent in the body.[17] Leaving Virno aside for the moment, I do understand your position much more clearly now. Certainly, you have addressed many of my concerns—especially with respect to the different genealogies, implications, and functions of the concepts of multiplicity and of multitude. There is an aspect of my objections, however, that I think still remains unaddressed. In brief, I do not understand yet how it is possible that the common is complementary with the singular and yet mutually exclusive with difference of nature—especially if one follows Spinoza in understanding the latter as that essential difference that makes modes singular.

an: The point is that in Spinoza modality is not reducible to its essence. Furthermore, it is through the mechanism of the passions that modalities come together. In short, the common comes into being on the basis of social praxis—which is another way of saying, of course, that the concept of the common is a fundamentally Marxist concept. This does not mean, however, that the common is a reconfigured concept of working class. The task, rather, is to capture the antagonistic qualifications of the concept of expression, that is, to produce a concept that would describe adequately the antagonistic expression of singularity. Singularity posits itself qua singularity not to the extent to which it constitutes singular existence, singular essence, singular determination, or even singular faculty. Singularity posits and reassembles itself as singularity to the extent to which it is opposition and antagonism. This is, hence, what it means to produce a concept of class: this is not a concept of mass or unity determined on the basis of interest; it is, rather, a concept of antagonistic dynamics and relations, a concept of antagonism determined on the basis of expropriation.

cc: If I understand you correctly, you are not denying that there is difference of nature in singularity; you are denying, rather, that it is on the basis of difference of nature that singularity comes into being qua singularity. Put differently, you are asserting that that which makes singularity singular is not its essence but its existence, and, in particular, that singularity posits itself as such only to the extent to which its existence involves antagonistic praxis. In short, you are saying that my objection is at once accurate and yet misplaced to the extent to which you are dealing with antagonism as constitutive of singularity.

AN: Yes, precisely. Another way of looking at my position is to understand it as an attempt to develop the concept of expression—expression intended as creative element.

CC: Would you say that there is no expression without antagonism?

AN: Yes—to the extent to which there can be no creation without antagonism. I cannot overemphasize how fundamental the discovery of negativity as productive principle was in my earliest philosophical formation, as well as how fundamental such a principle has continued to be throughout my entire philosophical development.

CC: What exactly is the relation between dialectical negativity and the type of negativity you are invoking here?

AN: They are one and the same! It is not the case that there are different types of negativity; rather, there are different ways of dealing with the one and only negativity that produces and never ceases to produce. The dialectic simply constitutes a largely inadequate, constrictive, and domesticating way of dealing with negativity. The point is that precisely because negativity produces, it destroys the dialectic, that is, it produces an unassimilable surplus [*eccedenza*]. This is a lesson that I learned from studying the history of philosophy as much as from being involved in class struggle. When I started frequenting the world of the factory and participating in its political struggles, for example, I was struck by the fact that all the factory workers knew perfectly well that they were heading for total defeat and yet did not refrain from fighting because they also knew perfectly well that there was an absolutely irreducible creative element within their defeat. And years later, my philosophical conversion, so to speak, took place precisely in the depths of despair and of defeat, namely, when I found myself in jail for the first time. It was there, in fact, that I started working on Spinoza and that I wrote *The Constitution of Time*.[18] The reason why these two books constituted such a pivotal moment in my philosophical development has all to do with the question of defeat: once defeated, one starts asking oneself what went wrong; once imprisoned, one starts looking around for ways to escape. In a sense, these two books constituted my attempt to identify exactly what was wrong with Marxism so as to escape it. More precisely, they constituted my attempt to unhinge Marxism so as to foreground that creative element which was indeed present in it but which was imprisoned within its dialectical strictures, namely, power.

CC: In short, it was defeat that forced you to reconfigure Marxism from the standpoint of power.

AN: Yes. Let me add, though, that I was extremely lucky: had it not been for the fact that—during the years of my first imprisonment, as well as during the years immediately after it—history, far from reaching its end, picked up speed exponentially instead, it is possible and even likely that my defeat would have done me no good and would have constituted only a miserable defeat pure and simple. Obviously, not all defeats are the same.

CC: This matter of defeat is as good a way as any to introduce my last topic for this conversation, namely, the question of war. As I hinted earlier, I found the first section of *Multitude* on war to be particularly powerful, illuminating, and timely. In brief, I have two points to make. As far as the first point is concerned, I am afraid that it will reconfirm my tic, that is, my incorrigible penchant for comparing *Multitude* to *A Thousand Plateaus*! Even though you and Michael never refer to that section of *A Thousand Plateaus* in which Deleuze and Guattari discuss at length what they call the war machine, it seems to me that, whatever else you are doing in *Multitude,* you are also commenting on, as well as elaborating further, their arguments regarding the complex triangulation of war, nomads, and the state.[19] Am I mistaken? My second point is more important as well as more difficult to substantiate—in other words, I am basing it largely on a gut feeling. It strikes me, in fact, that there might be significant similarities between this first section of *Multitude* and the last section of the book, that is, the section on democracy. Could one say perhaps that, much as in the last section of the book you attempt to rescue as well as to reclaim the concept of democracy by offering a series of critical genealogies of this concept, in the first section you elaborate a critical genealogy of the theory of war so as in the end to reclaim the concept of war for the multitude, that is, so as to produce a new concept of war altogether that might be used to wage war against the current and ongoing imperial wars? It seems to me that this first section of *Multitude* is trying to do more than merely produce a critique of war and, in particular, of the new and emergent forms of war that we are witnessing as we speak—although it certainly does all that extremely well.

AN: Let me begin with your second point. Our critical engagement with the question of war has two related sides, two related aspects: the first is primarily historical-political and the second is primarily theoretical-philosophical. As soon as we finished writing *Empire*—and especially after September 11, 2001—we realized that one could not speak of empire without dealing with the current exacerbation of monarchical forms and tendencies, which are best exemplified by the present governing elite of the USA and by its neoconservative project. In *Empire,* we had come up with the felicitous definition of empire as mixed government. This was a felicitous definition to the extent to which it enabled us in the following years to explain immediately, for example, the Franco–German outright opposition to the war in Iraq—as well as the skepticism and hesitation with which this war was met by certain strata of global capitalism—as an attempt on the part of the various global aristocracies to restrain and limit an increasingly absolutist monarchy. Initially, our decision to engage with the question of war was precisely an attempt to understand the current transformations of empire as mixed government: this is, in other words, the historical-political aspect or motivation of our analysis. The second and theoretical-philosophical aspect has to do with our attempt to produce a new theory of sovereignty, which in effect consists of the total dissolution of the concept of sovereignty. As far as I am concerned, this is the most valuable theoretical contribution of *Multitude:* after having laid down the premises of this argument in *Empire,* in *Multitude* we were able to state unequivocally that democracy and sovereignty nowadays are absolutely mutually exclusive with one another. *Multitude* constitutes an attempt to posit a radical anti-Hobbes: this attempt was already implicit in *Empire,* whereas in *Multitude* it is explicated on the basis of a recent phenomenology, that is, on the basis of the wars that are under way.

CC: Let me interrupt you for just a moment with two brief interjections. The first is something of a detour. The fact that you just brought up the question of sovereignty reminded me of something that you discuss on the last pages of *Multitude:* there you introduce a new term, which you had never used before and which, in fact, I had never heard before anywhere, namely, a "constituent state of exception."[20] Given that the state of exception is the prerogative par excellence of sovereignty, and given all the

connotations that the adjective "constituent" has in your work, a constituent state of exception can only sound like a contradiction in terms to me.

AN: You are absolutely correct. I think we made a mistake. At most, we should
have spoken of a regulating or formative state of exception—especially
when the state of exception is identified with war. At most, in other
words, a state of exception can construct—that is, reshuffle and reconfigure already preexistent and preconstituted norms; it can never constitute, that is, produce a new set of norms altogether. In short, the state of
exception can intervene only at the phenomenological and historical
level rather than at the ontological level.

CC: Fair enough. My second query is directly related to what you were saying regarding *Multitude* as an attempt to produce a new theory of sovereignty. You claim that your investigation of war has to do also with this
theory. How so? I am not sure I understand how the question of war fits
within this dissolution of the concept of sovereignty.

AN: War used to constitute the ultimate foundation of sovereignty. Today,
however, no form of sovereignty is able to use war as an effective instrument of government, as a stable institution of command.

CC: This might be a good point actually to return to my first question, that
is, to the relation between Deleuze and Guattari's theorization of the war
machine and your critical engagement with the question of war. It strikes
me that Deleuze and Guattari proceed quite differently and start from
elsewhere: whereas they begin with an analysis of how the war machine
is the defining invention of the nomads and then describe how it is appropriated by the state and institutionalized into war proper, you seem to
proceed the other way around, or, rather, to begin where they left off.

AN: Yes, of course. We begin from within monarchy, that is, we begin from
within the analysis of the concept of empire—and we do so because, evi-
dently, our historical conjuncture and hence our aims are quite different
from Deleuze and Guattari's. I am in agreement with just about everything they write in that section of *A Thousand Plateaus*. The point is,
however, that nowadays the capture, transfer, and transformation of the
nomad war machine into institutional instrument and repressive state
apparatus can no longer take place. In short, war is no longer the source
and foundation of Power. On the contrary, whoever wages war is bound
to lose it—period. In this sense, the Iraq war is a perfect example of how
military conquest amounts to nil and cannot be translated into government. As a matter of fact, the concept of government itself is no longer

given, is no longer operative: increasingly, we are confronted everywhere by the impossibility of managing government in a unitary manner, by the impossibility of reducing government to the One, by the impossibility of any form of government of the One. The multitude names this impossibility. The problem for the multitude nowadays is not exactly to reclaim the concept of war but to make war impossible *tout court*—or, as you put it very well, the problem is how to wage war against war.

Vicissitudes of Constituent Thought

Part I

CESARE CASARINO: I would like to begin this conversation by turning to those contemporary thinkers whom I believe come closest in some respects to your philosophical positions and political projects, namely, Gilles Deleuze, Félix Guattari, and Michel Foucault. Clearly, you have much in common with each of them. There are also important and substantial differences that separate your positions from theirs. You have at times drawn attention to such differences. At the end of your "Twenty Theses on Marx," for example, you acknowledge their importance for your work and also point out their limitations, which for you consist of the fact that ultimately they refuse to identify a constituent power, intended as the collective organ of subversive minorities (you are quick to add, however, that at times they implicitly overcome such limitations).[1] Moreover, at several points in *Empire,* you and Michael in essence reiterate this assessment of their positions.[2] I would like you to start from precisely such an assessment in order to discuss your relations to these thinkers. Could we begin perhaps with Deleuze?

ANTONIO NEGRI: My encounter with Deleuze took place via Spinoza. I had read Foucault quite carefully already in the 1970s, and in fact I wrote back then an essay on Foucault for the journal *Aut Aut,* which later became a chapter in *Macchina Tempo.*[3] In this essay I discussed and defended Foucault's methodology as being essential for any demystification of the great juridical–political institutions of modernity as well as for any analysis of the phenomenology of Power—which at the time we used to call "microphysics of Power." Yet I also reached the conclusion there that his methodology ultimately was stuck, was unable to open itself up to social recomposition. In other words, I felt that in the end Foucault's archaeology was unable to turn into an effective process of Power: the archaeological project always moved from above in order to reach below, while what concerned me most was precisely the opposite movement from below. For me, this was his project's main limitation. I never met Foucault, even though I knew well and saw frequently throughout the second half of the 1970s his Italian translators—such as Giovanna Procacci, etc.—as well as all the other figures who were working with Foucault as he was beginning his lectures at the Collège de France.

CC: But Foucault was perfectly aware of the limitations you ascribe to his project. It seems to me that it was precisely in order to overcome such an impasse that his research took a different turn precisely in those years, beginning at least with *Discipline and Punish,* but especially later with the first volume of *The History of Sexuality.*

AN: Yes, you are right. I heard him lecture a couple of times at the Collège de France, and each time his arguments were almost the arguments of a historian. He would always leave me profoundly dissatisfied—and it was evident to me that he shared such a dissatisfaction. At any rate, it was around this time that I returned to Spinoza. As usual, this return was dictated by my need to find conceptual forms that would adequately describe the positive recomposition of power taking place at the time, the exponential intensification of political struggles, the expansion of the political movement throughout the social terrain as a whole. While rereading Spinoza, I also studied all the major interpreters of his thought, and, above all, Matheron. And then I came across Deleuze's study of Spinoza, and so I began to attend his new lectures on Spinoza at Vincennes. My theoretical engagement with Deleuze begins precisely with his work on Spinoza, since I had never read any of his other works before—and I was right away extremely intrigued by him. Guattari and I were already very close friends by then. But in those years my friendship with Guattari revolved essentially around politics and we discussed philosophy very rarely. Guattari—who at the time still called himself a psychoanalyst—was at once very jealous as well as somewhat bashful with regard to his involvement with philosophy. It was very difficult to communicate with him about philosophy then, though he became much more open about it when I returned to France in 1983, which is what enabled us to begin cowriting *Communists Like Us.* To return to Deleuze. What struck me immediately about Deleuze was his ability to give a conceptual form to that ensemble of potentialities [*potenze*] which for me had begun to constitute and define the historical horizon, namely, that microscopic horizon of history which was crisscrossed by specific actions and intentions. In other words, what struck me in Deleuze was his ability to break the structural horizon. Up until that point, even within Marxist workerism, the definitions of force, of tendency, and of struggle were given only in terms of and within a general prefiguration of the system. The structure was always prefigured. Class action—and, more important, as far as we were concerned, the actions of emergent specific social groups and forces—were always understood within a necessary and structural teleology. My own handicaps when confronted with such emergent forces were perhaps more serious than those of thinkers who worked within more sociological paradigms, because I was too confined by the juridical framework; often, my focus on the state-form and its juridical institutions limited my research almost inadvertently. You know how apropos of Alessandro Manzoni we say that he went to wash his clothes in the Arno River; well, in that period I can truly say that I went to wash my clothes in the Seine! It was in Paris that I began to confront such impasses. My encounter with Deleuze eventually enabled me to overcome these limitations and constituted a radical break in my research. But at first, the most problematic and yet most inescapable thinker for me to contend with was Foucault, because his project consisted of an attempt to break the structure from within.

CC: It seems to me you are implying that you returned to Spinoza, and that you used your discovery of Deleuze in order to overcome at once Foucault's impasses as well as the impasses of the research you and your group were conducting in Italy at the time.

AN: Yes, exactly.

CC: I know I am jumping ahead in time almost two decades, but let me just point out that, in a sense, this explains why, when you reelaborate Foucault's concept of "biopolitics" in *Empire* and elsewhere, you read this concept through the filter of Deleuze's own reelaboration of Foucault in his essay "Postscript on Control Societies."[4]

AN: Yes, of course. You must keep in mind, however, that Deleuze's reading of Foucault in that late essay was strongly influenced by the relationship that by then he had established with me and Félix, as well as by all that Deleuze had learned in the meanwhile about the contemporary Italian context, in which an intense politicization of philosophical concepts was under way.

CC: Yes, I see what you are saying, and I think this influence on Deleuze is perhaps most evident in *A Thousand Plateaus,* in which they even refer to Tronti at several points.[5]

AN: Yes, it's quite evident there. But let me return now to my first encounter with Deleuze's work. After I came across his study on Spinoza, I immediately read all the other major texts he had written before *Anti-Oedipus,* among which *Difference and Repetition* is the fundamental work. It is in this text that Deleuze for the first time confronted and resolved the problems that hampered Foucault's project. And Foucault understood this right away: in a sense, Foucault's review essay on *Difference and Repetition* and *The Logic of Sense,* namely, *"Theatrum Philosophicum"*— in which he famously declared this to be the Deleuzean century—was all about his realization that Deleuze had found the conceptual solutions that he himself had been looking for and that he would find and elaborate in his own way a decade later. Deleuze's *Difference and Repetition* was a truly explosive event. And this was a philosophical event that corresponded exactly to what was taking place politically in Italy at the time. In this sense, I find the hypothesis that Michael put forth a few years ago quite compelling: namely, whereas in the nineteenth century France did politics and Germany did metaphysics, in the twentieth century France did metaphysics and Italy did politics.[6] I must add, though, that as I began to study Deleuze, I also resisted what rapidly became the fashionable interpretation of Deleuze: both in France and in Italy, Deleuze was immediately read as the philosopher of surfaces, as the first postmodern philosopher. Deleuze himself was quite incensed by these interpretations: this is the moment when he began attacking ferociously the "nouveaux philosophes" and hence began to make many enemies. I must say I am quite proud of the fact that, unlike many other comrades at the time, I understood most accurately not only the problems Deleuze too would eventually encounter but also the ways in which he finally would be able to solve them, namely, by identifying what we in Italy called "the tendencies" (such as the massive socialization of knowledge, the constitution of new forms of knowledge, the emergence of new forms of labor, etc.). And now I can finally address the issue you raised at very beginning, namely, the differences between Deleuze's project and my own project with regard to the question of constituent power. In Deleuze, the Event is often identified with singularity, is often centered on the insurgent birth of the singular—both in an ontological and in a historical sense. Such a conception of the Event, however, never intersects with the doing of history [*il fare della storia*]: the Event is never identified with the doing of movements in history. In Deleuze—and even in his last works—there is always a sense of astonished stupor in the face of singularity, there is always an inability to translate the ontological Event into a prefiguration or schematism of reason, into a constitution, or even into a merely virtual constitution that would nonetheless contain a constructive element. There is always surprise and chance.

cc: So, in effect you are saying that Deleuze is so thunderstruck when faced by the Event that he loses sight of that collective doing of which the Event is expressive and to which the Event could once again lead. It seems to me, however, that Deleuze is a thinker who puts much emphasis on the question of praxis, who repeatedly engages with collective practices of resistance—such as, for example, in the "Treatise on Nomadology" and "Apparatus of Capture" sections of A Thousand Plateaus.[7]

an: Well, I am not so sure—and, in any case, I wouldn't want to give you interpretive solutions as far as this matter is concerned. What I can tell you is that once I interviewed Deleuze on precisely these issues, that is, on the question of the political.[8] This is really a remarkable and beautiful interview, precisely because in it Deleuze insists on emphasizing both aspects of this question: on the one hand, he affirms the formidable and occasional apparition of singularity, and, on the other hand, he asserts the inescapable centrality of the Event. The problem is that whatever lies in between singularity and the Event does not come to the fore, is never articulated. What is the procedure enabling this passage? In other words, how can we translate the ontological substratum into logical dimensions? What kind of relation might be able to link a logical proposition to the Event—and might be able to do so not in a merely descriptive manner? These are questions that Deleuze does not address there. Admittedly, in A Thousand Plateaus they do provide us systematically with a series of enormous scenarios within which such a passage or transformation is given, within which such a continuous exchange among different orders of discourse is given. What concerns me most from a political standpoint, however, is to seize on the synthesis within the passage—and forgive me for resorting to a dialectical idiom here! To put it differently: what I consider most important is to capture the moment of decision within such passages and transformations. I must add that Félix, Gilles, and I discussed all these questions on numerous occasions, and that they never denied the crucial importance of the objections that I raised, of the problems I was forcing them to confront. In fact, Gilles was the more forthcoming of the two on these matters: he was always far more willing to admit to these kinds of difficulties and problems than Félix ever was. Ultimately, Félix was still hampered by some sort of residual positivism deriving from his interest in the French sociological tradition and, above all, from his early studies in the French tradition of philosophy of science, to which he remained always very attached. And one had to be extremely careful not to point this out to him, as he was very touchy on this matter, and he would easily fly into a rage at the very suggestion that the reluctance he had at times when faced by my criticisms might have been due to residual traces of positivism in his formation! In this respect, Gilles was completely different and not at all defensive. In essence, the problem that I was struggling with—and I think Gilles too was struggling with it, without nonetheless having any desire whatsoever to find a solution for it—was a classical problem of the phenomenological tradition, namely, the problem of the relation between intention and act. But if one lives this problem from a collective standpoint—that is, from the standpoint of collective subjectivities—this then becomes a fundamentally historical problem, the problem par excellence of constituent Power. And this is also the fundamental problem that the main traditions within the philosophy of right—namely, juridical formalism and critical realism—repeatedly faced, without ever being able to come to terms with it adequately, because within these traditions the birth of the norm is always a transcendent act. What is at stake for me, rather, is the internal apparatus: the task is to reach the level of immanence—which is not a horizon, a substitution for a divine scheme, or a pantheism; it is, rather, the discovery of the logic of collective actions, the constitution of such a logic in that moment of singularity. It is precisely such a constitution—rather than something coming from the outside—that turns that moment of singularity into an eternal one! In the end, I am not interested in talking about and adjudicating between immanence and transcendence—these are all meaningless debates. What concerns me is to find that force which is in there, which constitutes inside. I believe that a calculus of forces enabling one to understand and forecast what is taking place on the historical terrain is always available: there is always such a calculus that allows one to launch names, schemata, and projects forth—which are much like nets one casts to catch both the present and future.

CC: What I find most striking in your portrayal of Deleuze is that you identify some sort of ambivalence or hesitation at the very heart of his project: even though he understood perfectly the problem you have just outlined, he was nonetheless extremely hesitant when it came to identifying the moment of constituent decision, when it came to articulating a project or process of constitution. To what do you attribute such a hesitation on Deleuze's part? Why do you think he ultimately was not willing or able to solve this problem? Could we say, perhaps, that this simply was not his project? Could we say, in other words, that his project took him in other directions, that he was driven by different urgencies and priorities, and that he left it to others to contend with the question of constitution— others, such as yourself, whose philosophical and political formation or proclivities made them better equipped for this task?

AN: Well, this is a difficult question. Let's begin by reiterating the obvious: Deleuze's philosophical formation was in the Bergsonian tradition. Much like Félix, he too emerged from a world dominated by positivism, scientism, and relativism, a world in which the liberation of evolution from its naturalist cocoon was posed as a fundamental problem. Having said that, however, I must add that Deleuze found an escape from such a world by elaborating a particularly rich conception of immanence. Deleuze sensed how the crisis of the Bergsonian project could be identified with some of the outcomes of the Nietzschean project. Before being able to articulate such an identification, however, he tried out all sorts of different paths— from Kant to Hume, etc. And each time he would set out in a different direction, he did so with extreme intelligence and elegance: each time, he would critique thinkers from the standpoint of the present, thereby reactualizing them in the midst of contemporary debates and problematics.

CC: And by doing so, he also posited each thinker as the solution to the unresolved problems of another thinker. For me, that's most evident in *Nietzsche and Philosophy,* in which in effect he upholds Nietzsche's project as the solution and radicalization of the Kantian critique.

AN: Yes, absolutely. And such an intellectual trajectory eventually led him to clash with Marxism. Well, actually, he never clashed with Marxism directly; rather, he clashed with structuralism. You need to keep in mind, though, that structuralism in France was basically a Marxist heresy: in the mid-1950s, in fact, everybody at the École Normale was engaged in a debate concerning the relation between structure and superstructure— a debate whose ultimate aim was to ascertain exactly in what ways structure and superstructure were internal to each other, and, hence, to determine whether such mutual interpenetrations and overdeterminations between the two could any longer be adequately described in terms of dialectical relations. Lacan, on the one hand, and Lévi-Strauss, on the other hand, set the terms of the debate and constituted the system. Unlike Althusser, Foucault, and many others, Deleuze always remained on the margins of this debate. He circumvented it—and yet he nonetheless had to address it in some way. His answer was precisely *Difference and Repetition*—but it was not a completely successful one. The end of that work, in fact, constituted a crisis for Deleuze—even though it was an open crisis. It was in the midst of this crisis that he finally met Félix, in 1968—and this encounter enabled Deleuze to elaborate the relation between singularity and desire. And thus *Anti-Oedipus* was born! At the time, many wondered why such a fine philosopher would get together with such a dilettantish jack-of-all-trades as Guattari; what could possibly generate and sustain such an incredibly strange and symbiotic friendship; etc. And even nowadays, the history of philosophy still finds it impossible to accept their collaboration—thereby at best treating Félix like some kind of regrettable lapse in the expansion of Deleuzean rationality. Such an interpretation is unacceptable. It is thanks to this collaboration that Deleuze was able to confront not only the relation between singularity and desire but also their relation to the question of the body: this is, in other words, when we get the best Deleuze. This the Deleuze who then will work like a dog in order to build *A Thousand Plateaus*—because it is there that all the different parts of his project converge, it is there that he puts everything at stake so as to find what he had been looking for all along. And although I don't think in the end he finds it even there, *A Thousand Plateaus* is nonetheless an extremely rich work—one of the four or five most important philosophical works of the twentieth century.

cc: Actually, as I recall, in the early 1990s you wrote a review of Deleuze and Guattari's *What Is Philosophy?* in which you assert that *A Thousand Plateaus* is *the* most important philosophical work of the twentieth century! But let me return a moment to Deleuze's intellectual trajectory and, in particular, to the different roles that Bergson and Spinoza play in his work. It seems to me, in fact, that there are two main different tendencies, or perhaps even two opposite polarities, in Deleuze's work: a Bergsonian polarity and a Spinozian polarity—which at times coexist even in the same text. From everything you have said so far, I am inclined to think that, on the one hand, you have felt a close affinity with Deleuze precisely because of his Spinozian strain, and, on the other hand, you have always been very critical of his Bergsonian leanings. For example, in *Empire* you and

Michael borrow and reelaborate a series of concepts that Deleuze derives from Bergson, namely, the dyad of "virtual" and "actual," and the dyad of "possible" and "real." While Deleuze differentiates between these dyads and ultimately rejects the latter in favor of the former, you and Michael insist on the necessity to produce some sort of continuum between the two, and, above all, on the necessity not to reject the dyad of "possible" and "real" *tout court*.[9] Doesn't such a reelaboration of these concepts constitute precisely a critique of the Bergsonian strain in Deleuze?

AN: Yes, I completely agree. In *Empire*, Michael and I develop the concept of power—that is, the concept of the virtual as potential, the concept of the possible potential. The concept of the possible is linked to chance, while the concept of the potential is linked to a virtuality of the possible. In effect, we undertake an analysis of the concept of power in Spinoza as well as in Marx's *Grundrisse*. In any case, it is always very dangerous to discuss these matters simply in the context of philosophical references. There is something else of fundamental importance that lies behind the analysis of all these concepts, namely, the development and the overcoming of the concept of class—whether intended as social class or as political class. Or, to put it more precisely, what is at stake in our development of the concept of power is an attempt to revitalize the rational nucleus of the concept of political class through a new concept of corporeal singularity, to update such a rational nucleus by forcing it to confront the world of the immaterial, that is, the world in which the body is given a priori as wholly constructed and artificial, as always already a labor instrument. (And it goes without saying that I intend the body as indivisible from the mind.) But the moment when the body has thus become a body that already has undergone its specific *Bildung* and that already has been brought to a level of effective historicity and of real productivity— that is the moment when the possible is no longer ruled by chance and is, rather, that which is powerful [*potente*], that which is potentially able to take place. *This* is the virtual! From this standpoint, the Bergsonian paradigm becomes entirely irrelevant, while the Spinozian paradigm is integrated by the reelaboration of the concept of labor. When the human is conceived of and produced as tool, immanentism too becomes materialism, and the referent of a whole series of conceptual categories is incorporated, becomes incarnate.

CC: Yes, I understand. But let me return for a moment to the relation between those two dyads. In what you have said so far, you have not mentioned once the second half of each of the dyads, that is, you have not mentioned either the actual or the real. It's almost as if here the real has become subsumed by the possible and the actual has been subsumed by the virtual; or, at any rate, it's as if suddenly there is no longer much difference between the virtual and the actual as well as between the possible and the real. As I recall, however, what you and Michael undertake in *Empire* is quite different: there, you conceive of the possible as the passage from the virtual to the real, as that which transforms the virtual in a constitution of the real. I find this rather perplexing, because then the possible runs the risk of being turned into a category of mediation. In other words, it seems to me that suddenly you resort to a dialectical relation precisely there where you reject the possibility of any dialectical resolution.

AN: Well, if that's what we wrote, I immediately recant! If there is any possible mediation—which is then no longer a mediation at all—that is power itself. And this power needs to be understood in two ways at once: on the one hand, it must be singularized as unrepeatability, and, on the other hand, it must be universalized in its being instrument or tool. I believe that this concept of tooling [*utensileria*]—which is very important in Gilbert Simondon and which one can see here and there also in *A Thousand Plateaus*—is fundamental for a materialist reading of singularity and of its power.

CC: In any case, it seems to me that what differentiates you and Michael from Deleuze is the fact that you insist on the necessity of the concept of the real. And such a necessity is another version of what we were discussing earlier, namely, the necessity to identify a constituent Power.

AN: Yes, absolutely. When my *Insurgencies* was published, I had several discussions specifically on the question of constituent Power first with Félix and later with Gilles. Félix kept on saying that he agreed with me—even though actually he at once agreed with me and did not agree with me at all, in the sense that, as far as he was concerned, the problems I was trying to solve were already solved. For him, what I identified as problems did not constitute problems at all.

CC: Do you think that perhaps he had found the solution to the problem of constituent Power through his involvement in various political movements?

AN: No, no, Félix was not so uncouth or stupid to expect to solve such a problem simply by getting involved in politics! What he thought, rather, was that this was a preconstituted problem, for which one needed to find an explanation. In other words, he did think that the problem really existed, but he also thought that the explanations were already perfectly developed and available—so that what one needed to do at most was to refine one's own conceptual tools, which is precisely what he thought he and Gilles were doing in *What Is Philosophy?* In the late 1980s we were conducting a small seminar at Félix's house, and, as I recall, all these problems came to a head when Paul Virilio joined us. In Virilio, I saw a dispersion of the constituent horizon, which in the end becomes an elusive web. In Virilio, the charge of the constituent singularity is extremely strong, but in the end finds no resolution, or, rather, finds a resolution only in an explicitly theological transformation: the singularities engaging in the work of constitution ultimately disperse in the speed of the process, in the irrecuperability of the tendencies, in the lack or dissolution of center.

CC: This is a waste. This is a philosophy of waste.

AN: Yes, precisely. Or, rather, this is a philosophy of communication as waste.

CC: There is a precedent in French philosophy for all this, namely, Bataille.

AN: Yes, undoubtedly. I am sure that Bataille and others were enormously important for Virilio. But ultimately he is a technician before being anything else. All this philosophizing of his comes out somehow from being a specialist and a technician of urbanism. His cultural and intellectual formation is rather shallow. He is well connected—that's all. Even though he is often compared to or confused with somebody like Baudrillard, there is an enormous difference between the two. So, Virilio and I got into some pretty nasty fights, and we even stopped talking to each other for a while. The point of this story, in any case, is to stress that Félix would try all he could to help Virilio find a way to reformulate his conception of immanence into an immanence recuperated as and in concrete, positive acts. At the same time, I was conducting a seminar in Paris in which often we would engage with Bruno Latour. With Latour too the main problem was to try and identify the moment of constitution in his methodology: whereas for Latour such a moment was determined on the margins of the epistemological terrain, I was trying to imagine constitution as something that erupts from within that terrain. The impasse of Latour's research lies in an excessive emphasis on epistemological caesuras and on radical doubt intended as that which produces knowledge.

CC: In some ways, this is similar to Foucault's impasse: Foucault pushed the project of epistemological critique to its furthest limit—a limit beyond which such a project could not go without being turned into and reborn as a fully ontological project.

AN: Yes, definitively. And in his final years Foucault was attempting precisely such an ontological leap.

CC: Before turning to Foucault's final years, there are still a few matters I would like to discuss regarding your relation to Deleuze and Guattari. When Deleuze and Guattari undertake the project of identifying the emergence of new antagonistic and revolutionary subjectivities, they begin such a project by contending with psychoanalysis (and I am referring mainly but not exclusively to *Anti-Oedipus*). But why is it exactly that—unlike Deleuze and Guattari—a philosopher as concerned with the question of subjectivity as you are has never felt the need to engage with psychoanalytic discourse?

AN: First of all, psychoanalytic discourse did not play a central role in my intellectual formation. Second, I have some doubts regarding the scientificity of the psychoanalytic problematic. I have never quite understood either where the unconscious might be or even whether it exists. And I am not quite sure what else to say . . . I read Freud early on, but I never did much with it. After that, while I was working on German historicism, I studied much late-nineteenth-century psychological materialism, which I found enormously rich and interesting. When I was a student, I even took a couple of psychology courses, which focused on the old Viennese school and emphasized the physiological and neurological aspects of the question. And it was only later that I started reading Lacan. All in all, my assessment of Lacan is quite simple: I think of him as the intellectual figure who introduced and started doing philosophy of language in France. He did philosophy of language in exactly the same way in which it was being done in the Anglo-Saxon tradition—with one important difference. Whereas in the Anglo-Saxon countries the main research focus was the definition of meaning [*senso*] as well as its reference to reality, in Lacan the focus shifted to the relation between language and a hypothetical and ever so elusive soul. I never managed to become interested in such a project. Language and the analysis of language, however, do concern me enormously. But for me the analysis of language is nothing other than a way to enrich corporeality. Wittgenstein's finest insight—which is the reason why he is one of the greatest philosophers of the twentieth century— is precisely that language is a gestural form: he taught us that to speak is to gesture [*gestire*], that is, to manage the body [*gestire il corpo*]; he taught us that language is all there within the body. This is why psychoanalysis—with all its somersaults toward . . . toward what? Consciousness? The unconscious? A suffering interiority?—has always left me perplexed. Psychoanalysis truly is a science of pity, a compassionate science, a dubious science.

CC: But if your theory of subjectivity does not allow for a concept of the unconscious, whatever you mean by subjectivity is then very different from Deleuze and Guattari's conception of subjectivity.

AN: As far as I am concerned, there is no concept of the unconscious in Deleuze and Guattari. What we find in Deleuze and Guattari, rather, is simply a concept of desire. This is a concept of desire that is continuously referred to [as] a complex, undulatory subjectivity that moves about on the surface of a consistency—at once a historical and natural consistency—in which there is no space for the unconscious. In this sense, I think I reached the same conclusions that Deleuze and Guattari reached, without, however, going through the cesspool of psychoanalysis.

CC: Well, I don't really agree. But let's return to Foucault. In the last years of his life, Foucault was working on the concept of biopolitics. Clearly, this concept has been very important for your project. It seems to me that in reelaborating it for your purposes, you bring to the fore its latent aspects: in particular, you emphasize the element of productivity, of productive potentiality that had remained implicit in Foucault's articulations of this concept. Would you agree with this assessment?

AN: Yes, I would. The definition of biopolitics that I extracted from Foucault ultimately is not present in his work—even though all the elements enabling such a definition are certainly there. What I think is there in Foucault, above all, is an excavation of subjectivity that leads to the question of biopolitics. In the end, Foucault rediscovers and reformulates an old truth, namely, that human beings make, build, produce themselves. What emerges in the late Foucault is a humanism after the end of Man— a humanism in the best possible sense of the term.

CC: As I recall, you and Michael discuss this type of humanism in *Empire*.[10]

AN: Yes. And this is the humanism that comes after the end of any possible humanism of transcendence and that reaffirms human power as a power of the artificial, as the power to build artfully [*la potenza del costruire con arte*]. This is a humanism that understands and defines human beings at once as artificers and tools, and that is characterized by a Renaissance materiality of the human, by that religion of the human that was born in the Renaissance.

CC: But how is such a religion of the human to be intended nowadays?

AN: What I mean by a religion of the human is simply the richness and power of matter that continuously produces itself in each and every instant.

CC: Let me return to the concept of biopolitics. You said that you extracted the definition of this concept from Foucault's work. I take this to mean— among other things—that you also had to extract it from the original context in which Foucault was trying to elaborate this concept. Of course, there is nothing wrong with that: this is what we need to do whenever we want to reelaborate a concept so as to use it for our own purposes. I would like, however, to return to and reflect on that original context for a moment, namely, the last chapter in the first volume of Foucault's *History of Sexuality*. Within that context, the question of sexuality is the central focus of the whole investigation: in the last chapter of that work, Foucault posits the invention and deployment of sexuality as one of the fundamental technologies of Power in modernity, and understands sexuality as the crucial apparatus [*dispositivo*] used by both the modern state and modern capital to produce, organize, and manage life directly. In Foucault, in other words, sexuality is the principal mechanism of Power in modernity, the central apparatus [*dispositivo*] of biopolitics. I think that this crucial aspect of Foucault's project is lost or ignored in your own reelaboration of the concept of biopolitics.

AN: No, I don't think so. I believe the concept of sexuality as such cannot be reduced to the game of sex, to the specific and determined historical arrangement of the game of sex—and, of course, Foucault never reduced it to that. Sexuality, rather, is the fundamental element of human reproduction. I intend reproduction here in its strict Marxian sense: labor power [*forza lavoro*] reproduces itself above all through sexuality. This means that sexuality is crucial not only in the formation of social hierarchy—that is, in the reproduction of preexistent force relations—but also in the formation of styles of life, forms of life, and types of human beings. Foucault's interest in precisely these aspects of the question of sexuality is an index of the radical ontological turn that his project took from the middle of the 1970s onward—and it is not a coincidence that around this time he also began to engage with all the problems of identity. In any case, in articulating such a concept of sexuality, I don't think I am adding anything new to what contemporary feminism has been saying for a while, namely, that the choice of different styles of life and different styles of sexual play is overdetermined by the structuring of reproduction, which is as important as production itself. And this brings me to my own definition of biopolitics. In the world of immateriality in which we live, reproduction—which is the first possible definition of biopolitics—and production can no longer be distinguished from each other. Biopolitics becomes fully realized precisely when production and reproduction are one and the same, that is, when production is conducted primarily and directly through language and social exchange. I began elaborating such a definition of biopolitics in Paris—thanks also to the numerous discussions I had there with several dear comrades, such as Maurizio Lazzarato, Christian Marazzi, and Judith Revel, who at the time was director of the Foucault archives. Undoubtedly, the initial inspiration and crucial point of departure for my investigation into the question of biopolitics was the Deleuzean reading of Foucault. I took this reading, however, in a different direction: the concept of biopolitics for me ultimately needs to confront and address the question of labor. In any case, this is something I do with each and every concept I elaborate: I always try to bring concepts to bear on labor—which is why I still call myself a Marxist. In this sense, I see my definition of biopolitics as an expansion of Foucault's own investigation: rather than disregarding or neglecting Foucault's elaboration of biopolitics in the context of the deployment of sexuality, I assumed such an elaboration and expanded it so as to account for the overall construction of the body in the indistinguishable realms of production and reproduction, that is, in the realm of immaterial labor. Such an expansion of the investigation enabled me also to clarify something that in Foucault had remained relatively undefined, namely, the relation between biopolitics and bio-Power. I feel it is necessary, in fact, to introduce a distinction within the very concept of biopolitics, to distinguish between two different and antagonistic aspects or tendencies of that concept: biopolitics, on the one hand, turns into bio-Power [*biopotere*] intended as the institution of a dominion over life, and, on the other hand, turns into biopower [*biopotenza*] intended as the potentiality of constituent Power. In other words, in biopolitics intended as biopower, it is the *bios* that creates Power, while in biopolitics intended as bio-Power, it is Power that creates the *bios*, that is, that tries alternately either to determine or to annul life, that posits itself as Power against life. This is also to say that in reelaborating and expanding the concept of biopolitics, I attempted to turn it into a fully Spinozian concept. Spinozism is at once a formidable identification of the reason founded on the number two [*la ragione del due*] and a radical rejection of the reason founded on the number three [*la ragione del tre*]. Spinozism is a system of thought that knows no mediation: on the one hand, there is this power that creates life, that produces and reproduces, that defines the styles of life in which freedom, love, and knowledge continuously interact in the constitution of such a process of production, and, on the other hand, there is nothingness—the power of the nothing.

CC: So, much like Deleuze's work, your own work is replete with dualisms: the two versions of biopolitics, constituent Power and constituted Power, the theory of the two modernities,[11] etc. And all these dualisms are different forms and manifestations of this dualism you find in Spinoza.

AN: Yes, that's right: in the end, there is only one fundamental dualism.

CC: What I am wondering about is the relation between the polarities of this dualism. You emphasize that there is no possible mediation between the two. There must be, nonetheless, some kind of relation between them. It seems to me that you conceive of such a relation as one of capture and domination: constituted Power continuously endeavors to subject and exploit constituent Power.

AN: Or, to put it more precisely: Power takes away power from life. And I conceive of this life not at all as something personal or as a flux—which is why I am very much anti-Bergsonian. My conception of life is not a vitalism. I conceive of life, rather, as the multitude of singularities, which come together or apart, and in doing so they constitute, they produce together the moment of constitution. Such a multitude is continuously subjected to a subtraction of Power, which affects each and every aspect of its attempt to constitute. And this is then how the dualism turns into an infinity of concrete relations, rather than constituting a polarity of first principles awaiting some kind of metaphysical Zoroastrian resolution! But to return to biopolitics and bio-Power. It goes without saying that these concepts—like all other concepts—are to be evaluated according to their constitutive efficacy, according to the enabling efficacy that they might have for reasoning. There is no such a thing as biopolitics or bio-Power: they do not exist as such, as things. These are names that might or might not be useful for describing the real, or, rather, for capturing the real from the standpoint of the ones who are living it, who live in it, as well as for identifying tendencies and imagining projects of constitution that already exist *in potentia* here and now in the real. And for the time being, biopolitics and bio-Power are extremely useful names precisely in this sense.

CC: Let me return for a moment to your version of Spinozism and to that
fundamental dualism which manifests itself in a variety of other dualisms. On the one hand, there is a power that creates, produces, constitutes—which, I believe, is precisely what Deleuze and Guattari mean by
"desire"—and, on the other hand, there is a Power that subtracts and
negates, which is what you just referred to as the power of the nothing. I
would like you to clarify the ontological status of the latter. Whenever
you describe the various specific forms the latter takes—such as the
state's Power of domination, capital's Power of exploitation, etc.—you
always do so in negative, privative, subtractive terms, you always conceive
of them as negations of being. Now, my point is that in order not to misunderstand this fundamental dualism as some sort of Manichaeism, such
a negation of being cannot be thought of as an entity per se. In other
words, the power of the nothing is precisely nothing—not a power and
not a thing at all! And I suppose this also means that there cannot be any
kind of symmetrical relation between the polarities of the dualism. And
yet domination does exist, exploitation is real, etc. How does one deal
with this paradox?

AN: There is no paradox here. All this is worked out very clearly in Spinoza
when he engages with the problem of Evil, when he elaborates his own
concept of Evil. For Spinoza, Evil does not exist.

CC: Evil does not exist . . . and yet it subtracts and negates life?!

AN: No, wait, there is a misunderstanding here. Subtraction and negation are
not positive actions. Evil does not exist—and hence does not act, does
not do a thing. *We* are the ones who do not succeed, who are incapable
of action, who cannot act! In this sense, Spinoza completely reinterprets
Saint Augustine, for whom Evil is real, for whom there is such a thing
as hell, for whom, in other words, some kind of Manichaeism continues
to play the role of fundamental theological structuring principle. In any
case, it is a common feature of many religious traditions to need to conceive of Evil as a real entity: even when Evil is said not to exist from
a metaphysical standpoint, it is said nonetheless to exist from a moral
standpoint. For Spinoza, on the other hand, Evil is simply a limit—a very
real limit against which we continuously struggle. For Spinoza, Evil is the
limit of our desire.

CC: Yes, now I understand. The Spinozian dualism, in other words, is structured by, on the one hand, a productive power—namely, our desire—
and, on the other hand, a negative Power, which consists of the point at

which our desire runs into an impasse and for a time can no longer expand, can no longer develop any further.

AN: Yes, our desire reaches a limit, which then we identify with the state, etc. In other words, this limit is a negative reality that is actually produced—and it is produced at once by our need to develop and by our inability to do so. The existence of the state, for example, is determined by this impasse, is precisely a produced limit. But we must always go beyond such an impasse! And each and every time we are able to overcome the limit of our desire, we are able to do so only to the extent to which we express love rather than hatred or other negative passions. We overcome limits only by expressing positive passions, which increasingly constitute us collectively, that is, as collectivity. This means that we come to affirm and posit ourselves as democratic citizens only when we have been able to determine absolute democracy. This is the democracy in which the absoluteness of desire has developed collectively: to desire, in fact, is not an individual act; it is, rather, at once a singular and a collective act. In such a collectivity, there is no longer any contract; there is simply a founding, constitutive act of love. This is not utopia: this is the schema of reason, which enables us to select models, to link the ethical and the political, and, indeed, to abolish any difference whatsoever between ethics and politics, soul and body, private and public, the individual and the collective, in other words, between desire and its realization. None of this entails enacting a utopia; it entails, rather, analyzing what is in front of us—such as, for example, class struggle—from the standpoint of such a conception of collectivity. In this sense, class struggle ought to be understood as an ongoing attempt to produce love, as a great experiment of love.

CC: I would like to return to the question of biopolitics—but this time as a way to begin investigating the uncanny similarities as well as the crucial differences between your work and the work of Agamben. On the one hand, the two of you share several specific concerns—such as, for example, the question of biopolitics. And in more general and fundamental terms, you seem to share in an attempt to produce a philosophy of immanence centered on an ontology of potentiality. On the other hand, the two of you think about these common concerns and articulate such a shared project in strikingly different ways. Unlike Agamben, for example, you always emphasize the question of production, of the productivity of being. Such an emphasis leads you to critique Agamben's articulation of biopolitics and especially his concept of naked life: in *Empire*, you and

Michael argue that Agamben turns naked life into the negative limit of biopolitics, whereas you would rather conceive of it as the productive element par excellence in biopolitics.[12] Agamben, for his part, critiques your concept of constituent power in *Homo Sacer,* etc.[13] In any case, these are some of the issues I would like to discuss—but I want you to begin anywhere you like.

AN: Agamben is one [of] my best friends, one of my most intimate friends. I have known him for roughly two decades. We often spend summer vacations together; we get together for Christmas every year; we are basically family. In short, we love each other very much. I am older than he is. And, unlike myself, he was never involved in political struggles, for which he has an incredibly voracious curiosity, as they constitute a great lack in his life—and he very much regrets not having had such experiences. He is quite limited when it comes to understanding politics—and in his work this limitation takes the form of a radical Heideggerism. He is absolutely convinced that the human is a being-for-death. Such a conception of the human lends a paradoxical rhythm to his research, which is then founded on the idea that the world is continuously and miraculously reborn precisely at the limit of life, namely, on that threshold which is death. In a sense, one can already find such argumentations in Rosenzweig or in Benjamin. In Agamben, however, this problematic gets terribly complicated, because all in all he is also very much a materialist. Unlike Rosenzweig, Agamben has no interest in the problem of the individual. Unlike Benjamin, Agamben has no interest in the ambiguous relation between truth and eschatology. In the end, the questions he poses are historical questions concerning the nature of institutions: in his work, the fundamental questions have always been political questions. My polemics with Giorgio always have had to do with this tension in his thought: this is a tension precisely in the sense that he tends and stretches toward the extreme limit of being so as to extract from it some kind of new and purified language. Much like him, I too believe it is extremely important to analyze such a limit. As I was suggesting earlier, it's not a question of pitting the power of life and the power of the nothing against each other, as if in some sort of Manichaean agon; rather, it's a question of capturing the relation between these powers—intended as the relation between life and its real limits—in each singular nexus. If one looks at it from a subjective standpoint, such a relation becomes also our relation to death—a relation that is lived in each and every instant, since we can never be sure we shall live till the next instant. But it's one thing to give this limit the name of "death" and to believe that things signify only thanks to their contact with it, and it's something quite different to focus not on this limit but on our power continuously to overcome it and to believe, in other words, that such a power produces the world thanks not to its contact with such a limit but to its capacity to expand each and every time beyond it, to its ability to leave it behind over and over again. I am very often in agreement with Giorgio. But it's as if we looked at the same things from two different standpoints: we posit and engage with the same grand metaphysical-ontological schema—but he apprehends it from one side while I do so from the other side.

cc: Clearly, neither you nor Agamben conceives of death as the opposite of life; for both of you, rather, death is part of and immanent to life itself—much like what we see, for example, at some points in Foucault's *Birth of the Clinic.*

AN: Yes, of course.

cc: The two of you, however, are in complete disagreement when it comes to the concept of naked life. In your recent essay "The Political Monster: Power and Naked Life," you undertake a radical critique of Agamben's use of this concept, and, indeed, you denounce it as a purely ideological construct.[14] Such a critique is different from and, in fact, more uncompromising than the critique of naked life we see in Luciano Ferrari Bravo's essay on Agamben: rather than rejecting such a concept *tout court,* in fact, he attempts there to identify and criticize a fundamental ambiguity, dualism, or oscillation at the very heart of the concept, namely, the oscillation between nakedness and life.[15] But it strikes me that your most recent critique of naked life is also much more radical and scathing than the one you and Michael undertook in *Empire:* unlike what you wrote in that book—in which you suggest a different way of interpreting naked life from Agamben's—your essay now asserts that this concept is simply irredeemable. In any case, it seems to me that you have changed your mind about these matters since you wrote *Empire.* What has occurred in the meanwhile? Why did you feel the need for such a critique of this concept right now?

AN: Yes, Ferrari Bravo insists on asking: is it life that is naked or is it the naked that is life?

cc: Well, yes, but what do *you* think? And, in particular, what do you think about the fact that the concept of naked life has become so enormously and increasingly important for Agamben lately?

AN: I believe Giorgio is writing a sequel to *Homo Sacer,* and I feel that this new work will be resolutive for his thought—in the sense that he will be forced in it to resolve and find a way out of the ambiguity that has qualified his understanding of naked life so far. He already attempted something of the sort in his recent book on Saint Paul, but I think this attempt largely failed: as usual, this book is extremely learned and elegant; it remains, however, somewhat trapped within Pauline exegesis, rather than constituting a full-fledged attempt to reconstruct naked life as a potentiality for exodus, to rethink naked life fundamentally in terms of exodus.[16] I believe that the concept of naked life is not an impossible, unfeasible one. I believe it is possible to push the image of power to the point at which a defenseless human being [*un povero Cristo*] is crushed, to conceive of that extreme point at which Power tries to eliminate that ultimate resistance which is the sheer attempt to keep oneself alive. From a logical standpoint, it is possible to think all this: the naked bodies of the people in the camps, for example, can lead one precisely in this direction. But this is also the point at which this concept turns into ideology: to conceive of the relation between Power and life in such a way actually ends up bolstering and reinforcing ideology. Agamben in effect is saying that such is the nature of Power: in the final instance, Power reduces each and every human being to such a state of powerlessness. But this is absolutely not true! On the contrary: the historical process takes place and is produced thanks to a continuous constitution and construction, which undoubtedly confronts the limit over and over again—but this is an extraordinarily rich limit, in which desires expand, and in which life becomes increasingly fuller. Of course, it is possible to conceive of the limit as absolute powerlessness, especially when it has been actually enacted and enforced in such a way so many times. And yet, isn't such a conception of the limit precisely what the limit looks like from the standpoint of constituted Power as well as from the standpoint of those who have already been totally annihilated by such a Power—which is, of course, one and the same standpoint? Isn't this the story about Power that Power itself would like us to believe in and reiterate? Isn't it far more politically useful to conceive of this limit from the standpoint of those who are not yet or not completely crushed by Power, from the standpoint of those still struggling to overcome such a limit, from the standpoint of the process of constitution, from the standpoint of power? I am worried about the fact that the concept of naked life as it is conceived by Agamben might be taken up by political movements and in political debates. I find this prospect quite troubling, which is why I felt the need to attack this concept in my recent essay. Ultimately, I feel that nowadays the logic of traditional eugenics is attempting to saturate and capture the whole of human reality—even at the level of its materiality, that is, through genetic engineering—and the ultimate result of such a process of saturation and capture is a capsized production of subjectivity within which ideological undercurrents continuously try to subtract or neutralize our resistance.

cc: And I suppose you are suggesting that the concept of naked life is part and parcel of such undercurrents. But have you discussed all this with Agamben? What does he think about your critiques?

AN: Whenever I tell him what I have just finished telling you, he gets quite irritated, even angry. I still maintain, nonetheless, that the conclusions he draws in *Homo Sacer* lead to dangerous political outcomes and that the burden of finding a way out of this mess rests entirely on him. And the type of problems he runs into in this book recur throughout many of his other works. I found his essay on Bartleby, for example, absolutely infuriating. This essay was published originally as a little book that contained also Deleuze's essay on Bartleby: well, it turns out that what Deleuze says in this essay is exactly the contrary of what Giorgio says in his! I suppose one could say that they decided to publish their essays together precisely so as to attempt to figure this limit—that is, to find a figure for it, to give it a form—by some sort of paradoxical juxtaposition, but I don't think that this attempt was really successful in the end.[17] In any case, all this incessant talk about the limit bores me and tires me out after a little while. The point is that, inasmuch as it is death, the limit is not creative. The limit is creative to the extent to which you have been able to overcome it qua death: the limit is creative because you have overcome death.

cc: Yes, and the creativity—indeed, the productivity—that derives from having overcome this limit is the creativity of absolute freedom in the Spinozian sense. This is, in fact, one way of understanding what Spinoza means when he says that one must free oneself from the fear of death and that nobody is freer, as well as more powerful and more dangerous, than somebody who no longer fears death: in Spinoza, absence of the fear of death is at once absolute freedom and untrammeled productivity, namely, the expression of the most creative potentials, the zenith of creativity; or, more precisely, in Spinoza that moment of absolute freedom which is the absence of the fear of death constitutes the indispensable condition of possibility for such an exponential leap in expression, production, creation (without, perhaps, guaranteeing it necessarily).

AN: And while Spinoza tells us to free ourselves from the presence of death, Heidegger tells us the contrary.

CC: But let's return one last time to the question of naked life. In *Kairòs, Alma Venus, Multitudo,* you discuss at length the question of poverty; in fact, one could say that you elaborate there a specific conception of poverty, that you produce the concept of poverty. I want to return to this concept later.[18] What interests me for the moment is to note that in those pages on poverty you also engage with the question of nakedness, you often speak of the nakedness of poverty. At one point, for example, you write that—far from being an object constituted by the suffering inflicted by biopolitics—the poor is precisely the biopolitical subject, and, moreover, that the poor "is the naked eternity of the power to be."[19] As I was reading these passages, it occurred to me that your insistence on the question of nakedness here is a reference and a reply to the nakedness of Agamben's naked life.

AN: Yes, I completely agree: the fact that I took this term up again and redeployed it is a clear indication of Giorgio's presence and influence in my work—and I must say I am pleased about it, and I am glad that you noticed it. Undoubtedly, there is always ongoing dialogue, exchange, discussion between Giorgio and myself.

CC: What is the nature of the exchange in this specific case? What is the difference between the nakedness of poverty and the nakedness of naked life?

AN: The nakedness of poverty is immediately linked to love, that is, to a positive power. Such nakedness is always already there as element of being.

CC: And hence it is part and parcel of constituent Power—the concept with which we began this conversation and which you claim differentiates your project from Foucault's as well as from Deleuze and Guattari's projects. Unsurprisingly, the concept of constituent Power turns out to mark a crucial difference also between your project and Agamben's project. Agamben has commented on this matter. In *Homo Sacer,* he briefly discusses your *Insurgencies,* and, in particular, he critiques the way in which you separate constituent Power and constituted Power from each other in that work: he maintains that you are not able to find a plausible criterion according to which a distinction between these two Powers can be made, and, furthermore, that it is not possible to sustain or even to posit any separation between them anyway.[20] What do you think about such a critique?

AN: I am not really sure. Giorgio has always tried to show how juridical categories as well as the juridical as a category cannot be raised or made to answer to coherent metaphysical criteria. His critique, in other words, is a purely negative critique: what I mean by this is not that he criticizes the substance of what I say about constituent Power; what I mean, rather, is that he does not want to solve this problem, that he believes it is not even advisable to look for a solution to this problem at all. In the end, I find this type of critique to be rather banal.

CC: Could you be more specific?

AN: Giorgio's main critique of my positions consists of arguing that constituent Power and constituted Power cannot be distinguished from each other according to any juridical-political criterion. Well, thank you very much! That's entirely obvious—and, in fact, my analysis of constituent Power begins precisely from this problem. All jurists argue that constituent Power does not exist unless it is codified, that it ruptures the juridical system and its continuity, that it cannot come into being unless it has been recognized and validated by constituted Power. According to such arguments, hence, constituent Power paradoxically can take two forms at once: on the one hand, it lives outside the law, and, on the other hand, it lives inside the law, that is, in the form of the Supreme Court's power to innovate the legal system [*ordinamento giuridico*].

CC: And in the latter case constituent Power is already part and parcel of sovereign Power. So, if I understand you correctly, you are suggesting that this problem—namely, the problem of ascertaining, defining, and containing the existence of constituent Power—is not at all constituent Power's problem; it is, rather, a problem for constituted Power.

AN: Yes, precisely! Constituent Power does not need to ask itself whether or not it exists: it does exist, and it leads a parallel life with respect to constituted Power. The enormous social phenomena that are in the process of determining themselves nowadays—such as the antiglobal movements—bear witness not only to the fact that constituent Power exists but also to the fact that constituent Power makes its influence felt on constituted Power: these movements, in fact, express extremely powerful juridical as well as political aspirations that inevitably affect the legal system and that hence will end up having to be acknowledged in some way or other. These new movements, in other words, always contain a constituent function. Such a reply to his critique, however, is completely beside the point, because it does not address what is most problematic about his critique in the first place. Giorgio's most serious problem ultimately is that he does not allow for any kind of constitution of the political whatsoever. And this is why his critique remains external to my arguments, foreign to my way of reasoning: more than a critique, it constitutes an opposition, a counterpoint.

cc: This claim regarding Agamben's failure to think the constitution of the political has made me think of the sentence with which he ends his discussion of your arguments about constituent Power. Let me read it to you. He writes: "Until a new and coherent ontology of potentiality (beyond the steps that have been made in this direction by Spinoza, Schelling, Nietzsche, and Heidegger) has replaced the ontology founded on the primacy of the act and its relation to potentiality, a political theory exempt from the aporias of sovereignty remains unthinkable."[21] On the one hand, I completely agree with what he is saying here, and, on the other hand, I would like to take all this in different directions from the ones I think he pursues. I do share his concerns regarding that dominant ontological tradition which is willing and able to conceive of potentiality only as mere means to that all-important end which is the act—thereby not only subordinating potentials to acts but also failing to understand and indeed to think potentiality *tout court* (even though, as Agamben rightly points out, the foundational text of this tradition—namely, Aristotle's *Metaphysics*—is far more complex and astute with respect to the question of potentiality than such a tradition has often dared to admit).[22] Such concerns lead him in the end to attempt to produce a concept of potentiality without making recourse to the mediating passage or transformation from potentiality to act—that is, to conceive of potentiality no longer in relation to the act, and, indeed, to think potentiality at once without any relation and without any act whatsoever.[23] (And, clearly, this is also tantamount to producing a concept of means without end.) Whereas I agree that it is necessary to banish this mediating relation from any thought of potentiality—a relation that in the end has always had the effect of enslaving potentiality to act—I also feel that by getting rid of the relation one does not somehow get rid of the act too, that it is one thing to dispense with this relation and quite another to imply that the whole question of actualization will also vanish into thin air or become irrelevant once such a relation has been finally dispensed with. On the contrary! Doing without this relation should lead to a radical and global reconceptualization of both potentiality and act as immanent to each other, that is, as distinct yet indiscernible from each other. It is only by rethinking both at once in such a way that a "new and coherent ontology of potentiality" can at all come into being. And this is why, whereas Agamben suggests in the sentence above that such an ontology is yet to come, I think that it already exists in some form, and that, in particular, Deleuze took important steps in this direction. If we understand Deleuze's deployment of the dyad of "virtual" and "actual" as one of his ways of posing the question of the relation between potentiality and act, for example, we can see that Deleuze does not dispense with the actual just because only too often it has been used to suppress and indeed repress the virtual, and does not theorize the virtual in isolation from the actual. In Deleuze, the virtual and the actual form an immanent circuit, in the sense that each of the two is the obverse side of the other—and hence the actual always has virtual facets, always leads parallel virtual lives, and vice versa.[24] The virtual and the actual, thus, are two different ways of apprehending the very same thing. Importantly, this also means that the actualization of the virtual never constitutes an impoverishment or mortification of the virtual because such an actualization always produces yet other virtual realities in its turn. In Agamben, on the other hand, one often gets the feeling that potentiality always pulls back at the last moment from realizing itself in the act precisely because he understands such a realization to constitute nothing other than the depletion and death of potentiality: it's as if potentiality, by realizing itself in the act, would be reduced and relegated at best to playing the role of a haunting yet fossilized presence within the act, not unlike a mummy within the sarcophagus, or, better yet, within a pyramid. And yet, having said all this, I also think that there are elements in Agamben's work that point in different directions, which might be more reconcilable with Deleuze's positions on this matter (I am thinking, for example, of that beautiful chapter on the question of halos in Agamben's *The Coming Community,* about which I have commented elsewhere).[25]

AN: Well, I am not sure about this last point, that is, I am not sure that Agamben's and Deleuze's positions are reconcilable in the end. In any case, I agree with much of what you just said, but I would push it even further. The act always contains a surplus, always constitutes surplus.[26] That which is realized has a surplus with respect to that which is possible (and I intend this surplus as a very specific and precise concept, which is something I have worked on in *Kairòs, Alma Venus, Multitudo,* among other places). In undergoing the process of actualization, potentiality repotentiates itself, re-creates itself to the second power: far from being mortified, potentiality thus becomes more powerful precisely by actualizing itself. But such an ontology of potentiality is nothing other than Marxian ontology: the productive act does not decree the death of labor; the productive act, rather, is that act which exalts and accumulates labor—and once it does that, one can then take off once again, starting from a new and higher level. Living labor can never exhaust itself, can never be consumed! Not only its mortification but also its consumption cannot take place: there is only multiplication and expansion.

CC: And surely this is how things look like from the standpoint of labor rather than from the standpoint of capital.

AN: Well, obviously! I am speaking of living and not of dead labor! Capital can only subtract life, can only mortify labor.

CC: In a sense, then, that act which mortifies labor not only is not a productive act but also cannot be said to be—strictly speaking—an act at all: it is, rather, the manifestation of a limit; it is itself a limit to being. An ontology of potentiality founded on a reconceptualization of potentiality and act as immanent to each other, on the one hand, would understand potentiality as being reborn richer and fuller through the act, as expanding each and every time it determines itself in a process of actualization, and, on the other hand, would understand the act as giving more power to power, more life to life.

Part II

CC: The question of constituent Power is probably as good a question as any to begin interrogating the role that Gramsci plays in your work. I have always felt that Gramsci constitutes a surreptitious, difficult, yet important presence in your work: you rarely refer to him—directly or otherwise—and yet these are significant references. Most of these references take the form of an attempt to reelaborate the Gramscian concept of hegemony. In *The Constitution of Time* as well as in *Empire*, for example, you briefly deploy the concept of hegemony in a way that goes counter to the dialectical, humanist, and, ultimately, authoritarian interpretations of this concept—almost as if to suggest that it might be possible as well as useful to wrest this concept away from those more canonical interpretations, or that, indeed, such interpretations and deployments missed or perhaps ignored an antihumanist potential in Gramsci's own understanding of this concept.[27] It seems to me not only that there is such a potential in Gramsci but also that, if such a potential is taken into consideration and further elaborated, some of your most crucial concepts—such as constituent Power and autonomy—cannot be too far behind. In short, I am wondering, first of all, to what an extent such concepts in your work share in the same political-philosophical genealogy as the concept of hegemony—or, put differently, to what an extent such concepts have benefited from an implicit reelaboration of the Gramscian project—and, second and more generally, what is the exact nature of the difficulties you have had in engaging with Gramsci. As far as the latter issue is concerned, of course, I realize that for a long time Gramsci was so monopolized and instrumentalized by the Italian Communist Party as its own founding father that it was nearly impossible to extract him from that specific ideological context and to reclaim him for different political projects. In fact, you suggested as much earlier.[28] And yet, is that the only reason why Gramsci is a problematic figure in your thought, as I think he is?

AN: It's not the first time that I hear this: many friends, comrades, and readers have asked me about my position on Gramsci. First of all, I never read Gramsci well—in the sense that I never read him systematically. I was so annoyed by the dogmatic way in which he was interpreted and presented that I never took the time to read him carefully.

CC: The problem, in other words, was not with Gramsci per se but with how he was deployed and with what he came to represent in a certain historical moment.

AN: Yes. The problem was that Gramsci was used so as to avoid the very possibility of actually having a debate: I despised the fact that whenever he was mentioned or quoted, he was invoked biblically so as to put an end to all discussion. Furthermore, two different readings of Gramsci circulated among my comrades in the 1960s. (Keep in mind, of course, that the Gerretana edition of the *Prison Notebooks* had not yet been published, and hence that what we read of Gramsci at the time—namely, the little volumes published by Einaudi—had been edited and approved for all intents and purposes by Palmiro Togliatti himself, regardless of whoever the specific editor happened to be.)[29] On the one hand, Tronti was trying to recuperate the young, Soviet-leaning Gramsci by interpreting him in terms of a constituent philosophy. On the other hand, Asor Rosa was going in the opposite direction by undertaking a project whose main focus was no longer Gramsci as such but Gramscism and whose main concern was to investigate the relation between literature and people: he posited Gramscism as the perfect example of that scholasticism which was dominant in Italian Marxism and critiqued it as the theoretical and ideological matrix of indiscriminate and dubious political alliances. Asor Rosa, in other words, attacked Gramscism as the recuperation of a conception of people that had nothing to do any longer with the Marxian category of class, that is, as an attempt to return either to an organic or to a liquid conception of the social—neither of which could provide the foundation for the communist and workerist political project we were pursuing at the time.

cc: If I am not mistaken, the primary target of Asor Rosa's attack on Gramscism was Pasolini.

AN: Yes, it was an attack on Pasolini's populism, which Asor Rosa saw as a Gramscian interpretation of Togliatti that was fundamentally continuous and congruent with the development of Italian populism from Vincenzo Gioberti—that is, from the popular Catholicism of the Risorgimento—onward.

cc: I find this to be a rather ungenerous and ultimately stereotypical interpretation of Pasolini, who might have been guilty of a certain populism at times, but who was also far more and far better than a mere regurgitation of the Italian populist tradition. I think that Pasolini was the most important inheritor of Gramsci in the postwar period, in the sense that he was the intellectual who took most risks with Gramsci and who pushed the Gramscian project furthest—thereby inheriting undoubtedly some of Gramsci's less edifying aspects, such as his inveterate humanism. The point, in any case, is that—all humanism notwithstanding—neither Gramsci nor Pasolini can be reduced to sheer populism. But let's leave Pasolini aside for the moment, and let's return to my queries regarding Gramsci.

AN: My point was precisely that Asor Rosa's project in the end produced a series of stereotypes, on which I relied for a long time. So, on the one hand, I bought into Asor Rosa's stereotype of Gramsci as the philosopher of Italian populism, and, on the other hand, I was also intrigued by Tronti's tentative proposal to interpret Gramsci in insurrectionalist terms rather than in terms of hegemony and of class. And so my position on Gramsci remained unresolved well into the 1980s. There was, however, an aborted attempt to come to terms with Gramsci before the 1980s. In the winter of 1978—after having completed my seminar on the

Grundrisse at the École Normale during the spring of that year—I started teaching another seminar there, also at Althusser's request: this was a seminar on Gramsci, which, however, was interrupted after a couple of classes because of my arrest in April 1979. I taught this seminar with Robert Paris—an excellent historian who had studied Amadeo Bordiga very well and who was the French editor of the *Prison Notebooks*.[30] He and I were in complete agreement when it came to critiquing Gramsci, even though his point of view was quite different from mine, in the sense that he understood Gramsci fundamentally as the enemy of Bordiga's quasi-Blanquist positions—which were dominant in the Communist Party at first—and as pursuing instead a proto-Trotskyite project of class army and of people's army. As it happens, even though Gramsci eventually won over Bordiga, the political projects of the Communist Party ended up being dominated by Bordiga's doctrines throughout the period of the antifascist resistance, because Togliatti, who had been a follower of Bordiga before his switch to the Gramscian line, in effect returned to his earlier Bordigist positions when he won the leadership of the party after Gramsci's arrest. In any case, it was only once I returned to France in the 1980s that I finally started engaging with Gramsci more carefully. And that was the moment when I had to confront Ernesto Laclau and Chantal Mouffe's sociological, revisionist, and reductive interpretation of Gramsci. Laclau and Mouffe turn Gramsci into a hero of juridical realism by transforming the concept of hegemony into a concept of expanded social consensus on reformist projects, into a concept that designates the ability to participate actively in reforms: their version of hegemony, in the end, lacks any understanding of radical class divisions and ends up being no more than a saccharine-sweet concept of interclass collaboration.

CC: Well, this doesn't sound like a very novel version of Gramsci to me! Reading Laclau and Mouffe for the first time in the late 1980s felt much like experiencing some sort of déjà vu, which is probably why I never shared the enthusiasm with which their project was greeted in academic circles in the USA then. In other words, I don't think that their Gramscism is significantly different from the type of alliance politics pursued by the Italian Communist Party—with largely disastrous results in the end, I might add—as I was growing up in Italy in the 1970s.

AN: Precisely! Such a reformist interpretation of Gramsci is indissolubly tied to the crisis of the Italian Communist Party. As the party gradually let go of Stalinism, its ideologues were desperately in search of an ideology that would hold the party up, hold it together, and justify its existence. What better solution than turning once again to Gramsci, who always had been a revisionist *in potentia*? This is how Gramsci then became the great democratic author capable of creating precisely that which they had in mind, namely, the great party of the Left. But this might as well be Tony Blair's version of Gramsci! A nauseating Gramsci! So, my first attempts to get to know Gramsci in the 1960s clashed with the radicalism of my comrades at the time, who shunned him because they thought of him as a populist, while my later attempts clashed with this Gramscian reformism of the 1980s and 1990s, in which the concept of hegemony was reduced to a sociological concept of consensus.

cc: My point in bringing up Gramsci had been also to find out whether or not you agree with me that it might be not only possible but also potentially very productive to reread and reelaborate Gramsci differently today.

AN: Yes, I do agree. First of all, there is a historical and historicizing rereading of Gramsci that is long overdue: this would be an interpretation of the Gramscian concept of hegemony as a specifically Leninist concept. Gramsci is absolutely clear on this point from the very beginning to the very end: hegemony is the condition of possibility for the dictatorship of the proletariat. This was the main thrust of Gramsci's anti-Blanquist, anti-Bordigist, and anti-Stalinist polemical position: he never believed that the proletariat could possibly come to Power through an insurrection; for him, rather, coming to Power meant to construct a formidable class force, a vast class formation that would express itself through the dictatorship of the proletariat. I don't think there can be any doubt about this aspect of Gramsci's thought. And beyond this, there is much more that is still extremely useful in Gramsci and that, in a sense, has little to do with his Marxism. Gramsci, for example, introduced the concept of revolution from above, which constituted an immensely important contribution to political science, and which enabled him to understand fascism as a phenomenon of negative hegemony. Gramsci was perhaps the only eyewitness who saw fascism exactly for what it was, who described fascism precisely as a revolution from above—and this alone already suffices to make him a political thinker of enormous importance.

cc: In a sense, it is precisely his trenchant analysis of fascism that makes him so relevant nowadays: I believe, for example, that a Gramscian approach would go a long way in explaining the current ascendance of a figure such as Silvio Berlusconi.[31]

AN: Yes, I find Gramsci to be particularly useful in this case because Berlusconi's regime bears a striking resemblance to the initial phase of fascism. Having said all this, however, I must add that I disagree with you on a specific point you made earlier: I just don't see how one can use Gramscian tools in order to build the concept of constituent Power; or, rather, I think that Gramsci's usefulness here is limited. In short, the concept of hegemony is not a concept of multitude; to the extent to which the concept of hegemony is a concept of dictatorship of the proletariat, to that extent it is still a concept that is completely imbued with modern sovereignty.

CC: I find your characterization of the concept of hegemony as a Leninist concept to be convincing. And I also agree that Leninism partakes of some of the worst—that is, most authoritarian—tendencies of the tradition of modern sovereignty. What I will not concede, however, is that hence one ought to draw the conclusion that Leninism has completely lost its relevance today. I think that Lenin's analysis of imperialism, for example, is very useful in order to understand fully the passage from imperialism to empire.

AN: Well, I suppose it's fine to flirt and play around with Leninism a little bit once in a while! It's fine to say that we need to go and take a dip in Leninism so as to reinvigorate our sense of insurrection and sabotage, so as to give their due to the small groups that march united and rebuild the world one thing at a time, etc. But all of these are elements that specifically concern militancy rather than the ontology of liberation. And in Gramsci the Leninist elements dominate all the rest. Ultimately, Gramsci is completely soaked in the modern concept of the state.

CC: But what about Pasolini's Gramsci? Pasolini was definitively a Gramscian and yet he had absolutely no illusions about the state. First of all, he was one of the very few intellectuals who asserted repeatedly that World War II had not marked a radical break in Italy and that—on the contrary—there was a fundamental continuity between the political and social institutions of the fascist regime and those of the postwar democratic state. Second, whenever he expressed his profound longing and admiration for the immense creativity and capacity of resistance that he found in the poor and in the oppressed everywhere—even though he adopted a populist tone at times—he never suggested that such capacities would or should eventually find their adequate expression in the state and in its institutions, namely, that the political strengths of the poor and of the oppressed would be best served as well as best employed by being integrated into a reformed and more just state. And this is why I have always felt that his populism—if that is what we are dealing with here—was at worst some kind of residual rhetorical tic or ideological bad habit and at best a Trojan horse bursting with far different energies, since it never sought or trusted state solutions to the political problem of "the people." In short, Pasolini's Gramscism had little to do with what you identify as the most problematic aspects or potentials in Gramsci: Pasolini did not take Gramsci either in the direction of liberal-democratic reformism or in the direction of Leninist authoritarianism—both of which, it could be argued, ultimately have similar conceptions of the state as transcendent order of the social and share in the same tradition of modern sovereignty. The direction taken by Pasolini, especially during his last decade, had little to do with that tradition, which, in fact, repeatedly constituted one of the targets of his scathing attacks. Pasolini, rather, managed to articulate a series of critiques that were very similar to the positions of antihumanist thinkers such as Foucault, without ever relinquishing the fundamental Gramscian and Marxist substratum of his formation. Take, for example, his largely polemical—if at times cantankerous—critiques of the student movements of the 1960s and of the student revolts of 1968 as being complicit in some ways with the very logic of consumerism they were trying to fight: I think that such critiques are at the very least congruent with Foucault's implicit critiques of those same political movements and of their enthusiasm for sexual liberation as being fundamentally continuous with the crucial apparatus of capture of the modern state, namely, with what he calls the deployment of sexuality. In the late 1970s, Foucault tells us that when we think we say no to Power by saying yes to sex, we are simply fooling ourselves.[32] Wasn't this precisely what Pasolini was telling us a few years earlier in films such as *Porcile* and *Salò*, as well as in the public abjuration of his earlier film cycle, the Trilogy of Life?[33] And—to suggest another relevant link—if Pasolini's films and film theory play such an important role in Deleuze's philosophy of the cinema, that is so not only because Deleuze was able to transform, recuperate, and enlist in the service of his projects even the most unlikely of materials but also because Pasolini had already anticipated some of his theoretical positions.[34] And one could go on with the examples . . . All I am trying to say is that, if there is an antihumanist Gramsci, he is to be found in Pasolini and in his Gramscian experiment.

AN: No, please, don't misunderstand me: I am actually in complete agreement with what you are saying. I think that the interpretation of Pasolini you have suggested is not only a very good interpretation but also a far more radical one than what has been circulating in Italy on Pasolini for the past few decades, which is largely unreadable. I have had very long and very similar discussions with Michael, and he too would agree with you: in some ways, Michael was the first person to make me realize that Pasolini is far too rich and complex a figure to be simply dismissed as a populist. I must confess that—as you have probably understood by now—for a long time I underestimated Gramsci and I did not bother to get to know Pasolini very well. I must add, however, that I agree with you more when it comes to Pasolini than when it comes to Gramsci. Gramsci knew extremely well how to combine the analysis of modernization and the analysis of cultural and aesthetic forms—see, for example, his reading of Futurism—and, in a sense, this ability to complicate the relation between structure and superstructure was one of his strongest points. This is also an aspect of Gramsci, however, that makes him too similar to Lukács for me. Gramsci's and Lukács's evaluations of Lenin, for example, are very close to each other, largely because they are both imbued with German Idealism. Pasolini, on the other hand, was always far less of an idealist than Gramsci. Despite his critiques of the student movements of the 1960s, I have no doubt that today Pasolini would have been in full support of the antiglobalization movements! I think that his Third Worldism—which was undoubtedly problematic at times—would have taken him in this direction today.

CC: What you have just said goes a long way in identifying possibly the most important difference between you and Gramsci. This may be obvious, but it may be important to reiterate it here: while the question of the relation between structure and superstructure constitutes a crucial problematic in Gramsci, it is hardly present in your work. I take it that this is the case because all the insoluble problems arising from and associated with this classical Marxist question are solved *ab ovo*—and, in fact, largely constitute false problems—when considered from a strictly Spinozian standpoint, which is, in a sense, what Althusser was trying to say in *Reading Capital*.[35] In any case, it is a fact that this has never been a productive question for you. This fact, however, has not kept you completely from engaging with much of what in traditional Marxist terms used to be called the superstructural, including cultural and aesthetic forms. And yet such forms don't play a very important role in your thought. Take, for example, the question of literature: this has been an immensely productive and absolutely crucial question for many—perhaps for most—thinkers of the twentieth century, from Heidegger to Benjamin, from Sartre to Lukács, from Derrida to Foucault, from Lacan to Kristeva, from Deleuze to Agamben, etc. Aside from your book on Leopardi, the question of literature has not been an important question in your works (and even in that book, the question of literature—e.g., the question of what constitutes the literary, of how it functions, etc.—is not exactly central, since there you are interested for the most part in reading Leopardi in effect as a philosopher and an ontologist, as the thinker who was able to reintroduce the question of time in Italian thought, as a Spinozian and materialist thinker, etc.).[36] Of course, I am not suggesting that the question of literature—or, more generally, the question of the aesthetic—*should* be important for you! I am simply wondering about this because the fact that such questions have not been crucial for you sets you apart from most contemporary thinkers, including those—such as Foucault or Deleuze—to whom you are otherwise very close.

AN: Much like everybody else in my generation, I read enormous amounts of literary texts in my youth. As they used to say: "Initium philosophandi est literarium!" [The beginning of philosophical investigation is literary!]. It's not an exaggeration to say that I really started thinking for the first time through literature. And what I read in those years was essentially the literatures of the European cultivated classes: all the Russians, all the Germans, all the French, as well as the English eighteenth century and the American nineteenth and twentieth centuries. I read, however, very few Italian authors: I read what they gave us to read in high school, while later I did read much contemporary Italian literature, but always with great detachment. And much later I read many Latin American authors too. Besides the book on Leopardi, by the way, I have written on the book of Job, and, in general, the biblical texts have always been extremely important for me.[37] The point, however, is that I have given much thought to philological and textual issues especially when writing about philosophical authors: it's precisely when analyzing philosophical texts as texts that I have put most effort into investigating the question of the textual. The Hegel translations I did between the end of the 1950s and the beginning of the 1960s were fundamental in my formation, as they forced me to think about and experiment with the practice of writing [*la scrittura*]. In this sense, reading and writing about Marx as well as Descartes were crucial experiences for me—much more so, somehow, than reading and writing about Spinoza, since his way of writing [*la sua scrittura*] is so unique, so inimitable. Other than that, my efforts in this area have been limited.

cc: And yet, when reading your long, complex, beautiful, and passionate book on Leopardi one gets the feeling that your investment in these matters is less limited than you are suggesting here. There seems to be something particularly urgent about this book . . .

an: To be quite frank: I was in jail, I had just finished the book on Spinoza, I felt my time there would never come to an end, I didn't know what else to do, I felt completely beaten. So, I told myself: "Let's look around for somebody else who went through such an experience of total defeat." And so I slowly started working on Leopardi (and I finished the book once I got out of jail). Your reading of this book—namely, that the question of time constitutes the central and guiding question in my interpretation of Leopardi—is only partially accurate. It is true that while in jail I had also written *The Constitution of Time* and hence that the question of time inevitably was fresh in my mind when I started working on Leopardi. But even more than the temporal problematic as such, what compelled me most in this project was the question of the political: above all, I wanted to assert the primacy of the political in Leopardi's ontology. To this purpose, I had to situate Leopardi in a specific historical conjuncture (namely, the moment of Late Romanticism in Europe) when to ask the question of time meant inevitably to ask about the time of the Restoration, to ask about the time when the revolutionary project is in crisis—in short, to ask what becomes of time in a time of reaction. This was the central theme of the book.

cc: The primary urgency of this book, in other words, derived from the fact that you too were living through a time of reaction, that you too felt defeated by the time of reaction.

an: Yes, of course. I felt an elective affinity for Leopardi. I felt—rightly or wrongly—that our situations were unisonous. This means that, admittedly, I was moved at first by some sort of psychologizing aestheticism, which, however, was rescued by and substituted with a historicizing analytics. Put differently, this book for me constituted an attempt to understand what the hell one can do when one feels so completely defeated, what ontological forces might be able to break through such a stifling, regressive, reactionary crisis—much like the one we were going through in the 1980s. I wanted to clarify what the crisis of the revolutionary project had meant for Leopardi and what it meant for us in the 1980s. The revolution haunted Leopardi: his whole life and his entire thought were marked indelibly by that event and by the attempt to understand it. Leopardi is someone who never stopped asking himself: What happened? All his works echo with that question. In this sense, the book on Leopardi does not constitute a deviation in my work: all my historiographical works—that is, all those works that constitute interventions in the history of philosophy, including my books on Leopardi and on Spinoza—share the same concern, namely, to assess the significance of the reply one gives to crisis, to evaluate how one acts in the face of total defeat. All the works that I began in jail, as well as most works that I wrote right after my time in jail, are works of this type, namely, works that are trying hard to find out what comes after defeat, how not to be defeated by defeat. And all these works were driven by the anxiety—shared by many of my comrades at the time—of trying to identify the paradigm of the postmodern.

cc: Much of what you are saying reminds me of the Benjamin of the "Theses on the Philosophy of History." He writes there of that secret affinity the present has for a specific moment in the past, of that fleeting image of the past which flares up at a moment of danger in the present.[38] You describe the relation between Leopardi's historical conjuncture and your own similarly here. I find this Benjaminian moment to be very interesting, given that your position on Benjamin is somewhat ambiguous, contradictory—or, at the very least, can shift and change drastically depending on the situation. For example: in *The Constitution of Time,* you write a scathing critique of Benjamin's conception of the *Jetztzeit;* in the "Introduction" to *The Constitution of Time* —written more than fifteen years later—you acknowledge the important role Benjamin has played in your projects; in *Labor of Dionysus,* you and Michael find much that is still useful and relevant in Benjamin's essay "Critique of Violence"; and in *Empire,* you comment at times positively and at times negatively on various aspects of his work; etc.[39] Clearly, each of these different positions is based on different and at times conflicting elements of Benjamin's thought, and hence it is perhaps to Benjamin rather than to your position on Benjamin that one ought to attribute ambiguity or contradiction. And yet, there seems to be in general something undecided or unresolved about your engagement with Benjamin that cannot simply be blamed on the—at times admittedly evasive or hermetic—character of his writings. (Incidentally, I think his writings are far less evasive and hermetic than often they have been made out to be: friends and enemies alike have had at times an unfortunate tendency to overemphasize the purportedly esoteric aspect of Benjamin's thought.) You seem to oscillate between wanting to denounce and wanting to reclaim Benjamin, between a negative and a positive hermeneutic of his work.

AN: I must say you are absolutely right: I do approach Benjamin in very different ways at times. Every time I reread something by Benjamin, I feel differently about it. As a thinker, Benjamin is not organically structured. He is, though, a thinker of stunning intuitions that he develops then with great elegance. As I recall, the first time I read Benjamin—at some point during the second half of the 1950s—I was at once truly impressed and somewhat unconvinced. I was really struck by the "Theses on the Philosophy of History," and yet I was left also quite perplexed by them: what I found difficult to accept was his articulation—which, paradoxically, was also a disarticulation—of the Marxist conception of history and the Judaic interruption of time, of a fundamentally materialist analytics of the historical process and these myriad caesurae that incessantly intervene from the outside in religious—or, at least, eschatological—form. In Benjamin, the materialist conception of the historical process—namely, a conception of the historical process that proceeds from past to future as well as from that which is below to that which is above—is repeatedly capsized into a series of breaks and then turned into so many mystical illuminations that proceed from the future to the past, from that which is above to that which is below. It's no surprise, then, that the *Angelus Novus* is someone who looks backwards, over his shoulders.[40]

CC: You are saying, in other words, that the temporal caesura of the *Jetztzeit* is a moment of transcendence in an otherwise immanent historical process and, perhaps, constitutes even an attempt to transcendentalize such an immanent process.

AN: Yes. And this is precisely what Giorgio and even Derrida like so much about Benjamin! It is this aspect of Benjamin's thought that makes him such an attractive figure for all those who want to reinsert a transcendental tension—or, at least, a transcendental intuition—inside a materialist process. *The Arcades Project,* for example, is fully immured in Soviet cultural critique; it's a work that would make any old Stalinist quite happy!

cc: How so? I am not sure I understand.

an: The method of *The Arcades Project* is the same method you find in Bakhtin and in all other great Soviet literary analysts. Soviet literary criticism shouldn't be mistaken for Andrey Zhdanov. The qualitative level of materialist and philological analysis in the Soviet Union remained very high throughout. In any case, the point is that—all his materialism notwithstanding—in Benjamin there always is something that is not born from within, that does not emerge from the inside. It's not a coincidence, for example, that his essay on the "Critique of Violence" is a Schmittian essay (without, however, any of Schmitt's juridical concerns). In this essay, the irrationalist interpretation of power reaches its highest point, takes its most extreme form. In general, what I see in Benjamin is the utmost attempt to turn irrationalism inside out, to turn irrationalism against itself by emptying it out. And, in a sense, this is exactly what was taking place in Lukácsian Marxism around the same time (I am referring specifically to the early Lukács, to what Lukács wrote between 1914 and the early 1920s). The crucial difference is the Judaic dimension, which was always very powerful in Benjamin and which he derived and reelaborated not only from Gershom Scholem but also from Rosenzweig. In fact, a comparison between Benjamin and Rosenzweig might be instructive here. In Rosenzweig, there was a break between two quite different philosophical and political tendencies: before World War I, Rosenzweig wrote a truly splendid, remarkably lucid book on Hegel, which was the powerful expression of a very advanced democratic thought, and in which he attempted to use the liberal Hegel in a way that is reminiscent of Croce (without exhibiting, however, the vulgarity and heaviness of Croce's prose); and then he came back from the war and wrote *The Star of Redemption,* that is, a book in which the *Jetztzeit* produces—and, indeed, is—nothing other than mystical illumination.

cc: Let me interrupt you for a moment, because I think a clarification is in order here. It seems to me that at times you have the tendency to equate mysticism with transcendence, and transcendence with reactionary thought and reactionary politics. I completely agree with the second part of this equivalence, in the sense that I don't know of a transcendent concept that in the end is not reactionary, as well as of any concept of transcendence that is not also a reactionary political fantasy of sorts. The first part of this equivalence, however, I am not willing to accept: I don't think that all mysticism necessarily constitutes a flight into transcendence and is thus reactionary; on the contrary, I think that mystical discourse has at times constituted an attempt to express immanentist and materialist conceptions of life, politics, and the world. In other words, it seems to me that there have been thinkers and writers for whom mysticism was the only discourse available for articulating their profound dissatisfaction with the reactionary traps constituted by transcendence in all of its various forms, as well as for attempting to find escapes from such traps, alternatives to such forms. William Blake would be an exemplary case of such a figure, I think.

AN: I don't think I am confusing the mystical with the transcendent and the reactionary, and, in fact, I agree with what you are saying about mysticism. When writing my book on Job, for example, I had to go back and reread much Jewish mysticism and to engage with one of its most recurrent concerns, namely, the relationship between human beings and God, the relation between the human and the divine. In Jewish mysticism, such a relation is a direct one. This is much unlike what we see in Catholicism, where everything is so highly structured, so well organized . . .

CC: In Catholicism, in other words, there is always mediation.

AN: Yes. Even in the great, insane mystics—such as Saint Teresa of Avila—there are always highly structured mediations. Not so in Jewish mysticism. There, the relation to God is always direct. Such a relation can take the form of a relation to nature, to the family, or to much else: the point is that each and every time, you rediscover God inside concrete, material things. In Jewish mysticism, to see God—that is, to participate of God by and through seeing him—can be at times almost a way of reclaiming and reappropriating the divinity in materialist terms (one can see this, for example, in a certain revolutionary Talmudism). In this sense, I agree with you. Nonetheless, this is not the case with Rosenzweig: burdened as it was by the tragedy of the war, his vision remained completely mystical *and* transcendent. So—to return to my earlier comparison—while Rosenzweig at a specific historical conjuncture shifted from a certain tendency to quite a different one, Benjamin continuously alternated one of these tendencies with the other throughout his life.

CC: Yes. Sometimes, I think of Benjamin's thought as having developed in wavelike motions, as a series of ebbs and tides, or, perhaps, of oscillations. In youth, he went through that Schmittian phase you mentioned earlier, which included what I think is his best and most important work, namely, his stunning book on the *Trauerspiel;* and then . . .

AN: Yes, yes, and then there was the discovery of Marxism—which was simultaneous with the rise of fascism and Nazism—etc. He went through phases. Different phases aside, however, the alternative or alternation I am referring to was internal to each of these phases and remained unresolved up until and including the very end, that is, the "Theses on the Philosophy of History." In fact, the theses constitute the most extreme and most unresolved point of such an alternative, in the sense that there the alternating tendencies not only are present within the very same text but also are juxtaposed to one another without any mediation whatsoever.

CC: Yes, actually, I was about to say something similar. In Benjamin, there is a continuous oscillation between two polarities: at one extreme, a decidedly idealist and transcendent discourse, and, at the other extreme, a sustained and far-reaching experimentation in nondialectical historical materialism. (Incidentally, I believe that Adorno sensed very clearly the presence of these polarities in Benjamin; his mistake, however, was to think that they were ultimately equivalent as well as equally misguided, or, in other words, that they were both idealist in the end.) This oscillation in Benjamin takes at least three different forms. It is an oscillation from one phase of his thought to another (e.g., from an early Schmittian phase to a subsequent Marxist one, etc.); but—as you point out—it is also an oscillation that is present within each of these phases as well as within the very same work at times. For example, the "Epistemo-Critical Prologue" to the *Trauerspiel* book is terminologically steeped in Romantic Idealist discourse and yet conceptually already quite different from that discourse: on the one hand, the terms that Benjamin uses and discusses there—as well as the ostensible problematic of the whole piece, namely, the relation between truth and representation—are derived from Romantic Idealism; on the other hand, these terms and the problematic they immediately evoke seem at times to have been emptied out of their original conceptual content and reinjected with a more materialist content. In this text, in other words, the oscillation between those two polarities occurs in the gap between terms and the concepts to which these terms purportedly refer—almost as if words here begin to function like so many Trojan horses. This is also to say that at times the gap between these polarities is so narrow that the oscillation itself looks almost like an encryption of sorts, almost like a hologram—in which the two polarities become two layers that inhere in one another, that are distinct yet indiscernible from each other . . . for better and for worse! And it occurs to me that the opening of the "Theses on the Philosophy of History"—in which Benjamin describes the theological hunchback hiding inside the automaton of historical materialism—constitutes in effect a thematization of such dynamics.[41]

AN: Yes, in Benjamin we have both a highly coherent historical-materialist conception of the world and a theological pull toward the transcendent, which are at times very difficult, even impossible, to separate from each other. And there is no doubt in my mind that the tension between these two different tendencies often proved to be extremely productive for Benjamin. There is no doubt that it is also because of such a tension that he was able to produce some of the very finest historical-materialist analyses of nineteenth-century French culture, in which the typological classifications alone suffice to show that he had an unparalleled attentiveness to forms and styles of life. I have no doubt about any of that. But let's be frank here: where is the revolution in all that? *This* is the question I want to ask Benjamin ultimately! And it's also the question I want to ask Giorgio! It's the question I want to ask all these brilliant people who understand so clearly the epoch in which they live and who can describe so effectively the current modes of existence, without, however, having an intuition of how to break with them. The *Jetztzeit* is nothing other than the way in which the need for such a radical break with an intolerable existence is entrusted to transcendent instances and appeals.

CC: The *Jetztzeit* is a transcendent expression of an urgent need for change.

AN: Exactly! Benjamin's vision of God ultimately is a biblical one. In Agamben, at least, all of this takes place at history's limit, rather than beyond it.

CC: And yet I still find Benjamin's experimentations in nondialectical historical materialism to constitute a powerful and useful example. The method he adopted in his cultural analysis shows that he understood all the problems inherent with the category of mediation as well as that he tried to find solutions for them. His jarring and unmediated juxtapositions of apparently unrelated modern forms of life—say, on the one hand, the bodily gestures involved in striking a match, and, on the other hand, the gestural regime imposed on the worker's body in factory production—bear witness to his attempts to do away with mediation and to circumvent the dialectic altogether. Do you remember that moment in *Discipline and Punish* when Foucault asks whether it is surprising that prisons resemble factories, schools, barracks, hospitals, which all resemble prisons? I think that at times Benjamin was asking similar questions—especially in *The*

Arcades Project. I think that at times Benjamin was looking for precisely that which Foucault later will call the diagram, namely, that function which is immanent in the fabric of the social, which changes at different historical conjunctures, which does not coincide with any specific use or form of life, and of which institutions such as the prison or the factory—and their attendant forms of life—are material expressions and exemplary instantiations. It is this aspect of Benjamin—namely, his method, his attempt to go beyond dialectical thought—that I still find very compelling, even when it was not entirely successful.

AN: I certainly agree that Benjamin was trying to go beyond the dialectic. But for me that's not the real issue! In and of itself, to go beyond the dialectic—or even to avoid it altogether—is not enough! The dialectic constitutes an answer to a real problem. You may well think that the way in which the dialectic solves this problem is insufficient or misguided, and hence you avoid the dialectic at all costs. The problem, however, is not simply going to disappear if and when you no longer think dialectically! The problem will continue to constitute a problem, and you will still need to give an adequate answer to it. Take another book that is exemplary of the type of modernity—or, if you will, antimodernity—that we are investigating here: Adorno and Horkheimer's *Dialectic of the Enlightenment.* Even there the dialectic doesn't work! In that book, they tell us a terrifying story with extreme elegance and with exquisite articulation. Their account is characterized by brutal necessity: the inclusive force that the process of commodification exerts on cultural phenomena hinders and forbids any type of relation. In the end, they posit the historical summation and terminal fruition of the process of alienation as something inevitable, inescapable. But, surely, this is where the dialectic is over and done with! This is precisely the end of the dialectic! Their account does not include or allow for even a dialectic of liberation. Incidentally, this is exactly what Grigory Zinoviev reproached Lukács for.

CC: If I understand you correctly, you are saying that neither Benjamin with his attempts to circumvent the dialectic nor Adorno with his attempts to produce a negative dialectics were able to solve the problem to which the dialectic was thought for so long as having been the right solution. They understood that the dialectic was the wrong solution, but in the end they were not able to produce a better solution themselves.

AN: The real task is to succeed in constructing a mode of thought that would at one and the same time refuse the dialectic as well as solve the problem of the passage from the simple to the complex, from singularity to multitude, etc. Neither Adorno nor Benjamin succeeded in this.

CC: In the end, I agree with you. And yet I also think that both Benjamin and Adorno—in their own different ways—always thought in the vicinity of such a nondialectical mode of thought. For example, for all of Adorno's insistence on the need for a reelaboration of dialectical thought from the standpoint of the negative—that is, from the standpoint of the nonidentical—the mode of negation that he deploys no longer has anything dialectical about it, in the sense that it recuperates or transforms nothing of that which it negates. Adorno's negation is not even *negatively* dialectical; it is, rather, absolute. This is evident above all in his devastating critiques of that apotheosis of the identical which is the commodity form in all of its insidious varieties. In fact, these are no longer even critiques: they are unmitigated destructions pure and simple! In this respect, Adorno was even better than Nietzsche precisely there where Nietzsche was at his best. Adorno knew, as very few have ever known, how to negate absolutely that which negates life. In Adorno, there is an admirable nondialectical *pars destruens* that—sadly—is never followed by a *pars construens*.

AN: It sounds as if Benjamin and Adorno were very important for you for a long time and then they suddenly let you down! Unlike Benjamin, Adorno certainly was very important for me at a certain point.

CC: How so?

AN: There was a moment in my life when I was struggling very hard to extricate myself from Hegel without much success. And then I discovered Adorno. He was music to my ears! Reading Adorno was a sublime experience: it was sheer pleasure. Adorno was crucial for me because he embodied the exhaustion of Idealism. Here was this thinker who understood perfectly well the problems posed by the Hegelian dialectic, who tried all he could to solve these problems from within the dialectic by turning the dialectic inside out, and who still wasn't able to do it! What I felt at the time was that if Adorno had not been able to solve such problems from the inside, then these were problems that simply could not be solved in that way. If he could not do it, nobody could! Reading Adorno convinced me that one had to take an entirely different approach to the dialectic.

CC: You learned much more from Adorno's failures than from Hegel's successes!

AN: Adorno's failures certainly were very instructive. The question I was asking Adorno in the 1950s was the same question that his students asked him in 1968: "Yes, yes, Herr Professor, this is all fine and good, and we all agree on it, but could you now please explain to us how to get beyond it?" In a certain sense, I never had any problems with what Adorno was saying. What I could not stomach, rather, were the truly perverse effects of what then we used to call "critical thought," namely, the attempts to identify use values, pure values, alternative values outside the logic of capitalism. Such attempts used to be particularly evident in certain types of Third Worldism, as well as in much ecologism, which was always bordering on nature worship. I have always found such attempts to be absolutely unacceptable. I have never believed that there could be something that could place us outside of that historical process which is capitalism. If there was anything outside, it was precisely inside such a process: for example, the struggling working class, the struggling mass intellectuality, perhaps even the early phase of the Bolshevik Revolution, etc. All of this was nowhere other than inside there! Those values that many conceived of as existing outside were always values that we had constructed in the first place: a first, a second, a third, an nth nature; first, second, third, nth needs; new and emergent desires—in short, the relation between production and self-reproduction, the whole process of self-valorization. It was all this that Adorno completely misrecognized or could not even see.

CC: He never showed any interest for the question of production in general.

AN: Yes, but he was always very interested in one of the crucial effects of production, namely, in alienation. In any case, the point is that in negative dialectics there is always an anxious yearning for purity. When you read Adorno, sooner or later you will hear him whispering to himself: "Somewhere, there is a God."

CC: I must confess, though, that I hear something quite similar also when I read your books! Or, rather, what I hear there at times is quite simply: "There is God"—which is, admittedly, a different matter. Let me explain. According to you, Adorno in the end both believes in the existence of and longs for a transcendent principle, which, nonetheless, he cannot find or see anywhere: in short, Adorno yearns for a God that turns out to be always already hidden. This is another way of saying that Adorno never extricated himself completely from negative theology, and ended up precisely in the same place as Benjamin did, albeit via a different route. Clearly, this is not at all what I see in your works. I do see there, however, something that for lack of a better term I will call religiosity. First of all, this is a question of rhetoric, or, more generally, a question of writing style. You write with religious fervor: at times, the enthusiasm, excitement, and passion of your writing are so intense as to reach almost mystical, visionary heights. Or, to put it more precisely, the tone you adopt in your writings—characterized as they are by tropes such as exclamatory phrases, apodictic statements, etc.—is at times reminiscent of the tone found in certain kinds of religious texts. Second, this is also a terminological and conceptual question. Very often, in fact, you deploy terms as well as concepts that belong to theological, religious, or even mystical traditions (see, for example, your reelaboration of the concept of poverty in *Kairòs, Alma Venus, Multitudo,* or your references to Saint Francis of Assisi in *Empire*). Such a religiosity, which ranges from the rhetorical to the conceptual, is rather different from the melancholy yearning you identify in Adorno's work in at least one crucial respect, namely, yours is a fully positive religiosity that—far from seeking a hidden God—knows, affirms, and exclaims that God is here and now. Positive though it is, however, it is still a religiosity: as such, it might still bear a vague family resemblance to those elements you critique in both Benjamin and Adorno; as such, it might not be completely insensitive to the temptations of the transcendent. This may sound like an accusation, but it is not one. After all, I do believe that transcendence is the risk one always runs when one thinks ontologically (and that's not at all a good reason not to think ontologically). All I am saying is that I do see you running this risk in what I have been referring to here as religiosity.

AN: There is no doubt that there are elements of religiosity in my thought. They are, however, profoundly different from Benjamin's mysticism. If there are elements of religiosity in my thought, they are linked to everything else that is to be found there; unlike with Benjamin, in other words, these elements in my work do not constitute an abstraction that stands outside my work, do not constitute a state of exception. What you call religious fervor is not something that can be separated from the way I write or isolated in the way I write: it *is* my way of writing. It's not as if you find it in some works and not in others, in some passages and not in others! I can assure you that religiosity is omnipresent in my work—even though it is expressed in different forms and at different levels of intensity throughout my works.

CC: So, I am being reproached not for going too far but for not going far enough! You are saying that religiosity constitutes nothing less than the very fabric of your thought, that it is completely immanent in your thought.

AN: Well, I am not sure about that. All I know is that mine is very much a peasant religiosity. Such a religiosity is absolutely never an exalted illumination or epiphany. It's a religiosity that is intimately related to the rhythms of peasant life, to the passing of peasant time, to the proximity of domestic animals and wild beasts, even to a sense of maternity . . . It's a very pagan, very pantheistic religiosity. It's a way of considering each and every thing as sacred. It's a way of extending such sacredness to everything.

CC: This is pure Saint Francis!

AN: Actually, I think that my religiosity is much closer to Giordano Bruno's religiosity. Whenever I think of Bruno, the first image that crosses my mind is the immense expanse of tomato fields all around Nola.[42] In my mind there are these unforgettable images of leaving Naples behind by train and then crossing through the plain around Nola and being surrounded by this lush, exuberant, uncontainable nature! A nature that is so hyperproductive, so intensely beautiful—and always bursting at its seams! How could they possibly burn at the stake somebody who simply describes all this? So, yes, one can find all this also in my work—this type of nature, as well as this type of love for this type of nature. There are a couple of differences, however. First of all, *my* nature—that is, nature as it is where I am from in northern Italy—is perhaps a little calmer, quieter (in other words, no more than two harvests per year, rather than, say, seven, as is the case around Nola!). Second, and more important, mine is a nature that had experienced a process of capitalist modernization from the fourteenth century onward. In any case, the point is that for me nature is always fully cultivated nature, in which the irrigation canal is just as sacred as the tomato or the peach.

CC: Such a religiosity of nature, hence, is different from the nature worship you criticized earlier in certain types of ecologism because in the latter nature is posited as an outside to history or even as opposite to history.

AN: Precisely. There is nothing that is not fully historical about a tomato field! Moreover, it's because it is fully cultivated and fully historical that I am willing and able to love nature in the first place. This is a relation to nature that I established early on as a child and that undoubtedly I inherited from my mother. In this sense, I am truly from the Po Valley [*sono veramente un Padano*]. I could be a Po Valley philosopher! And this, of course, has nothing to do with Umberto Bossi's Padania![43]

cc: It strikes me that such a conception of nature immediately implies a conception of the subject as working subject, producing subject, creating subject. If one relates to nature in the way you have just described, then, each and every time one looks at nature or looks at oneself as part of nature, what one sees in effect is the sedimentary history of human labor—layers upon layers of work, production, exploitation, suffering, joy, creation . . . Yours is really a religiosity of labor! This is a religiosity of labor intended at once as *natura naturans* ["naturing" or active nature] and as *natura naturata* ["natured" or passive nature]—in short, a religiosity of labor as the producing product.[44]

an: This is the way I would put it: mine is a religiosity of the tool [*utensile*], a religiosity of doing, of making [*del fare*]. In any case, I would insist that it is a completely pagan religiosity and that it has nothing to do with mystical illuminations: I am constitutionally unable to envision or experience God as the transcendent lightning bolt that suddenly rends our dark skies, transfixes our gaze, and transforms our life by throwing some tablets at us from above!

cc: So, you are not exactly a Po Valley philosopher: more precisely, you are a Po Valley *pagan* philosopher! In any case, you have convinced me by now that it is your pagan and pantheistic sensibilities that make you allergic to God as epiphany and revelation. What I am beginning to wonder about, rather, is the relation between, on the one hand, your type of religiosity, and, on the other hand, philosophical discourse, or, more precisely, philosophical practice. A moment ago, after all, when I compared your religiosity to the religiosity of a mystic (namely, Saint Francis), you replied by pointing to the religiosity of a philosopher (namely, Giordano Bruno) as representing a better term of comparison. I am wondering what is at stake here. I am wondering, for example, whether the religiosity you are describing is specific to a certain type of philosophical practice, or whether instead it is common to various discourses and practices, philosophy being only one among them—and the latter possibility all in all makes more sense to me than the former. I am wondering, in other words, whether your understanding and definition of philosophy itself as a practice may be at stake in what we are discussing here, as well as how important it is for you to call yourself a philosopher, to identify with philosophical practice, or even just to think about such definitions at all—and it goes without saying that by "philosophy" and "philosophical practice" I don't mean necessarily the academic discipline of philosophy. Let me give you a concrete example of what I have in mind. In *What Is Philosophy?*, Deleuze and Guattari claim that they had never really asked themselves the question of the title while they were doing philosophy—either together or alone—over the span of several decades, and that only late in life they found it necessary to ask themselves what exactly they had been doing all these years.[45] As I see it, their answer to this question in that work involves not only an explicit definition of philosophy as the practice of producing concepts but also an implicit and powerful affirmation of the right as well as of the necessity of philosophy. This is an affirmation at once of a domain of thought that appertains properly to philosophy and to philosophy alone, as well as of an urgent and insistent need to use the term and concept of philosophy at a time when philosophy is increasingly under attack in the hostile and anti-intellectual environment of the society of the spectacle, is increasingly dismissed as obsolete and irrelevant by the reifying practices of global capitalism—such as marketing and advertising—which lay a claim on the concept and, in general, on the domain and function of philosophy.[46] In short, are these types of reflections on the philosopher as a specific intellectual figure and on philosophy as a specific practice at all relevant or important for you?

AN: I am not really sure. Certainly, I have given much thought to these matters. Truth be told, I have always considered philosophy as a hobby. I am aware, though, that this is an incredibly reductive and rather silly way of answering your question. It is the case, after all, that many of the analytic instruments that have been fundamental for my research were produced within philosophical contexts in the first place. Philosophy, nonetheless, has always been a hobby for me—in the sense, for example, that I have never taught philosophy. When I was an academic, I had always the good luck not to have to teach philosophy.

CC: Do you mean to say that you have never taught the history of philosophy as such, and that instead you have taught philosophy by other means and in other forms such as political theory, legal theory, political economy, etc.?

AN: Yes. I have taught all sorts of things, but never philosophy per se.

cc: And yet, regardless of the specific topics or disciplinary discourses you engaged with when teaching, wasn't your method always a philosophical method?

AN: That's probably true. In any case, I never taught philosophy as such because, frankly, I would have found it embarrassing. Doing philosophy always involves a direct, immediate, personal element: it involves a form of rhetorical argumentation that often touches upon one's own most intimate moments. This means that when teaching and discussing philosophy one uses often a personalizing rhetoric—and this makes me feel very uncomfortable. Somehow, I have never been willing or able to let go of a sense of modesty [*pudore*], reserve, shyness . . . There have been times in my life, nonetheless, when I tried to be a public philosopher—and failed. It was always a failure because I exaggerated, I tried too hard to play the part of philosopher—and these failures marked me deeply. In a sense, philosophy for me has been at once a hobby and a scar. In any case, none of this is very important. What is much more important is that at this point there is one type of philosophy that is truly over and done with, namely, modern philosophy, the philosophy of modernity. There is simply no point in teaching this philosophy any longer.

cc: Really? I find this statement very hard to accept, especially coming from someone who knows the philosophy of modernity extremely well!

AN: It is useless to teach it, but, of course, it is useful to know it! What should be covered and taught, however, is the *other* philosophy: namely, those forms of materialist thought that were able to survive within modernity and to resurface in postmodernity. For example, it would be essential to study carefully Renaissance philosophy—which is hardly known or taught any longer, and which I would read as a form of poetry. I am thinking about figures such as Ficino and, of course, Machiavelli—but also about someone like Ludovico Ariosto.[47]

cc: During the Renaissance, after all, the distinction between philosophical and literary discourses was not at all as clear and significant as it was later, from the seventeenth century onward.

AN: Yes—and that is one of the main reasons why I am interested in Renaissance philosophy and why I believe it is important to teach it. Moreover, I would teach all these literary-philosophical materials alongside the visual arts of the period. If I were to teach philosophy, in other words, I would not teach it as a disciplinary, technical, or specialized discourse; I would treat it, rather, as a vast and heterogeneous space for the excavation of the past. As far as philosophical concepts are concerned, on the other hand, I would be very careful and discriminating. Philosophy is enslaved by its own tradition: in particular, the classical Platonic-Aristotelian tradition—which ends with Hegel—has enslaved and suffocated thought for too long, and we must simply get rid of it. The dialectic corresponds to nothing that is real: it is sheer falsification. To get rid of the dialectic is for us just as important as getting rid of medieval theology was for modern philosophy. One of the greatest merits of figures such as Deleuze and Foucault—as well as of the whole Nietzschean tradition in general—is that, before being postmodern, they constituted above all an antimodern tradition, by which I mean that they destroyed the conceptual structures of modern philosophy. Among such structures, possibly at once the most impervious and the most pernicious still are the theological transcendent and the Kantian transcendental. In particular, the transcendental—in the form in which it was developed by Descartes, Kant, and Husserl—is truly the enemy. It is telling that the philosophical profession as we know it is founded upon the concept of the transcendental, without which it would not be able to exist and to reproduce itself. Indeed, this is the main reason why the philosophical profession cannot let go of this concept and will continue to defend its validity as long as it can. Think, for example, of the contemporary descendants of the Vienna School—namely, of Anglo-American academic philosophy from W. V. O. Quine onward—who have managed to turn philosophy into a grotesque and reactionary neometaphysical inquiry by reinventing all the transcendentals of knowledge [conoscenza]. Contemporary logicians aside, this has been absolutely clear at least since Descartes: the professional philosopher posits himself as mediator of thought. That is all that the social and political function of the philosophical profession amounts to: mediation. To my mind, Pascal and Spinoza constitute the first cluster of thinkers who reject and negate this function absolutely, while Marx and Nietzsche constitute the second cluster.

cc: In a sense, you have just explained why it is that philosophy is taught at all, that is, why it was formalized as a disciplinary and institutional knowledge in the first place.

an: Yes. Take, for example, the Italian case. As soon as Italy is born, a specifically Italian philosophy needs to be invented so as to justify the existence and function of this bourgeois national entity as mediation of political conflict. This is, in effect, what Gentile did by inventing more or less from scratch at once a philosophy and a history of philosophy, which became rapidly the staple of high school as well as of university curricula throughout Italy.

CC: We can assume safely by now that you do not see yourself as a professional philosopher! In a sense, you have also explained here why it is that you find it difficult to reconcile the very idea of teaching philosophy with your intellectual project.

AN: No, I do not identify with philosophy as academic discipline or profession. Neither do I identify, by the way, with philosophy understood as production of concepts, that is, with philosophy as Deleuze and Guattari define it in *What Is Philosophy?*. When it comes to the question of the concept and to its relation to philosophy, actually, I have a strong affinity for the intellectual iconoclasm of those philosophical-scientific thinkers who took it upon themselves to demolish systematically one concept after another: I am thinking of the best among the Physicalists as well as of Rudolf Carnap—but also of certain moments in John Dewey's thought and in American pragmatism in general.

CC: Yes, but what conception of philosophy do you identify with—if any? I am beginning to feel as if you are dodging, as if you are avoiding saying explicitly what *your* definitions of philosophy and of the philosopher are!

AN: Are you asking me what a philosopher is? What else could a philosopher be? The philosopher is merely a residue of the past. And as far as philosophy is concerned, the reason why I do not agree with Deleuze and Guattari's definition of philosophy has all to do with the way in which they handle the question of the concept. It is not exactly the case that their definition of philosophy as production of concepts is incorrect or misguided: this definition does capture an important element of philosophical activity—and yet it is still inadequate. Neither is it the case, of course, that concepts are unnecessary or unimportant—on the contrary. What is crucial, however, is not to mistake the definition of a concept—which at most constitutes a propaedeutic instrument—for a real transformation in history, which is what the concept should help us analyze and understand. As long as you work on a purely conceptual terrain, everything remains too formalized, too abstract—and, indeed, this is the main problem with *What Is Philosophy?*. The title of the book itself is indicative of this problem: I think that Deleuze and Guattari ended up choosing this title almost as a way of hiding the fact that they had not been able to define what it is exactly that philosophy should concern itself with—which is what I believe they had been after in the first place.

CC: On your reading, the book they had wanted to write originally would have had to formulate a very different question as well as to bear an altogether different title, namely, *Why Philosophy?* You are saying, in other words, that they ended up focusing too much on the concept and hence on the "what" of philosophy and too little on the "why" of philosophy, that is, on its political task or ethical raison d'être.

AN: Yes. We ought to live thought—and everything else, for that matter—in a way that enables us to be fundamentally linked to practices, because practices always refer to something real. I understand perfectly someone who wants to concern himself with, for example, the analysis of a literary text or, for that matter, with the analysis of a philosophical text. But once I have analyzed this or that text, I still need to attend to the most important thing: namely, I still need to attend to the fact that philosophy—or literature or whatever else—has any value at all for me only to the extent to which it constitutes a decision on life, only to the extent to which I am willing and able to interrogate it regarding the direction of my life. To attend adequately to this fact means in effect to posit philosophy as an instrument of struggle like many others. This is as much of a definition of philosophy as I think I will offer you: philosophy is nothing if it is not an instrument of struggle. Philosophy is nothing if it does not help me decide whether I want to go up toward God or whether I want to go down toward the Earth, whether I should work for a pacification—that is, for a transcendental mediation—of my problems or whether instead I should push self-interrogation and self-analysis as far as they can go. Philosophy has nothing to do with critique. Whereas the modern philosophical tradition has constituted nothing less than the solution or *Aufhebung* of critique, we ought instead to dissolve, and hence to erase, philosophy completely into a reflection on praxis and on existence.

CC: I completely agree with you: philosophy is nothing if it does not constitute an ethics of existence—and, incidentally, I believe this is precisely what Foucault was trying to say in the last few years of his life. I would like, however, to defend Deleuze and Guattari—at least in part. It seems to me that, even though they can be taken to task for overly emphasizing the "what" rather than the "why" of philosophy, there is nothing in their account that contradicts what you have been saying here. On the contrary, their emphasis on the fact that philosophy is a practice of thought just like many other practices, and hence that it does not have primacy or take precedence over other practices, as well as their insistence on using this practice to denounce all contemporary forms of *doxa* ranging from journalism to marketing, are congruent with the political-ethical functions of philosophy you have outlined so far. Far from negating or obscuring what you have said here about philosophy, it seems to me that in *What Is Philosophy?* they were simply trying to say something else, namely, that philosophy is a specific practice of thought that produces specific objects—that is, concepts—and that functions according to specific rules and regulations. In short, their account of philosophy is complementary to yours. If I were to criticize this work, rather, I would take a different approach: I would say that in it they do not emphasize nearly enough the fact that philosophy understood as production of concepts is a necessary element intrinsic to any practice, or, put differently, that any practice involves something like a philosophical moment to the extent that it needs to produce its own concepts in order to function.

AN: Our specific disagreements regarding *What Is Philosophy?* aside, I do agree with your last point—as long as we understand, however, that it is far more *your* point than theirs. There is no doubt that any form of knowledge [*conoscenza*] needs to go through an epistemological phase, during which it produces and defines its own concepts so as to formalize and transmit knowledge. But why should all this be called philosophy? Call it conceptual activity. Call it practice of thought. Call it anything else you like. Possibly the most damning and baneful aspect of the history of philosophy is that whenever this conceptual activity or practice of thought has been given the name of philosophy, it has been turned immediately into a function of Power and domination. It ceases to be, in other words, a sophistic function. The Sophists maintained precisely that each and every discourse has its own specific concepts and rules, as well as that these concepts and rules are not preexistent or eternal but need to be invented from within that specific discursive practice which needs them in order to exist in the first place. But then there comes Plato and says: "No, it is not true that every science has its own rules. There exist, rather, general rules that enable us to conduct and pursue all sciences." And then there comes Aristotle—who is even shrewder and who says: "Not only there exist general rules. These rules are also inscribed in the very order of nature!" And it's downhill from there! From then on, in other words, this form of thought will be unstoppable and will continue to haunt philosophy to the present day because it constitutes a formidable instrument of domination: once you have managed to secure and to own these eternal rules, in fact, you can conquer and dominate the world. It is not a coincidence that Plato travels all the way to Sicily to put philosophy in the service of the tyrant Dionysius—and this event is not an exception or aberration in the history of philosophy. Should *this* history of philosophy be taught? Perhaps so—but very, very carefully. Should I defend and fight for *this* history of philosophy? No—because, unfortunately, it is almost impossible by now to make sure that such a defense would not end up constituting also a glorification of a long and sad tradition of enslavement of thought by sovereignty. I have better things to do than act like those revisionist socialists who, in order to defend the existence of socialism within the state, ended up glorifying the state itself! It is truly unfortunate that nowadays we still need not only to reiterate the obvious—namely, that the history of philosophy is the product of a selection conducted according to the worst of political criteria—but also to act on the basis of such an obvious fact and hence to write another history of thought, to write the history of the *other* thought, that is, the thought of the poor, of the rebels, of the outcasts, of all those who had a different image of the world. Why is it that when it comes to medieval philosophy we remember those theologians who concerned themselves with the conflict between church and state while we do not remember Carlo Ginzburg's miller who thought that the universe was made like cheese (and whose cosmology clearly was still medieval, even though he lived during the Renaissance)?[48] Crude and simplistic as this may sound, the answer to this type of question for me is actually very simple: the history of philosophy is the history of victors.

cc: Arguably, a significant part of Deleuze's project consisted in articulating one possible version of this other history of thought, in producing a very different selection and genealogy of thought.

an: Yes, of course. Do not underestimate, however, how comical and futile our efforts at producing this other history can be. Take Spinoza, for example. He survived oblivion largely thanks to Hegel's codification of the history of modern philosophy: the reason why Hegel resurrected him, however, was that Hegel needed an object around which to annul, or at least to neutralize, the materialist temptation.

cc: This is an exorcism rather than a resurrection! It seems to me you are suggesting that Hegel in effect brought Spinoza back so as to co-opt him by putting him in the service of idealism before anybody else would rediscover him and be tempted by his materialism instead.

AN: And since then we have rediscovered Spinoza, that is, we have been able to extract him from the idealist shell to which Hegel had sentenced him. One would think that such a rediscovery has been successful: our books sell, some are even well received, etc. But—I swear—in twenty years Spinoza will be talked about once again in the way in which Hegel talked about him rather than in the way in which Matheron or Deleuze rediscovered him. In short, Spinoza—much like all the other thinkers of this other history of thought—needs to be rediscovered and reinvented anew in each and every historical epoch. One can hardly say the same about Hegel or, for that matter, about Plato.

CC: Arguably, Plato too needs to be rediscovered and reinvented anew in different epochs. It strikes me, in other words, that one could indeed say the same about any thinker. I am not saying that all resurrections are the same: I am saying simply that all thinkers must be resurrected in some way or other in order to be redeployed in the present. Obviously, the difference must lie somewhere else.

AN: I suppose it depends—among other things—on who performs the resurrection and why! Jokes aside, the point is that one of the best and one of the worst aspects of the history of philosophy consists of the fact that it foreshortens distances, it produces close encounters. In this respect, the history of philosophy is very different from the history of literature. When you read, say, Sappho or Sophocles, you get at best less than a third of what they are talking about—which may well be still enough to go by and to make us want to reread and reinterpret them anew in different epochs. In the history of literature, the distances are enormous: in general, each epoch is highly distinct from the preceding one, as well as from the next one. The history of philosophy, on the other hand, has the tendency to manipulate repeatedly the same conceptual heritage and to present it to us in a synchronic package. In this sense, Plato is just as modern as Hegel. In each and every epoch, you will always find the Aristotelian philosopher arguing with the Platonic philosopher about the question of ideal forms, and so on and so forth. Such is philosophy's enormously mystificatory sleight of hand: the history of philosophy produces, reproduces, posits, and presents itself as eternal—and it is able to do so because its foundational categories, from the transcendent to the transcendental, are incredibly useful for the continued existence and exercise of sovereign Power.

cc: This is why, then, a thinker who was never canonized in the history of philosophy because of his opposition to sovereign Power has a very precarious afterlife, and why his rediscovery is not the same as the rediscovery of a thinker who is central and dominant in that history.

AN: And this is also why at times I think that it is simply undignified to call oneself a philosopher.

Notes on a Politics of the Future Anterior

The Political Monster

Power and Naked Life

Antonio Negri

TRANSLATED BY MAURIZIA BOSCAGLI

Monstrous Genealogies

Classical Eugenics

"Eugenia" means that one is "well born," that one will be "beautiful and good." Classical metaphysics has given body to this concept and developed systems of definitions that pertain to it. Therefore, the universal will be, in the metaphysical tradition that originates from the classical world, always interlocked with eugenic values. Consequently, only those who are good and beautiful, eugenically pure, are entitled to command. This is the dimension (the original matrix and the future *dispositif*) of *Greek parlance in philosophy*. Indeed, to speak of *arché* is to speak at the same time of "origin" and of "command"—in the universal and/or in the essence are simultaneously inscribed the beginning and the hierarchical order of being. Aristocratic blood, good birth are constantly the causal source of a hierarchical order.

Through this reading of the metaphysical plot of classical philosophy, we go beyond the critiques that materialist and democratic thought have offered of it, even beyond the most spirited ones; after all, they have limited themselves, even though proceeding with great sophistication, to recognizing in slavery the origin of Greek political theory (as well as of its metaphysical developments).[1] For us now it's possible to grasp also the "form" in which classical thought takes shape and gets applied in metaphysical terms, that is, that "eugenic" form of the universal that does not include but excludes, that does not produce equality but rather intrinsically legitimates slavery. When Reiner Schürmann, interpreting the Heideggerian legend of that constitutive episode of Western tradition, stresses the relation between beginning and leadership implicit in the concept of *arché,* and unearths its constitutive dynamics ("the connection between the notions of beginning and leadership is possible when the metaphysics of cause has been put in place. Once we assume that the phenomenon [as totality] is understandable from the point of view of causality, then it will be possible to say that the true cause is only that which begins its [own] actions and 'never ceases to begin them'—which means that it is a cause that commands"),[2] he tells us that aristocratic blood and constant presence, as articulated in the causal relation, are the foundation of ontology and Power. Thus, in the great Greek philosophy, eugenism—Martin Heidegger *dixit*—"reveals" the truth of being and the foundation of authority.[3] That "revealing" is a masterpiece of ambiguity and mystification. *On the other side there's the monster . . .*

The monster is outside this economy of being. In the Greek language, ontology disqualifies the monster. If he inhabits classical antiquity, he can only do so by accepting to be demonized in metamorphic mythology.[4] The monster wanders in the dream and in the imaginary of folly: he is a nightmare for those who are "beautiful and good": it can exist only as catastrophic destiny that must be atoned, or as divine event. Classical rationality therefore dominates the monster in order to exclude him, because the monster's genealogy entirely exceeds eugenic ontology.[5] Greek metaphysics can foresee the corruption of the causal process of becoming, either natural and/or ethical, but it cannot understand, or even simply expect, the explosion of the monster as "other," different from the causal regime of being's becoming. Not even Neoplatonism, at the twilight of the Greek world, manages to imagine the monster ontologically: if the monster ever existed, he couldn't but be part of nothingness, and belong to the absolute limit of being, to matter (which is not capable of being and cannot be, absolutely, *eugenia*—in fact, it not even is). Then let the Gnostics, or a mythically or religiously contaminated metaphysics, affirm the presence of the monster in life—a fable that ontology cannot accept![6]

At the beginning of modernity, the monster is excluded from the order of reason for a motive different from that given by classical metaphysics: he is partially readmitted into the philosophical order. How? Here the monster appears as a "metaphor" in the political field, a metaphor of the transcendence of Power, which, even though it cannot be reduced to the order of reason, to causal rationalism, must nonetheless appear and be part of the world. Leviathan and Behemoth, monsters out of the book of Job and products of the Judeo-Christian tradition, are crucial to mediating a multitude that can no longer be subjected immediately to the hierarchical order merely in the name of the origin and of its consequent causality, namely, command. The problem is another, the situation completely different: here there's no longer any presumed *eugenia*, the "political ontology" of the "Doric power." The multitude upon which Power must be exercised is "Gothic," the hybrid product of barbarian invasions and the mixing of different races, languages, and political orders. Differently from classical antiquity, then, the Leviathan is a monster that, if he dictates an order, is nevertheless deprived of any naturalness—but it's an order that is considered *internal* to the world.[7]

This is not the case: it's rather a matter of appearance. The modern philosophy of the state, at the moment when it seems to make the monster reasonable, actually makes all the rest, the whole of life and society, monstrous. Rather than the Leviathan, what's monstrous now are the plebs or the multitude, the anarchy and disorder that they express: upon them and against them the monster constructs the central sovereign Power—the untimely event of a necessary epiphany. Leviathan stops being a monster insofar as he is a "deus ex machina." Thomas Hobbes's argumentations clearly say so: within the logic of monstrous reason Leviathan is disarmed; in fact, he is completely effective in the order of rational causes: here he is no longer a monster, but an instrument.[8]

Let's pay attention to the genealogy of modern sovereign Power. As Hobbes will do later, already Jean Bodin tried to free this genealogy from any diabolical homology or assonance, while restricting its genesis and form to monarchic legitimacy—a eugenic genealogy as no other.[9] Only a century later James Harrington and radical Englishmen of all sorts take up once again—and explicitly—the Saxon *eugenia* as the foundation of the Protestant republic, and around it they delude themselves and others: no, it's not yet democracy![10] Both on the Right and on the Left then, the eugenic essence of Power is maintained. I could go on for pages and pages to show how the monstrous event of Leviathan has not eliminated classical *eugenia*, but rather, by transforming it and making it immanent, confirmed it. A little later, in the development of the modern idea of the state, between J. G. von Herder and Thomas Carlyle, between Alexis de Tocqueville and Hippolyte Taine,[11] not to mention those authors who fall into a deep racism,[12] we witness newly an explicit reaffirmation of eugenic Power—whether monarchic, aristocratic, popular, it doesn't matter. What matters is that an absolute, physical criterion of authority runs through and develops the genealogy of Power. When nationalism, the eugenic legitimation of Power, and racism explode once again fiercely in the nineteenth and twentieth centuries, they have an incredibly deep, ancient, and continuous ideological origin and credibility: here classical *eugenia* reappears, taking over reason, and subordinating the concepts of a secular and immanent idea of Power.[13]

It's interesting to notice that, vis-à-vis the eugenic tradition, not even the humanist revolution was able to do much.[14] Classical eugenism, in fact, doesn't only present itself as the content of the Western philosophical tradition, and as the figuration of its image of authority. In fact, it has also a lot to do with its "rational form." Thus the humanist revolution, and humanism in general, have, in spite of themselves, repeated the ancient concept of Power because, even though they attacked and modified its contents, they did not renovate its form. It was not enough; one needed to go much further. Only in the last past thirty years, *feminist thought* has partially moved in this direction: however, often it has limited its perception of this phenomenon to the critique of patriarchal Power.[15] Instead, we must recognize in the texture of Greek rationality, as well as in the order of modern reason, the domination of the eugenic criterion: even better, we must consider eugenism as a *dispositif* operating in a period as long as the history of Western rationality. The humanist revolution was only capable of challenging the (feudal, clerical, patriarchal, etc.) contents of the eugenic tradition. But until it attacks the "rational form" coextensive with those contents, such a challenge is weak and ineffective. We must go deeper and reclaim the monster, and by doing so go radically beyond the eugenic rationality of classical tradition.

Monstrous Resistances

At a certain point in the history of Western ideology, the picture changes radically. *Class struggle* comes to occupy the whole scene and becomes generalized. Marx is the first to assume it as paradigm of historical development: consequently, the old eugenic schema wanes. The monster becomes a subject, or different subjects—he is neither excluded in principle nor reduced to a metaphor. No, he's there, he exists, he's really there. If in classical antiquity and also in modernity everything seemed to be predisposed to eliminate even the mere possibility of the monster ("In the eyes of God nobody is a monster," says in fact that perfect mediator of antiquity and modernity, Montaigne),[16] with capitalism the picture gets turned upside down, and this turning, with monstrous force, represents a radical and irreversible innovation.

The scene is paradoxical. Indeed, Marx depicts the entire capitalist development as monstrous. He himself is an ironic monster, an excess of intelligence who, when describing, critiques and destroys. So, for Marx the way in which "bourgeois science" shows us the world around us is certainly "rational"; nonetheless, it's very "philistine"! Here classical metaphysics, which connects origin and command, is turned on its head: under capitalism, says Marx ironically, science is as rational as the pope, the czar, or even Metternich . . . To be more explicit, science is as "bastard," spurious, as is Power . . . Likewise, "the riddle of the commodity," that is, that effective and hard conundrum constituted by the congealing of the product (of labor) in reified and fetishistic object and/or its monetary transfiguration, is "rational."[17] Just as "rational" would be also the capitalist mode of production and the natural laws that claim to be able to describe it—as much as political economy and (natural or positive) right. The closer political economy and legislation come to labor, to man's living labor operating in history, the more "rational" (by now we can get rid of irony and call them with their real name, "monstrous"), the more monstrous the techniques of logical abstraction and of ontological extraction of value become.[18] All the more, thus, properly monstrous laws of exploitation become established. Shylock, the merchant of Venice, demands human flesh as compensation for his credit: the capitalist tears human flesh from those who don't even have a contract of debt with him. And this monstrous (rational?) game of the flesh and of its exploitation expands and becomes intensified: Marx describes these developments synchronically in his theory of surplus labor (of value), and diachronically in his analysis of the different periods of exploitation, in their changing and advancing between slavery and capitalism, between absolutism and democracy, in the continuity of the mode of accumulation as well as in its uncertain wavering and metamorphosing . . . Thus we find again in the critique of political economy the fantastic, mythological, and ancient history of natural metamorphoses, but, so to speak, turned upside down: it no longer shows us how the monster is excluded, but rather the forms in which capitalist "rationality" has been invested by the "monster" of class struggle, and how they have been monstrously transformed and subjected to an irresistible pressure. The metamorphosis, that is, "from utopia to science."[19]

But there's also the metamorphosis "from science to experience," the daily experience of the fatigue and mortification produced by labor. When, subjected to exploitation, every worker recognizes himself abstractly as commodity, but also concretely sees himself as a monstrous member of a class of poor, then he understands that he must resist and, if he can, rebel . . . The more he will develop this kind of self-consciousness, the more monstrous he will become.[20]

To be more explicit . . . For more than a century now we have been accustomed to accept, as part of our perception of life, not only the violent experience of the capitalist relations of production (and of the consequent relation to the state), but also the individual suffering of the subjects submitted to it. We identify less and less with the "rationality" of Power, and more and more with the "monstrosity" of suffering. The twentieth century, with fascism and Nazism, colonialist abuses, imperialism, as well as nuclear and environmental terrorism, has taken us to the highest degree of suffering consciousness. Thus *monstrous resistances* have taken shape during these two last centuries. Realist writers and existentialist philosophers have offered us extreme and exciting phenomenologies of this ontological situation of the subject.[21] There exists more evidence: people deported in concentration camps, tortured in wars of liberation; evidence from apartheid, from the Palestinians in their struggle, from the African American ghettos, etc.[22] The classical metaphysical tradition and Western rationality excluded the monster from the ontology of the concept: these experiences instead register his powerful presence. Indeed, he who tries to resist against the development of the capitalist relations of production *is only a monster;* and it's only a monster he who obstructs the logic of monarchic, aristocratic, popular Power, eugenic in all cases; it's a monster he who refuses violence and expresses insubordination, hates the commodity and explodes in living labor . . . We start seeing history from the point of view of the monster, that is, as product and limit of those struggles that have freed us from slavery through escape, from capitalist rule through sabotage, always through revolt and struggles.[23] This is a long process, ambiguous and often contradictory: but the "line of the monster" is the only one that, in the end, can explain the development of history, the way we experience it—and, above all, the way what-is-to-come (*l'a-venire*) will present it to us.[24]

Between a monster and another, from that which is the metaphor of capital to that which embodies the multitude of the exploited, there lies nonetheless a great space of ambiguity, of *pourparler:* I would like to pause on this problem for a moment.[25] This parenthesis, or better, this interval of uncertainty, has been represented as a world of specters.[26] But if the specter is a dialectical metaphor and points to a passage (perhaps an alternative that lies on the margin and is difficult to express), the ontological indexicality attached to the monster is much deeper: it doesn't waver between (capitalist) subject and (proletarian) object of exploitation, but rather lies *between subject and subject*. The monstrous opposition is ontological, relentless, irreversible—the spectral one, instead, a little faded.[27] The monstrous opposition makes the subject grow—it makes his existence epidemic and wants to exterminate his enemy. Monstrous subjectivity attacks ambiguity, doesn't acknowledge it, comes to clash on the limit, doesn't accept the margin, acknowledges the other subject as the enemy and, against this, it becomes power. Here is perhaps the place where ambiguity affirms itself: when the new monstrous subject, through his own movement, induces that of the enemy, and the monstrous multitude of the exploited produces the cycle of capital ... Here the monster is like the great worm that is overcome by desire in the desert of *Dune*. Or perhaps he is like the monstrous images of the insurrectional masses in Eisenstein's films . . . Or like the delirious nights of the tropical jungle that García Márquez's heroes turn into their infinite destinies. In short, the monster leaves behind the ambiguity upon which his most recent history (after the rupture of the eugenic tradition) had pinned him; instead, the metamorphosis of being that the struggles have determined reveals itself to be, as event, irreversible. And also against (classical) linguistic evidence, the monster is not only event, but *positive event*.[28]

Let's be careful: not even Marx understands that the monster is definitely other from capital. When Marx, in fact, goes beyond the dialectics he has inherited from Hegel, he almost does so unwillingly, and in any case only from a logical-political point of view.[29] It's necessary instead to dig deeper and foreground ontology: it's upon this terrain, in fact, that *labor power becomes class, by destroying, that is, its own ambiguous presence in capital*. By separating itself from it. *Thus it becomes class by recognizing itself as monster.* A monstrous subject that produces monstrous resistances. The existence of class is no longer spectral but monstrous—even better, such is its essence, which carries the inscription of the force that refuses capital's productive labor. The subalternity of labor power to capital is thus turned upside down. Labor power, living labor, are present as political power ... Monstrous power ... This is the end of any homology and also of any analogy, of any common name, and also of any singular communication, between capital and living labor.

When this metamorphosis has been realized, classical eugenic metaphysics can no longer either approach, or understand, or register the dance steps and war drums in which these monstrous resistances express themselves. From antiquity to postmodernity, not only the names change (names were the things that changed the least in Western tradition and Eurocentric culture), but rather the ontological determination of becoming changes. *The monster becomes beautiful and good:* eugenism fades into infamy. Each one of its attempts to impose upon the monster the ancient definition, the classical definition of the beautiful and the good, shatters against discursive impossibility, against linguistic separation. In the capitalist regime, when monstrous resistances have grown to such a degree of physical consistency, any dialectic and any linear transformation—on the whole, any eugenic intensity—has become ridiculous and impossible. If the monster exists, the rest gets transformed and doesn't remain. The concept of ontological foundation and that of order, *origin and command,* cause and hierarchy, *become split.* As Nietzsche has explained—but before him Marx, Spinoza, and Machiavelli—what philosophy has imposed upon us, from Plato to Hegel, can be considered a strange thing. A wasp's nest that has withered when the tree of life (that contained it) expands, greener and greener.

In the feminism of *métissage* and of hybridization, these antidialectical truths, this correct apprehension of the end of any "rational" form of domination (either patriarchal or solely political) in favor of the supersession of any disciplinary boundary, in epistemology as much as in natural sciences—this power of the monster has been by now completely affirmed.[30]

Res Gestae

A Monster Is Wandering Through . . .

"A specter is (was) wandering through Europe." Today instead, what's wandering through the world resembles rather a monster. We will no longer be concerned with the conditions of development of the ideology of the political (or biopolitical, or common) monster, we will instead be concerned with his real genealogy, with his presenting itself—outside literature—as a mechanism of destruction and/or (material and/or utopian) construction, in the history of struggles and around the possibility of new worlds.

We have already said it: the biopolitical monster is a positive ghost, in any case a form of opposition, better, an ontological alternative against the eugenic claim of Power (in this case it will be difficult not to single out its figures, that is, not to name the powerful ones, the masters, the privileged, the heirs, etc.). During the twentieth century that ghost and this opposition have been called *communist movement:* this is what the rich, the master, the capitalist have regarded with spite, hatred, at times with terror. If the good bourgeois, so kind with his own children, pious in religious matters, and with an Oedipus well under the control of the psychoanalysts, becomes nonetheless a fascist—why does he do so but because, terrified, he wants to terrify others in turn? Can this become possible once again? The wider the world becomes, the more widespread monstrosity becomes. We encounter the monster everywhere, and he truly scares the masters of the world. The romantic game of dialectics, that had allowed one to hold up the adversaries by making them spectral, now gets jammed—revealing the irrepressible solidity of the subjects in action.[31]

But doesn't this happen each and every time when a great historical transformation erupts? Doesn't this always happen when man discovers himself as new? Then the past world seems to be, and is, a parasite—but the new humanity (which is already in place) is slow to appear, to represent its hegemony, and this slowness can become tragic. Already in the Renaissance François Rabelais has shown us, through his creative giants, the impossibility of medieval dialectics. Yet today the scenario is much more tragic, because the dimensions of the transformation, of the Power of command and of the power of the new man, have become enormous. Therefore, if there are no longer specters but only rising giants, violence, destruction and creation, corruption and generation close ranks all around us . . . We don't know what will happen.[32]

Let's go back to our ancient monsters. Peasant communism was monstrous, we know that. From the sixteenth-century German peasant war till the anticolonial wars of liberation of the twentieth century (in Latin America, in Africa, in Asia), honored by the heroic extremism of Patrice Lumumba, of Ho Chi Minh, of Che, the attack on land property (whose ownership was presented as natural) was considered monstrous by those who held Power. Here we are on the terrain of "one's own property," of the natural conditions of the reproduction of life. If nature is, from the beginning of time, property of Power, eugenic trace of authority (Roman law interpreted, expressed and developed this very idea of a claim upon nature), here we have, then, the denunciation of the "monstrous" character of the reappropriation of the land, and the definition of the revolt against those ancient conditions of the reproduction of life, as an attack against a necessary metaphysical condition (which is not mentioned as such, but whose eugenic logic is not denied).[33] The peasants crucified in Saxony or in Silesia upon the incitement of Martin Luther or of the pope's "emissaries," and those massacred and tortured in the Vietnamese countryside, have been considered first of all demons. Slaves, lowest servants, poor peasants—here is the irredeemable monster! Indeed, they were monsters. They had nothing to do with the eugenic history of the Western world, with its elites and their doctrine of Power, of inheritance and/or filiation! Even today peasant wars are imagined as extremely fierce loci, something that reason cannot recuperate: from the jacqueries to the brigands' revolts, in Spain, and then in southern Italy; from the Cossack wars of resistance to the chiliastic insurgencies in the Brazilian Nordeste, etc.— they continue to act against this memory. The mere memory of peasant communism is scandalous and blasphemous.[34]

Also, the communism of the industrial worker was monstrous, and perhaps even more than the peasant's. Indeed, if the peasant's existence was (in part) outside the accumulation of capital,[35] that of the worker, as generic labor power, was inside it. This "being inside" was what determined the frightened acknowledgment, the hatred, and the repression: the more resistance and opposition are internal (and here they were such to the point of touching the heart of Power in the production of wealth), the more frightening they are. It's a "rational" fear, which creates the enemy—not a delirium (even though it can appear to be so in the fascist forms of the organization of social movements), but the lucid intelligence of a force relation, more and more fragile the more intimate are opposition, resistance, rebellion to it . . . *It's the fact that the monster is positioned internally to Power that makes the latter fragile* . . . and terrified. Consequently, state violence (inspired by the dominant classes) has never expressed itself in such an extreme, continual, and coherent manner as in the case of the Parisian workers' class struggles.[36] From the Florentine revolt of the Ciompi to the proletarian insurrection of 1793, between Shays's sedition in Massachusetts and the Paris Commune, from June 1848 to October 1917, and the Shanghai massacres in 1927 and the fascist ones (from Giacomo Matteotti on), and then the repression of the communist opposition in the country of the Soviets and the great pogroms . . . And then Sacco and Vanzetti, the thousands and thousands of workers killed by the Pinkertons, and the anticommunist witch hunting, in the United States and in all the Western countries, repeated over and over again . . . Which American president, novel Constantine, will claim the equal right of *all* men, of all *the citizens* of the American Empire, to work, to participate in public life, and in the distribution of the riches of collective work? The massacre and the martyrdom will continue till that time!

Also because the communist monster—that *facies* of the insurgent peasant (first), of the struggling working class (later), and perhaps in the end (according to the new sociological definition of the proletariat) of the new intellectual labor force—is a *dispositif* that mobilizes, develops, and exasperates all the forms of opposition and of struggle on the side of the exploited. It's for this reason that class war has become, in the twentieth century, the point where any other struggle for liberation converges, the conceptual schema and the soul of national and peasant, anti-imperialist and anticolonial wars, wars of modernization and, in any case and always, anticapitalist wars. A monster has wandered through the world, capable of gathering and organizing any aspect of the workers' opposition, of proletarian resistance, and of the insurgency of the poor.[37]

Is this period over? Perhaps yes. In any case, we hope so. Why? Because it has represented an ambiguous moment when, in the distorted and capsized forms that capital has imposed upon life, the *res gestae* (what really happens) and certain modernizing aspects of capital have met. We have registered and described this bloc of vital experiences, convergent and antagonistic, in the very concept of capital (the labor force that is part of capital, the working class that produces capital).[38] Now this copresence must be destroyed because *it is already destroyed in reality, to the extent to which the powerful apparition of the monster takes place.* (When we talk of the end of dialectics, we talk about this definitive, monstrous eclipse of mediation.) Therefore, today is the moment to verify whether dialectics has truly ended; whether, consequently, the monster (as hegemony, through the resistance of the class of those who work and are exploited) can triumph; whether the proletarian class can oppose, really, as monster, the masters' eugenic Power, *kaloi kai agatoi.* We say: long live the monster! Long live his capacity to dissolve any idea or project of capitalist development and of order (both old and new) that organizes it! To sum up, it seems to us that the relation between capital and proletariat (the *multitude* of those who produce and are exploited) is founded upon an ontological imbalance in favor of the proletariat. Today the monster is the event waited for . . . neither miscarriage nor wreckage . . . even though it could be such . . . but it's not![39]

The fear that the current (twentieth-century) capitalist triumph over the revolution might be episodic and contingent can be recognized (as spoken in a very loud voice) in all historical and contemporary revisionism, that is, in the monstrous configuration of communism according to the revisionist reading . . . From François Furet on, through the "Black Books,"[40] and above all in the new palimpsests of cultural propaganda, after the fall of the Wall, we witness a curious experience. It has nothing to do with classical *eugenia:*

this, in fact, excluded that evil, the monster, the other, were part of reality—
at most it identified them as negative limit, as dark and atavistic, that thing
there at the bottom, irredeemable even in its eternity. In the counterrevo-
lutionary theories of the end of the eighteenth century, *chez* Furet and his
followers, we have instead some sort of (fantastic) ontology of the monster's nature, opposed to the historical ontology of the revolution. Furet as
Edmund Burke? Perhaps so . . .[41]

But the terrain on which these polemics take place is not stable: on the
contrary, it is incapable of immobilizing the stereotypes of the debate. The
monster crosses this terrain: more and more visible, he is within it. Historical revisionism underscores its uncontainable presence. While the past is
depicted as evil, as sin, we stumble, instead, upon something that is still, and
violently so, the capability to open onto what-is-to-come (*l'a-venire*). Facing
the negative passions of his critics, the monster presents itself as positivity.
The spectral ambiguity is now over: here the monster doesn't run away, is
not wrapped in fog, but rather prefers to declare his existence and his capability to change, to be a metamorphic being. He, the monster, is a web of
existence.

The Biopolitical Monster

If a monster is wandering in the world, we need to catch him, imprison him,
cage him. The philosopher of Power must be committed to this task. There
are, however, different ways—and none certain—of catching the monster.
Often it's even difficult to identify him the first time he appears: the know-
it-all is forced to humility, the judge to silence. Saint George risks being
thrown off the horse. But Power (and the capitalist mind), leaning as it does
toward omnipotence, cannot in any case avoid facing this problem. If there
is a monster, there must be the capability to catch him; and if there isn't,
or not yet, or no longer, the capability of destroying him, there must be that
of keeping him under control, or of normalizing him. This is true in general, but it's particularly adequate to the eugenic conception and practice of
Power.[42] Eugenism must indeed and above all prevent the original entitlement to Power from being put into question. For eugenism, Power is always
implanted in an infinite regression that ends up in the present hypothesis.
Blut und Boden, Heimat und Volk in the latest caricatural, and no less horrible, literary expressions of the twentieth century . . . In the presence of the
entitlement to Power, in the permanent naturalist legitimation, there are

not, in any case, either spatial plurality of sources, or temporal diffusion that may explain the modalities of existence of Power: here lies a void that must be predetermined and is so: the monster must be always *sub-jectum*.[43]

But nowadays, as we have already stressed, this capability of containment, that is, of normalization, is more and more marginal. Good were the times when, with Hobbes, one could tell the fable according to which the foundation of Power consisted of imposing on the multitude a contract that took any right away from it, except that of reproducing life in peace. Through the contract, order was imposed against anarchy, and the monarch turned the plebs, the multitude, into the people. That transfer of rights authorized "reason" to oppose the monster, and legitimized its action in the continual reaffirmation of this foundation. But, as I said, today it's no longer so: the monster has definitely brought *eugenia* to a crisis, today we have democracy! And democracy means weak and fleeting controls, mobile and flexible controls . . . What does it mean, then, to live or survive with the monster, in his presence?[44]

Does it mean perhaps, first of all, that the monster is not there? That he is pure illusion? It's a hypothesis. This is confirmed by the fact that we manage to give a name to the monster with difficulty. The end of strong social sciences seems to have taken place around this problem.[45] We are left with ethnomethodologies, or with the more and more minute phenomenologies of the monster. We cannot even circumscribe his sphere of action: statistical surveys and cognitive networks, which claim to be meaningful and are only ineffectual, follow one another—ill-timed and precarious moves, casual, and arrogant at times—while that extremely singular being that is the monster is more and more elusive.[46] He mingles with us, moves among us: to catch him in order to hold him up is impossible, there in the midst of that confusion, those hybridizations. To kill him would be a suicide. In fact, when you discover to be yourself in front of the monster, inside a *multitude* that is monster (but you are part of it, you cannot separate yourself from it), there's nothing left but to shudder in unison with the multitude. Saint George is the monster! Even better: this *monster is common*.

It's curious to notice how, once the possibility of conceiving the monster as an "outside" is over, all the ambiguous performative experiments that try to turn that "outside" into an "almost inside" or into a "little inside" soon themselves go into a crisis. Dialectical theologies, teleologies and/or theodicies of the monster . . . these experiments go on. The nineteenth and twentieth centuries, in political science and constitutional engineering, have invented tens, if not hundreds, of these useless (monstrous?) mediations. The American eagle or the Soviet bear have been made symbols of opposite alternatives (opposite, and yet how homogeneous) in the construction of systems of control and/or domestication of the monster.[47]

In fact, the monster had won. He had flooded, like a river in full spate, all the spaces that, around its course, had been kept free in order to avoid the big inundation—it went beyond. At this point Power—that Power which always expressed the same eugenic command regardless of the different shapes it took—doesn't know what to do anymore. And does not do anything . . . The solution has been imposed on it. It's the monster to impose it, invading any terrain and flooding the space of the political. Through his mass mobilization in the wars of the nineteenth and twentieth centuries, the *monster* becomes the real *political and technical subject* of the production of commodities and of the reproduction of life.[48] *The monster has become biopolitical.*[49] From Otto von Bismarck to Walter Rathenau in Germany, during the entire Third Republic and until the Popular Front in France, between the Soviet New Economic Policy and the American New Deal, this process is performed and accomplished. After World War II, it steadily represents the figure of capitalist production in the industrialized world. And afterwards the biopolitical qualification of the system has done nothing but improve and intensify itself.[50]

Naturally, this attempt to *control the caesura* of lived experience and of the forms of politically organized social life has been direly opposed. As far as political science (philosophy) and the Power of those who produce it are concerned, its intervention was in fact very circumscribed. Political science is sick, its servile activity is paltry, its innovative proposals vile. In sum, as when a river has changed its course through gigantic catastrophes, human intervention can do nothing, and can only wait for the new course to stabilize itself and become calm—so now it won't be the fierce politics of reduction of public expenditure or of repressive control of welfare to regulate the new biopolitical course of democratic life. The control won't affect (and even less break through) that ontological tension running through, constituting, strengthening the new, contemporary anthropological fabric. The dominant classes' will to control, ultimately repressive, cannot measure up to, or even fully understand the magnitude of, the multitude's will to power. (Certainly, the continual attempt to control is not, however, useless or ineffectual. In the eugenic tradition, from Plato up, *mimesis and metessi*, representation and participation, have always constituted models for the penetration of

Power into the improper—into what has been constituted as other; and it's off these operations that pieces of *res gestae*, scraps of history, live: they live of this ambiguity that claims to be ontology, and that instead is only rhetoric. But not even these experiments, in the current case—that is postmodern—manage to do so: their legitimization is yet another shipwreck.) By winning, *the monster has imposed the common* as substance of any productive *development* and as *power* of the citizens.

There are those who don't accept it. The constitution of the biopolitical subject is then conceived as *technological drift* (and there follows an attempt to impose command upon these technologies);[51] alternatively, what's given is a fleeting and wretched image of the monster, and of his rebellious life as destined to an adverse fate.[52] We will soon come back to this debate. But here, what man's life seems to have affirmed, beyond any doubt, is that the monster, always *common*, has now become, in some way, *subject*. He is no longer a margin, a residue, a leftover: he is internal, totalizing movement, a subject. He expresses *power*.[53]

Let's once again take up the discussion from the beginning. Power has been, forever, Power upon life, bio-Power. In the tradition of Western command and thought, it is so to such a point that any definition of Power *tout court* is eugenic, it wants to affect life and make life. The eugenic conception of Power creates life and, above all, creates those who reign upon life. Instead, those who must not command are pushed out, they are the monster. But little by little in the history of the world, the monster, from his position "outside," comes to occupy the "inside." Better said: the monster has been *inside* all the time, because his political exclusion is not the consequence, but the *premise*, of his productive inclusion. The hierarchical instruments of bio-Power define and fix him into an ambiguous position—labor power within capital, the citizen within the state, the slave within the family . . .[54] And this is in force, works, goes on until the biopower of the monster breaks the hierarchical connections. In the history of humanity this has happened often. We could say that its entire development is dominated by this insubordination of life (the power of life) against Power (the domination of life). Any development must be brought back to this continual insubordination. Today, however, rather than yet another continual revolt of power against Power, we are facing the common affirmation and victory of power (probably irreversible). Here the political monster is right up front. Until yesterday subordinated, classified, organized within Power, *the monster's power has managed to get around Power through the invasion of bios, of life.* The monster has become hegemonic in biopolitics. Which is to say: he has infiltrated himself everywhere, rhizome, he is now common substance.[55]

The Monster Monstrified

Naked Life

At the point when the monster has taken over life, there are those who claim that this is, in any case, "naked life." Against the reality of the biopolitical, the hardship of the struggles that take place within it, is pitted the name, or the illusion, of "naked life" (or, more often and dangerously, at the other extreme, the powerful machinations of biological engineering emerge . . . yet another way of acting upon/against the biological monster). But let's stay with "naked life."[56] As Socrates wanted, in fact, it's necessary to understand what lies behind this name. Thus "naked life": but what might this mean when what we are interested in is to recognize from which place our bodies can organize not only resistance but an attack, not only the force of opposition but the power that transforms? There is no naked life in ontology, much as there is no social structure without rules, or word without meaning. The universal is concrete. What precedes us in time, in history, always already presents itself as ontological condition, and, as far as man is concerned, as (consistent, qualified, irreversible) anthropological figure. Thus we understand the ideology of "naked life" (as much as the genome industry, biogenetic engineering, and the claims to dominate the species) as a mystification that must be antagonized.[57]

Were the Vietnamese at war or the blacks in the ghettos naked? Were the workers or the students during the 1970s naked? Not so, if we look at the photographs. Unless we consider the fighting Vietnamese as stripped by napalm, or the students in revolt as deciding to bear witness, naked, to their freedom. Rather, our heroes were covered, encrusted with passion and thick scales of power . . . they were dressed up, sometimes they made fashion and music . . . in any case, they could not be naked because they were carrying too much history upon themselves. *They were dripping historicity.* And yet there are those who claim that man can present to Power a naked body. The sense of this vision remains dubious: whether it's man to be naked or nakedness to become man, and which the most simple and obvious thing might be—whether to consider man first and then nakedness, or vice versa.

But it is also true that there is a moment when a nakedness imposed by ideology and by the violence of Power has imposed itself upon humankind.

There has been a moment when these experiences have become terribly confused.[58] This historical episode is being obsessively reproposed to us today. It seems that Power continually needs to show us the nakedness of the eternal suffering in order to terrorize us. (A proletarian nakedness as heteronomous effect of the revolutionary passion that rocked the world and made the bourgeoisie naked? Or, rather, the posthumous revenge, a symbolic sign of punishment, the bourgeois reaction, a Hollywoodian parable of the suffered defeat, of the avoided catastrophe, of the developed counterreformation?)[59] In sum, ideology makes nakedness an absolute and assimilates it to the horror of a Nazi concentration camp! But why? There is an extreme disproportion and an impossible homology between these images, between the propagandistic urgency of Power and the actual historical reality.[60] Let's go back, then, to the fundamental alternative of the naked and the human. When the human quality is reclaimed through and/or flattened upon nakedness, what gets affirmed is a sort of natural-right assertion of man's innocence, an innocence that is impotence, in the sense of the "Muslim." To declare human, and only for this reason, he who is naked is an act of mystification, because it mistakes the man who struggles for those massacred by Nazi Power, he who refuses eugenism for an improbable naturalistic innocence. No, life and death in the camps represent nothing other than life and death in the camps. An episode of civil war in the twentieth century. A horrible spectacle of the destiny of capitalism and of the ideological disguises of its will, of the machinery of capital against the demands of freedom.[61] To use nakedness to signify life means to homologize the nature of the subject and the Power that made it naked, and to confuse in that nakedness any power of life. But life is more powerful than nakedness, and neither can "naked life" explain the terrible violence that ideology and history have perpetrated against being in the century through which we have lived.[62]

The claim of "naked life" is ideological. "Ideological" means that a statement is at the same time false with respect to the true and functional with respect to Power. We have already said that it is false: it's not possible to reduce ontology to nakedness, and man to negative essence. What "naked life" denies is the power of being, the capability of spreading into time through cooperation, struggle, and constitution. But not only is the hypothesis of "naked life" false: above all, it's correlative to the affirmation of a eugenic constitution of being, against the monster's possible power. The theory of "naked life" is so radical in its negation of power that it sees an act of terrorism in any expression of the latter. It neutralizes ontologically the very possibility of the expression of power. "Naked life" doesn't allow that "monster" which by now represents our only hope: it tries to dissolve him from within, it dilutes him into a deposit of all the violence suffered—the "Muslim," once again. Any act of resistance is in vain.

It's strange to notice that the theory of "naked life" repeats the same scenario upon which Hobbes's *Leviathan* is founded. This is the scenario of an undefended life, and as such pushed to the limit of an impossible resistance. A new *Leviathan* would have then appeared, and would have led us to this condition. It would advance all the same demands as the old ones, but more radically: it doesn't even promise us "peace," but only "life." Thus are revealed the paradox and the mystification of "naked life." When man's thought and his experience have invested life, making it common, making it *full* in its singular and creative constitutions, at this point, then, must the language of political Power declare void man's power upon life in order to reduce his actual capability to resist, and to once again subjugate his productive force. "Naked life" represents man, or, rather, presents bodies—these above all matter—on the brink of an unspeakable risk and destitution. "Naked life" is what remains after the terrorism of dying capital has been practiced upon the life and labor of the multitude. It's a scream of impotence, which resounds within a mass of defeated individualities, to make this defeat eternal, to transfer it from the individual to the singular, from the mass to the multitude. "Naked life" reaches right down there, close to matter, as Neoplatonism defines it: with this "beginning of nothingness" it constitutes bodies.[63] *Naked life is the opposite of any Spinozian power and joy of the body.* It's the exaltation of humiliation, of pity, it's medieval Christianity—not yet an experience nourished by the humanist revolution, no longer that what-is-to-come [*a-venire*] which the common hope of the proletarians had built.

In sum, through "naked life" imperial capitalism returns to the origins, and attempts—on the basis of the new intellectual and cybernetic accumulation of capital—an *operation of transfer* of the individual's and the community's rights to the sovereign.[64] Thus "naked life" is not only a falsification of poverty, an apology of alienation, but above all it puts in place new mystified images. By channeling the absolute violence of Power onto the destitution of the masses, and by intensifying extremely both the destitution and the violence, by pushing them to the point where only the necessity of staying alive emerges, the theory of "naked life" comes to represent a "return to the origins" of the capitalist state, to the imaginary of its founding myth.

The subtle consequential logic of this theory finally must be underlined: if the terrorism tied to the image of the Shoah were to fail, the one tied to the image of Hiroshima would immediately come into play. It's to be expected. Once again we have naked men, escaping death while having already been subjected to it, a senseless movement of burned and dying men . . . The fact remains that, either "Muslim" or "irradiated," in opposition to what the narrative of "naked life" claims, we are dealing first with men rather than with "naked life," with the monstrous rather than with the helpless.[65]

Bio-Power and Genetics

The other way of containing the monster (of turning him into one) is to destine him once again to the original function he had in the eugenic hierarchy—to unveil thus the spirit that inhabited the ontology, anthropology, and political science of classical antiquity—and to impose such spirit once again. The slave, the worker, he who is excluded from Power is a monster. But today there are tools to *fabricate the eugenic teleology:* why not use them? It's thus that in contemporary *genetic engineering* a will to power gets expressed that scandalizes the pious, and, on the other hand, excites the evil: there is the possibility of creating monsters/bodies that are born outside the autonomy of the genetic subject and that can be modified or corrected according to necessity—or, further, pieces of the body that can help modify other bodies, sometimes to correct genetic or pathological defects, other times to correct nature. There is the possibility of creating monsters, not those that Power feared because they subverted it, but those who are useful to eugenism so that the system of Power may function and reproduce itself such as it is.[66]

Bio-Power, therefore, is configured as Power upon the reproduction of man. Already in the past, the intervention, whether self-aware or not, upon the environment at large (which is typical of productive action from time immemorial) transformed, it's true, the general conditions of the reproduction of the world; now, however, the supporting axis of this reproduction, man's very essence, is articulated by the syntax of Power. (Heidegger has pointed out how pitiable the rehashing of the modern theories of Power appeared vis-à-vis this revolution. The poor Max Weber, as much as the followers of Machiavellianism, are all ridiculed both by scientific practices and by the theories legitimating bio-Power. Heidegger sneers in experiencing the end of humanism and the drift of technology. Isn't this what Nazism consists of? Maybe yes, maybe no: nonetheless these tendencies, translated into destiny, constitute a not so secondary element of it.)[67]

But that's not how things go. Within this great transformation, as we have seen, *the subject of the modern* (that productive and massified subject, whose capability of resistance we have encountered) has radically transformed itself—the monster has become biopolitical. By becoming biopolitical he has spread out, he is in any place where life is, he is production and communication—the monster has occupied the *postmodern scene.*

What can be done with him? After the mystification attempted by the ideological fantasy of "naked life," now it's a matter of organizing a new manipulation (at least of the metaphor proposed by this monster) through biological engineering . . . Here we are confronting, then, the attempt to dissolve the biopolitical into the biological: if man, with Charles Darwin and Marx, was the key to understanding the ape, now, in the renewed eugenic ideology, the ape becomes man's destiny . . . we must put it to work . . . bodies must be tampered with to adapt them to the eugenic order and to Power's control . . . the social division of labor must be reorganized according to this same *dispositif.* Already today, the division of labor is articulated prominently along lines of color and/or race, a logic fully at work in global economy and one that imprisons the worker's biopolitical mobility in an ignoble and destructive cage of exploitation.[68] However, simultaneously, other cages begin to appear that predispose the organism to function within the hierarchy, attuning it to a systemic performativity that brands and pigeonholes the workers into the totalitarian beehives. That these mechanisms take life as their target and get encrusted on its very Power of expression appears now possible—even more, from the point of view of the scientists of postmodern capitalist politics and economics, it appears desirable.[69]

Thus, here we are at the showdown: the monster who, by becoming *bios* and by occupying with his immaterial labor force the entire space of production, had emancipated himself from subjectifying relations (as eugenic rationality had defined them); the monster that had turned himself into "*full life*"[70]—this monster must be "re-monstrified," that is, taken back to a "rational" subordination. Here eugenics is no longer, as in the good old days, an ontological principle *plus* an abstract norm of social organization; it has become, rather, the engineering of the living predisposed to become a technique of political domination.[71] In this case, the political metaphor is just as strong as capitalism's ferocious capacity to realize materially this project. Technology posits itself in place of ontology and "the eugenic of the good and beautiful" is not ashamed to yield to such manipulations.[72]

Nonetheless, behind genetic engineering, and also behind these frightening machinations of Power, real forces do act, the very forces that the biopolitical organizes within itself. And here that violence contained in the technologies of Power can be disarmed and turned, on the contrary, into a formidable tool for alleviating in men, in singularities, in the multitude, the fear of poverty, of sickness, and of death . . . but above all it can help to free us from fear *tout court*. If we would like to define the monster in his new location (into which the postmodern forces him and against which he rebels)—and this is what we will do later—we would have then to define him as a network of stimuli and an architecture of forces (these we will call "flesh" and "body without organs"), nonetheless open, tending toward metamorphosis, toward the production of a body, and in it already chaotically caught.[73] Now, this mighty spontaneity determines the new sense of the political scene.[74] Life is enriched by the monster's presence. "Naked life" is obliterated by "flesh"—and the technological monster will not be able to deny himself to the biopolitical power of the new bodies.

Is this an enormous "heteronomy of ends"? And what if the postmodern would truly free man from fear? Because this is the real crux of the ancient and modern philosophy of Power: to create fear in order to affirm the leadership of the elites. Eugenics is a political science that doesn't give up its firstborn rights to anyone: from Plato on, it dominates the scene of knowledge, of the ruling upon public life. How can fear be eliminated from the public scene?[75]

The Monster as *Angelus Novus*

Crisis, Metamorphosis

No longer an element of resistance to, and rupture of, teleology, the monster becomes now, here, technological production of eugenics (project and predetermination of domination): this seems to be the *Grundnorm* of postmodernity. After the debacle of the modern, the theory of Power is reconstructed upon monster-subjects, included in, or (possibly) excluded from, the synthesis of Power. The biological monster, product of bio-Power, thus takes the place of the teratological monster: the *good* (as functional product of the technology of Power) takes the place of the *evil* (insofar as it is fleeting) produced by natural teleology.

However, this is the point: this description forgets (or it would even like to erase the fact that) the biopolitical monster has not only constituted the means of this development, but it has been its motor and subject. Our attention must now, therefore, return to the monster, to his strange power, to the change of his moods, and to the expression of his force: we must turn to him not as caught in the turmoil of the passage, but in its result, in the postmodern realized. We must understand how the monster lives, changes, and singularizes at once consistency and resistance.[76] Which is to say: we must ask ourselves how this biopolitical monster not only has sanctioned the crisis of the modern, but how it presents himself today, here, in the common life of the *post-*, as transformed, irreducible, with a new life power.

The identification of this strange character is certain: he is the "*General Intellect.*"[77] *General Intellect* and biopolitics lie under the same blanket, where they perform beautiful and powerful games, and present themselves as the "*full life*" of the *intellectual labor force*.

The genealogy of this biopolitical subject is very difficult to describe. It's not linear, but rather proceeds by sudden innovations, with strange and innovative curves. In the last quarter of the twentieth century, many authors tried to describe this line of chaotic constitution.[78] A first moment: the "*Cso,*" "*Corps sans organes*" [BwO, Body without Organs], that is, the indetermination of the flesh, destined to a subject who is in the process of discovering on the one thousand plateaus of existence the necessity to reorganize life and productivity beyond any determination or paradigm of the modern . . ."[79] Here there is an accumulation of power that doesn't yet correspond to the definition of a body. If singularity wants to become body, if the multitude demands to become such, at this point they are not yet one: they are flesh, but a flesh transfigured by the desire for a figure, by a will to power. Certainly, in the crisis of the modern, there is a moment when the search for subjectivation positions us at a zero point. We are flattened upon that horizon. Not for this reason is "naked life" requalified here: flesh tosses and turns *to become body*. This crisis is known.[80] It has been defined by that passage (and, beforehand, by that caesura of the modern) which took place between hegemony of material labor and hegemony of the immaterial one in production, between disciplinary world and the universes of control, between localization and globality of existence.[81] Now, through this passage, the flesh—this monstrous existence of the *General Intellect*—resists. It resists, as Deleuze says, because it *consists.*[82] Here resistance is no longer only a form of struggle but a figure of existence. Ontology is, so to speak, at its boiling point. It deposits metamorphic consistencies that are unrecoverable, irreversible. Here resistance is the hardness of the flesh, change of paradigm that reveals itself in mobility, in the color of the sea, the superficial yet ontologically mighty waves that modify the mass of the waters. What will be the productive expression of this new consistency, *what will be the form of its subjectivity?*

The answer to these questions is contingent upon the intensity of the processes of crisis and metamorphosis that interrupt and relaunch the tumultuous movements of the flesh that wants to become body of the *General Intellect*. Monstrous in this case are the change of the nature of the process and the radical modification of the figures and of the dynamics. If we were referring to the classical model of permanence and dynamic of being, that is, to the fourfold figure of the causal principle (in Aristotle), we could observe that in the transformation that we are following, there is neither a homology of forms, nor of finality; and neither continuity of matter—nor, finally, is it possible to grasp the efficient cause, because what is before us is not only a process, an accumulation, but above all a transfiguration, an explosion . . .[83]

Once we have eliminated Aristotle, have we perhaps also eliminated, definitely, the *eugenia* of Power? It would be too easy. And yet, we are there, within these experiences of metamorphosis: and if it is true that ideological proposals in the eugenic mode present themselves continually, attempt to repropose a shady continuity, and try to affirm the "rationality" of the process, it's also true that the multitude, as flesh of the *General Intellect,* searches furiously for other, corporeal genealogies, reaching out toward subjectivation. Migrations, nomadism, multidirectional movements of the multitude provoke experiences of hybridization.[84] But let's be careful: this nomadism, these dynamics of transformation and of production of subjectivity, are not, nonetheless, simply spatial experiences: there is something that in the microcosm repeats the macro, that penetrates the singular being and that traverses multiplicity;[85] finally, there are also many paths, forces, and lines that cross the borders of the species;[86] and all this, in the end, is always and continually manipulated (rigged in a positive sense) and progressively constructed . . .[87] Great metaphor or impossible practices?

We have thus described a second field of expression and of repression in the genealogy of the monster. Such field is nourished by the expansion of passions that tend toward the formation of a *new body*. By traversing flesh to open itself to subjectivity, the genealogical process is like a great motor advancing upon an unknown territory. In order to be followed, it sets signals, fixes stops, defines strata—all this configures the pathway. Here, thus, is the monster made up by a figure that is *other:* as free mass intellectuality, suddenly constituting himself with self-assured power, he has already modified any condition of life and of reproduction around himself. The monster, or, better, that intellectual movement that, from flesh, wants to turn the *General Intellect* into a body, spreads, gets defined, and is capable of taking shape more and more. Any moment of time promotes new openings for being, perhaps hopes, certainly drives, desires, and upon this tension the monster opens himself to the future. Benjamin had presented us with the slightly ominous image of the *Angelus Novus,* looking at the past as a *continuum* of defeats. In the crisis of modernity, probably, the innovation of the subject (so fatiguing in this traversing the flesh to become body) has created an ontological fabric that allows the metamorphosis to resolve the crisis itself. The postmodern monster, resistant because consistent upon another ontological foundation, is thus already, somehow, expression of the new genealogy.

The Body of the *"General Intellect"*

There are joyous passions through which we can cathect that metamorphosis that turns the monster into a subject. What moment can be more creative than that when flesh becomes body? Even the old God of Genesis, not at all inclined to benevolence, was satisfied with his work!

The fact that joy invests the self-manifesting of the subject means that the body is joyous. A great literature has developed the utopia of a world happy from the "down below" of the body: at the beginning of modernity, in the middle of the Renaissance, poetry has given a corporeal shape to the "low" joy.[88] Today it's the moment to identify in the "high" of the body, in that intellect that gives shape to common names and is the subject of processes of communication, the source of a new joy, the signal of the happy anthropological transformation. But only on the same materialist basis of that earlier apology of the low passions, because, here too, at the *center* of this discourse, lies *production.*[89]

Why turn to these images? Because they tell us, outside of any dialectics, what "to be monster" means today: a common subject, a collective force, a being other. And just like those carnivalesque masses (whose joy comes from the "below" of the body) who, as I was mentioning before, never became "people," but only multitude of desires, subverting any manipulation and any mystification, so these new intellectual multitudes, whose pleasure and productivity lie in the possibility to communicate and in collective interaction, will not become empire's *demos* but will exist in their resistance to any attempt to manipulate their power: besides the power to resist, they reclaim also the plenitude and the richness of the passions of life. The body of the *General Intellect* takes shape upon this altogether monstrous path.[90] We need a new Rabelais in order to narrate it. But not only: any materialist writer, at least once in his poetic experience, has attempted this type of imagining: Leopardi's *Batracomiomachia*, Ezra Pound's or Céline's grotesque . . . not to talk about Bertolt Brecht or Heiner Müller.

By becoming body, the *General Intellect* therefore gives shape to the monster as subject. It takes the flesh out of contact with the elusive matter of corruption and decay, it subtracts it from the cruel fantasies of "naked life." It returns the flesh to joy, and it's this progressive movement of joyous passion that (in a Spinozian manner) produces subjectivity!

But why must joy produce an ontological substratum? Because joy is constituted there where intelligence becomes collective and reason constructs common names and real community. Any mystification of what exists is, first of all, attacked by joy—which is the subversion of the existent, the capability to decide as opening and progress from flesh to common bodies, as a furthering of the capacity of doing, building, inventing being.[91]

However, his capability to decide doesn't grant the monster the *actuality* of decision. The possibility is not effective per se. On the other hand, we have already explained how the biopolitical is an ill-timed and paradoxical motor, subversive of any eugenic teleology: we have explained how the biopolitical necessarily interrupts any continuity on which the systematic quality of Power feeds. Now, it's exactly when *bios* and politics, the force of life and collective violence are coupled in a tight and rich manner—it's only then that an extreme overdetermination can still give Power a grip on the monster (that is, on the life and the commonality that he represents). But this overdetermination is so extreme as to resemble a catastrophe. From this moment on, any social struggle, any struggle of mass intellectuality, will take place in an entirely new manner, because it invests the very paradigm of the metamorphosis of Power. Whether the eugenic product or the monstrous innovation will win we really don't know: this is what's at stake.

To decide we would need a most radical democracy.[92]

In fact, what needs to be decided here is not whether or not to access the practices of biological engineering, but rather *what to do with these techniques*. The struggle has now shifted on the paradigmatic alternatives of *bios*, and the multitude is called to fight about the idea and the reality, the type, model, language of the body that it wants to assign to the *General Intellect*. There takes place, so to speak, a strange battle, a phantasmagoria of class struggle: *on the one side*, a biopolitics of the multitude, and, *on the other*, a bio-Power that takes place in terms of eugenic bio-domination. *The object of these struggles is the technology of life* as the ultimate figure of capital's technological domination upon life . . . but also as *the chance for mass intellectuality to decide upon a paradigm totally alternative to capitalism.* If the aim of the struggle is no longer a compromise about wages or about the political structures that intervene in the redistribution of profit, but rather a decision about bodies, then the dialectic is over, and the conflict is immediately about life. Subversion opens to constitution. And the "nonplace" upon which the normal movements of the multitude have been taking shape so far, now becomes *place:* it metamorphoses and gives material dimension to time and space, to struggle and decision. Indeed, it's the movements of the multitude that fix and configure the place from which decisions are made.[93]

Thus the monster who shattered eugenic teleology stands as a form of full independence, or, better, as autonomy of the multitude, as expression of the common. He is *constituent Power.* Until we haven't grasped (that is, until we have not identified with) the biopolitical monster, until then constituent Power cannot be defined. When we have grasped it, then we move within the monstrous creativity of *common living.* Finally we have gone beyond the monster: on the one hand, it has robbed the dialectic of any ability to express itself and to put in place linear paths of development, and, on the other, it produces the common.[94]

But the monster remains monster. It can be constituent Power (and thus develop a paradigm of common life) and/or body of the *General Intellect* (so that mass intelligence may have a common body)—fine, we could acknowledge all this, describe it, get used to the monster to the point of not being scared of it anymore . . . and further, he could give many cues to a philosophy of sympathy and to a phenomenology of common constitution . . . And yet, having said all that, there will still be a eugenic metaphysics and practice of domination, and therefore there will still be *an enemy:* this decides about war and is disposed to catastrophe rather than giving up the possibility to control and to use the monster, to renounce to manipulate him. Once again we have the classical tradition of Power, its celebration of war in order to subjugate the monster and to destroy freedom. But the biopolitical monster—we have seen it—is the common power of being. To destroy him is by now impossible, unless we destroy—with the monster—the world, unless we take away—with the monster—being itself. It could happen. It will not happen: the monster in which we recognize ourselves, in which we identify our destiny, is guaranteed by an indestructible genealogy of what-is to-come [*dell'a-venire*].

Time Matters

Marx, Negri, Agamben, and the Corporeal

Cesare Casarino

> *Economy of time, to this all economy ultimately reduces itself.*
>
> —Karl Marx

Time Incorporated

On the first page of an essay written in 1978, "Time and History: Critique of the Instant and the Continuum," Giorgio Agamben writes:

> The original task of a genuine revolution . . . is never merely to "change the world," but also—and first of all—to "change time." Modern political thought has concentrated its attention on history, and has not elaborated a corresponding conception of time. Even historical materialism has until now neglected to elaborate a concept of time that compares with its concept of history. Because of this omission it has been unwittingly compelled to have recourse to a concept of time dominant in Western culture for centuries, and so to harbor, side by side, a revolutionary concept of history and a traditional experience of time. The vulgar representation of time as a precise and homogeneous continuum has thus diluted the Marxist concept of history: it has become the hidden breach through which ideology has crept into the citadel of historical materialism.[1]

Having sounded such a call to arms so as to arouse this besieged and in-filtrated citadel from its bourgeois slumber, Agamben proceeds to offer his tactical-conceptual services for this most decisive battle in the ongoing philosophical war between materialism and idealism—a war that, as Althusser reminds us in "Lenin before Hegel" and elsewhere, must always be understood as a form of class struggle in its own right. It can be only destructive and self-destructive, however, to wage war without an adequate knowledge of the enemy—especially when the latter is virtually indistinguishable from oneself and indeed is incarnated in the self—and hence Agamben begins by outlining a critical genealogy of the dominant conception of time in the West. One could conceive of Agamben's account of such a dominant temporality as the unhappy offspring of the arranged marriage between, on the one hand, the circular and cyclical time of Greco-Roman antiquity, and, on the other hand, the continuous and linear time of Christianity—and the two patriarchs arranging, presiding over, and officiating at such a marriage turn out to be Aristotle and Hegel. The point is that—all important differences notwithstanding—these two conceptions of time intersect at one point, namely, the instant: in both cases, time is imaged as a homogeneous and quantifiable succession of instants in which each instant is understood as always fleeting and hence as inconsequential in and of itself, or, put differently, as acquiring significance only insofar as it negates itself. Each instant can find its realization and fulfillment only in the next instant, and so on ad infinitum—or, in Hegel's words: "'Time' . . . 'is the thing existing which is not when it is, and is when it is not.'"[2] During such a time, we are always waiting—as our redemption is always already being deferred to that impossible instant which will end all instants and abolish time altogether. This is time understood as lack, negation, and destruction that conspires against the works of human history by bringing them down to ruination and reducing them to a heap of dust—a time against which humans must fight tirelessly by spatializing, measuring, and quantifying it. Clearly, as Agamben implies at one point in his essay, such a spatialized, measurable, quantifiable, homogeneous, empty, and teleological time found its apotheosis with capitalist modernity and its purest expression in the specular and complementary temporalities of industrial wage labor and of bourgeois historicism. Against such an enemy, Agamben attempts to sketch the elements of a theory of time understood not as emptiness and negation but rather as plenitude and affirmation. To this purpose, he searches "the folds and shadows of Western cultural tradition"[3] for those forgotten, marginalized, yet always latent temporalities of interruption, discontinuity, and undeferred fulfillment that might be recuperated and marshaled in the service of a revolutionary theory of time. He finds good allies in Gnosticism and especially in Stoic philosophy and in its concept of *cairós*, namely, the event, or, as he puts it, "the abrupt and sudden conjunction where decision grasps opportunity and life is fulfilled in the moment."⁴ Unsurprisingly, Agamben sees in this concept a precursor of Heidegger's *Ereignis* as well as of Benjamin's *Jetztzeit,* namely, that time of the now that Benjamin calls upon to blast the continuum of the "homogeneous, empty time" of bourgeois historicism in his "Theses on the Philosophy of History."⁵ Agamben indicates that it is precisely to this Heidegger and to this Benjamin that we need to turn if we want to begin to think time anew and to explore the revolutionary potential of what he calls "cairological" time.

I will return to Agamben and to his proposal of a cairological time— a proposal that I find at once compelling and yet unsatisfactory, crucial and yet crucially incomplete. ⁶ For the moment, I would like to point out that— even though his critiques of the dominant conception of time are accurate as well as still relevant for our time, and even though his invocations of Heidegger and Benjamin are not to be dismissed—his arguments are nonetheless founded on a series of important omissions.

The first of such omissions may not necessarily undermine his arguments and may indeed complement them. It seems to me, in fact, that one can find alternatives to the Aristotelian-Hegelian conception of time already within Greco-Roman antiquity. I am thinking here of the temporality implicit in the ancient theory of atomism and in its concept of the *clinamen.* It is precisely to these aspects of antiquity that Althusser turns toward the end of his life so as to complete a project strikingly similar to the one Agamben articulates at the beginning of his essay, namely, to banish any residual idealism from the citadel of historical materialism. In an important 1984 interview, Althusser begins to theorize what he calls "aleatory materialism." I will quote at length:

—Do you conceive of aleatory materialism as a possible philosophy for marxism?

—Yes . . . Now we can return to Democritus and to the worlds of Epicurus. Let's remember the main thesis: before the formation of the world, an infinite number of atoms were falling parallel to each other through the void. The implications of such a statement are important: 1) before there ever was a world, absolutely nothing existed that had a *form,* and, at the same time, 2) all the elements of the world already existed separately and for all eternity before any world had come into being.

The implication of all of the above is that before the formation of the world there existed no cause, no end, no reason, and no unreason. This is the negation of all teleology—whether rational, moral, political, or aesthetic. I would add that such a materialism is not the materialism of a subject—such as God or the proletariat—but rather the materialism of a process without a subject that governs the order of its own development, without any assignable end . . .

And then the *clinamen* suddenly appears: an infinitesimal declination that one doesn't know whence, when, or how it originated. What's important is that the *clinamen* causes the atom to deviate the course of its fall through the void and causes an *encounter* with the nearest atom—and from encounter to encounter . . . a world is born.

—Are we to deduce that the origin of the whole world and of reality, of all necessity and sense is due to an aleatory deviation?

—Exactly. What Epicurus posits is that this aleatory deviation is at the origin of the world rather than the First Cause or rather than Reason. It is crucial to understand, however, that the encounter does not create any of the world's reality and that it provides atoms themselves with their own reality; without any deviation or any encounter, in fact, atoms would be no more than abstract elements without either consistency or existence. It is only after the world is constituted that the realm of reason, of necessity, and of sense is established . . .

Rather than thinking of contingency as a modality of necessity or as an exception to necessity, one ought to think of necessity as the becoming-necessary of the encounter of contingencies.

It is my intention here to insist on the existence of a materialist tradition that has not been acknowledged by the history of philosophy. This is the tradition of Democritus, Epicurus, Machiavelli, Hobbes, the Rousseau of the second discourse, Marx, and Heidegger—along with all its attendant categories, such as void, limit, margin, absence of center, displacement of the center to the margin (and vice versa), and freedom. This is a materialism of the encounter and of contingency, in other words, a materialism of the *aleatory*, that opposes itself to those materialisms that have been acknowledged as such, including that materialism that is commonly attributed to Marx, Engels, and Lenin. The latter is a materialism of necessity and teleology, which is to say, a form of idealism in disguise.[7]

Even though before the world comes into being one is faced here by the formless, undifferentiated, static, and, indeed, atemporal temporality of eternity, the atomic collisions occasioned by the deviation of the *clinamen* incept a wholly different temporality. It is only at the moment of such collisions—that is, it is only as the world comes into being through a series of contingent encounters—that one can speak of necessity. This means that one cannot conceive of contingency as the ancillary opposite of a preexisting necessity that the latter negates, incorporates, masters, and subordinates through a process of sublation. Necessity, rather, consists of a contingent encounter that is immediately posited as necessary. Things happen: all sorts of encounters take place all the time, and we have no say in the matter—but as they are taking place they can be affirmed as necessary and can be actively turned into lives and worlds of our own making over and over again.[8] Within this paradigm, time and history are not inimical to each other: with the onset of the *clinamen*, there is no other time outside of a fully human and fully historical time, there is no temporality other than the temporality of human history intended as the product of a praxis of freedom that has no predetermined beginning, end, or telos. Such a praxis is governed neither by absolute necessity nor by pure contingency, which is another way of saying that freedom is available to us neither within the realm of traditional metaphysics nor within the realm of contemporary critiques of metaphysics of the constructivist, culturalist, discursivist, or historicist varieties. The realm of freedom, rather, is always already being constituted here and now in our daily struggle to live the events of our lives as fully contingent and yet urgently necessary at one and the same time. This is the struggle, on the one hand, to forbid either contingency or necessity to be turned into the transcendental determinations of our histories, and, on the other hand, to think contingency and necessity as immanent to each other and as different—distinct yet indiscernible—aspects of the very same reality. Or, put differently, freedom consists of the productive moment when a contingent encounter becomes necessary—that is, when, for better and for worse, such an encounter is seized and claimed as irreparably our own—thereby producing another contingent encounter, and so on.[9] Clearly, such a moment is closely related to that *cairós* that Agamben defines as "the abrupt and sudden conjunction where decision grasps opportunity and life is fulfilled in the moment." It seems to me, however, that while Agamben's *cairós* is not steeped in the flux of becoming and is not productive of other such fulfilled moments, the deviations and collisions occasioned by Althusser's *clinamen* repeatedly produce these moments in a chain reaction of unforeseeable becomings. The temporality that appertains to such a chain reaction of becoming—which is the temporality of the infinite productivity of being—is a temporality of radical experimentation. (And I believe this is also the temporality regulating what Marx and Engels first, and Leon Trotsky later, referred to as "permanent revolution.")

In Agamben's account of these matters, however, there is yet another and more glaring omission. There is indeed another thinker who articulated a radical critique of bourgeois temporality as well as produced elements toward a revolutionary theory of time—and his name, of course, is Marx. I do not mean to suggest that Agamben does not engage with Marx in his essay. What I mean, rather, is that Marx is missing there as a theorist of time in his own right. After having discussed Marx's theory of history as praxis—or, more precisely, his theory of praxis as "the founding act of history" by which human beings hence reveal and produce their nature as essentially historical—Agamben writes: "Marx did not elaborate a theory of time adequate to his revolutionary idea of history, but the latter clearly cannot be reconciled with the Aristotelian and Hegelian concept of time as a continuous and infinite succession of punctual and precise instants."[10] Agamben suggests, in other words, that a theory of time adequate to Marx's revolutionary theory of history is somehow somewhere already implicit in the latter. This is all true. And yet I think it is important to go further and to insist that the thinker who wrote many pages on the relation between socially necessary labor time and surplus labor time—to mention just one among the many relevant questions in Marx's work to which I will return—is a thinker who found it indispensable to grapple explicitly and directly with the possibility of another temporality that would be qualitatively different from, as well as antagonistic to, that homogeneous temporality of quantifiable and measurable units that during capitalist modernity found its perfected historical form par excellence in the temporality of the wage. There is a Marx who understood well what Agamben accurately claims that many—perhaps most—Marxists have never understood, namely, the necessity to change time.

It is precisely to this Marx that Antonio Negri turns in order to elaborate his own revolutionary theory of temporality, or, rather, what he calls at once "the communist idea of time" and "a new proletarian practice of time."[11] Such a reconceptualization of time is implicit already in his 1968 essay "Marx on the Cycle and on the Crisis" as well as in his 1978 work on Marx's *Grundrisse,* namely, *Marx beyond Marx.* It becomes fully explicit, however, in what I consider to be one of his most important works, *The Constitution of Time: The Timepieces of Capital and Communist Liberation*—written in prison between 1980 and 1981. This breathtaking tour de force, which engages with all the main figures and turning points of the Western metaphysics of time, clearly deserves a more thorough engagement than the one I am about to undertake. For my present project, what I wish to highlight and to investigate in particular is the following complex of relations between Negri's and Agamben's meditations on time: while several of Negri's theoretical premises in *The Constitution of Time* coincide with Agamben's own conceptual points of departure, the respective reconceptualizations of time that result from such shared premises, on the one hand, are quite different from each other, and, on the other hand, ultimately reach very similar impasses. Let us proceed gradually.

Much like Agamben, Negri maintains that the dominant concept of time in the history of Western thought—including in most historical materialism—has been dictated by the Aristotelian-Hegelian logic that spatializes time by dividing it into discrete units, namely, that subordinates and enslaves time to space so as in effect to neutralize its most fructiferous and disquieting aspects. This shared premise, however, leads Negri in a different direction, namely, to Marx: he theorizes—via selective analyses of both the *Grundrisse* and *Capital,* volume 1—the heterogeneous temporalities of the real subsumption of all social relations by capital, or, the temporalities of what in a different intellectual idiom is referred to as the moment of late capitalism.[12] Even though these contemporary temporalities have a crucial feature in common with Agamben's cairological time—as in both cases we are faced with a decidedly nonquantifiable and nonmeasurable time—Negri, unlike Agamben, is concerned ultimately with the question of production, that is, with the productivity of time, and hence articulates a concept of time as essentially *productive,* as constitutionally *collective,* and as potentially *constitutive* of new, antagonistic, and revolutionary subjectivities.

For Negri, the temporality of production—that is, the time most expressive of our productive and creative energies—is at once a temporality that cannot be measured as quantity and yet the temporality that capital endeavors to quantify and to measure all the time so as to control it and employ it in the extraction of surplus value: the logic of equivalence is identified here as the harness of the incommensurable, as the strategy of containment that becomes instrumental for the continued exploitation of that which is fundamentally uncontainable about time. It seems to me, moreover, that for Negri there is no time outside such a time beyond all measure, that is, there is no time other than what I called earlier the temporality of the infinite productivity of being: time *is* the turbulent and intractable becoming of substance, time *is* productivity—and nothing else. It is then under capitalist modernity that time as productivity is at once exponentially intensified and denigrated, at once exponentially potentiated and objectified: this is the historical conjuncture when the double-edged liberation of productive forces from the various yokes of premodern social arrangements increasingly realizes the vital potentials latent in time since time immemorial as well as increasingly turns time into dead and deadening time. It is also in this sense that postmodernity can be said to constitute the full fruition of the projects of modernity: if the real subsumption of society by capital has entailed that there is no longer virtually any aspect and indeed any time of our lives that is not productive for capital, time then—Negri seems to suggest—is that which capital needs now more than ever and yet that which capital always hopes against all hope to reduce to zero. The impossible dream of capital, after all, has been always to have production and circulation in no time and without time, that is, to disengage production from time and to relegate time to its ontologically mortified and increasingly inadequate role of measure.[13] (Incidentally, this impossible dream is nowhere so powerfully expressed and succinctly encapsulated as in that now very old British Airways advertisement for a Concorde flight that left London at 10:30 a.m. and arrived in New York City an hour earlier—an advertisement whose triumphant slogan was "speed: the conquest of time.")

I believe it is precisely such an emphasis on the productivity of time that leads Negri toward the end of *The Constitution of Time* to undertake a scathing critique of Benjamin's conception of the *Jetztzeit* as well as of Agamben's recuperation of the latter. Negri writes:

> Capital presents itself not only as measure and as system but also as *progress*. This definition is essential for its internal as well as external legitimization. From this perspective political economy is entirely directed towards drawing the *innovative element* that history—in any case—produces inside the time of administration (that is, the time of accumulation as administration, the reversible and cyclical time of the eternal return). *Jetzt-Zeit*, innovative punctualness, utopia: capital considers them as its own. Progress is the eternal return lit up by the flash of a *Jetzt-Zeit*. Administration is illuminated by charisma. The demonic city is enlightened by grace.

The elements of innovation are reduced to numerical and quantitative units, and only as such are they channeled back into ordained and enlightened progress. Progress is the figuration of a process that proceeds by leaps and bounds and yet in which all the factors can be recast in terms of proportion. The difference is only quantitative. The economic cycle is the clearest example of capitalistic progress: all of its terms are modified according to essentially quantitative effects and trajectories. In short, *Jetzt-Zeit,* utopia, present themselves as innovation—as the touch of the real—*within the routine* of the temporal being of command. Utopia and routine present themselves as *abstract identity,* as necessity. Economic determinism, the invisible hand that is natural law and that hence transforms itself into law of the state while retaining the numinous and inescapable character of the law of nature: here we have reached the hard kernel in which *necessity* identifies itself with *interest* and with the progressive *self-representation* of capital.[14]

In this perverse reading of Benjamin's theory of time, the *Jetztzeit* is identified as the true motor of progress. Far from being disruptive of the bourgeois myth of progress, the *Jetztzeit* is that creative flash in history which—after its sudden, glorious, and only too episodic flare—is retranslated into quantified and measured time, and hence flattened back into the relentless march of progress precisely because it was only a flash. Far from being disruptive of capital, the *Jetztzeit* provides capital with invaluable elements of innovation, with indispensable creative energies. The problem with conceiving of innovative and creative time in Benjamin's terms, in other words, is that the *Jetztzeit* is always eminently co-optable. It is thanks to the endlessly repeated co-optation of the *Jetztzeit* that capital can represent itself as it needs to, namely, as the progressive force of history. Or, put differently, it is only from the standpoint of such a self-legitimizing self-representation of capital that the productive time of creativity and innovation can be understood (and hence seized and recuperated) as *Jetztzeit*—which is how utopian yearning becomes then indistinguishable from routine labor. After all—Negri seems to be implying—since when have not epiphanies and illuminations of all sorts been ultimately useful for oppressive and exploitative systems of command? Since when has capital not been able to learn and bounce back from revolutionary impulse thus conceived?

Negri's critique goes even further. While discussing how such a capitalist conception of the *Jetztzeit* has also informed the socialist theory of revolution, he comments thus on Benjamin's fourteenth and sixteenth theses on the philosophy of history:

Such a conception of time is ruinous. Far from being the destruction of historicism and of its perverse political outcomes, the conception of the messianic *Jetzt-Zeit* is the utmost modernization of reactionary thought: it is the conversion of historical, plural, multi-versatile, and punctum-like materials into the thaumaturgical illusion of empty innovation. The conception of the messianic *Jetzt-Zeit* reduces the tautology of subsumption to *mysticism,* and mysticism always stinks of the boss (no matter what Agamben and Fachinelli say about it). In Benjamin, one relives a paradox that is at once the equivalent and the opposite paradox of stoicism, namely the paradox of the creationist conception of time-as-measure. Saint Augustine writes: "time was made simultaneously with the world, and with the creation of the world change and movement were also created, as appears clear from the order of the first six or seven days.'" Precisely. If an innovative methodology establishes itself in a formal universe, it loses the flavor of the materialism and of the creativity of the only creative time—the time of the masses. The historical continuum, thus, is reduced to an elementary series and hence can be then reorganized systemically. The only real practice of "the time of the now" is that of the abstract rupture, of the abstract unit of productive time—and hence we have a mechanical and methodical dimension of the equilibrium. *The time of the now, the Jetzt-Zeit, is a particular form of time-as-measure.* From this point of view, a construction of time such as Benjamin's functions perfectly as a mediation between, on the one hand, the productive monism of the systemic conceptions of the later [Max] Weber and of the later [Hans] Kelsen, and, on the other hand, the *socialist and insurrectionalist practice* of the state. Revolutionary rationality is grafted onto, and co-inserted into, technocratic rationality: all in all, what we are dealing with here is an implosion of development towards zero time that is anticipated by the zero of insurrectional initiative, the zero of insurrectional time. Recently, Erik Olin Wright—in his 1979 *Class, Crisis and the State*—has reconstructed the concept of administrative rationality in Weber and Lenin by tracing synoptic correlations between the two. The negation of real time in the dimension of measure and of administrative reversibilty, hence, is everywhere equally a medium and instrument of "rationality," that is, of that formal and atemporal rationality that is sealed in illusory fashion in the original act of the *Grundnorm,* of charisma, or of *insurrection*—all of which are foundational *Jetzt-Zeiten.*[15]

Much to Benjamin's chagrin, he is cast here in the sadly farcical role of a messianic dispatcher shuttling back and forth in history from the bourgeois assemblies of the Reichstag to the proletarian storming of the Winter Palace—both of which, it turns out, were informed by the same understanding of the state and by the very same rationality. (And, of course, we must keep in mind that when Negri was writing these polemical pages, so-called real socialism was still alive—if not well and if not for long.) Bourgeois order and socialist revolution alike found the state by a flight into transcendence and hence attempt to put a stop to that truly creative time which never can stop and which is always already there, namely, the immanent and revolutionary time of the multitude. (In a different intellectual idiom, one could say that they both at once exploit and foreclose the unconscious, that they exploit the unconscious by foreclosing it.) It matters little whether such a flight into transcendence takes the historical form of *Grundnorm* or of insurrection, as both these forms share in the identical structure of a *Jetztzeit* that serves a rationality inimical to all time. What Negri finds so pernicious about the *Jetztzeit* is that it transcendentalizes the plane of immanence constituted by time as productivity. The time of the now is zero time, that is, the negation of the real time of production. The problem faced by Benjamin was real enough: bourgeois historicism sublates time into the history of progress. The solution he found to this problem, however, backfired: in attempting to escape the history of progress, the *Jetztzeit* ends up escaping time altogether. Benjamin's "Messianic cessation of happening"[16] in the end turns out to be precisely that negation of time as productivity which capital itself—whether in its bourgeois or in its socialist forms—at once yearns for and can never accomplish. Now we can see that if the *Jetztzeit* is so co-optable, that is so because it has cut itself loose from the productive flux of becoming: once separated from its life supply, it becomes easy enough to reduce it to the abstract unit of time as measure and to put it in the service of the time of death.[17]

These are harsh words indeed. And I believe that such a reading of Benjamin is at once accurate and yet ungenerous: Negri—much like Agamben—is ultimately wrong by virtue of being only partially right. I will return to such an assessment of these matters. For the moment, I would like to show briefly how this same problematic reappears and is negotiated in an apparently very different form, idiom, and context. In a 1994 essay titled "Desire and Pleasure," Gilles Deleuze clarifies and elaborates further some of the engagements with Michel Foucault that he had articulated a decade earlier in his work on the latter:

> The last time we saw each other, Michel told me, with much
> kindness and affection, something like, I cannot bear the word *desire:*
> even if you use it differently, I cannot keep myself from thinking or
> living that desire = lack, or that desire is repressed. Michel added,
> whereas myself, what I call pleasure is perhaps what you call desire;
> but in any case I need another word than *desire.*
> Obviously . . . this is more than a question of words. Because
> for my part I can scarcely tolerate the word *pleasure.* But why? For
> me, desire implies no lack; neither it is a natural given. It is an
> *agencement* [assemblage] of heterogeneous elements that function . . .
> And above all, it implies the constitution of a plane of immanence
> or a "body without organs," which is defined solely by zones of
> intensity, thresholds, gradients, flows. This body is as much
> biological as it is collective and political; the *agencements* of desire
> are made and unmade upon it, and it supports the cutting edges of
> deterritorialization or the lines of flight of the *agencements.* It varies
> (the body without organs of feudalism is not the same as that of
> capitalism) . . . I cannot give any positive value to pleasure because
> pleasure seems to me to interrupt the immanent process of desire;
> pleasure seems to me to be on the side of strata and organization;
> and it is in one and the same movement that desire is subject to the
> law from within and scanned by pleasures from without; in both
> cases there is the negation of the field of immanence proper to
> desire. I tell myself that it is not by chance that Michel attaches a
> certain importance to Sade, and myself on the contrary to Masoch.
> It would not be enough to say that I am masochistic, and Michel
> sadistic. That would be nice, but it's not true. What interests me in
> Masoch are not the pains but the idea that pleasure interrupts the

positivity of desire and the constitution of its field of immanence . . .
Pleasure seems to me to be the only means for a person or a
subject to "find itself again" in a process that surpasses it. It is a
reterritorialization. And from my point of view, desire is related to
the law of lack and to the norm of pleasure in the same manner.[18]

Deleuze's reservations with regard to pleasure are the same reservations
Negri expresses with regard to the *Jetztzeit*: both pleasure and the *Jetztzeit*
interrupt becoming and transcendentalize the plane of immanence constituted by an infinitively productive principle that is to be understood not as an
originary and pregiven natural life force other than and outside of time and
history but rather as a fully natural, fully temporal, and fully historical force
at one and the same time. (And it matters little that Deleuze calls such a principle "desire" while Negri calls it "time" because both are modeled upon, and,
indeed, are different names for, Spinoza's substance.) It would not be enough
to say that Negri and Deleuze are Spinozians while Agamben and Foucault
are Heideggerians. That would be nice, but it's not true. It is only partially
true. Ultimately, one must refuse to choose and must insist on retaining and
affirming both these sets of apparently mutually exclusive positions at once.
I am not, however, calling for a synthesis between the two that would inevitably beget some hapless average progeny. Thankfully, these are not synthesizable elements: rather, they are different—distinct yet indiscernible—
aspects of the same reality; they are alternately virtual and actual, contingent
and necessary facets of the very same immanence; they are part and parcel of
the same torque of time. And lest you think I have forgotten about Marx, let
me add here that I believe he is precisely the thinker who refuses to choose.[19]

Having articulated the general scope of Negri's and Agamben's important projects on time, I want now to pause and reflect on their shared limit.
What concerns me here is that—all points of tangency, of intersection, and
of divergence aside—both projects in the end butt up against the intractable
matter of corporeality. It seems that at the end of time there stands the body
and its demands forever waiting to be attended to.

Let us now retrace our steps. After having invoked Heidegger and Benjamin, Agamben suddenly offers these brief speculations on the last page of his
essay:

Yet for everyone there is an immediate and available experience on
which a new concept of time could be founded . . . : it is pleasure.

Aristotle had realized that pleasure was a heterogeneous thing in relation to the experience of quantified, continuous time. "The form . . . of pleasure"—he writes in the *Nicomachean Ethics*—"is perfect at any moment," adding that pleasure, unlike movement, does not occur in a space of time, but is "within each now something whole and complete" . . .

This does not mean that pleasure has its place in eternity. The Western experience of time is split between eternity and continuous linear time. The dividing point through which the two relate is the instant as a discrete, elusive point. Against this conception, which dooms any attempt to master time, there must be opposed one whereby the true site of pleasure, as man's primary dimension, is neither precise, continuous time nor eternity, but history. Contrary to what Hegel stated, it is only as the source and site of happiness that history can have a meaning for man. In this sense, Adam's seven hours in Paradise are the primary core of all authentic historical experience. For history is not, as the dominant ideology would have it, man's servitude to continuous linear time, but man's liberation from it: the time of history and the *cairós* in which man, by his initiative, grasps favorable opportunity and chooses his own freedom in the moment . . .

True historical materialism does not pursue an empty mirage of continuous progress along infinite linear time, but is ready at any moment to stop time, because it holds the memory that man's original home is pleasure. It is this time which is experienced in authentic revolutions, which, as Benjamin remembers, have always been lived as a halting of time and an interruption of chronology. But a revolution from which there springs not a new chronology, but a qualitative alteration of time (a *cairology*), would have the weightiest consequence and would alone be immune to absorption into the reflux of restoration. He who, in the *epochē* of pleasure, has remembered history as he would remember his original home, will bring this memory to everything, will exact this promise from each instant: he is the true revolutionary and the true seer, released from time not at the millennium, but *now*.[20]

As we saw earlier, there is a strict homology between pleasure and the *Jetzt-zeit*—and hence it should come as no surprise that Agamben's *cairós* finds its purest expression precisely in the moment of pleasure. By now, we can already hear what Negri and Deleuze might have to say about such a cairology of pleasure—namely, it interrupts becoming, it transcendentalizes the plane of immanence of the infinite productivity of being, and so on—and I believe that their critiques would be largely sound. And yet I am not convinced that to forgo completely a conception of pleasure is a desirable or even feasible solution. Agamben's proposal, after all, has the merit of making the question of corporeality inescapable for any historical-materialist and revolutionary theory of time—and vice versa. It might be possible to begin to push Agamben's arguments further by affirming and drawing attention to that which in these arguments at best remains entirely implicit, namely, to the *collective formation* of the cairological moment of pleasure, when contingency is turned into necessity and history is made. I take pleasure to be always collective by definition: there is no such a thing as a solitary pleasure because any pleasure at the very least puts corporeal boundaries into question by instantiating a condition in which a body literally comes out of itself—and it goes without saying that this is also the case with the pleasures of thought. If I insist on the fact that any pleasure implies a collective process of formation, that is so because it is precisely such a formless, nonquantifiable, nonmeasurable process that is at once fomented and neutralized, exploited and mortified by capital in the various forms of pleasure-as-commodity that continuously interpellate our bodies as subjects of that all-subsuming and all-consuming postmodern form of production which is consumption. Indeed, the fact that in the moment of real subsumption we witness in the First World an exponential proliferation of prepackaged pleasures to be safely consumed according to the guidelines of the most complacent and anodyne hedonism—that very fact is an index of how increasingly difficult yet necessary it is for capital to anchor firmly the collective formation of pleasure to the commodity form, that is, of how increasingly productive yet threatening such a collective process is for capital today.[21]

As one might expect, it is the question of the collective that constitutes the focus of Negri's own attempt to conjugate the temporal with the corporeal. Toward the end of *The Constitution of Time*, Negri increasingly alludes to, yet repeatedly defers, the necessity to study what he calls "the phenomenology of collective praxis," namely, "the series of phenomenological relations that *from the bodies of individuals* extend to *the materiality of collective composition.*"[22] Finally, in a section titled "The Body and the Time of Constitution," Negri decides that the time has come to take up this analysis directly, and hence poses the question of what he calls "collective corporeality," namely, "the individualization of the social subjectivities that make up the class composition emerging at the level of subsumption."[23] Even though Negri importantly shows here how it is just such collective corporeality in the first place that constitutes the corporeality of individual bodies rather than the other way around, it is also here that the analysis becomes increasingly unsure and makes recourse to repeated leaps of faith. On the one hand, Negri insists that the "phenomenology of collective praxis is a *process* without laws . . . an ensemble of multiple times that only with the fullness of liberation will achieve definite determinations"[24]—thereby implying also that at present one cannot be more precise regarding the specific modalities of being of this process. On the other hand, he also insists that such a liberation of time "entails and demands the acknowledgement of collective antagonism, the molding of antagonism into constitutive instrument, and the capacity to reach higher forms of *collective corporeality* (beyond individuality, beyond the family—and towards increasingly complex and versatile communities)."[25] On the one hand, he declares that "the recomposition of bodies" attendant to and constitutive of such higher forms of collective corporeality "exhibits and manifests the highest level of recomposition and self-determination of the versatile multiplicity of the singular times of liberation: the body and the choruses, the forms of love and of collective recomposition,"[26] and proceeds to envisage rapturously a "temporal, collective, corporeal body" as well as what he calls a "corporeal communism."[27] On the other hand, he also gives up and defers the whole project yet again: "All this should undergo a description and a definition that we cannot provide here in these 'prolegomena.'"[28] And there is no doubt that such a project still awaits its time and indeed constitutes a crucial and unresolved question in Negri's thought. Twenty years later, for example, toward the end of Hardt and Negri's *Empire*, we come across a section titled "Time and Body (The Right to a Social Wage)" that, on the one hand, is at the very least as suggestive and compelling as anything we can read in *The Constitution of Time*, and, on the other hand, does not yet offer anything more concrete than what we found there either.[29]

To recapitulate: In both Agamben and Negri, an attempt to formulate a revolutionary theory of time leads to and ends with the question of corporeality. While both thinkers declare this question to be essential for such a reconceptualization of time, they ultimately fall short of attending to its demanding singularity: their projects are—if in different ways—at once indispensable and insufficient for the symbiotic articulation of a revolutionary time and a revolutionary body, that is, for the production of communism. These are pathbreaking projects precisely in the sense that they open up paths that subsequently they do not explore much further.

Marx's Pleasure

We need to go further. But how? Here, I would like to take a detour through the Marx of the *Grundrisse,* so as to return in the end to the symbiosis of time, body, and communism. The first two notebooks of the *Grundrisse* are entirely centered on an analytic of money.[30] For our present purposes, these lengthy and intricate arguments can be summarized by saying that money is understood by Marx as having three semiautonomous and at times simultaneous functions: (1) money as measure of value, (2) money as medium of exchange and circulation, and (3) money as money. What concerns me here is money in its third role, in which it sublates the other two and transcends the process of precapitalist circulation in order to become the independent and general form of wealth. Or, as Marx puts it: "From its servile role, in which it appears as mere medium of circulation, [money] suddenly changes into the lord and god of commodities. It represents the divine existence of commodities, while they represent its earthly form"—and, in a sense, what Marx refers to as a sudden change in the money form succinctly describes the passage from the feudalist premodern to capitalist modernity.[31] As soon as it becomes independent from specific forms of wealth—that is, as soon as it realizes in modernity that potential for abstraction that had been latent in it all along—money, however, suddenly splits further into two mutually negating and mutually determining functions: on the one hand, money as money, that is, money as "the general form of wealth," and, on the other hand, money as capital, that is, money as "the material representative of general wealth." Marx writes:

> Money in its final, completed character now appears in all directions as a contradiction, a contradiction which dissolves itself, drives towards its own dissolution. As the *general form of wealth,* the whole of riches stands opposite it. It is their pure abstraction—hence, fixated as such, a mere conceit. Where wealth as such seems to appear in an entirely material, tangible form, its existence is only in my head, it is a pure fantasy. Midas. On the other side, as *material representative of general wealth,* it is realized only by being thrown

back into circulation, to disappear in exchange for the singular, particular modes of wealth. It remains in circulation, as medium of circulation; but for the accumulating individual, it is lost, and this disappearance is the only possible way to secure it as wealth. To dissolve the things accumulated in individual gratification is to realize them. The money may then be again stored up by other individuals, but then the same process begins anew. I can really posit its being for myself only by giving it up as mere being for others. If I want to cling to it, it evaporates in my hand to become a mere phantom of real wealth. Further: [the notion that] to accumulate it is to increase it, [since] its own quantity is the measure of value, turns out again to be false. If the other riches do not [also] accumulate, then it loses its value in the measure in which it is accumulated. What appears as its increase is in fact its decrease. Its independence is a mere semblance; its independence of circulation exists only in view of circulation, exists as dependence on it . . . If negated as the mere *general form of wealth*, it must then realize itself in the particular substances of real wealth; but in the process of proving itself really to be the *material representative* of the totality of wealth, it must at the same time preserve itself as the general form. Its very entry into circulation must be a moment of its staying at home and its staying at home must be an entry into circulation. That is to say that as realized exchange value it must be simultaneously posited as the process in which exchange value is realized. This is at the same time the negation of itself as purely objective form, as a form of wealth external and accidental to individuals.[32]

Money qua money cannot keep still. Within a fully developed system of capitalist circulation, to stop money—that is, merely to accumulate it—is tantamount to relegating and reducing it once again to its first two and limited functions, in which it no longer appears as the independent and general form of wealth. If it is to realize its full potential for abstraction, money must circulate. And yet, as soon as it circulates it loses precisely its fixed abstract form of independent and general wealth and becomes indistinguishable from the process by which specific forms of wealth—namely, commodities—are exchanged. In order to realize itself as an abstract form, money must negate itself qua abstraction by continuously realizing itself in the circulating commodity instead. This means that money becomes independent of commodities only to the extent that it becomes fully dependent on the circulation of those commodities: this transcendent god achieves its transcendence only by abjuring it in repeatedly being brought back to earth and reincarnated in each and every successive instant of an immanent process of circulation that is nonetheless ruled by such a transcendence in the first place. Amid such mesmerizing dialectical somersaults, we witness the beginning of an investigation concerning the temporality of capitalist circulation that Marx will proceed to develop in later sections of the *Grundrisse*. The temporality governing such circulation is a homogeneous succession of quantified instants in which each and every instant realizes itself only in the next instant, thereby negating itself in and as the present instant: money realizes itself by accruing to money; but money accrues to money only in the next transaction, only in the next instant of realization—and so on ad infinitum. If Hegel says that "'Time' . . . 'is the thing existing which is not when it is, and is when it is not,'" Marx says that money is the thing existing which is not when it is, and is when it is not (and even though they might be articulating the same paradox, they offer very different solutions for it). The time of money is the time of circulation, and the time of circulation is Aristotelian-Hegelian time: it is only within such a paradigm of spatialized, quantifiable, measurable time that time = money. In a world ruled by such an equation, we are always kept waiting because money is always already waiting for itself. It is a short leap from here to arguing—as Marx does argue in some of the most prophetic pages of the *Grundrisse*—that such a process of circulation leads to a society ruled by debt and to a definition of the human as always already indebted.[33] These pages are not far from that remarkable essay in which Deleuze uses Foucault as a springboard to dive into and articulate the passage from modern disciplinary society to postmodern control society in which "a man is no longer a man confined but a man in debt."[34]

Such meditations on the money form lead Marx also in the direction of a historical-materialist genealogy of affect. In a passage that is as powerful and as perceptive regarding the political historicity of affect as the best pages of the third and fourth sections of Spinoza's *Ethics* as well as of Nietzsche's *Genealogy of Morals,* Marx produces the concept of greed as that peculiarly modern affect that appertains to money in its third, fully realized, fully abstract, and fully modern form:

> Money is therefore not only *an* object, but is *the* object of greed. It is essentially *auri sacra fames* [that accursed hunger for gold]. Greed

as such, as a particular form of the drive, i.e. as distinct from the
craving for a particular kind of wealth, e.g. for clothes, weapons,
jewels, women, wine etc., is possible only when general wealth,
wealth as such, has become individualized in a particular thing, i.e.
as soon as money is posited in its third quality. Money is therefore
not only the object but the fountainhead of greed. The mania for
possessions is possible without money; but greed itself is the
product of a definite social development, not *natural*, as opposed to
historical. Hence the wailing of the ancients about money as the
source of all evil. Hedonism [*Genussucht*] in its general form and
miserliness [*Geiz*] are two particular forms of monetary greed.
Hedonism in the abstract presupposes an object which possesses
all pleasures in potentiality. Abstract hedonism realizes that
function of money in which it is the *material representative of
wealth;* miserliness, in so far as it is only the general form of wealth
as against its particular substances, the commodities. In order to
maintain it as such, it must sacrifice all relationship to the objects of
particular needs, must abstain, in order to satisfy the need of greed
for money as such. Monetary greed, or mania for wealth, necessarily
brings with it the decline and fall of the ancient communities.
Hence it is the antithesis to them. It is itself the community, and
can tolerate none other standing above it. But this presupposes the
full development of exchange values, hence a corresponding
organization of society.[35]

If greed is that affect that realizes its full potential as soon as money is
posited in its third function, and if money in its third function immediately
splits off into two mutually negating and mutually determining forms, then
greed too is revealed here to consist of two such opposite and complementary forms, namely, miserliness and hedonism—which name a cathexis on
money as money and on money as capital, respectively. It should come as
no surprise, thus, that the Janus-faced affect of greed is steeped in the self-
contradictory temporality of circulation. Both miserliness and hedonism
are governed by the time of money—the former negatively and the latter
positively. Miserliness can achieve pleasure only through an absolute sacrifice of time: the miser renounces the present and the future by attempting
to step outside of time altogether; the miser forgoes all possible present and
future pleasures that money can buy for the pleasure of money in its form

of atemporal and transcendent abstraction. Such a pleasure, however, is not only a terminally impoverished form of pleasure; it is also an impossible one. In order to satisfy what Marx calls "the need of greed for money as such," the miser stops the relentless movement of money by withdrawing it from circulation and by accumulating it. Whereas such an accumulation might have satisfied this need in the context of premodern circulation, within a fully developed system of capitalist circulation, to accumulate money as money is to forgo precisely that which the miser yearns for—namely, its characteristic of abstraction—because that characteristic now can realize itself only by negating itself in circulation. Hedonism too is essentially sacrificial: if miserliness sacrifices time through abstinence, hedonism sacrifices it through incontinence. Marx writes that hedonism "presupposes an object which possesses all pleasures in potentiality"—and that object is money as the material representative of general wealth, that is, money as capital. As we saw earlier, however, this object is eminently slippery and fluid as it is indistinguishable from that immanent process that is nonetheless ruled by money as transcendence and that is the endlessly repeated exchange of commodities. The hedonist, hence, is caught in circulation and is forever leaping from commodity to commodity in search of that final commodity that will surely grant the ultimate pleasure—the testosterone-activating new H3 Hummer, the sexiest new model of BlackBerry® smartphone, the hottest new compact disk by the trendiest new band, the latest theoretical paradigm in the marketplace of ideas, the faster, slicker, cutting-edge, state-of-the-art, new-generation, MacBook laptop computer on which this whole book was written, and so on. This is "man in debt" indeed. If money as capital "possesses all pleasures in potentiality," each actual pleasure can then be realized only in the next pleasure, each present pleasure is always already waiting for the coming pleasure—and hence pleasure is achieved only by not having any pleasure at all. In the end, both the hedonist and the miser may come into money—but their pleasure never comes. And it cannot come by definition because the miser is addicted neurotically to eternity and the hedonist is addicted hysterically to an always already deferred future—and they both share in a metaphysics of time as lack, negation, and death.

But there are yet other pleasures waiting to be attended to in the *Grundrisse*. While discussing the relation between socially necessary labor time and the wage, Marx wages a powerful critique of the discourse of "*self-denial.*" This is a critique of the capitalist injunction that the worker ameliorate his condition by (a) "saving, cutting corners in his consumption" as well as by

(b) "denying himself more and more rest, and in general denying himself any existence other than his existence as worker, and being as far as possible a worker only."[36] Marx draws attention to the crucial difference between these two forms of self-denial. From the standpoint of capitalist circulation, the injunction to save and to cut consumption should not be implemented by workers "generally . . . and as a rule": if all workers were to comply with this injunction to the letter, in fact, there would be catastrophic consequences for capital, given the damage that this "would do to general consumption . . . and hence to production."[37] In other words, the boss wishes only his own workers qua workers to practice this form of self-denial, for he experiences all other workers not as workers at all but rather as potential consumers. Such an injunction, thus, serves mostly the ideological function of supporting the bourgeois myth of parthenogenesis: it was precisely by practicing such asceticism that the capitalist became a self-made capitalist in the first place—or, at any rate, that is how the story goes. That other form of self-denial that enjoins the worker to be nothing other than a worker, however, would really constitute the proverbial dream come true of capital: in this case, all of the time socially necessary to reproduce that most precious of commodities which is the bodily existence of the worker would be sublated by surplus labor time and swallowed back into the process of production. In the context of a critique of both forms of self-denial, Marx writes:

> The most [the worker] can achieve on the average with his
> self-denial is to be able to better endure the fluctuations of prices—
> high and low, their cycle—that is, he can only distribute his
> consumption better, but never attain wealth. And that is actually
> what the capitalists demand. The worker should save enough at the
> times when business is good to be able more or less to live in the
> bad times, to endure short time or the lowering of wages . . . That is,
> the demand that [workers] should always hold to a minimum of
> life's pleasures and make crises easier to bear for the capitalist etc.
> Maintain themselves as pure labouring machines and as far as
> possible pay their own wear and tear. Quite apart from the sheer
> brutalization to which this would lead—and such a brutalization
> itself would make it impossible even to strive for wealth in general
> form, as money, stockpiled money—(and the worker's participation
> in the higher, even cultural satisfactions, the agitation for his own
> interests, newspaper subscriptions, attending lectures, educating his

children, developing his taste etc., his only share of civilization
which distinguishes him from the slave, is economically only
possible by widening the sphere of his pleasures at the times when
business is good, where saving is to a certain degree possible),
[apart from this,] he would, if he saved money in a properly ascetic
manner ... conserve his savings and make them fruitful only by
putting them into banks etc., so that, afterwards, in times of crisis
he loses his deposits, after having in times of prosperity foregone all
life's pleasures in order to increase the power of capital; thus has
saved in every way *for* capital, not for himself.[38]

Even though the pleasures invoked here are bought with money, they are not
necessarily ruled by the time of money: in not forgoing all of "life's pleasures"
and indeed in "widening the sphere of [their] pleasures," workers already
point to a crisis in the time of money and in effect posit a different type of
temporality altogether. *In the Grundrisse, the question of pleasure is indissoluble from the question of crisis:* if by practicing self-denial workers "ultimately
make crises easier to bear for" capital, by "widening the sphere of [their]
pleasures," they presumably would make such crises unbearable for capital,
they might, in other words, bring about a real crisis—that is, perhaps, the
Benjaminian *wirklich Ausnahmezustand,* the real state of emergency. In a
powerful discussion of the above passage in *Marx beyond Marx,* Negri elaborates further the notion of such a "widening" of the sphere of pleasures and
identifies it as an essential moment in the antagonistic movement of autonomy from capital: "the workers' opposition, the proletarian struggle, tries
continually to broaden *the sphere of non-work,* that is, the sphere of their own
needs, the value of necessary labor."[39] For Negri, such a "widening" is ultimately tantamount to "the ontological broadening of [the worker's] use value,
through the intensification and elevation of the value of necessary labour."[40]
To increase the value of socially necessary labor, of course, is immediately to
decrease surplus labor and hence surplus value and profit. Such a quantitative decline of profit would already constitute a crisis for capital—but this is
not merely a question of quantity. Negri speaks not only of an "elevation" but
also of an "intensification" of the value of socially necessary labor: while the
former constitutes a change of degree, that is, a quantitative change, the latter constitutes a change of nature, that is, a qualitative change. It is precisely
because this is not only a quantitative but also and more importantly a qualitative shift that such a shift can effect an ontological broadening of the use

value of labor, which is to say, can incept the production of new forms of subjectivity and new types of human beings antagonistic to surplus labor time, to the time of exploitation. Demanding and dangerous pleasures indeed are those that would harbor the potential for such antagonism. *The demand of pleasure is indissoluble from revolutionary aspirations.* Capital is well aware of the dangers inherent in this irrefragable demand, which is why in our time such a demand was met by capital through the self-negating pleasures of what Marx calls "hedonism" and of what now we can call by its proper name, namely, consumerism. Consumerism has constituted one of the most effective solutions for the problems posed by the constant widening of the sphere of pleasures, one of the most efficient ways to dispel the threat of a real state of emergency intrinsic in the increasing and intensifying demand of pleasure. Consumerism is the apparatus of capture used by capital to reclaim the broadening sphere of nonwork, thereby killing two birds with one stone: in this way, such a sphere is made productive once again through consumption and its revolutionary potentials are frozen and neutralized. Do you want pleasure? I'll give you pleasure. I'll give you all the pleasures money can buy as long as you renounce any collective process expressive of such pleasures, as long as you enjoy them in the time of money, as long as you fulfill them always already in the next pleasures, as long as you realize them by negating pleasure and time *tout court.*

Lest this picture look too grim, we need to look at it once again from the standpoint of Marx's reflections on pleasure. In the passage just cited, in fact, we are in the presence of a series of important conceptual and political achievements. First of all, Marx here produces an analytic distinction—which is no less concrete and effective for being analytic—between pleasure and the pleasure of consumerism: the latter may indeed be instrumental in containing and exploiting the former, but that does not mean that they are one and the same, even when they prove to be virtually indistinguishable from one another.[41] Whereas—Marxist as well as non-Marxist—critiques of pleasure unwittingly conflate the two, and hence in attacking consumerism in effect also erase the antagonistic power of pleasure, Marx insists on their irreducible difference. Second, the temporality of consumerism—which is the temporality of circulation—is likewise indiscernible and yet distinct from the temporality inherent in the widening of the sphere of pleasures and in the broadening of the sphere of nonwork. Admittedly, in both cases we are faced with a temporality that is figured spatially in terms of spiraling expansion, and hence it may seem as if they both share in a temporality of infinite deferral that in effect negates time altogether.[42] But let's pay closer attention to the specificities of the temporal dynamics involved here. Both consumerism and the widening of the sphere of pleasures are posited as productive. What do they produce? Consumerism is essential in the production of that which at once produces it and governs it, namely, money as capital: consumerism negates pleasure and time so as to accrue capital to money and hence its ultimate function is not to produce pleasure but rather to annul time by deferring it so as to produce capital for capital. To widen the sphere of pleasures, on the other hand, means to produce more and more pleasures that in the end capital must pay for. Within such a widening, pleasure is affirmed each and every time because it is not made accountable to money, but rather to pleasure itself. Within such a widening, pleasure is asserted in the very moment when it is seized, and in being so asserted it is made productive of yet another moment of pleasure, it becomes productive of more and more pleasurable encounters, in which the necessity of pleasure—namely, its demand—is precisely the becoming-necessary of the encounter of contingencies. The temporality expressive of the insistent widening of the demand of pleasure, in other words, is the one implicit in Althusser's account of the ancient theory of atomism. According to such a temporality, time and history as well as contingency and necessity are immanent to each other and are different aspects of the turbulent vitality of substance and its modes, or of matter and its bodies, or, in short, of corporeality. (And this might be as good a moment as any to recall that Marx's 1841 dissertation dealt with the Democritean and Epicurean philosophy of nature.) As the sphere of pleasures widens, it does not foreclose the present and yet also projects itself toward an undetermined future of experimentation: it materializes, incorporates, and, indeed, incarnates the temporality of the infinite productivity of being, the temporality of becoming.

Marx's double achievement consists in having differentiated and disengaged pleasure from consumerism, as well as in having sensed and shown how pleasure—far from interrupting or disrupting desire—is indissoluble from the infinitely productive, self-positing, self-differentiating, extensive and intensive movement of desire. The reason why neither Negri nor Agamben ultimately quite succeeds in articulating that corporeality that they nonetheless believe to be indispensable for any revolutionary theory of time is that the latter can be articulated only by taking into account both the fulfilled moment of the *cairós* (namely, pleasure) and the time of productivity (namely, desire). It is only by insisting on retaining both these concepts and on finding them embedded and pulsating in each other that, on the one hand, to theorize and to live the *cairós* would no longer constitute a flight into transcendence, and, on the other hand, to theorize and to live time as production would not only allow for but also necessitate a historical-materialist conception of pleasure. Within such a reconfigured double articulation of pleasure and desire, the fulfilled moment of pleasure would constitute the point at which desire folds back upon itself so as to go on producing other such points, other such moments. *Pleasure is the fold of desire:* it is the immanent point of tangency between our bodies and desire (that is, between modes and substance understood as the immanent and absent cause both of itself and of modes). And this is another way of saying that the pleasure of our bodies can come at any point and at any moment—because desire is always already there. We need to understand and practice time as fully incorporated, as nowhere existing outside of bodies and their pleasures, as inalienable from the historical and collective body of pleasure. It is only deep from within the folds of such a temporality that one can begin to ask—as Spinoza does ask in the *Ethics*—what the body can do, what a revolutionary and liberated body might be.[43]

Does Marx ever really pose this question? Or—to put it differently—in exactly what ways are Marx's pleasures corporeal? The term "pleasure" appears five times in the brief span of the three pages from which the passage above is excerpted: clearly, the question of pleasure is not a fleeting thought or passing remark here. And yet, the specific pleasures to which Marx refers in these pages all seem to fall under the rather narrow and humanist heading of the purportedly civilizing influences of education and culture. In no way can such pleasures not be considered corporeal in their own right, and yet Marx does not indicate whether there are other corporeal pleasures that can or ought to enter the antagonistic political arena he outlines here; he does not suggest how his conception of pleasure might also necessitate a political reconceptualization of the realm of the corporeal.

To excavate and to elaborate Marx's conception of pleasure further, so as to find the question of corporeality there, however, is not a difficult task—and one can easily enlist Marx himself for this very purpose. If it is the case—as Negri suggests—that to widen the sphere of pleasures is to incept an ontological expansion of the use value of labor, we might want to recall exactly how Marx conceives of such a use value in the first place. Throughout the *Grundrisse*, Marx understands the use value of labor not just as one among other use values but rather as the use value par excellence, inasmuch as it is "the general possibility of all wealth."[44] In this sense, such a use value should not be understood as a value at all, but rather as the condition of possibility of a system founded on value and of the very notion of value itself— or, as Marx puts it: "not as itself *value,* but as the *living source* of value."[45] The point is that Marx repeatedly emphasizes how such a living source of all value exists exclusively as a potential incorporated in the "bodily existence,"[46] "bodiliness,"[47] and "muscular force"[48] of the worker—a corporeal potential for exponential leaps of production, creativity, and liberation that fully came into its own with capitalist modernity. (Such an invocation of the corporeal, in other words, is not an ahistorical and essentialist vitalism, as Marx is always attentive to the determining historicity of the mode of production, that is, to the political forms and social relations that organize— and, indeed, produce—bodies for production.) But once the use value of labor has been found thus to be incarnated as a potential in the very flesh of the worker, the ontological expansion of the worker's use value—and the attendant and constitutive production of subjectivity that is effected by widening the sphere of pleasures—must also necessarily pass through and innervate the level of the corporeal *tout court.* The body and its pleasures emerge in Marx as the critical site for any form of class struggle and indeed constitute the battlefield on which the class war between materialism and idealism continues to be fought. (And I believe Foucault is not far from precisely this Marx when he invokes "bodies and pleasures" as the "rallying point for the counterattack against the deployment of sexuality" on the final pages of the first volume of *The History of Sexuality.*)[49] This also means that corporeal communism is a tautology and that there can be no communism other than a corporeal one—either inside or outside the embattled citadel.

Notes

Surplus Common

1. Mikhail Bakhtin, "The Problem of the Text in Linguistics, Philology, and the Human Sciences: An Experiment in Philosophical Analysis," in *Speech Genres and Other Late Essays*, trans. Vern W. McGee (Austin: University of Texas Press, 1992), 125, but see also 117–28.

2. Ibid., 172.

3. Kojin Karatani, *Architecture as Metaphor: Language, Number, Money*, trans. Sabu Kohso, ed. Michael Speaks (Cambridge: MIT Press, 1995), 111, 112, 113.

4. Mikhail Bakhtin, "From Notes Made in 1970–71," in *Speech Genres*, 147. Later in the same work, Karatani does acknowledge Bakhtin: "[W]hat is commonly presupposed as a normal case—a dialogue *with* a common rule—is rather exceptional . . . Bakhtin would call this a monologue" (116).

5. Cesare Casarino and Antonio Negri, "It's a Powerful Life: A Conversation on Contemporary Philosophy," *Cultural Critique* 57, no. 2 (spring 2004): 151–83.

6. This essay first appeared as "Il mostro politico: Nuda vita e potenza," in *Desiderio del mostro: dal circo al laboratorio alla politica* (Desire of the monster: From the circus to the laboratory to politics), ed. Ubaldo Fadini, Antonio Negri, and Charles T. Wolfe (Rome: Manifestolibri, 2001), 179–210.

7. Cesare Casarino, "Time Matters: Marx, Negri, Agamben, and the Corporeal," *Strategies* 16, no. 2 (fall 2003): 185–206.

8. Gilles Deleuze and Félix Guattari, *What Is Philosophy?*, trans. Hugh Tomlinson and Graham Burchell (New York: Columbia University Press, 1994), 16.

9. Ibid., 11.

10. My exercise here consists less in juxtaposing two distinct moments in the history of philosophy so as to do justice equally to both, and more in showing how contemporary elaborations of the common (including my own) have found significant inspiration in—and hence have fabricated their own conceptual genealogies starting from—the likes of Dante, among other late-medieval and early-modern thinkers. (Hardt and Negri's account of the "two modernities" and their respective thinkers in *Empire*, among which Dante also figures, is a particularly adept example

of such a posteriori genealogical fabrications. Such fabrications constitute the necessary fictions for any conceptual practice and also foreground the collective and composite nature of thought. See Michael Hardt and Antonio Negri, *Empire* [Cambridge: Harvard University Press, 2000], 70–90.) This is to say also that my main aim here is not to give a comprehensive critical assessment of Hardt and Negri's collaborative project but rather to activate and learn from their project so as to be able, hopefully, to go further in the elaboration of the concept of the common.

11. Giorgio Agamben, "Form-of-Life," in *Means without End: Notes on Politics*, trans. Vincenzo Binetti and Cesare Casarino (Minneapolis: University of Minnesota Press, 2000), 9–11; idem, Agamben, "Forma-di-vita" in *Mezzi senza fine: Note sulla politica* (Turin: Bollati Boringhieri, 1996), 17–19. See also Negri's remarks on Dante in "On *Empire*" in this volume.

12. Dante Alighieri, *De vulgari eloquentia* (bilingual edition), ed. and trans. Steven Botterill (Cambridge: Cambridge University Press, 1996), 3; translation modified.

13. Ibid., 7; translation modified.

14. See, for example, Marx's comments on linguistic and economic production as similarly collective by definition. Karl Marx, *Grundrisse: Foundations of the Critique of Political Economy (Rough Draft)*, trans. Martin Nicolaus (Harmondsworth, U.K.: Penguin Books, 1974), 84.

15. Ibid., 221–35. See also my "Time Matters" in this volume, in which I discuss Marx's understanding of money in more detail.

16. A. Kiarina Kordela, "Capital: At Least It Kills Time (Spinoza, Marx, Lacan, and Temporality)," *Rethinking Marxism* 18, no. 4 (October 2006): 540, but see also the whole essay, 539–63.

17. Dante, *De vulgari eloquentia*, 2 and 9.

18. Unlike Kordela, I prefer not to qualify that abstract symbol that is value as "immaterial," because I find the whole materiality–immateriality dyad to constitute an idealist, dialectical binary opposition rather than a historical-materialist conceptual apparatus. In the end, however, my disagreement is more terminological than conceptual (i.e., even though I find the term "immaterial" to be misleading and hence counterproductive, I am in basic agreement with Kordela's conceptual articulation of "value"). I discuss this question in more detail with respect to Negri's very similar use of the term "immaterial" in note 23 below.

19. On this matter, see also this provocative statement by Deleuze and Guattari: "Speech communities and languages, independently of writing, do not define closed groups of people who understand one another but primarily determine relations between groups who do not understand one another: if there is language, it is fundamentally between those who do not speak the same tongue. Language is made for that, for translation, not for communication" (Gilles Deleuze and Félix Guattari, *A Thousand Plateaus: Capitalism and Schizophrenia*, trans. Brian Massumi [Minneapolis:

University of Minnesota Press, 1987], 430). Obviously, I have been calling "communication" precisely what Deleuze and Guattari call "translation." Moreover, what they call "communication" is precisely what Dante attributes only to animals (rather than to human beings) (Dante, *De vulgari eloquentia*, 5 and 7).

20. Dante, *De vulgari eloquentia*, 9. In understanding communication as including both semantic and nonsemantic forms, I follow—among others—Jacques Derrida; see, for example, his well-known remarks on this matter as well as his arguments regarding J. L. Austin's differentiation between constative and performative utterances (Jacques Derrida, "Signature Event Context," in *Limited Inc*, trans. Samuel Weber [Evanston, Ill.: Northwestern University Press, 1988], 1 and 13–19).

21. This type of universalism was considered to be heretical and protosecular already in its own time—within both Christian and Islamic contexts. Shortly after Dante died in exile, his *De monarchia* was banned and burned by order of Pope John XXII—and was listed in the Index of Forbidden Books from its inception in the mid-sixteenth century up until the nineteenth century—because of its Averroism as well as its argument for the necessity of a single secular world monarch, who would oversee all temporal matters (thereby relegating the pope and the church to spiritual matters only). Similarly, in the late twelfth century Ibn Rushd himself (better known in the Christian West as Averroës) had been tried and exiled—and his works had been banned and burned—by order of the caliph Yaqub Al-Mansur, because of that thinker's rationalism (e.g., his argument that truth can be attained not only through religious faith but also through philosophical reason). In both cases, what was seen as dangerously heretical in effect constituted a crucial antecedent of modern secular arguments for the separation of church and state, religion and philosophy, faith and reason, and so on. On a different yet related note, I believe it is not a coincidence that many among the most important thinkers of the common—all their vast differences notwithstanding—share in having suffered censorship, ostracism, imprisonment, exile, or worse. Ibn Rushd, Dante, Giordano Bruno, Spinoza, Marx, Oscar Wilde, Antonio Gramsci, Rosa Luxemburg, Leon Trotsky, Jean Genet, Pier Paolo Pasolini, and Antonio Negri himself along with several other Italian thinkers and political militants of his as well as of the following generation (such as Paolo Virno)—to mention just a few. On the one hand, they suffered such dire fate because of their various articulations of the common. On the other hand, it was arguably such a fate that determined in significant ways their articulations in the first place. The complex and mutually determining relations between the concept of the common and the spatiotemporal phenomenology of exile and of prison have not yet been properly attended to and still await their adequate theorization. On this matter, however, see Negri's powerful meditations on the biblical book of Job, written in prison in the early 1980s (Antonio Negri, *Il lavoro di Giobbe* [The labor of Job] [Rome: Manifestolibri, 2002]; see especially his 2002 preface, 7–16).

But see also Michael Hardt's essay on Jean Genet, "Prison Time," *Yale French Studies* 91 (1997): 64–79.

22. Walter Benjamin, "Theses on the Philosophy of History," in *Illuminations*, trans. Harry Zohn (New York: Schocken, 1969), 254. On the significance of Benjamin's work (and especially of his theses), see also "Vicissitudes of Constituent Thought," as well as "Time Matters," in this volume.

23. A few clarifications are in order. First of all, my definition of postmodernity as "the era of the real subsumption of all forms of life and of *bios* itself under capital" is simply a variation on a by now familiar theme. Marx was the first to distinguish between the formal and the real subsumption of society under capital. See Karl Marx, *Capital: A Critique of Political Economy,* vol. 1, trans. Ben Fowkes (New York: Vintage, 1976), 1019–38. Negri, among others, has reelaborated this distinction further—so as to articulate the transformations in capital–labor relations within the post-Fordist process of production—in many of his works (including all the ones coauthored with Hardt); for a succinct recapitulation of Negri's past and present arguments regarding these matters, see Hardt and Negri, *Empire,* 254–56 and 271–72. Second, it goes without saying that forms of life for me include both so-called inorganic and so-called organic matter. In short, I define "forms of life" simply as forms that persist in being, up until the moment when an event takes place that forces them to change in form, to metamorphose. This is another way of saying also that I do not know of compelling arguments for differentiating between "life" and "being," as well as that I follow Spinoza in understanding "death" simply as the moment when the various parts of a form of life "are so disposed that they maintain a different ratio of motion and rest to one another"—that is, as the moment of metamorphosis—and hence in understanding "life" and "death" not at all as mutually exclusive with but as immanent to one another; see the Scholium to Proposition 39 in Part IV of Spinoza's *Ethics* (Spinoza, *Ethics,* ed. and trans. G. H. R. Parkinson [Oxford: Oxford University Press, 2000], 256–57); Benedicti de Spinoza, *Ethica Ordine Geometrico Demonstrata*, in *Opera: Tomus Primus,* ed. J. Van Vloten and J. P. N. Land (The Hague: Martinum Nijhoff, 1914), 212–13. Third, when I refer to intellectual, linguistic, and affective communication as "the increasingly dominant and determining" form of labor for contemporary capitalism, I use these adjectives in strictly qualitative rather than quantitative terms: other forms of labor—such as the labor involved in modern industrial production organized according to Taylorist principles, or the labor involved in premodern processes of agricultural production—not only are alive and well but also may well still constitute quantitatively the most common forms of labor nowadays. However, such modern and premodern forms of labor are increasingly determined by and dependent on more properly postmodern forms of communicative labor for their continued existence and profitability; for a similar and more detailed version of this argument, see Michael Hardt

and Antonio Negri, *Multitude: War and Democracy in the Age of Empire* (New York: Penguin, 2004), 107–15 and 141–42. My only objection to Hardt and Negri's formulations there has to do with their use of the term "immaterial labor" for indicating what I have been calling here "communicative labor": my objection has to do specifically with the term rather than with its corresponding concept, which I do find to be extremely useful. The origin of the term "immaterial labor" is collective, in the sense that it originated in the late 1980s and early 1990s from the debates that took place on the pages, as well as during the editorial meetings, of *Futur Antérieur*—the journal founded by Negri in Paris, around which many of the Italian thinkers and political militants in exile there as well as French intellectual figures coalesced for a decade. It is very likely that Maurizio Lazzarato was the one among them who coined the term in the first place; in any case, he is the one who has theorized it in most detail. See Maurizio Lazzarato, "Immaterial Labor," in *Radical Thought in Italy: A Potential Politics*, ed. Paolo Virno and Michael Hardt (Minneapolis: University of Minnesota Press, 1996), 133–47. For an account of the brief yet intense life of *Futur Antérieur*, see Negri's 2003 "*Postface à la publication sur le site de Multitudes de la collection complète de Futur Antérieur, 1989–1998*," at http://multitudes.samizdat.net/-Postface-de-Toni-Negri-.html). In brief, I find the term "immaterial labor" to be unserviceable and even counterproductive to the extent to which it appeals to an untenable distinction between the "material" and the "immaterial," and to the extent to which, thus, it may lead easily to fatal misunderstandings. In retrospect, for example, it seems to me that many of the otherwise lively debates that were sparked by the publication of *Empire* often were bogged down, sidetracked, and ultimately impoverished by the disproportionate attention given to such misunderstandings, even though Hardt and Negri had defined this term very clearly in that work (see, for example, Hardt and Negri, *Empire*, 289–94). Eager to avoid similarly less than useful and tiresome debates with the publication of *Multitude*, Hardt and Negri further clarify this term in the latter work by pointing out that what is "immaterial" in "immaterial labor" is not the labor itself but its product (e.g., from online financial transactions to call-center services, from customer-satisfaction management to forms of knowledge of all sorts) (Hardt and Negri, *Multitude*, 109). I would argue, however, that there is nothing immaterial even about such products. My point, in other words, is that the whole material–immaterial binary opposition is an idealist conceptual apparatus rather than a historical-materialist one and hence cannot be deployed effectively in the context of historical-materialist arguments. I am implying, of course, that from a historical-materialist standpoint nothing at all is immaterial, and hence that in the context of such a paradigm one needs to argue exclusively in terms of different modalities of the material and of their specificities, much as Louis Althusser, among others, pointed out long ago. See Louis Althusser, "Ideology and Ideological State Apparatuses (Notes towards an Investigation)," in *Lenin and*

Philosophy, and Other Essays, trans. Ben Brewster (New York: Monthly Review Press, 1971), 127–86, especially 165–70. Last, but not least, I am aware of the fact that the numerous literatures on these matters are hardly in agreement regarding the role played by communicative labor in the contemporary phase of the capitalist mode of production. All in all, I find the various arguments regarding the hegemonic tendency of this type of labor nowadays—some of which I have already referred to—to be very convincing. That said, an original and compelling counterpoint to Hardt and Negri's arguments regarding these matters in *Empire* and *Multitude* can be found in Brynnar Swenson's excellent dissertation *The Corporate Form: Capital, Fiction, Architecture,* from which I have learned a great deal. In particular, Swenson argues convincingly that those forms of labor that Hardt and Negri identify as characteristic of the post-Fordist process of production were an essential component of the corporation as a capitalist entity already in the nineteenth century—and, in some respects, also from its very inception in the seventeenth century—and hence that they preceded Fordism as such. Furthermore, he argues that the "immaterial labor which Hardt and Negri 'discover' as the dominant form of work at the beginning of the twenty-first century was the *cause* of Fordist models of production, not the *effect,*" as well as that this "discovery" is the result of "the level of *visibility* that these forms of work have attained in contemporary society" (Brynnar Swenson, "The Corporate Form: Capital, Fiction, Architecture," unpublished dissertation).

24. Some might object that the central concern of *Multitude* is the multitude rather than the common per se. As Hardt and Negri weave the complex fabric of the relations binding multitude, capital, and empire, however, they find it necessary also to continue to elaborate and refine a conceptualization of the common that had begun—in Negri's case—arguably at least since the early 1960s; I am referring to Negri's 1964 essay "Labor in the Constitution," now included in *Labor of Dionysus* (Michael Hardt and Antonio Negri, *Labor of Dionysus: A Critique of the State-Form* [Minneapolis: University of Minnesota Press, 1994], 53–136 and especially 58–63). (See also Negri's comments on this essay in "A Class-Struggle Propaedeutics, 1950s–1970s" in this volume.) At one point in *Multitude,* for example, they assert that there are "mutually defining relations between the production of the multitude and the production of the common" (Hardt and Negri, *Multitude,* 348). Elsewhere, they go as far as to define the multitude as "an open network of singularities that links together on the basis of the common they share and the common they produce"—thereby implying that in order to articulate conceptually as well as to constitute socially the multitude, it is imperative to ascertain exactly what it is that singularities share and produce in common in the first place (*Multitude,* 129). In short, the common in a crucial sense is the unofficial yet inescapable protagonist of *Multitude.* Indeed, even though it is an advisable hermeneutical practice not to take an author's words at face value, it may be nonetheless relevant to relate a conversation I had with

Hardt on this matter (which occurred on May 27, 2007, and which he has given me permission to report here). During this conversation, he explained that now he feels that "the common" was central to the project of *Multitude* but was not yet adequately conceptualized in that work, much as "multitude" was central to the project of *Empire* but was not yet adequately conceptualized in that work either—and he added that he likes the idea of one book posing a problem that the next book will then take up and attempt to solve. As far as Negri's own latest, most explicit, and most compelling efforts to conceptualize the common are concerned, they are to be found in his *Kairòs, Alma Venus, Multitudo* (Antonio Negri, *Kairòs, Alma Venus, Multitudo: Nine Lessons to Myself,* in *Time for Revolution,* trans. Matteo Mandarini [London: Continuum, 2003], 137–261; see especially 147–58 and 181–93; Negri, *Kairòs, Alma Venus, Multitudo: nove lezioni impartite a me stesso* [Rome: Manifestolibri, 2000], especially 19–34 and 67–82). In many respects, this important work—which Negri wrote at the same time as he was cowriting *Empire,* and which appeared in Italian at the same time as *Empire* appeared in English—provides many of the philosophical foundations for the variations on the same common theme that are found later in *Multitude.* I discuss *Kairòs, Alma Venus, Multitudo* in more detail in note 91 below.

25. See, for example, Hardt and Negri, *Multitude,* 148, 188, 213, 310, 348–50, as well as the entire section titled "Production of the Common," 196–202, and part of the following section titled "Beyond Private and Public," especially 202–4. Whereas Hardt and Negri absorb fully and elaborate further the first two features of the earliest definitions of the common, they might not seem to inherit its third feature: nowhere do they write explicitly about the common in universalist terms or otherwise argue explicitly for any kind of universalism whatsoever. Nonetheless, I would argue that their conception of the common does exhibit a specific kind of universalism that is quite different from the essentialist varieties of universalism encountered in protomodern, modern, or postmodern environments. In short, I believe that their project can be enlisted for a specific kind of nonessentialist universalism based on common potentials and common projects, as opposed to those (either Kantian or Hegelian) universalisms that find their stable ground in shared and essential identities and that ought to be fought by all means necessary. (I conceive of these two dominant varieties of universalism in the following manner: Hegelian varieties of universalism function according to synthesizable contradictions, and determine the identity of the totality by means of a relative and recuperative negation of all that is perceived as not sharing in the essence of the totality—that is, by selectively sublating the different into the identical. Such Hegelian universalisms find their complement in those Kantian universalisms that function according to dynamic and nonsynthesizable antinomies, and that determine the identity of the totality by means of a relative yet nonrecuperative negation of all that is perceived as not sharing in the essence of the totality—that is, by selectively excising the different from the

identical. If the most dangerous political manifestations of the former amount to total assimilation and domestication, the most dangerous political manifestations of the latter amount to complete ostracism and extermination; both, in any case, ultimately lead to the same end, that is, the obliteration of difference.) Whether or not Hardt and Negri share my specific understanding of the nonessentialist universalism of common potentials and common projects that I have both invoked and endorsed here, I believe that they belong to a series of otherwise quite different contemporary thinkers who, on the one hand, critique (and rightly so) the current relativist and particularist orthodoxies—for example, the discourse of multiculturalism—as specifically capitalist ideologies that function as barely disguised universalisms of the aforementioned Hegelian or Kantian varieties, and, on the other hand, assert explicitly the need to reconceptualize and endorse universalism on nonessentialist grounds. I am thinking, for example, of Alain Badiou, who, in his book on Saint Paul, denounces particularist solutions to the problem of difference, and attempts to recuperate Saint Paul as a thinker of "universal singularity" who articulated universalism in effect as an egalitarianism that is respectful of difference (Alain Badiou, *Saint Paul: The Foundation of Universalism*, trans. Ray Brassier [Stanford, Calif.: Stanford University Press, 2003], 104–6; but see also 6–7 and 14). Similar positions can be found in Slavoj Žižek: see, for example, his exchanges with Judith Butler and Ernesto Laclau (Judith Butler, Ernesto Laclau, and Slavoj Žižek, *Contingency, Hegemony, Universality: Contemporary Dialogues on the Left* [London: Verso, 2000]). I am not fully sure that either Badiou's or Žižek's attempts to produce nonessentialist concepts of universalisms are successful in the end. In a different—and, as far as I am concerned, more effective—way, Deleuze and Guattari had made analogous arguments already two decades earlier, when discussing the question of minorities in *A Thousand Plateaus,* to which I return in note 39 below (Deleuze and Guattari, *A Thousand Plateaus,* 469–73).

26. Hardt and Negri, *Multitude,* 147. Hardt and Negri argue also that such a present state of affairs constitutes the full fruition of a tendency that had been there all along—"Capital has always been oriented toward the production, reproduction, and control of social life"—as well as that Marx had intimated such developments already (146). Indeed, it is to their credit that they begin their attempt to update Marx's insights here with the following admission: "Strangely . . . after beginning to walk ahead of Marx . . . we continually have the haunting suspicion that he was already there before us" (141).

27. Ibid., 148.

28. Ibid., 150; but see also 149–51. For a more detailed account of the privatization of the common, see also the entire section titled "Life on the Market" (179–88).

29. My arguments in this paragraph (a) do little more than recast the question of the common in terms of Spinoza's understanding of substance as the immanent

cause of itself as well as of modes, and (b) articulate such a recasting by drawing in part on Virno's remarkable discussion of the relation between potentiality and actuality in his important treatise on time, which is, astonishingly, yet to be translated into English. See Paolo Virno, *Il ricordo del presente: Saggio sul tempo storico* [The remembrance of the present: An essay on historical time] (Turin: Bollati Boringhieri, 1999), 49–118, especially 54–56, 67–74. On this relation, see also "Vicissitudes of Constituent Thought" in this volume. For Spinoza's understanding of substance as immanent cause, see Definitions 1, 3, 5, and 6, Axioms 1 and 2, and Proposition 18, in Part I of the *Ethics* (Spinoza, *Ethics*, 75–76 and 93 [*Opera: Tomus Primus*, 37–38 and 54]).

30. If I say "so-called anti-globalization movements," that is because very often the demands articulated by these movements are (implicitly or explicitly) global in nature. I understand such movements, in other words, to constitute *globalization movements in their own right*, in the sense that they express a desire for a globalization radically different from the capitalist one that is taking shape currently under the aegis of neoliberal political-economic policy. On these matters, see Hardt and Negri, *Multitude*, 268–306.

31. Ibid., 226 and 227. For my disagreements on the question of democracy, see "On *Multitude*" in this volume.

32. In invoking the notion of an "ideological revolution," I follow Althusser's understanding of ideology—as that which produces *all* forms of subjectivity—with one crucial proviso. I take Althusser's definition of ideology at once as having "*no outside* (for itself)" and as being "*nothing but outside* (for science and reality)" more seriously than Althusser himself took it in the end. In brief, if one is to push such a definition to its logical conclusions, it would follow—contrary to what Althusser argues—that there cannot be such a thing as a subject-less discourse, namely, a purely nonideological science (Althusser, *Lenin and Philosophy*, 175 and 171, respectively). Even the Spinozian-Marxian method of "symptomatic" reading, as articulated by Althusser in *Reading Capital*, is not a science in this sense, as inevitably it too is constituted by its own sets of ideological postulates and driven by its own sets of ideological imperatives—not least of all being the postulate of a synchronic "structure" posited as "cause immanent in its effects" and hence as "nothing outside its effects," as well as the imperative to articulate a philosophical discourse and a political project radically antagonistic to capital (Louis Althusser and Étienne Balibar, *Reading Capital*, trans. Ben Brewster [London: Verso, 1997], 28 [but see also all of 18-30], 69, 189 [but see also all of 182–93]). Or, as Fredric Jameson puts it in a sentence that constitutes an implicit critique of Althusser: "every 'system' of thought (no matter how scientific) is susceptible to *representation* . . . such that it can be apprehended as an ideological 'vision of the world'" (Fredric Jameson, *Postmodernism; or, The Cultural Logic of Late Capitalism* [Durham, N.C.: Duke University Press, 1991],

245). All of this is to say that the spell of ideology can be broken only by another, altogether different and more powerful, ideological spell—where "more powerful" means literally more full of power, more full of potential, that is, more capable of tarrying and engaging with potentiality qua potentiality. On this matter, see also Kordela's reelaboration of the question of ideology in her *$urplus: Spinoza, Lacan*—a work that I discuss at some length below (see especially notes 39 and 97). See A. Kiarina Kordela, *$urplus: Spinoza, Lacan* (Albany: State University of New York Press, 2006), 117.

33. Hardt and Negri, *Multitude*, 150; "*the expropriation of the common*" is in italics in the original, while "*some*" is not.

34. Ibid., 212; but see also 211–19.

35. In the pages of this volume, Negri comments on this other surplus in the following way: "The act always contains a surplus, always constitutes surplus. That which is realized has a surplus with respect to that which is possible . . . In undergoing the process of actualization, potentiality re-potentiates itself, re-creates itself to the second power: far from being mortified, potentiality thus becomes more powerful precisely by actualizing itself. But such an ontology of potentiality is nothing other than Marxian ontology: the productive act does not decree the death of labor; the productive act, rather, is that act which exalts and accumulates labor—and once it does that, one can then take off once again, starting from a new and higher level. Live labor can never exhaust itself, can never be consumed! Not only its mortification but also its consumption cannot take place: there is only multiplication and expansion" (see "Vicissitudes of Constituent Thought" in this volume).

36. It is clear throughout *Multitude* that the production of the multitude as a political subject is inseparable from the political project of reappropriation of the common. See, for example, Hardt and Negri, *Multitude*, 222, and 348–50, as well as note 24 above.

37. Strictly speaking, "potential" in the passage quoted is attributed to "the poor" rather than to the surplus of the common: "the poor" are "the paradigmatic subjective figure of labor today"; they "are included in the circuits of production and full of potential, which always exceeds what capital . . . can expropriate." These qualifications regarding the poor, however, appear in this paragraph after the surplus of the common has been described already in the way in which the "potential" of the poor is described, namely, as exceeding capital's capacity to exploit, as unexploitable—which is why I feel it is legitimate to conclude that this surplus is "potential." As a syllogistic corollary, one might add that the poor thus defined are the materialization and incorporation par excellence of the surplus of the common, or, as Negri puts it succinctly: "the poor are the common of the common." Moreover, it is precisely because such a surplus is "potential" that Negri can define the poor also as "the naked eternity of the power of being" (Negri, *Time for Revolution*, 195 and 194,

respectively; Negri, *Kairòs, Alma Venus, Multitudo*, 85 and 83, respectively). On the question of the poor, see Hardt and Negri, *Multitude*, 129–38, and *Empire*, 156–59, as well as Negri, *Time for Revolution*, 194–208; Negri, *Kairòs, Alma Venus, Multitudo*, 83–102. But see also our discussion of these matters in "On *Empire*" in this volume.

38. Marx, *Grundrisse*, 296, but see also 295. It seems to me that Hardt and Negri's effort to rethink the poor today as the source of all wealth is rooted in—and constitutes an attempt to elaborate further—these Marxian formulations regarding the double life of labor power as "absolute poverty" and "*general possibility* of wealth." On these matters, see also note 37.

39. My elaborations of the concept of surplus—in this paragraph as well as throughout this preface—owe a crucial debt to Kordela's important work on this matter, *$urplus: Spinoza, Lacan.* (Kordela does not use the term "potentiality" to describe surplus, however.) On my reading, this book—whose rare conceptual acuity is matched only by its rare conceptual precision—asks as well as answers the following question: how would the concept of secular capitalist modernity have to be redefined if one were to understand Spinoza's dictum "truth is the standard both of itself and of the false" as its foundational epistemological and ontological principle? (For Spinoza's definition of truth, see the Scholium to Proposition 43 in Part I [Spinoza, *Ethics*, 150 (*Opera: Tomus Primus*, 108)]). Kordela's compelling answer to this question involves surplus at all levels (and, while in the process of finding surplus everywhere, produces original reinterpretations of, primarily, Spinoza, Kant, Marx, and Lacan). In particular, she writes: "Spinoza is the first philosopher to grasp the structure of secular causality, as immanent or differential causality, as we know it since its popularization by linguistics. Here the cause is itself an effect of its own effects. What enabled Spinoza to see this structure was the fact that, as we shall see, he conceived of nature, insofar as it is inhabited by human beings, as a system of signifiers. Far from being autonomous physical things with inherent qualities, signifiers are differential values, and differential values, by structural necessity, constitute a system of disequilibrium, that is, a system that always produces a surplus" (Kordela, *$urplus*, 1). I will discuss Spinoza as a thinker of immanence, of surplus, and of the common later in this preface, and I will return to Kordela's work particularly in note 97. For the moment, I would like to point out that, even though I agree with the fundamental arguments of her book, I find its characterization of Hardt and Negri's philosophical and political project to be ungenerous. About the political demands put forth by Hardt and Negri at the end of *Empire*, for example, Kordela writes: "Their political manifesto is reducible to three major demands: "'The Right to Global Citizenship,'" so that illegal immigrant labor is officially recognized as legal; "'The Right to a Social Wage,'" so that everybody contributing to production, including its aspects of reproduction and unproduction, be equally paid; and "'The Right to Reappropriation,'" so that the multitude have control over the means of production (the

technology of information)—though one might wonder, how can the multitude have control over something that is anyway already "'increasingly integrated in the minds and bodies of the multitude'"? . . . More importantly, one might also wonder in what, then, does the revolutionary "'telos of the multitude'" differ from the telos of capital itself? . . . Or, conversely, wouldn't the Empire's legislation itself be more than happy to grant these "'rights,'" had it caught up with the pace of global, informatized capital—legislation being always slower in its development . . . ? Capital itself demands the abolition of national boundaries, involves a system of production in which what traditionally was considered reproduction or unproduction is equally a part of production itself (both leisure and unemployment being necessary for the sustenance of capitalism), and is already increasingly entrusting the means of production to the multitude, since the latter is itself constituted by them, reproducing them in body and mind . . . [F]or Hardt and Negri, these rights, far from being the path towards the system's collapse or future transformation, themselves constitute the transformation of the present Empire into the ideal state in which the multitude's power will have found its true expression. There is no reference to any further transformation required for their ideal state of communism. In short, there is no distinction in Hardt and Negri's "'Neo-Spinozist'" monism between the full realization of the force of capital and the full realization of the multitude's power" (ibid., 4–5). First of all, the reduction of "The Right to Global Citizenship" to the demand "that illegal immigrant labor" be "officially recognized as legal" is misleading. Hardt and Negri write also: "If in a first moment the multitude demands that each state recognize juridically the migrations that are necessary to capital, in a second moment it must demand control over the movements themselves. The multitude must be able to decide if, when, and where it moves. It must have the right also to stay still and enjoy one place rather than being forced constantly to be on the move. *The general right to control its own movement is the multitude's ultimate demand for global citizenship*" (Hardt and Negri, *Empire*, 400). I take this passage to imply that this "second moment" would constitute precisely the moment when "the system's collapse or . . . transformation" would take place, because movement or rest would be decided then on the basis of the multitude's rather than capital's necessities. Obviously, this "second moment" presupposes a distinction between capital and the multitude, which is the distinction Kordela argues Hardt and Negri do not make. I will return to this point shortly. All this aside, on the one hand, I do agree with Kordela that there is nothing revolutionary—that is, anticapitalist—in these three demands in and of themselves, and, on the other hand, I believe that these three demands can be interpreted also as constituting the tactical preconditions for revolutionary transformation in our particular historical conjuncture. In *A Thousand Plateaus*, Deleuze and Guattari engage with this political predicament when discussing the question of minorities. (Importantly, they do not understand the difference between minority and majority in terms of quantity; or, more precisely, they define minority as multiplicity, that is, as a nondenumerable set that changes qualitatively each and every time an element is added to or subtracted from it, as opposed to majority understood as magnitude, that is, as a denumerable set that never changes qualitatively regardless of the number of elements composing it. As I will show, this is also the difference between the common and community in Spinozian terms: see note 77. In short, Hardt and Negri's concept of multitude is closely related to Deleuze and Guattari's concepts of multiplicity and minority.) In this context, Deleuze and Guattari argue that political struggles centered on demands for rights are not revolutionary in and of themselves and yet constitute "the index of another, coexistent combat" on the basis of which they might become revolutionary: "[M]inorities do not receive a better solution of their problem by integration, even with axioms, statutes, autonomies, independences. Their tactics necessarily go that route. But if they are revolutionary, it is because they carry within them a deeper movement that challenges the worldwide axiomatic. The power of minority, of particularity, finds its figure or its universal consciousness in the proletariat. But as long as the working class defines itself by an acquired status . . . it appears only as "capital," a part of capital (variable capital), and does not leave the *plan(e) of capital*. At best, the plan(e) becomes bureaucratic. On the other hand, it is by leaving the plan(e) of capital, and never ceasing to leave it, that a mass becomes increasingly revolutionary and destroys the dominant equilibrium of the denumerable sets" (Deleuze and Guattari, *A Thousand Plateaus*, 472; but see also 469–73). Simply because the political demand for a specific juridical right becomes necessary as a tactical operation at a given historical conjuncture, it does not follow that the right in question is the solution to the problem that produced the necessity for its demand in the first place. There are times when one may need to start from demands and rights because one may be unable to start from anywhere else; the crucial point is never to forget that revolutionary potential lies neither in the demand nor in the right but in the desire for change that not only is the presupposition of any demand whatsoever but also was unable to express itself at the time in forms more radical than demands or rights. In short, it is crucial never to mistake one for the other or to conflate the two, and hence, whenever possible, to pursue political struggles by means other than demands for rights. After all, to have been forced into a mode of existence so unbearable that one's own desire can express itself only as demand for acknowledgment and recognition of such an unbearable existence is to be in the position of the slave. Elsewhere, I have made similar arguments with respect to the act of coming out in the context of gay and lesbian as well as queer political struggles (Cesare Casarino, *Modernity at Sea: Melville, Marx, Conrad in Crisis* [Minneapolis: University of Minnesota Press, 2002], 188–92). As far as the distinction between capital and multitude is concerned, I would like to note that, since the publication of *Empire*, Hardt and Negri have modified and rectified some of the more problematic aspects of that work in *Multitude*—a work to which Kordela does not refer. In *Multitude*, for example, they write: "the multitude does not arise as a political figure spontaneously and . . . the flesh of the multitude consists of a series of conditions that are ambivalent: they could lead toward liberation or be caught in a new regime of exploitation and control" (Hardt and Negri, *Multitude*, 212). Overall, I find this to be a more sober and more adequate understanding of the multitude than the one articulated in *Empire*, as well as an understanding of the multitude that has come much closer willy-nilly to Virno's (slightly earlier) formulations on this matter: "The multitude is a *mode of being*, the prevalent mode of being today: but, like all modes of being, it is *ambivalent*, that is, it contains within itself both loss and salvation, acquiescence and conflict, servility and freedom" (Paolo Virno, *Grammar of the Multitude: For an Analysis of Contemporary Forms of Life*, trans. Isabella Bertoletti, James Cascaito, and Andrea Casson [New York: Semiotext(e), 2004], 26; translation modified; Virno, *Grammatica della moltitudine: Per una analisi delle forme di vita contemporanee* [Rome: DeriveApprodi, 2002], 17–18). Furthermore, as I have been trying to show in my discussion of *Multitude*, the distinction between capital and the common—which, as I point out in note 24, Hardt and Negri understand as linked inextricably to the concept of multitude—is indeed present in *Multitude*. In short, I find there are better—that is, politically more useful and more productive—ways of reading Hardt and Negri's project than the ways in which Kordela reads it in her *$urplus*. On these matters, see "On *Empire*" and "On *Multitude*" in this volume.

40. Marx, *Grundrisse*, 267.

41. Marx, *Capital*, vol. 1, 138–39. I am grateful to Kordela for having reminded me of this crucial passage in Marx.

42. I am referring to Marx's 1841 dissertation "The Difference between the Democritean and Epicurean Philosophy of Nature."

43. Marx, *Capital*, vol. 1, 151.

44. Ibid., 151–52.

45. Ibid., 152.

46. Curiously, Althusser—who reads Marx precisely as a reader of gaps, blanks, omissions, and absences—does not see, or, at any rate, does not concern himself with, this gap in Marx's reading of Aristotle. For Althusser's reading of Marx's reading of Aristotle, see Althusser and Balibar, *Reading Capital*, 123. For Althusser's reading of Marx as a reader of absences, see *Reading Capital*, 19–30.

47. Marx, *Capital*, vol. 1, 151–52.

48. More precisely, in Aristotle potentiality is itself indeterminate matter, as opposed to actuality, which has always a determinate, specific form (in the sense that a "block of wood" is the potential material of an actual form, for example, "a statue of Hermes"). On this question, see the opening paragraph of Part 6 as well as the

entirety of Parts 7 and 8 of Book Theta of *Metaphysics* (Aristotle, *Metaphysics,* in *The Basic Works of Aristotle,* ed. Richard McKeon, trans. W. D. Ross [New York: Random House, 1941], 825–26, 827–28, and 828–31, respectively).

49. Aristotle defines "primary" potentiality as "an originative source of change in another thing or in the thing itself *qua* other," that is, a thing's potentiality of "acting" on something other than itself; while he defines the other type as a potentiality of "being acted on, i.e. the originative source, in the thing acted on, of its being passively changed by another thing or by itself *qua* other." Aristotle adds that, in a sense, these two types of potentiality are one, "for a thing may be 'capable' either because it can itself be acted on or because something else can be acted on by it," but that, in another sense, they are qualitatively different, since the former lies "in the agent" while the latter "is in the thing acted on" (ibid., 820–21; translation modified). Aristotle differentiates also between irrational and rational potentiality: the latter appertains only to human beings. On this difference, see Part 2 of Book Theta of *Metaphysics* (ibid., 821–22).

50. I am following here Agamben's more literal translation of this passage in his essay "On Potentiality," which is entirely devoted to the question of potentiality in Aristotle (Giorgio Agamben, "On Potentiality," in *Potentialities: Collected Essays in Philosophy,* ed. and trans. Daniel Heller-Roazen [Stanford, Calif.: Stanford University Press, 1999], 181–82). Ross's translation of this same passage reads as follows: "And 'impotence' and 'impotent' stand for the privation which is contrary to potency of this sort, so that every potency belongs to the same subject and refers to the same process as a corresponding impotence" (Aristotle, *The Basic Works of Aristotle,* 821).

51. For Aristotle, "actuality is prior both to potentiality and to every principle of change"—where "prior" is intended in logical, ontological, as well as temporal terms. This means, among other things, that an incomplete actuality retains the potentiality to change or be changed into something other than itself. It is in this sense that *adynamia* adheres to both. On the priority of actuality, see Part 8 of Book Theta in *Metaphysics;* the quotation above is the last sentence of Part 8 (828–31).

52. Ibid., 821.

53. Ibid.

54. Marx, *Capital,* vol. 1, 270. Importantly, Aristotle defines potentiality also in terms of setting in motion, that is, as "movement." On this matter, see the end of Part 6 of Book Theta in *Metaphysics* (Aristotle, *The Basic Works of Aristotle,* 826–27).

55. And yet, it is not insignificant (a) that three of the recurrent examples chosen by Aristotle to explain the relation between potentiality and actuality in Book Theta of the *Metaphysics* are the "builder," the "house," and the builder of the house, and (b) that the house appears also in the exchange relation as developed in the *Nicomachean Ethics.* Moreover, the house (*oikos*) is, of course, also the etymological root and conceptual foundation of the economy (*oikonomia*), which was intended originally

as management of the household, including the acquisition of those things that are useful for the household. (For further discussion of the importance of Aristotle's definition of *oikonomia* for Marx, see note 58 below.) This is all to say that the question of the house—as a privileged example at once of the relation between potentiality and actuality as well as of the relation of exchange—constitutes a potential link in Aristotle's thought between the realm of the metaphysical and the realm of the economic. For Aristotle's examples of the builder and the house, see Parts 1, 2, 6, 7, and 8 of Book Theta of the *Metaphysics*, in ibid., 821, 822, 826, 827, 828, 829, 830.

56. Marx, *Grundrisse*, 324.

57. Ibid.

58. If in the aporetic loop between the *Nicomachean Ethics* and the *Metaphysics* Aristotle steps and stops on the threshold of value as *adynamia* without crossing it, in the *Politics* Aristotle knocks quietly on the door of surplus value without opening it. The key to this door is the question of excess. In Book I of the *Politics*, Aristotle contrasts two related yet crucially different arts, namely, economics (*oikonomia*) and what he calls *chrematistics*—both of which involve "the art of acquisition" and hence the exchange relation. Economics is "the art of managing a household," namely, the "natural art of acquisition which is practiced by managers of households and by statesmen." For Aristotle, economics is necessary and limited, in the sense that there is a limit to the number of things to be acquired that are "necessary to life, and useful for the community of the family or state." Such things "are the element of true riches; for the amount of property which is needed for a good life is not unlimited." By contrast, chrematistics is the art of acquiring wealth simply for the sake of acquiring wealth. For Aristotle, this art is unnecessary and unlimited, in the sense that there is no limit to how much wealth can be acquired and that such unlimited acquisition of wealth is not necessary for the management of the household. If these two arts often are confused for one another or thought to be one and the same—Aristotle argues—that is because "the measure" and "the unit of exchange" is the same in both, namely, money. Each of these arts—he writes—"is a use of the same property, but with a difference": whereas the telos of economics is the satisfaction of needs by exchanging money for things, the telos of chrematistics is "accumulation" of money—which is why those who confuse the latter for the former think that "the whole idea of their lives is that they ought either to increase their money without limit, or at any rate not to lose it." The question, then, is: Whence chrematistics? How could such an unnatural art come to be? One can count on Aristotle to pose this question as well as to answer it: "The origin of this disposition in men is that they are intent upon living only, and not upon living well; and, as their desires are unlimited, they also desire that the means of gratifying them should be without limit. Those who do aim at a good life seek the means of obtaining bodily pleasures; and, since the enjoyment of these appears to depend on property, they are absorbed in getting wealth: and so

there arises the second species of wealth-getting [i.e., chrematistics]. For as their enjoyment is in excess, they seek an art which produces the excess of enjoyment; and, if they are not able to supply their pleasures by the art of getting wealth, they try other arts using in turn every faculty in a manner contrary to nature . . . [Thus] some men turn every quality or art into a means of getting wealth; this they conceive to be the end, and to the promotion of the end they think all things must contribute." Much ought to be said about this astonishing passage, which shows clearly, among other things, that Aristotle—even though he refuses to bring the realm of the economic and the realm of the metaphysical to bear on each another—is nonetheless acutely aware of the fact that it is impossible to theorize the realm of the economic and the realm of the psychological in separation from each other (and the discovery of the necessary nexus between these two realms constitutes an insight whose explicit elaboration and full implications will have to wait at least till the Enlightenment). Here, I will limit myself to pointing out that "excess of enjoyment" is posited in this passage as the final cause of an infinite process of accumulation whose direst consequence is the subordination of labor power as such (i.e., "every faculty," "every quality") to money *tout court*. It is not hyperbolic to state that for Aristotle "excess" is at the root of all evils. The Aristotelian notion of excess, of course, is quite different from the Marxian conception of surplus value as the excess of value. And yet, Aristotle has sensed already in excess as final cause of chrematistics the motor of a machinic assemblage that will eventually undermine and destroy social relations as he knew them. This is why, for example, his condemnation of usury could not be more uncompromising: "The most hated sort [of chrematistics], and with the greatest reason, is usury, which makes a gain out of money itself, and not from the natural object of it. For money was intended to be used in exchange, but not to increase at interest . . . Wherefore of all modes of getting wealth this is the most unnatural." No wonder, then, that in the *Grundrisse* Marx writes: "Money is therefore not only the object but the fountainhead of greed. The mania for possessions is possible without money; but greed itself is the product of a definite social development, not *natural*, as opposed to *historical*. Hence the wailing of the ancients about money as the source of all evil . . . Monetary greed, or mania for wealth, necessarily brings with it the decline and fall of the ancient communities. Hence it is the antithesis to them. It is itself the community, and can tolerate none other standing above it. But this presupposes the full development of exchange values, hence a corresponding organization of society." I comment on this passage in detail in "Time Matters" in this volume. For the moment, I would like to note that Aristotle's discussion of the relation between economics and chrematistics will prove to be of crucial importance for Marx, who reformulates it in *Capital* thus: "The simple circulation of commodities—selling in order to buy—is a means to a final goal which lies outside circulation, namely the appropriation of use values, the satisfaction of needs. As against this, the circulation of money as capital is an end in itself, for the valorization of value takes place only within this constantly renewed movement. The movement of capital is therefore limitless." For Aristotle's discussion of economics and chrematistics, see chapters 8, 9, and 10 in Book I of the *Politics* (Aristotle, *Politics,* in *The Basic Works of Aristotle,* 1135–41). The quotations are from 1135, 1137, 1139, 1139–40, and 1141, respectively. For Marx's discussion of these passages in Aristotle's *Politics,* see *Capital,* vol. 1, 253–54. For Marx's commentary on monetary greed among the ancients, see *Grundrisse,* 222–23.

59. *Grundrisse,* 321.

60. Ibid., 335.

61. Quoted by Althusser in *Reading Capital,* 79, but see also 80.

62. In this passage, Althusser is writing specifically about surplus value (ibid., 180–81). On the difference between surplus value as such and its particular forms, see 79–81, 91, and 161.

63. In this passage, Marx actually is discussing Ricardo as the only classical political economist who "understood the surplus" as well as the fact that "surplus value is the presupposition of capital," and who nonetheless was unable to grasp surplus value as such because in the end he always reduced it to one of its various particular forms (Marx, *Grundrisse,* 326, but see also 326–27).

64. Antonio Negri, *Marx beyond Marx: Lessons on the Grundrisse,* trans. Harry Cleaver, Michael Ryan, and Maurizio Viano, ed. Jim Fleming (Brooklyn: Autonomedia, 1991), 82, but see also 83 (Antonio Negri, *Marx oltre Marx* [Rome: Manifestolibri, 1998], 104, but see also 105).

65. See above all Althusser's "Marx's Immense Theoretical Revolution," in *Reading Capital,* 182–93.

66. See the second section of my "Time Matters" in this volume.

67. Marx, *Grundrisse,* 334–35. See also Negri's excellent discussion of this passage in *Marx beyond Marx,* 81, but see also 80–83 (Negri, *Marx oltre Marx,* 103, but see also 102–6).

68. Marx, *Capital,* vol. 1, 254.

69. This formulation builds on Deleuze and Guattari's discussion of immanence in *What Is Philosophy?,* 35–49. I borrow the term "absolute immanence" from Agamben's homonymous essay, which discusses the question of immanence in relation to Deleuze, Foucault, and Spinoza, among others (Agamben, *Potentialities,* 220–39).

70. For a discussion of the relation between capital and that which lies outside and beyond measure, see also Hardt and Negri, *Empire,* 354–59.

71. Despite the fact that much has been made of the emergence of a Spinozian Marxism (as an alternative to the dialectical orthodoxies of Hegelian Marxism) during the last four decades, the scholarly literature relating Spinoza and Marx to one another in a direct, explicit, and sustained manner is surprisingly scarce. It is

possible that such a scarcity constitutes a symptom in its own right—and yet I am not sure of what exactly it is a symptom (other than of the fact that a full-fledged and rigorous comparative study of these two thinkers is surely a daunting prospect). During these four decades, there have been, of course, thinkers who have written about both Marx and Spinoza in separate yet closely related works (such as Negri in *Marx beyond Marx* and *The Savage Anomaly* as well as Étienne Balibar in *Reading Capital* and *Spinoza and Politics*), thinkers who refer implicitly or in passing to the relation between Spinoza and Marx (such as Althusser in *Reading Capital* and in his autobiographical writings as well as Warren Montag in *Bodies, Masses, Power: Spinoza and His Contemporaries*), thinkers whose entire weltanschauung is imbued thoroughly with the Spinozian and the Marxian problematics regardless of whether or not they acknowledge it explicitly as such (see, among others, Deleuze and Guattari in both volumes of *Capitalism and Schizophrenia,* Hardt and Negri in all their collaborative works, as well as Paolo Virno in *Grammar of the Multitude*), and thinkers who confront the Spinoza–Marx relation indirectly yet significantly via the examination of a third and related thinker (see, for example, Pierre Macherey's important study *Hegel ou Spinoza* as well as Nicholas Thoburn's recent *Deleuze, Marx, and Politics*). Arguably, among these various and immensely valuable attempts to combine Spinoza's and Marx's systems of thought, the most influential one remains Althusser's pioneering contribution to *Reading Capital,* which in many respects is still unsurpassed and to which I have referred several times already. All significant differences notwithstanding, what these thinkers share in common is at the very least an understanding of Spinoza's immanentist materialism as a crucial precursor of Marx's philosophical and political project (where "precursor" ought to be understood not only in historical but also in logical terms, in the sense that both Spinoza's and Marx's systems of thought shared the same condition of possibility or cause in the immanent structures of thought and life inaugurated by capitalist modernity, rather than one system being the direct and transitive cause of the other). In short, the body of Spinozian Marxism is abundant—yet the literature on Spinoza and Marx is thin. Thin as it is, however, it is notable and significant nonetheless. In particular, I would like to refer the reader to two important works, namely, Eugene Holland's 1998 essay "Spinoza and Marx" (which discusses some of the works mentioned above as well as cites three earlier precursors: Maximilien Rubel's "Marx à la rencontre de Spinoza," Alexandre Matheron's "Le Traité Théologico-Politique vu par le jeune Marx," and Albert Igoin's "De l'ellipse de la théorie politique de Spinoza chez le jeune Marx," all published in 1977 in the journal *Cahiers Spinoza*), as well as Kordela's *$urplus* (which constructs a tetradic philosophical structure, whose complementary conceptual personae, as Deleuze and Guattari might call them, consist of Spinoza, Kant, Marx, and Lacan). For Holland, possibly the most important insight that Spinozian Marxism stands to gain from a direct confrontation between Spinoza and Marx is the eradication of "teleologism from the forces/relation of production model in two ways: there would be no guarantee that forces of production will continue to develop even in the face of restrictive or destructive relations of production; and even if they were to, there would be no guarantee that such development will eventuate in any increase in human freedom" (Eugene Holland, "Spinoza and Marx," at http://clogic.eserver.org/2-1/holland.html). Judging from Kordela's pointed critiques of Hardt and Negri's teleological tendencies, I believe she is in full agreement with Holland on this matter (Kordela, $surplus, 2–5, and 127–30). Kordela's project, however, goes beyond the level of critique, as the examination of Spinoza and Marx in her work constitutes an explicit attempt to produce what she refers to as an ontology of "*differential (non-)substance*," according to which "the registers on which Being needs to be named are the following: *(1) being as the imaginary univocity of abstract thought, that is, as simulacrum (exchange-value or signifier); (2) beings as the multiplicity of being (use-value or physical beings); and (3) the primary, transcendent, yet immanent, differential (non-)substance that at once institutes the above duplicity and is the effect thereof (surplus)*" (46–47; this is the culmination of a complex argument, and hence I refer the reader at the very least also to 38–49, in which the intermediary, logical steps leading to this conclusions are taken). I have found both Holland's and Kordela's direct engagements with the Spinoza–Marx relation (as well as all the aforementioned indirect engagements) to be provocative, illuminating, and productive. To my knowledge, however, what I am about to suggest has not yet been suggested, namely, that there is much to be gained, philosophically as well as politically, from articulating the relation between these two thinkers on the basis of Marx's understanding of surplus value and Spinoza's understanding of the third kind of knowledge and the love that arises from it.

72. See the Corollary to Proposition 32 as well as Proposition 33 in Part V of the *Ethics*, 308 (Spinoza, *Opera: Tomus Primus*, 265–66).

73. As Deleuze has pointed out, in Spinoza the "different kinds of knowledge are also different ways of living, different modes of existing" (Gilles Deleuze, *Expressionism in Philosophy: Spinoza*, trans. Martin Joughin [New York: Zone Books, 1992], 289).

74. See the second Scholium to Proposition 40 in Part II of the *Ethics*, in which Spinoza describes briefly all three kinds of knowledge (Spinoza, *Ethics*, 148–49; Spinoza, *Opera: Tomus Primus*, 106). Spinoza discusses in more detail his theory of knowledge in Part II (especially from Proposition 13 onward) as well as in Part V (which is primarily devoted to the third kind of knowledge) (*Ethics*, 124–62 and 287–316, respectively; Spinoza, *Opera: Tomus Primus*, 83–119 and 245–73).

75. Genevieve Lloyd, *Spinoza and the Ethics* (New York: Routledge, 1996), 67.

76. See Definition 2, Proposition 10, the second Scholium to this Proposition, as well as Proposition 37 in Part II, Spinoza, *Ethics*, 113, 121–22, and 145; *Opera: Tomus*

Primus, 72, 80–81, and 102. On the relation between essence and existence, in substance as well as in modes, see Definitions 1, 3, 5, 6, 8, as well as Axioms 1 and 7 in Part I, *Ethics*, 75–76; *Opera: Tomus Primus*, 37–38.

77. One of the major political implications of such a concept of essence as singularity is that in Spinoza the common has nothing to do with community understood as *Gemeinschaft*. Whereas the latter is fundamentally essentialist and exclusionary—in the sense that all of its members must share in the same transcendent essence as identity, such as race, religion, nation, language, and so on, thereby excluding by definition all others whose essence is defined as different—the former consists of modes that are essentially different from one another and that come together on the basis of that which agrees in them, such as, for example, common trajectories and common projects. Importantly, for Spinoza all modes "agree in certain things"—and hence the common in principle does not exclude any mode. See Lemma 2, but see also its Demonstration, Axiom 1, the Definition of Axiom 2, as well as Propositions 38 and 39 and their Corollaries in Part II, Spinoza, *Ethics*, 126, 127, 128, and 145–46; *Opera: Tomus Primus*, 85, 86–87, 103–4. On this matter, see also our discussion of the common in "On *Empire*" in this volume.

78. See, for example, the Scholium to Proposition 36 in Part V of the *Ethics*, 310–11; *Opera: Tomus Primus*, 267–68.

79. More than necessary, the first knowledge for Spinoza is, strictly speaking, unavoidable. On the complementary relations among the three kinds of knowledge, see Lloyd, *Spinoza and the Ethics*, 70, as well as Gilles Deleuze's discussion of Spinoza's theory of knowledge (Deleuze, *Expressionism in Philosophy*, 273–320, and especially 298–301).

80. See the Scholium to Proposition 33 in Part V, Spinoza, *Ethics*, 308–9, translation modified; Spinoza, *Opera: Tomus Primus*, 266. In his otherwise highly competent version of the *Ethics*, Parkinson translates *laetitia* as "pleasure" and *tristitia* as "pain." I find such a translation of these terms—which are of crucial importance in the *Ethics*—to be misleading in the context of Spinoza's thought: I believe they are translated more adequately as "happiness" and "sadness," respectively. Moreover, unlike Parkinson, I translate *beatitudo* as "beatitude" rather than as "blessedness" because the latter term implies a binary and transcendent relation between somebody who blesses and somebody who is blessed, which is not congruent with Spinoza's immanent understanding of cause and effect.

81. Negri—commenting on this same passage in Spinoza—makes the point that the intellectual love of God "is not a process but a condition" (Antonio Negri, *The Savage Anomaly: The Power of Spinoza's Metaphysics and Politics*, trans. Michael Hardt [Minneapolis: University of Minnesota Press, 1991], 178, but see also 179; idem, "L'anomalia selvaggia: Potere e potenza in Baruch Spinoza," in *Spinoza* [Rome: DeriveApprodi, 1998], 226, but see also 227). What I am suggesting is that, once

achieved, this kind of love is a condition—and, indeed, a precondition—as well as that its achievement does involve a process, by which one builds on the first and second kinds of knowledge so as to reach the third. I discuss Negri's interpretation of the third kind of knowledge in more detail in note 91.

82. See the Scholium to Proposition 20 in Part V, Spinoza, *Ethics*, 301–2; Spinoza, *Opera: Tomus Primus*, 258–60.

83. See the second Scholium to Proposition 40 in Part II, Spinoza, *Ethics*, 148; Spinoza, *Opera: Tomus Primus*, 106.

84. The sixth Definition of Part II of the *Ethics* reads as follows: "By reality and perfection I understand the same" (Spinoza, *Ethics*, 114; Spinoza, *Opera: Tomus Primus*, 74). This means that, even though we may very well experience the world and ourselves in it as lacking, the world in reality never lacks anything: everything is at any moment all it can be, that is, perfect. Spinoza's world, however, is not inert matter. Far from being an endorsement of the status quo, such a definition of perfection does involve the potential for change. Spinoza, in fact, understands perfection also in terms of potentiality: "the person who has a body which is capable of very many things has a mind which, considered in itself alone, is very conscious ["by a certain eternal necessity"] of itself, of God, and of things"—and such consciousness "of itself, of God, and of things" is the hallmark of the culmination of all ways of knowing in the third kind of knowledge. He adds shortly thereafter: "The more perfection each thing has, the more it acts, and the less it is acted on; conversely, the more it acts, the more perfect it is"—where action is understood in terms of self-determination, that is, as a modality of being and acting that strives to be ruled as little as possible by contingency, that strives as much as possible to posit itself as necessary instead. In short, in reality we are always as perfect as we can be, and because reality includes its own necessary and eternal cause, the more aware we are of this cause, the less dependent on contingency and the more capable of action we are. It is in this sense that we may achieve higher degrees of perfection, and that perfection involves, in effect, the potential for freedom. See Proposition 39, its Scholium, Proposition 40, as well as the Scholium to Proposition 42 in Part V, Spinoza, *Ethics*, 312–13 and 316; Spinoza, *Opera: Tomus Primus*, 269, 270, 273.

85. Elsewhere, I have discussed this experience of love as a love of potentiality that is mutually exclusive with relations of ownership and possession (Casarino, *Modernity at Sea*, xxvi–xxvii).

86. Theodor Adorno and Max Horkheimer, *Dialectic of Enlightenment*, trans. John Cumming (New York: Continuum, 1987), 72–73.

87. See the aforementioned Scholium to Proposition 33 in Part V, Spinoza, *Ethics*, 308–9; Spinoza, *Opera: Tomus Primus*, 266.

88. Spinoza ends the *Ethics* with the following sentences: "If the way that I have shown to lead to this [i.e., to the intellectual love of God] seems to be very arduous,

yet it can be discovered. And indeed it must be arduous, since it is found so rarely. For how could it happen that, if salvation were ready at hand and could be found without great labour, it is neglected by almost all? But all excellent things are as difficult as they are rare" (Spinoza, *Ethics*, 316; Spinoza, *Opera: Tomus Primus*, 273). Moreover, once achieved, the intellectual love of God is not necessarily achieved once and for all time, is not necessarily a permanent reality: even though this type of love is eternal and infinite, we still experience it fully within our modal existence of "duration" (i.e., diachrony) and finitude. Put differently, the spell of this love may well break, and, once broken, we are back once again solely within that modal existence which we had never left but to which eternity had been added while under the spell of this love. Spinoza does say, however, that the more we achieve such moments of love, the more capable of them we are and the more we desire them. See Proposition 26, its demonstration, as well as the Scholium to Proposition 34 in Part V, Spinoza, *Ethics*, 304–5 and 309, respectively; Spinoza, *Opera: Tomus Primus*, 262 and 266, respectively. For Spinoza's radical critique of teleological thought, see at the very least the Appendix to Part I. *Ethics*, 106–12; Spinoza, *Opera: Tomus Primus*, 66–72.

89. Louis Althusser, "The Only Materialist Tradition. Part I: Spinoza," in *The New Spinoza*, ed. Warren Montag and Ted Stolze, trans. Ted Stolze (Minneapolis: University of Minnesota Press, 1997), 18. For Spinoza's explanation of the way in which both body and mind are involved in the third kind of knowledge, see Proposition 39 and its Scholium in Part V, Spinoza, *Ethics*, 312–13; Spinoza, *Opera: Tomus Primus*, 269, 270.

90. Deleuze, *Expressionism in Philosophy*, 296 and 298–301.

91. I agree fully with Hardt and Negri when they argue—in the final chapter of *Multitude*—that it is necessary and urgent to rethink love as a political concept. I believe, however, that such a task requires a sustained engagement with Spinoza's intellectual love of God as love of surplus, which, on my reading, is present neither explicitly nor implicitly in their account. (I am not sure that their invocation of "the Christian and Judaic love of God" as not being "necessarily metaphysical" and as finding its expression "in the common material political project of the multitude" constitutes such an engagement in this context.) See Hardt and Negri, *Multitude*, 351–52, but see also 351–58. Negri does refer to Spinoza in his meditations on love in *Kairòs, Alma Venus, Multitudo*, without, however, engaging explicitly with Spinoza's third kind of knowledge: "That love is the constitutive *praxis* of the common is an ancient truth. Love is desire of the common, the desire (*cupiditas*) that traverses both physics and ethics—Spinoza said as much. Knowing that desire (*cupiditas*) is rooted in the eternity of being, we still need to demonstrate that the experience of love constitutes the dynamic of the innovation of being" (Negri, *Time for Revolution*, 209; translation modified; Negri, *Kairòs, Alma Venus, Multitudo*, 103). I have no doubt that love is at once "the constitutive *praxis* of the common" as well as "the

dynamic of the innovation of being"—if we intend love as determined by the third kind of knowledge. Is this the way in which Negri intends love here? It is unclear. I find the reference to Spinoza's conception of desire in this passage, for example, to be misleading or at least insufficient. Spinoza defines desire (*cupiditas*) as "appetite with a consciousness of the appetite" (see the Scholium to Proposition 9 in Part III, Spinoza, *Ethics*, 172; Spinoza, *Opera: Tomus Primus*, 129–30). Such consciousness is not necessarily consciousness "by a certain eternal necessity" (i.e., consciousness of cause), and hence only the latter rather than the former is necessarily "rooted in the eternity of being." *Cupiditas* may become "rooted in the eternity of being" only if and when it is consciousness not only of itself but also of its immanent cause, that is, only if and when it is capable of contributing and giving rise to the third kind of knowledge and its love. (And it is crucial to insist that there is no teleology in this passage: by the same token, in other words, *cupiditas* may well remain stuck within the confines of the diachronic forever.) In short, for Spinoza *cupiditas* in and of itself is the limited way in which we experience desire within the diachronic rather than constituting immediately desire intended as experience of the synchronic, namely, intellectual love of God. Only the latter "constitutes the dynamic of the innovation of being." Admittedly, earlier in the same work Negri also writes: "With Spinoza the ontology of materialism . . . is . . . invested and founded anew by desire. The rhythm of the constitution of the world is sustained—in a confusion of forms—by a living force that unfolds in the world so as to construct itself as divine. Freedom constructs itself in this development and interprets its continuity within the absolute productive immanence of a *vis viva*, a living force, that unfolds from physical *conatus* to human *cupiditas* on to divine *amor* [love]. Before interpreting the human world and sublimating itself in the divine world, ethics constitutes the physical world itself. Eternity is lived as presence, and the common is brought back in its entirety within the development of ontology. The composition of bodies is common; the object of *cupiditas* is common; the figure of the divine is common. The common is ontology considered from the point of view of passion, of the force that agitates and constitutes both world and divinity" (Negri, *Time for Revolution*, 186–87, translation modified; Negri, *Kairòs, Alma Venus, Multitudo*, 73–74). There is much that ought to be discussed in this rich passage. Leaving aside the thorny question of how to interpret Spinoza's definition of *conatus* as the endeavor by which modes persist in being—a question with which I cannot engage here, as it would take me even farther afield—I agree with what Negri argues here, as long as (a) the passage from *conatus* to *cupiditas* to *amor* is understood as the perfecting process by which the first and second kinds of knowledge culminate into knowledge of the third kind, (b) this passage is understood also in strictly nonteleological terms (i.e., there is no ontological necessity guaranteeing that this passage may ever come to pass), and (c) the "force" that causes this passage is understood precisely as surplus, that is, as absent cause immanent in its effects. The reason why I am not sure that Negri would agree with my assessment is that, shortly after the passage just quoted, he writes: "That said, despite [Spinoza's materialist affirmation of the common as immanence], one must add that Spinoza's asceticism is incapable of providing a full account [*dar senso pieno*] of its progression. For it forms an image of beatitude that, in separating itself from the production of desire, only touches upon the notion of beatitude without appropriating it" (Negri, *Time for Revolution*, 187, translation modified; Negri, *Kairòs, Alma Venus, Multitudo*, 74). This is where I diverge from Negri's interpretation of Spinoza. As I have tried to show in my—admittedly incomplete and somewhat hasty—reading of Spinoza's understanding of the third kind of knowledge, beatitude not only does not separate itself from the production of desire but also constitutes its fullest realization. Unlike Negri, therefore, I do not see the need to critique Spinoza's "asceticism." Negri's critique here constitutes a further elaboration of arguments he had made already in *The Savage Anomaly*, in which the third kind of knowledge is relegated to a somewhat marginal and ambivalent position within Spinoza's system (Negri, *The Savage Anomaly*, 174–75, but see also 168–82; Negri, *Spinoza*, 223–24, but see also 216–30). Arguably, however, *Kairòs, Alma Venus, Multitudo* in its entirety might lend itself to a different reading: given its recurrent and insistent emphasis on the experience of eternity, it could be argued that this work is so steeped in Spinoza's third kind of knowledge as to have turned such knowledge into a ubiquitous, imperceptible, and powerful presence throughout. In this work, for example, Negri argues explicitly that the production of the common is an index of eternity—and I find myself in complete agreement with this argument (Negri, *Time for Revolution*, 185; Negri, *Kairòs, Alma Venus, Multitudo*, 72). And yet, it remains unclear to me how it is possible to put such an emphasis on the experience of eternity without placing the third kind of knowledge at the very center of the Spinozian problematic.

92. Deleuze and Guattari, *What Is Philosophy?*, 2.

93. Ibid., 48. Throughout *Expressionism in Philosophy*, Deleuze argues that in Spinoza the power of being involves also the power of acting and the power of thinking involves also the power of knowing. See, for example, Deleuze, *Expressionism in Philosophy*, 120–22.

94. Deleuze and Guattari, *What Is Philosophy?*, 41 and 59–60.

95. Gilles Deleuze, "On the Difference between the *Ethics* and a Morality" in *Spinoza: Practical Philosophy*, trans. Robert Hurley (San Francisco: City Light Books, 1988), 9.

96. Ibid., 29.

97. For our discussion of "the void," see "On *Multitude*" in this volume. The expression "degree zero" comes from Virno, who refers to it also as "neutral kernel," and who deploys it to describe the structure of certain ethically negative affects and modes of behavior—such as cynicism and opportunism—that appertain to

contemporary capitalist forms of subjectivity. His point is that the structure itself is precisely neutral, and hence that it may be materialized in ways that are radically different from its current and dominant instantiations: "Our theoretical challenge lies . . . in the identification of a new and important *modality of experience* through the forms in which it may for the moment be manifest, without, however, reducing that experience to them" (Paolo Virno, "The Ambivalence of Disenchantment," trans. Michael Turits, in Virno and Hardt, *Radical Thought in Italy*, 25, but see also 26). This is what I have been arguing with respect to surplus understood as the neutral matrix of both capital and the common: our philosophical and political challenge lies at once in disengaging the matrix from its current and ruinous forms as well as in incorporating (rather than foreclosing) such a matrix in gestures of love. In essence, this is also Kordela's argument in *$urplus*. There, she argues (about Marx, and, mutatis mutandis, she argues in effect the same about Spinoza): "What Marx tells us . . . is that Being is a Nothing, a Zero, which is simultaneously a surplus, and which needs to be said in a single sense both from the viewpoint of the unity of its exchange-value (the One abstract form that renders all beings equivalent) and from the viewpoint of the multiplicity of use-value, the multiple concrete and divergent empirical manifestations of Being. Neither the unity of exchange-value nor the multiplicity of use-value, neither being-for-others nor being-in-itself is the "'power'" that determines the other, as they are both determined by the power of Being and Thought (Surplus) of which both are the empirical "'modes of existence.'" Crucially, she adds: "Given that, as I have shown, capitalism is not an ontological necessity but one of the theoretically infinite manifestations of Being and Thought within the realm of the possible as determined by them, the only other alternative for Marxians, therefore, is to rethink communism as an economic, political, and cultural system that includes the surplus on all levels" (Kordela, *$urplus*, 106–7 and 108, respectively). To which I have nothing to add, and from which I have nothing to subtract.

98. Desiderius Erasmus, *The Praise of Folly*, trans. Hoyt Hopewell Hudson (Random House: New York, 1941), 1; originally published in 1511. The title of this work has been translated also as *In Praise of Folly*.

99. See note 11 above. On this matter, see also Virno's comments on the contemporary relations between "intellect" and "multitude" (Virno, *Grammar of the Multitude*, 37; Virno, *Grammatica della moltitudine*, 27–28).

100. Deleuze and Guattari, *What Is Philosophy?*, 3, but see also 2–5.

101. Ibid., 41.

102. Deleuze and Guattari, *A Thousand Plateaus*, 3.

A Class-Struggle Propaedeutics, 1950s–1970s

1. Azione Cattolica Italiana is an Italian nonclerical Catholic organization that played an especially important social and political role in the period immediately

after World War II. Its origins date back to the foundation of Società della Gioventù Cattolica Italiana (Society of Italian Catholic Youth) in 1867.

2. Leonardo Bruni (1370–1444)—multifaceted scholar, historian, and political figure—is regarded as one of the most important figures in the Humanist intellectual movement. Poised between Humanism and Renaissance, Marsilio Ficino (1433–99) was one of the most important philosophers of his time, whose works had a profound influence on Renaissance thought throughout Europe.

3. The Scuola Normale di Pisa is a famous research institute in Pisa, which was founded in 1810 by Napoleon as a branch of the Parisian École Normale Supérieure.

4. Antonio Negri, *Saggi sullo storicismo tedesco: Dilthey e Meinecke* [Essays on German Historicism: Dilthey and Meinecke] (Milan: Istituto Giangiacomo Feltrinelli, 1959); idem, "Studi su Max Weber (1956–1965)" [Studies on Max Weber (1956–1965)], in *Annuario bibliografico di filosofia del diritto* (Milan: A. Giuffrè, 1967).

5. Giovanni Gentile (1875–1944), Hegelian philosopher and political figure, dominated Italian intellectual life during the first half of the twentieth century, along with Benedetto Croce (1866–1952).

6. On Gramsci, see also "Vicissitudes of Constituent Thought" in this volume.

7. The PSIUP was born in 1964 from a left-wing split of the Socialist Party.

8. Cossutta, Alinovi, and La Torre were all prominent figures in the Italian Communist Party at the time.

9. In the political milieu in which Negri was operating at the time, the term *inchiesta operaia* designated research on the working class conducted from the standpoint of the workers' own realities and projects, as well as involving workers themselves, as opposed to the type of research that was conducted from the standpoint of state's or capital's needs, from the standpoint of official leftist organizations such as the Communist Party, or from the standpoint of the traditional theoretical and methodological discourses of the academic social sciences.

10. Porto Marghera is located across the Venice lagoon.

11. Antonio Negri, *Political Descartes: Reason, Ideology, and the Bourgeois Project*, trans. Matteo Mandarini and Alberto Toscano (London: Verso, 2007). Originally published as *Descartes politico o della ragionevole ideologia* (Milan: Feltrinelli, 1970).

12. "[R]ank and file" is in English in the original.

13. The CGIL was and continues to be the most powerful labor union in Italy; traditionally, it had close links to the Communist Party. *L'unità* was founded by Gramsci in 1924 as the official newspaper of the Communist Party.

14. For the latest reelaboration of the argument regarding the two modernities, see Michael Hardt and Antonio Negri, *Empire* (Cambridge: Harvard University Press, 2000), 69–92, as well as "On *Empire*" in this volume.

15. Antonio Negri, *Books for Burning: Between Civil War and Democracy in 1970s Italy*, trans. Arianna Bove, Ed Emery, Timothy S. Murphy, and Francesca Novello, ed. Timothy S. Murphy (London: Verso, 2005).

16. Antonio Negri, *La forma stato: Per la critica dell'economia politica della Costituzione* (Milan: Feltrinelli, 1977).

17. Michael Hardt and Antonio Negri, *Labor of Dionysus: A Critique of the State-Form* (Minneapolis: University of Minnesota Press, 1994), 53–136.

18. The first article of the Italian Constitution is "Italy is a Republic founded on Labor."

19. "[B]ig business" and "big labor" are in English in the original.

20. Hardt and Negri, *Labor of Dionysus,* 23–51.

21. In March 1977, during clashes between the police and students at the University of Bologna, a student was killed by the police, after which riots ensued throughout the city for several days.

22. The English term "power" corresponds to two distinct terms in Italian, *potenza* and *potere* (roughly corresponding to the French *puissance* and *pouvoir,* the German *Macht* and *Vermögen,* and the Latin *potentia* and *potestas,* respectively). *Potenza* resonates often with implications of potentiality as well as with decentralized or mass conceptions of force and strength. *Potere,* on the other hand, refers more typically to the might or authority of an already structured and centralized capacity, often an institutional apparatus such as the state. Unless otherwise noted, here and throughout the sections of this book that were translated from Italian into English—namely, "A Class-Struggle Propaedeutics, 1950s–1970s," "Sounding the Present," "Vicissitudes of Constituent Thought," and Negri's essay "The Political Monster"—we have translated *potere* as "Power" and *potenza* mostly as "power," and occasionally as "potentiality." We have indicated in the main body of the text the instances in which *potenza* is translated as "potentiality." The English term "labor power," however, always translates as the Italian term *forza lavoro* throughout.

23. The term *operaio sociale* (socialized worker) designates the new forms of work and of class composition appertaining to the post-Fordist process of production, as opposed to the *operaio massa* (mass worker) of the Taylorist and Fordist models of industrial production and organization. For a concise overview of the arguments and periodizations corresponding to these terms, see Negri's essay "Twenty Theses on Marx: Interpretation of the Class Situation Today," in *Marxism beyond Marxism,* ed. Saree Makdisi, Cesare Casarino, and Rebecca Karl, trans. Michael Hardt (New York: Routledge, 1996), 154–56.

24. Ibid., 149–80, and especially 164–78.

On *Empire*

1. Michael Hardt, *Gilles Deleuze: An Apprenticeship in Philosophy* (Minneapolis: University of Minnesota Press, 1993).

2. For a brief history of *Futur Antérieur,* see note 23 in "Surplus Common."

3. The figure of the "socialized worker" is discussed briefly in "A Class-Struggle Propaedeutics, 1950s–1970s"; see especially note 23. On the question of "immaterial labor," see note 23 in "Surplus Common."

4. Giovanni Arrighi, *The Long Twentieth Century* (London: Verso, 1994). Hardt's arguments about this work are reiterated in Michael Hardt and Antonio Negri, *Empire* (Cambridge: Harvard University Press, 2000), 237–39.

5. Antonio Negri, "The Political Monster: Power and Naked Life," in this volume. For the original bibliographical reference, see note 6 in "Surplus Common."

6. Antonio Negri, *Macchina Tempo: Rompicapi, Liberazione, Costituzione* [Time machine: Conundrums, liberation, constitution] (Milan: Feltrinelli, 1982).

7. Antonio Negri, *Insurgencies: Constituent Power and the Modern State*, trans. Maurizia Boscagli (Minneapolis: University of Minnesota Press, 1999). Originally published as *Il potere costituente: Saggio sulle alternative del moderno* (Carnago: SugarCo., 1992).

8. Karl Marx, *Grundrisse: Foundations of the Critique of Political Economy (Rough Draft)*, trans. Martin Nicolaus (Harmondsworth, U.K.: Penguin Books, 1974), 407–8 and 410.

9. Gilles Deleuze and Félix Guattari, *A Thousand Plateaus: Capitalism and Schizophrenia*, trans. Brian Massumi (Minneapolis: University of Minnesota Press, 1987), 463.

10. C. B. Macpherson, *The Political Theory of Possessive Individualism: Hobbes to Locke* (Oxford: Oxford University Press, 1962).

11. Delio Cantimori, *Eretici italiani del Cinquecento* [Italian heretics of the sixteenth century] (Florence: Sansoni, 1967).

12. For Negri's meditations on this concept, see his *Kairòs, Alma Venus, Multitudo: Nine Lessons to Myself*, in Antonio Negri, *Time for Revolution*, trans. Matteo Mandarini (London: Continuum, 2003), 181–223 (*Kairòs, Alma Venus, Multitudo*, 65–121).

13. Hardt and Negri, *Empire*, 396–407.

14. Roberto Esposito, *Communitas: Origine e destino della comunità* [Communitas: Origin and destiny of community] (Turin: Einaudi, 1998).

15. On *Moby-Dick* as novel of the common, see Cesare Casarino's "White Capital; or, Heterotopologies of the Limit," in *Modernity at Sea: Melville, Marx, Conrad in Crisis* (Minneapolis: University of Minnesota Press, 2002), 63–183.

16. On this matter, see notes 37 and 38 in "Surplus Common."

17. In "Vicissitudes of Constituent Thought," in this volume, Negri refers to himself as a pagan thinker.

18. Ibid.

19. Here and throughout, "naked power" translates *nuda potenza*.

20. "[S]howdown" is in English in the original.

On *Multitude*

1. On this thesis, see Michael Hardt and Antonio Negri, *Empire* (Cambridge: Harvard University Press, 2000), 69–92, as well as "On *Empire*" in this volume.

2. Félix Guattari and Antonio Negri, *Communists Like Us* (New York: Semiotext[e], 1990).

3. Gilles Deleuze, *Cinema 2: The Time-Image*, trans. Hugh Tomlinson and Robert Galeta (Minneapolis: University of Minnesota Press, 1989), 20–21.

4. Michael Hardt and Antonio Negri, *Multitude: War and Democracy in the Age of Empire* (New York: Penguin, 2004), 64–67.

5. Karl Marx, *Grundrisse: Foundations of the Critique of Political Economy (Rough Draft)*, trans. Martin Nicolaus (Harmondsworth, U.K.: Penguin Books, 1974), 105.

6. On Spinoza's definition of perfection, see note 84 in "Surplus Common."

7. Hardt and Negri, *Empire*, 415n4.

8. On this matter, see Antonio Negri, *Time for Revolution*, trans. Matteo Mandarini (London: Continuum, 2003), 147–80; idem, *Kairòs, Alma Venus, Multitudo*, 19–64.

9. Louis Althusser, "Une philosophie pour le marxisme: 'La ligne de Démocrite'" [A philosophy for Marxism: Democritus's line], in *Sur la philosophie* [On philosophy] (Paris: Gallimard, 1994), 40–42. On the concept of aleatory materialism in Althusser, see also Casarino's "Time Matters" in this volume.

10. Gilles Deleuze and Félix Guattari, *A Thousand Plateaus: Capitalism and Schizophrenia*, trans. Brian Massumi (Minneapolis: University of Minnesota Press, 1987), 482–88.

11. Hardt and Negri, *Multitude*, 105.

12. Ibid., 105–6.

13. Ibid., 107.

14. On the concept of essence and its relation to the common in Spinoza, see "Surplus Common," especially notes 76 and 77.

15. Antonio Negri and Anne Dufourmentelle, *Negri on Negri*, trans. M. B. DeBevoise (New York: Routledge, 2004), 111–18.

16. Paolo Virno, *Scienze sociali e "natura umana": Facoltà di linguaggio, invariante biologico, rapporti di produzione* [Social sciences and "human nature": Linguistic faculty, biological invariant, relations of production] (Catanzaro: Rubbettino, 2002), 13–24; idem, *Quando il verbo si fa carne: Linguaggio e natura umana* [When the word becomes flesh: Language and human nature] (Turin: Bollati Boringhieri, 2003), 143–84; as well as idem, *Grammar of the Multitude: For an Analysis of Contemporary Forms of Life*, trans. Isabella Bertoletti, James Cascaito, and Andrea Casson (New York: Semiotext[e], 2004), 35–41 and 55–61; Paolo Virno, *Grammatica della*

moltitudine: Per una analisi delle forme di vita contemporanee (Rome: DeriveApprodi, 2002), 25–34 and 49–58.

17. Virno, *Grammar of the Multitude,* 81–84; Virno, *Grammatica della moltitudine,* 81–86; as well as Virno, *Scienze sociali e "natura umana,"* 23–24.

18. Antonio Negri, *The Constitution of Time,* in *Time for Revolution,* 19–135. This work was written in jail between 1980 and 1981, and was first published in 1997 as *La costituzione del tempo: Prolegomeni: Orologi del capitale e liberazione comunista* (Rome: Manifestolibri, 1997).

19. Deleuze and Guattari, *A Thousand Plateaus,* 351–423.

20. Hardt and Negri, *Multitude,* 357.

Vicissitudes of Constituent Thought

We thank Brynnar Swenson for his help with the editing of Part I of this conversation.

1. Antonio Negri, "Twenty Theses on Marx: Interpretation of the Class Situation Today," in *Marxism beyond Marxism,* ed. Saree Makdisi, Cesare Casarino, and Rebecca E. Karl, trans. Michael Hardt (New York: Routledge, 1996).

2. Michael Hardt and Antonio Negri, *Empire* (Cambridge: Harvard University Press, 2000), 22–30.

3. For bibliographical reference, see note 6 in "On *Empire.*"

4. Hardt and Negri, *Empire,* 22–27; Gilles Deleuze, "Postscript on Control Societies," in *Negotiations,* trans. Martin Joughin (New York: Columbia University Press, 1995), 177–82.

5. Gilles Deleuze and Félix Guattari, *A Thousand Plateaus: Capitalism and Schizophrenia,* trans. Brian Massumi (Minneapolis: University of Minnesota Press, 1987), 571n66 and 571–72n67.

6. Michael Hardt and Paolo Virno, eds., *Radical Thought in Italy: A Potential Politics* (Minneapolis: University of Minnesota Press, 1996), 1.

7. Deleuze and Guattari, *A Thousand Plateaus,* 351–473.

8. Gilles Deleuze, "Control and Becoming," in *Negotiations,* 169–76. Originally published in *Futur Antérieur* 1 (spring 1990).

9. Hardt and Negri, *Empire,* 356–59 and 468n8.

10. Ibid., 91–92.

11. Ibid., 69–90, but see also Michael Hardt and Antonio Negri, *Labor of Dionysus: A Critique of the State-Form* (Minneapolis: University of Minnesota Press, 1994), 283–86.

12. Hardt and Negri, *Empire,* 366–67.

13. Giorgio Agamben, *Homo Sacer: Sovereign Power and Bare Life,* trans. Daniel Heller-Roazen (Stanford, Calif.: Stanford University Press, 1998), 42–44; Agamben, *Homo Sacer: Il potere sovrano e la nuda vita* (Turin: Einaudi, 1995), 50–51.

14. See "The Political Monster: Power and Naked Life" in this volume.

15. Luciano Ferrari Bravo, "*Homo Sacer:* Una riflessione sul libro di Agamben" [*Homo Sacer:* A reflection on Agamben's book], in *Dal fordismo alla globalizzazione: Cristalli di tempo politico* [From Fordism to globalization: Crystals of political time] (Rome: Manifestolibri, 2001), 279–86.

16. Giorgio Agamben, *The Time That Remains: A Commentary on the Letter to the Romans,* trans. Patricia Dailey (Stanford, Calif.: Stanford University Press, 2005).

17. Giorgio Agamben, "Bartleby, or On Contingency," in *Potentialities: Collected Essays in Philosophy,* ed. and trans. Daniel Heller-Roazen (Stanford, Calif.: Stanford University Press, 1999), 243–71; Gilles Deleuze, "Bartleby; or, The Formula," in *Essays Critical and Clinical,* trans. Daniel W. Smith and Michael A. Greco (Minneapolis: University of Minnesota Press, 1997), 68–90.

18. On the concept of poverty, see also "On *Empire*" as well as notes 37 and 38 in "Surplus Common."

19. Antonio Negri, *Time for Revolution,* trans. Matteo Mandarini (New York: Continuum, 2003), 194.

20. See note 13 above.

21. Agamben, *Homo Sacer,* 44; translation modified; Agamben, *Homo Sacer,* 51.

22. On Aristotle's *Metaphysics,* see also "Surplus Common."

23. Agamben, *Homo Sacer,* 47; Agamben, *Homo Sacer,* 54–55.

24. Gilles Deleuze, *Cinema 2: The Time-Image,* trans. Hugh Tomlinson and Robert Galeta (Minneapolis: University of Minnesota Press, 1989), 68–70 and 78–83.

25. Giorgio Agamben, *The Coming Community,* trans. Michael Hardt (Minneapolis: University of Minnesota Press, 1993), 53–56; Agamben, *La comunità che viene* (Turin: Einaudi, 1990), 36–39. See also Casarino, *Modernity at Sea: Melville, Marx, Conrad in Crisis* (Minneapolis: University of Minnesota Press, 2002), xxxv–xxxvii.

26. Here and throughout this paragraph, "surplus" translates the Italian term *eccedenza.*

27. Hardt and Negri, *Empire,* 233; Negri, *The Constitution of Time: The Time-pieces of Capital and Communist Liberation,* in *Time for Revolution,* 90. Negri, *La costituzione del tempo. Prolegomeni. Orologi del capitale e liberazione comunista* (Rome: Manifestolibri, 1997), 128.

28. See "A Class-Struggle Propaedeutics, 1950s–1970s."

29. Palmiro Togliatti (1893–1964) was the leader of the Italian Communist Party from 1927 to 1964. With Gramsci, he cofounded the weekly *L'ordine nuovo* in 1919.

30. Amadeo Bordiga (1889–1970) cofounded the Italian Communist Party with Gramsci in 1921, and continued to be one of the most prominent figures in the party for several decades.

31. At the time of this conversation, Silvio Berlusconi (born 1936) was Italy's richest man and one of the richest men in the world. His economic empire started from real estate and includes now a vast media network throughout Europe (ranging from

newspapers and magazines to radio and television stations). He became involved actively in politics in the early 1990s: he founded the party Forza Italia (Go Italy!) in 1993 and has been prime minister three times at the head of self-declaredly right-wing government coalitions (in 1994–95, 2001–6, and 2008). He has stood trial numerous times for corruption and conflict of interest; he has always been acquitted.

32. Michel Foucault, *The History of Sexuality,* vol. 1, *An Introduction,* trans. Robert Hurley (New York: Vintage Books, 1990), 157.

33. Pasolini's Trilogy of Life included *The Decameron* (1971), *The Canterbury Tales* (1972), and *The Flower of the Arabian Nights* (1974). He rejected these films in his 1975 essay "Abjuration of the Trilogy of Life." See Pier Paolo Pasolini, "Trilogy of Life rejected," in *Lutheran Letters,* trans. Stuart Hood (New York: Carcanet, 1987), 49–52; translation modified (i.e., "Abjuration of the Trilogy of Life" is a more literal translation of the essay's title than Hood's translation); Pasolini, "Abiura dalla Trilogia della Vita," in *Lettere Luterane: Il progresso come falso progresso* (Turin: Einaudi, 1976), 71–76.

34. Deleuze, *Cinema 2,* 35–36, 148–49, 183.

35. On Althusser's *Reading Capital,* see also "Surplus Common," especially notes 32, 46, 71.

36. Antonio Negri, *Lenta ginestra: Saggio sull'ontologia di Giacomo Leopardi* [Slow broom: Essay on Giacomo Leopardi's ontology] (Milan: Mimesis Eterotopia, 2001); originally published in 1987.

37. For full bibliographical reference, see note 21 in "Surplus Common."

38. Walter Benjamin, "Theses on the Philosophy of History," in *Illuminations,* trans. Harry Zohn (New York: Schocken, 1969), 255.

39. See Negri, *Time for Revolution,* 107–14, and "Introduzione," in *La costituzione del tempo,* 18–19, as well as Hardt and Negri, *Labor of Dionysus,* 293–94, and *Empire,* 214–15 and 377.

40. Benjamin, "Theses on the Philosophy of History," 257.

41. Ibid., 253.

42. Giordano Bruno was born in the southern Italian town of Nola, which is famous for the fertility of its countryside and for its agricultural products. He was tried for heresy by the Inquisition, and, when found guilty, he was burned at the stake on February 17, 1600, in Rome.

43. Umberto Bossi (born 1941) founded the Lega Nord [Northern League] in 1989, and has been its leader ever since. The Lega Nord is a northern Italian right-wing party: its platform has been openly xenophobic from its inception, and its political program was secessionist at first (i.e., it argued for the secession of northern Italy from the rest of Italy and for the foundation of a new nation-state to be named Padania, after the name of the Po River Valley) and federalist later (i.e., more recently, it has argued for Italy to adopt a federalist model not unlike the Swiss one).

Bossi and his party have been crucial political allies of Berlusconi and have played a very important role in Berlusconi's government coalitions.

44. On the relation between *natura naturans* and *natura naturata*, see Spinoza, *Ethics*, trans. G. H. R. Parkinson (Oxford: Oxford University Press, 2000), 100.

45. Gilles Deleuze and Félix Guattari, *What Is Philosophy?*, trans. Hugh Tomlinson and Graham Burchell (New York: Columbia University Press, 1994), 1–2.

46. Ibid., 10–12.

47. Ludovico Ariosto (1474–1533) was one of the most important poets of the Italian Renaissance. His works have had a lasting influence on modern European literatures.

48. Carlo Ginzburg, *The Worm and the Cheese: The Cosmos of a Sixteenth-Century Miller*, trans. John and Anne C. Tedeschi (Baltimore: Johns Hopkins University Press, 1980).

The Political Monster

Throughout this essay (as throughout the other sections of this book that were translated from Italian into English) the Italian terms *potenza* and *potere* have been translated as *power* and *Power*, respectively. See also note 22 of "A Class-Struggle Propaedeutics, 1950s–1970s."

1. George Thomson, *Studies in Ancient Greek Society*, vol. 2, *The First Philosophers* (London: Lawrence and Wishart, 1955). It's worth remembering that this refined approach was inspired by Alfred Sohn-Rethel (above all by his book *Intellectual Labor and Physical Labor*) and used by scholars such as J.-P. Vernant and Pierre Vidal-Naquet.

2. Reiner Schürmann, *Heidegger on Being and Acting: From Principles to Anarchy*, trans. Christine-Marie Gros (Bloomington: Indiana University Press, 1987), 99.

3. Johannes Fritsche, "Genus and Essence in Aristotle and Socrates," *Graduate Faculty Philosophy Journal* 19, no. 2, and 20, no. 1 (1997): 163–202.

4. On my reading, Karol Kerényi's work moves entirely in this direction and remains paramount in the literature about classical mythology. For a critical illustration of this direction on mythological thought, see Theodor W. Adorno, *Interpretazione dell'Odissea* [Interpretation of the *Odyssey*] (Rome: Manifestolibri, 2000).

5. It must be emphasized that there is a singular convergence between the thought of scholars of ancient philosophy, such as Schürmann and Fritsche, and those of culture, or historians such as Vidal-Naquet and Vernant. But see already E. R. Dodds, *The Greeks and the Irrational* (Berkeley: University of California Press, 1951).

6. Henry-Charles Puech, *En quête de la Gnosis* [In search of gnosis] (Paris: Gallimard, 1978), but see already Hans Jonas, *The Gnostic Religion: The Message of the Alien God and the Beginnings of Christianity* (Boston: Beacon Press, 1971).

7. I have studied this problem in chapter 3 of *Insurgencies: Constituent Power and the Modern State,* trans. Maurizia Boscagli (Minneapolis: University of Minnesota Press, 1999), 99–139.

8. Here I am referring to Hobbes scholars, "all included," from right to left (in chronological order, from Michael Oakeshott to C. B. MacPherson, from Gérard Mairet to Yves Charles Zarka).

9. The six books "on the republic" (that is to say on monarchy) by Jean Bodin, of 1576, are followed in 1578 by *La Démonomanie des sorciers,* a manual that describes witchcraft practices, and above all the way to recognize and punish them.

10. Here I am again referring to the studies mentioned in note 8, and in particular to the relations between the thought of the secular theoreticians (Harrington) and of the religious theoreticians (Milton) of democracy in the English Glorious Revolution—the theoreticians of a democracy that is not yet able to think of itself as an association of equals.

11. For some reason, it's above all in the tradition of German *Historismus* (and in its French versions) that these tendencies are revealed little by little. On the authors cited above, see Eduard Fueter, *Geschichte der neueren Historiographie* (Munich: Oldenbourg, 1911).

12. Starting from Joseph-Arthur de Gobineau: to understand the dynamics of his thought, and the influence of his *Essai sur l'inégalité des races humaines* [Essay on the inequality of human races], see the contribution of Philippe Raynaud, in *Dictionnaire de philosophie politique* [Dictionary of political philosophy] (Paris: Presses Universitaires de France, 1986).

13. See Ernst Cassirer, *The Myth of the State* (New Haven: Yale University Press, 1946), and Léon Polyakov, *Le mythe aryen* (Paris: Calmann-Lévy, 1971).

14. Ferguson's very famous (and justly celebrated) study on the interpretations of the Renaissance doesn't contain any relevant idea about this point. Not even the Warburg School has ever turned to this theme.

15. Judith Butler is the preeminent figure regarding this problematic. Indeed, no matter how powerful and effective her attack on patriarchal Power is, its continual assertion of Hegelian dialectics limits its critical impact, that is, the destruction of classical *eugenia.*

16. Michel de Montaigne, *The Complete Essays,* trans. M. A. Screech (London: Penguin, 1987), 808.

17. It's the "Communist Left" of the 1920s, and in particular Georg Lukács, who articulate the critique of rationality in fetishistic, monstrous, and, in some ways, Nietzschean, terms—thereby, on the one hand, being ostracized by the Marxist orthodoxy, and, on the other, spreading its models among the new generations of critical thinkers.

18. This sequence is signaled by the Frankfurt School in all its variants. Further-more, it is once again taken up and celebrated by the French school "headed" by Althusser. It's important to point out that neither in the first nor in the second case are we facing a "catastrophist" perspective: the (critical) negation of capitalist ratio-nality opens up to the search for an *other* rationality . . . for a *monstrous* rationality.

19. Yann Moulier-Boutang, in his excellent *De l'esclavage au salariat* [From slav-ery to wage labor] (Paris: Presses Universitaires de France, 1998), has exemplified the presence of the monster, of metamorphosis, of *métissage* . . . in sum, of emigration and of the movements of labor power, at the center of the development of capital . . . It's not a paradox. It's perhaps the only way to make a history of freedom.

20. Perhaps it will be important, in a further stage of our analysis of the anthro-pological transformations determined by postmodernity, to critique the mythologies of development invented by Goethe, and theorized dialectically by Hegel: we must, that is, debunk the unidirectional universalism of the *Bildung* (à la Wilhelm Meister) and of the master–slave dialectic. A first step in the direction of this critique is Michael Hardt and Antonio Negri, *Empire* (Cambridge: Harvard University Press, 2000).

21. From Émile Zola to Jean-Paul Sartre, from Giovanni Verga to Antonio Gramsci, from Tolstoy to the major authors of the Soviets, not to mention American realism (which probably is superior to all of the above), and not to talk of cinema (which, without doubt, has been capable of the most powerful realist denunciation of exploitation) . . .

22. Besides those mentioned in the preceding note, we can begin to recognize as witnesses of the "monster" Primo Levi for the victims of the camps, Frantz Fanon for the anticolonial wars of liberation, Jean Genet for the Palestinians . . . and so many others!

23. For the method of "the struggles that produce reality"—"it's the monsters who produce the real"—there are three or four great schools that must be remem-bered: that of African American historiography, that of Indian anticolonial histo-rians, that of Italian workerism, and finally that which constitutes the communist dissidence in the countries of "real socialism" (at least since 1956) as the motor of political and social development.

24. In *Empire*, Hardt and I have amply summed up the results of those researches (partially mentioned in the previous notes) that take the act of revolt as the creative moment of history.

25. As far as the method is concerned, it's that of the negotiation between "mon-strous subjects" well theorized by Gilles Deleuze in his *Pourparlers* (Paris: Éditions de Minuit, 1990); Gilles Deleuze, *Negotiations*, trans. Martin Joughin (New York: Columbia University Press, 1995).

26. Jacques Derrida, *Specters of Marx: The State of Debt, the Work of Mourning, and the New International*, trans. Peggy Kamuf (New York: Routledge, 1994).

27. Antonio Negri, "The Specter's Smile," in *Ghostly Demarcations: A Symposium on Jacques Derrida's Specters of Marx,* trans. Patricia Dailey and Costantino Costantini (London: Verso, 1999), 5–16.

28. I am having fun here, playing at being Heideggerian, so to speak. In German, "monster" is *Ungeheuer,* where *geheuer* means "safe," while *heuer* is an adverb meaning "this year," *heute* means "today," *heu* means "hay," and *Heuernte* means "hay harvesting." Therefore, *das Ungeheuer* is the name of a peasant event, insecure, untimely, rural—the event that implies a possible rupture, a disappointed and strange wait, of an instantaneous overturning . . . the elderly person's wisdom about the countryside has been betrayed . . . the hay of a year that is there and isn't . . . a phenomenon now dominated by insurance companies . . . how ridiculous to be Heideggerian!

29. It's what I argued in *Marx beyond Marx.*

30. For this issue, these are the fundamental texts: Donna Haraway, *Symians, Cyborgs, and Women: The Reinvention of Nature* (New York: Routledge, 1991), and Rosi Braidotti, *Madri, mostri e macchine* (Rome: Manifestolibri, 1996).

31. We owe to Bertolt Brecht and Heiner Müller the strongest and most formidable images of this epiphany of the poor. The philosophy of the monsters numbers these playwrights among its greatest authors.

32. At other times, in transitional epochs, the monster has become a sort of Saint Christopher, carrier of men from one era to another. Rabelais has described these heroes of transition. Lucien Febvre and Mikhail Bakhtin have sung again, through Rabelais, the *gesta* of the transition from the Middle Ages to modernity . . . Today these songs must be written once again to celebrate and describe the passage from modernity to postmodernity.

33. H. J. C. von Grimmelshausen has written an immortal *Simplicissimus* in order to affirm peasant freedom, a Rousseauian figure in the atrocious event of the Thirty Years War, and Franz Mehring has set the definitive standard of the historical analysis of that epoch in his *Deutsche Geschichte vom Ausgange des Mittelalters* (Berlin: J. H. W. Dietz, 1947). But why don't the historical "revisionists" return to those tragic dawns of communism?

34. Eric Hobsbawm's reconstruction of the histories of the *Rebels* is, in this case, exemplary.

35. Edmund Burke ("that vulgar Sophist and famous sycophant": Karl Marx) had no doubt in considering the agricultural laborer as *instrumentum vocale,* while donkeys were considered *instrumentum mutum.* See his *Thoughts and Details on Scarcity* (Whitefish, Mont.: Kessinger Publishing, 2005).

36. Karl Marx, "The Class Struggles in France, 1848–1850," in *The Marx-Engels Reader,* ed. Robert C. Tucker (New York: W. W. Norton, 1972), 586–93.

37. Against the image of the twentieth century as a time of defeat and implosion of the struggles against labor. Recently, this "weak" ideology has been proposed

in Italy by Marco Revelli in his *Oltre il Novecento* [Beyond the twentieth century] (Turin: Einaudi, 2001). By contrast, we posit, now and later in our discussion, the politico-historiographical path of E. P. Thompson in his *The Making of the English Working Class* (New York: Vintage Books, 1966) as the general direction to follow.

38. It is in the *Grundrisse* above all that Marx has managed to describe dynamically the reciprocal insertion of the proletariat into the relations of productions dominated by capital, and of capital into the constitution of the working class.

39. All the Leninist experience and science have worked to identify this monstrosity of the revolutionary event. In the conference on Lenin's *What Is to Be Done?* (held in Essen in winter 2001 and organized by Slavoj Žižek), the sentiment of revolutionary monstrosity, as Lenin had foreseen it, was recuperated.

40. How many are they? What economic incentive do they represent in book production and political propaganda? What horrible stupidity is being transmitted by these blackest of books, or what terrible truths and horrors are here distorted and bent to the nontruth of political hatred and revenge? When Furet gave scientific dignity to historical revisionism, could he have imagined these drifts?

41. An excellent answer to Furet is proposed by Denis Berger and Henri Maler in *Une certaine idée du communisme: Répliques à F. Furet* (Paris: Éditions Du Felin, 1996).

42. Were this study to be continued in greater depth, we should certainly insert a chapter here about "*eugenia*" and "performativity" of the enunciations of this practice.

43. Here, permit me to refer you to the reflections on transcendental philosophy contained in my *Kairòs, Alma Venus, Multitudo*, in *Time for Revolution*, trans. Matteo Mandarini (London: Continuum, 2003).

44. It is on this point that the "real" political science from the beginning of the twentieth century, as founded by Max Weber, takes shape. After 1917, the "monstrous" accentuation of the problematics of political science becomes exclusive (as a response to the October Revolution).

45. See the recent work by Eve Chiappello and Luc Boltanski, *Le nouvel esprit du capitalisme* (Paris: Gallimard, 1999).

46. An older book, but very important for the social sciences, had anticipated this perception: Alvin W. Gouldner, *The Coming Crisis of Western Sociology* (New York: Basic Books, 1970).

47. Elias Canetti's mighty study *Massen und Macht*, whose gestation goes from the end of the 1920s to 1960, is perhaps a classic example of the anxiety and difficulty of grasping (or not) the monster. In any case, it's impossible to study the European twentieth century *entre-deux-guerres* without posing this problematic.

48. See Ernst Jünger's *L'operaio: Dominio e forma*, in the latest Italian edition (Parma: Guanda, 2001), with a beautiful introduction by Quirino Principe.

49. It has now become the norm, and rightly so, to turn to Michel Foucault's work to define the hegemony of the "biopolitical" scenario in the human, political (not to mention historical) sciences.

50. "Critical theory," in the work and teaching of Horkheimer and Adorno, can be described as an unceasing effort to follow these processes of "colonization of life." Its limitation was its inability to perceive the subjective metamorphoses that were taking shape within this colonized life: but the phenomenology presented in Horkheimer and Adorno's work is often insurmountable. Even today.

51. Martin Heidegger, in his writings about technology between the 1930s and the 1950s, has been capable of giving an unquestionable force to this model.

52. In the 1970s and 1980s, "weak thought" has done its task (its apology of capitalism) above all by ridiculing the constitutive power of the subaltern classes.

53. In twentieth-century thought there runs, along functional rationalism, a utopian thought that, between Ernst Bloch and Deleuze-Guattari, between Lukács and Tronti, proposes the basis of the monster's power (of the revolutionary or metamorphic monster).

54. On the development of public law of mature capitalism, on its alternatives and evolutions, see Michael Hardt and Antonio Negri's *Labor of Dionysus: A Critique of the State-Form* (Minneapolis: University of Minnesota Press, 1994).

55. The reference obviously is to Gilles Deleuze and Félix Guattari's *A Thousand Plateaus: Capitalism and Schizophrenia*, trans. Brian Massumi (Minneapolis: University of Minnesota Press, 1987).

56. Giorgio Agamben, *Homo Sacer: Sovereign Power and Bare Life*, trans. Daniel Heller-Roazen (Stanford, Calif.: Stanford University Press, 1998). On this theme, and for the discussion that interests us, see the special issue of the journal *Aut Aut*, no. 298 (July–August 2000), titled "Politica senza luogo" (Politics without place).

57. See Luciano Ferrari Bravo's extraordinarily pertinent critique of the aforementioned book by Agamben, now in *Dal fordismo alla globalizzazione* (From Fordism to globalization).

58. This confusion, between man and nakedness, and about the question of whether one or the other comes first, is the foundation of the historical revisionism of postmodernity. The sharpest anti-Heideggerian philosophers had foreseen these conclusions: see Karl Löwith's *From Hegel to Nietzsche: The Revolution in Nineteenth-Century Thought*, trans. David E. Green (New York: Columbia University Press, 1991), and *Meaning in History: The Theological Implications of the Philosophy of History* (Chicago: University of Chicago Press, 1949).

59. But on these themes, in a nonrevisionist mode (the Shoah, far from being its negation, concludes modernity), see Zygmunt Bauman's *Modernity and the Holocaust* (Ithaca, N.Y.: Cornell University Press, 1989). Hannah Arendt's 1963 work

Eichmann in Jerusalem: A Report on the Banality of Evil (New York: Penguin Books, 1977) denounces in advance these ideological distortions.

60. In *Remnants of Auschwitz: The Witness and the Archive,* trans. Daniel Heller-Roazen (New York: Zone Books, 1999), Giorgio Agamben stresses with great intensity the impossibility of these historical homologations.

61. It's once again Hannah Arendt who, in the theoretical struggle that opposes her to Heidegger throughout her life, is witness to this confrontation, for vital and political reasons, as well as philosophical ones.

62. The experience of Primo Levi (but also the narrations of other less known deported people: for me, in my childhood, Piero Caleffi was important) is a testimonial of the profound, irrepressible historicity of the Shoah.

63. Once again we are now confronting that heap of transcendental philosophy that makes no distinction between the drifting toward nothingness of historical becoming and the becoming insignificant of constitutive thought. As it has happened in other ages of crisis, not even idealism is allowed any longer to the masters of the world. In an age of transformations they slide, through weak conceptions of knowledge, toward nihilistic ideological positions. As a consequence, politics becomes fascist.

64. This operation of transfer obviously has the characteristics of the new accumulation (of immaterial, cybernetic, communicative labor). Habermas had grasped this passage, in the mystified manner that characterizes him, without being able to interpret it, except formally (through the ridiculous exhumation of the Kantian model). On the other hand, in Rawls we see the more explicit attempt to reorganize the "consent" for accumulation on an "individualist basis" (a multitude of "terrorized" individuals). But for all these themes, and on the variegated series of authors who fight to hegemonize ideologically the new processes of accumulation and the formulation of adequate schemes of legitimization, see Hardt and Negri, *Labor of Dionysus.*

65. Deleuze's essay "Bartleby, or The Formula" is exceptionally important because it has stressed the extraordinary "power" of the character—a power that expresses itself also in the absolute negativity of his behavior: the power of intention prevails upon the nothingness of the end.

66. See Marco Bascetta's essay "Verso un'economia politica del vivente" [Toward a political economy of the living] and the indications it offers, in *Desiderio del mostro,* 149–62. For a full bibliographical reference, see note 6 in "Surplus Common."

67. See Johannes Fritsche's *Historical Destiny and National Socialism in Heidegger's "Being and Time"* (Berkeley: University of California Press, 1999). This is truly a useful book if one wants to avoid the shame of European philosophical good society and to consider Heidegger for what he is.

68. Sandro Mezzadra, "Cittadini della frontiera e confini della cittadinanza" [Border citizens and the borders of citizenship], in *Aut Aut,* no. 298 (July–August 2000).

69. As I already pointed out in note 66, this situation must be analyzed more in depth theoretically and politically.

70. To theorize this concept of "full life" we must turn above all to Deleuze. In his work, this concept is, so to speak, paradigmatic. The new builders of systems, of the state, and of the dialectic consequently turn to him the way Hegel turned to Spinoza: they accuse him of not compromising on "singularity," they denounce him for not being a slave to the exigencies and urgencies of the "totality" of Power. Hegel says that Spinoza is a "consumptive," but none of us feels "consumptive." Rather, in the manner of Spinoza, we know how to unite in a forceful denunciation of Hegel. In fact, our conception of life is powerful and armed, "full"—the way it emerges from all of Deleuze's work. Not to mention Guattari's folly, which runs by itself or together with Deleuze in the great work they build—there is always repetition of a "refrain," invention of "*agencements*," and, above all, determination of a positive teleology set up by subjects.

71. The problems, however, are never posed in these explicit terms, but rather in terms of medical and health opportunities and/or of economic profitability. The structure of research (and the necessity for very large investments, particularly in invention and labor power) predominates at the moment, and delegates leadership to the multinationals (rather than directly to political structures). It's clear that the struggle on property rights (and on copyright) has become fundamental also in this context of biopolitics, in order to determine, that is, its development.

72. On all these questions, I refer the reader to a special issue of the journal *Posse* on the concept of the "biopolitical" (Rome: Castelvecchi, 2001).

73. See Deleuze and Guattari's concept of BwO (Body without Organs) in *A Thousand Plateaus*.

74. In Guattari's last works we are fully inside a new ecological and biopolitical horizon of philosophy, and of political decision making. See, especially, Guattari's *Chaosmosis: An Ethicoaesthetic Paradigm*, trans. Paul Bains and Julian Pefanis (Bloomington: Indiana University Press, 1995). See also my *Kairòs, Alma Venus, Multitudo*, in *Time for Revolution*.

75. Hardt and I debate this problematic knot extensively in *Empire*.

76. The relation between ontological "consistency" and political "resistance" is, as is well known, one of the central points of Deleuze's rereading/reinterpretation/reinvention of Spinozism. We find this relation all over Deleuze's work after 1968, that is, from the publication of *Expressionism in Philosophy* till the last book, *What Is Philosophy?*. On this theme, I refer you once again to my *Kairòs, Alma Venus, Multitudo*, in *Time for Revolution*.

77. [In English in the text.—*Trans.*]

78. The reference points once again to Guattari. Concerning this program of chaotic constitution, Paul Virilio, Pierre Lévy, and, earlier, Gilbert Simondon are no

less important. We could trace a similar path of theoretical development in studies of physics and philosophy in the Anglo-Saxon world in postmodernity.

79. It's between Antonin Artaud and Deleuze and Guattari's *A Thousand Plateaus* that the prolegomena of a *positive* philosophy of the *Cso,* that is, of the revolutionary monster, are thus put into effect for postmodernity.

80. It has been lived in the most singular and different manners in the most distant cultures, which are reunified in the name of and through this crisis. The passage of the modern (in all its categories) to the *post* (in all its aspects) hinges on this point. The process takes place between 1968 and 1989.

81. In *Empire,* Hardt and I have developed the chief themes of this passage.

82. See note 76. But see also Deleuze's last article, "Immanence: A Life . . . ," in *Pure Immanence: Essays on A Life,* trans. Anne Boyman (New York: Zone Books, 2001), 25–33.

83. On this problem, see Reiner Schürmann, *Des hégémonies brisées* (Toulouse: Ter, 1997).

84. Bruno Latour's research, first on laboratories and then on scientific paradigms, is insurmountable (especially the propaedeutic chapters). See Bruno Latour, *Pandora's Hope: Essays on the Reality of Science Studies* (Cambridge: Harvard University Press, 1999).

85. Gilbert Simondon, *L'individuation psychique et collective* (Paris: Aubier, 1989), and *Du mode d'existence des objets techniques* (Paris: Aubier, 1989).

86. Donna J. Haraway, *Modest_Witness@Second_Millennium. FemaleMan©_Meets_Oncomouse™: Feminism and Technoscience* (New York: Routledge, 1997).

87. On this topic, the reference is less approximate: we are referring in fact to the long series of essays by Georges Canguilhem collected under the title *La connaissance de la vie* (Paris: Vrin, 1971).

88. I am referring to Rabelais, but also, and above all, to the line of interpretation that has made of him a central paradigm in our critical tradition, from Febvre to Bakhtin.

89. To conclude this discussion, besides referring to our many interventions on the definition of "immaterial labor" and of "biopolitical horizon," we want to call the reader's attention to the development of literary, historical, and linguistic studies of Bakhtinian origin in Russia, after 1989; see the special issue of the journal *Critique,* no. 645 (Paris: Éditions de Minuit, 2001), titled "*Moscou 2001.*"

90. Negri, *Kairòs, Alma Venus, Multitudo,* in *Time for Revolution.*

91. On this matter, see Spinoza's *Ethics.*

92. It seems entirely evident, we think, that the analysis of bodies and of metamorphosis, the critique of nature and of capital, and a new political project of transformation intersect one another on this point. In recent years, the attempts to put back together the discourse of sociological critique, that of ontological analysis, and that of political reconstruction have multiplied. See note 39.

93. See Hardt and Negri's often cited *Empire*.

94. Antonio Negri, *Insurgencies: Constituent Power and the Modern State*, trans. Maurizia Boscagli (Minneapolis: University of Minnesota Press, 1999).

Time Matters

I thank Brian Meredith and the Marxist Reading Group of the University of Florida, Gainesville, for inviting me to present a previous version of this essay at the conference "Refusing Our Way of Life" in March 2002. I am also grateful to the friends whose thoughtful words helped me write and revise this essay: Richard Dienst, Eleanor Kaufman, Kiarina Kordela, Andrew Knighton, John Mowitt, Ross Prinzo, and Brynnar Swenson.

1. Giorgio Agamben, "Time and History: Critique of the Instant and the Continuum," in *Infancy and History: Essays on the Destruction of Experience*, trans. Liz Heron (London: Verso, 1993), 91; translation modified; Agamben, "Tempo e storia: Critica dell'istante e del continuo," in *Infanzia e storia: Distruzione dell'esperienza e origine della storia* (Turin: Einaudi, 1978), 95.

2. Agamben, "Time and History," 98; "Tempo e storia," 103.

3. Agamben, "Time and History," 100; "Tempo e storia," 106.

4. Agamben, "Time and History," 101; "Tempo e storia," 107.

5. Walter Benjamin, "Theses on the Philosophy of History," in *Illuminations*, trans. Harry Zohn (New York: Schocken, 1969), 261.

6. I discussed Agamben's concept of "cairological time" in "Pornocairology; or, The Communist Clinamen of Pornography," *Paragraph* 25, no. 2 (2002): 116–26. The arguments of this present essay constitute at once a corrective and a complement to what I argued in "Pornocairology."

7. Louis Althusser, "Une philosophie pour le marxisme," in *Sur la philosophie* (Paris: Gallimard, 1994), 40–42; the translation and the italics are mine. This interview took place in Paris during the winter of 1983–84, and the interviewer was the Mexican philosopher Fernanda Navarro; see Althusser's preface, in *Sur la philosophie*, 27–28.

8. This is akin to the temporality of the Nietzschean-Deleuzean throw of the dice, with which Althusser is likely to have been familiar. Deleuze writes: "The dice which are thrown once are the affirmation of *chance*, the combination which they form on falling is the affirmation of *necessity*. Necessity is affirmed of chance in exactly the sense that being is affirmed of becoming and unity is affirmed of multiplicity. It will be replied, in vain, that thrown to chance, the dice do not necessarily produce the winning combination, the double six which brings back the dicethrow. This is true, but only insofar as the player did not know how to *affirm* chance from the outset. For, just as unity does not suppress or deny multiplicity, necessity does not suppress or abolish chance. Nietzsche identifies chance with multiplicity, with

fragments, with parts, with chaos: the chaos of the dice that are shaken and thrown. *Nietzsche turns chance into an affirmation* . . . What Nietzsche calls *necessity* (destiny) is thus never the abolition but rather the combination of chance itself. Necessity is affirmed of chance in as much as chance itself is affirmed. For there is only a single combination of chance as such, a single way of combining all the parts of chance, a way which is like the unity of multiplicity, that is to say number or necessity. There are many numbers with increasing or decreasing probabilities, but only one number of chance as such, one fatal number which reunites all the fragments of chance, like midday gathers together the scattered parts of midnight. This is why it is sufficient for the player to affirm chance once in order to produce the number which brings back the dicethrow . . . We must therefore attach the greatest importance to the following conclusion: for the couple causality-finality, probability-finality, for the opposition and the synthesis of these terms, for the web of these terms, Nietzsche substitutes the Dionysian correlation of chance-necessity, the Dionysian couple chance-destiny. Not a probability distributed over several throws but all chance at once; not a final, desired, willed combination, but the fatal combination, fatal and loved, *amor fati;* not the return of a combination by the number of throws, but the repetition of a dicethrow by the nature of the fatally obtained number" (Gilles Deleuze, *Nietzsche and Philosophy,* trans. Hugh Tomlinson [New York: Columbia University Press, 1983], 26–27).

9. In some of the most powerful and beautiful pages Deleuze ever wrote, he describes precisely this moment—when a contingent encounter is claimed as our own—as well as the ethics that appertains to it. See Gilles Deleuze, *The Logic of Sense,* trans. Constantin V. Boundas (New York: Columbia University Press, 1990), 148–53, and especially 149–50.

10. Agamben, "Time and History," 99–100; translation modified; Agamben, "Tempo e storia," 105.

11. Antonio Negri, *The Constitution of Time,* in *Time for Revolution,* trans. Matteo Mandarini (London: Continuum, 2003), 21. Negri, *La costituzione del tempo: Prolegomeni: Orologi del capitale e liberazione comunista* (Rome: Manifestolibri, 1997), 23.

12. On the question of real subsumption, see also note 23 in "Surplus Common."

13. On this matter, see also my discussion of Marx's conception of surplus value in "Surplus Common."

14. Negri, *The Constitution of Time,* 108; translation modified; Negri, *La costituzione del tempo,* 154–55.

15. Negri, *The Constitution of Time,* 112–13, translation modified; Negri, *La costituzione del tempo,* 160–62.

16. Benjamin, "Theses on the Philosophy of History," 263.

17. It should be noted, however, that Negri's assessment of Benjamin is at times quite different from the one articulated in these passages. In the 1997 preface to *La costituzione del tempo,* after all, Negri acknowledges briefly Benjamin's importance

for his project (Negri, *La costituzione del tempo*, 19). Furthermore, in *Labor of Dionysus*, Hardt and Negri draw usefully from Benjamin's essay "Critique of Violence" in order to elaborate their own "practical critique of violence" (Michael Hardt and Antonio Negri, *Labor of Dionysus: A Critique of the State-Form* [Minneapolis: University of Minnesota Press, 1994], 290–95). And in *Empire*, they comment at once critically and appreciatively on different aspects of Benjamin's work (Michael Hardt and Antonio Negri, *Empire* [Cambridge: Harvard University Press, 2000], 215 and 377). Negri's assessment of Agamben's project, however, is far less ambivalent and far more critical throughout. Negri's critique of Agamben's concept of "naked life," for example, is particularly relevant here, as it is strikingly similar to his critique of Benjamin's *Jetztzeit* (Hardt and Negri, *Empire*, 366 and 421n11; but see also Negri's scathing attack on that concept in "The Political Monster").

18. Gilles Deleuze, "Desire and Pleasure," in *Foucault and His Interlocutors*, ed. Arnold Davidson (Chicago: University of Chicago Press, 1997), 189–90.

19. Spinoza too, however, is the thinker who refuses to choose between the positions that I have identified above, on the one hand, with Deleuze and Negri, and, on the other hand, with Agamben and Foucault. I believe it is possible and indispensable to read Part V of Spinoza's *Ethics* in a way—different from both the ways in which Deleuze reads it in *Expressionism in Philosophy* and in which Negri reads it in *The Savage Anomaly*—that could lend support to this hypothesis. Ultimately, the fact that Spinoza found it necessary to articulate a third type of knowledge as well as what he calls *amor Dei intellectualis* (intellectual love of God) is an index of such a refusal to choose between those positions and of an attempt to elaborate an altogether different one. But these thoughts belong to a different essay—even though they are fully immanent and operative in this present one. On Spinoza's conception of love, however, see my "Surplus Common."

20. Agamben, "Time and History," 104–5; Agamben, "Tempo e storia," 110–11.

21. For similar formulations regarding the politics and historicity of pleasure, see also Fredric Jameson's important 1983 essay "Pleasure: A Political Issue," which has inspired my present project in more ways than I can know (Fredric Jameson, "Pleasure: A Political Issue," in *The Ideologies of Theory: Essays, 1971–1986*, vol. 2 [Minneapolis: University of Minnesota Press, 1988], 61–74).

22. Negri, *The Constitution of Time*, 102; Negri, *La costituzione del tempo*, 145.

23. Negri, *The Constitution of Time*, 102; Negri, *La costituzione del tempo*, 146; translation modified.

24. Negri, *The Constitution of Time*, 102–3; Negri, *La costituzione del tempo*, 146.

25. Negri, *The Constitution of Time*, 104; translation modified; Negri, *La costituzione del tempo*, 148–49.

26. Negri, *The Constitution of Time*, 105; translation modified; Negri, *La costituzione del tempo*, 149.

27. Negri, *The Constitution of Time*, 105; translation modified; Negri, *La costituzione del tempo*, 150.

28. Negri, *The Constitution of Time*, 103; Negri, *La costituzione del tempo*, 147.

29. Much as Negri returns to the conjoined questions of time and of corporeality in *Empire*, Agamben too has returned several times to the question of corporeality since the 1978 essay with which I began my discussion. In particular, see the section titled "Dim Stockings," in *The Coming Community*, as well as the essays "Form-Of-Life," "Notes on Gesture," and "The Face" in *Means without End* (Giorgio Agamben, *The Coming Community*, trans. Michael Hardt [Minneapolis: University of Minnesota Press, 1993], 47–50, and *Means without End: Notes on Politics*, trans. Vincenzo Binetti and Cesare Casarino [Minneapolis: University of Minnesota Press, 2000], 3–12, 49–60, and 91–100, respectively; Agamben, *La comunità che viene* [Turin: Einaudi, 1990], 32–35; Agamben, *Mezzi senza fine: Note sulla politica* [Turin: Bollati Boringhieri, 1996], 13–19, 45–53, and 74–80, respectively). But see also his reelaborations of Foucault's notions of "biopolitics," as well as the related theorization of the concept of "naked life"—both in *Means without End* and in *Homo Sacer*. Whereas in "Time and History" the question of corporeality was strictly correlated with the question of time and indeed emerged from the latter, in these later texts, the question of corporeality is engaged with in relative autonomy from the question of time. Likewise, there is much in Hardt and Negri's *Multitude* as well as in Negri's "The Political Monster" that is of great interest for a historical-materialist theorization of the corporeal: see, for example, the repeated attempts in both these texts to articulate at once a distinction and a relation between "body" and "flesh" (Michael Hardt and Antonio Negri, *Multitude: War and Democracy in the Age of Empire* [New York: Penguin, 2004], 158–62, 199–200, 336–38; Negri, "The Political Monster," especially the last two sections ["The Monster Monstrified" and "The Monster as *Angelus Novus*"]; Negri, "Il mostro politico," in *Desiderio del mostro*, ed. Ubaldo Fadini, Antonio Negri, and Charles T. Wolfe [Rome: Manifestolibri, 2001], 193–203). Much like in Agamben's aforementioned later texts, however, in both *Multitude* and "The Political Monster" the question of corporeality is not theorized directly in relation to the question of temporality. My present project precisely hinges on and argues for the inseparability of these questions for any theory and practice of communism.

30. I have already discussed Marx's *Grundrisse*, and especially its engagement with the question of money, in a different context (Cesare Casarino, *Modernity at Sea: Melville, Marx, Conrad in Crisis* [Minneapolis: University of Minnesota Press, 2002], 63–183). Much of the second section of the present essay stems from and constitutes a further elaboration of arguments I did not have the time and space to articulate fully in that book.

31. Karl Marx, *Grundrisse: Foundations of the Critique of Political Economy (Rough Draft)*, trans. Martin Nicolaus (Harmondsworth, U.K.: Penguin Books, 1974), 221.

32. Ibid., 233–35.

33. Ibid., 366–67.

34. Gilles Deleuze, "Postscript on Control Societies," in *Negotiations,* trans. Martin Joughin (New York: Columbia University Press, 1995), 179.

35. Marx, *Grundrisse,* 222–23.

36. Ibid., 284–85.

37. Ibid., 285; for the full argument regarding both forms of self-denial, see 284–89.

38. Ibid., 286–87.

39. Antonio Negri, *Marx beyond Marx: Lessons on the Grundrisse,* trans. Harry Cleaver, Michael Ryan, and Maurizio Viano, ed. Jim Fleming (Brooklyn: Autonomedia, 1991), 71; Negri, *Marx oltre Marx* (Rome: Manifestolibri, 1998), 92.

40. Negri, *Marx beyond Marx,* 72; Negri, *Marx oltre Marx,* 93.

41. In effect, I make the same argument regarding the relation between surplus value and surplus common in "Surplus Common."

42. Marx writes that the circulation of capital is "a spiral, an expanding curve, not a simple circle" (Marx, *Grundrisse,* 266).

43. For a further elaboration of the arguments articulated in this paragraph, see my discussion of Marx and Spinoza in "Surplus Common."

44. Marx, *Grundrisse,* 296.

45. Ibid., 295–96.

46. Ibid., 282–83.

47. Ibid., 298.

48. Ibid., 300.

49. Michel Foucault, *The History of Sexuality,* vol. 1, *An Introduction,* trans. Robert Hurley (New York: Vintage Books, 1990), 157; but see also 135–59.

Index

Lenta ginestra (Negri), 65, 168, 169–70
Leopardi, Giacomo, 65, 168, 169–70, 217
Levi, Primo, 282n22, 286n62
Leviathan, 194, 195
Levinas, Emmanuel, 88
Lévi-Strauss, Claude, 115, 141
Lévy, Pierre, 287n78
Liberalism: radical, 107
Liberation, 176, 198, 226, 234, 245, 260n39; sexual, 166; struggle for, 203. *See* Ontological/ontology: of liberation; Theology: of liberation
Libération, 76
Libertarian/libertarianism, 55
Life, 14, 16, 115, 147, 148, 149, 150, 152, 153, 154, 160, 173, 177, 186, 203, 206, 207, 208, 209, 210, 212, 213, 216, 218, 220, 231, 250n23, 265n71, 285n50, 287n70; form(s) of, 14, 91, 147, 175, 176, 218, 250n23, 254n26; naked, 5, 91, 151–52, 153–55, 156, 208–11, 212, 213, 214, 217, 291n17, 292n29; styles of, 95, 149
Literary/literature, 88, 89, 95, 162, 168, 183, 186, 189, 204, 216, 280n47
Lloyd, Genevieve, 32, 267n79
L'ordine nuovo, 278n29
Löwith, Karl, 285n58
Love, 31–32, 33–35, 37, 44, 86, 87, 149, 151, 156, 234, 266n71, 268n85, 269–70n91, 272n97. *See also* God: intellectual love of
Lukács, Georg, 4, 45, 46, 47, 49, 167, 168, 172, 176, 281n17, 285n53
Lumumba, Patrice, 201
L'unità, 56, 273n13
Luther, Martin, 201
Luxemburg, Rosa, 78, 249n21
Lycurgus, 74

Macchina tempo (Negri), 71, 134
Macherey, Pierre, 265n71
Machiavelli, Niccolò, 68, 97, 103, 123, 125, 183, 200, 211, 222
Macpherson, C. B., 77, 281n8
Mairet, Gérard, 281n8
Malcolm X, 76
Maler, Henri, 284n41
Mandelbrot, Benoit, 123
Manichaeism, 150, 152
Manzoni, Alessandro, 136
Marazzi, Christian, 148
Martinetti, Piero, 47
Marx, Karl, 4, 6, 7, 10, 14, 34, 35, 47, 49, 50–51, 55, 67, 68, 75, 80, 86, 103, 109, 110, 117, 123, 134, 147, 160, 162, 169, 184, 196, 197, 199, 200, 212, 219, 222, 224, 231, 249n21, 254n26, 255n32, 257n39, 260n41, 260n46, 262n55, 263n58, 264–66n71, 272n97, 283n33; *Capital*, 23–25, 27, 28, 29, 31, 51, 55, 62, 225, 250n23, 263–64n58; "The Class Struggles in France, 1848–1850," 283n36; *The Communist Manifesto*, 114; "The Difference between the Democritean and Epicurean Philosophy of Nature," 23, 243, 260n42; *Grundrisse*, 6, 10–11, 23, 28–32, 49, 59–61, 62, 65, 72, 113, 116, 118, 142, 163, 224, 225, 235–45, 248n14, 248n15, 257n38, 263n58, 264n63, 264n67, 284n38, 292n30, 293n42
Marx beyond Marx (Negri), 30, 60–61, 65, 113, 163, 169, 224, 264n63, 265n71, 283n29
Marxism, 45, 49, 51, 53, 68, 83, 92, 115, 117, 128, 130, 136, 140, 148, 162, 164, 166, 167, 171, 172, 174, 219, 221,

CESARE CASARINO is associate professor of cultural studies and comparative literature at the University of Minnesota. He is coeditor of *Marxism beyond Marxism* and author of *Modernity at Sea: Melville, Marx, Conrad in Crisis* (Minnesota, 2002), as well as numerous essays on literature, cinema, philosophy, queer theory, and AIDS studies.

ANTONIO NEGRI is an independent scholar and political activist. He has taught political science at the University of Paris and the University of Padua. He is the author of more than thirty books, many of which have been translated into several languages. Among his translated works in English are *The Savage Anomaly* (Minnesota, 1991); *Marx beyond Marx; Insurgencies: Constituent Power and the Modern State* (Minnesota, 1992); *Time for Revolution;* and *Books for Burning.* He is coauthor, with Michael Hardt, of *Labor of Dionysus: A Critique of the State-Form* (Minnesota, 1994); *Empire;* and *Multitude.* He was the most prominent figure in the Autonomia movement in Italy in the 1970s, and he has participated several times in the Global Social Forum. Many of his works have inspired contemporary antiglobalization political movements around the world.